M000034590

QUEENSHIP AND POWER

Series Editors: Carole Levin and Charles Beem

This series brings together monographs, edited volumes, and textbooks from scholars specializing in gender analysis, women's studies, literary interpretation, and cultural, political, constitutional, and diplomatic history. It aims to broaden our understanding of the strategies that queens—both consorts and regnants, as well as female regents—pursued in order to wield political power within the structures of male-dominant societies. In addition to works describing European queenship, it also includes books on queenship as it appeared in other parts of the world, such as East Asia, Sub-Saharan Africa, and Islamic civilization.

Editorial Board

Linda Darling, University of Arizona (Ottoman Empire)
Theresa Earenfight, Seattle University (Spain)
Dorothy Ko, Barnard College (China)
Nancy Kollman, Stanford University (Russia)
John Thornton, Boston University (Africa and the Atlantic World)
John Watkins (France and Italy)

Published by Palgrave Macmillan

The Lioness Roared: The Problems of Female Rule in English History
By Charles Beem

Elizabeth of York
By Arlene Naylor Okerlund

Learned Queen: The Image of Elizabeth I in Politics and Poetry
By Linda Shenk

"High and Mighty Queens" of Early Modern England: Realities and Representations
Edited by Carole Levin, Jo Eldridge Carney, and Debra Barrett-Graves

The Monstrous Regiment of Women: Female Rulers in Early Modern Europe
By Sharon L. Jansen

The Face of Queenship: Early Modern Representations of Elizabeth I
By Anna Riehl

Elizabeth I: The Voice of a Monarch
By Ilona Bell

Tudor Queenship: The Reigns of Mary and Elizabeth
Edited by Alice Hunt and Anna Whitelock

The Death of Elizabeth I: Remembering and Reconstructing the Virgin Queen
By Catherine Loomis

Queenship and Voice in Medieval Northern Europe
By William Layher

The Foreign Relations of Elizabeth I
Edited by Charles Beem

The French Queen's Letters: Mary Tudor Brandon and the Politics of Marriage in Sixteenth-Century Europe
By Erin A. Sadlack

Wicked Women of Tudor England: Queens, Aristocrats, Commoners
By Retha M. Warnicke

A Monarchy of Letters: Royal Correspondence and English Diplomacy in the Reign of Elizabeth I
By Rayne Allinson

Three Medieval Queens: Queenship and the Crown in Fourteenth-Century England
By Lisa Benz St. John

Mary I: Gender, Power, and Ceremony in the Reign of England's First Queen
By Sarah Duncan

The Last Plantagenet Consorts: Gender, Genre, and Historiography, 1440–1627
By Kavita Mudan Finn

Fairy Tale Queens: Representations of Early Modern Queenship
By Jo Eldridge Carney

Mother Queens and Princely Sons: Rogue Madonnas in the Age of Shakespeare
By Sid Ray

The Name of a Queen: William Fleetwood's Itinerarium ad Windsor
Edited by Charles Beem and Dennis Moore

The Emblematic Queen: Extra-Literary Representations of Early Modern Queenship
Edited by Debra Barrett-Graves

The Queens Regnant of Navarre: Succession, Politics, and Partnership, 1274–1512
By Elena Woodacre

Queenship in the Mediterranean: Negotiating the Role of the Queen in the Medieval and Early Modern Eras
Edited by Elena Woodacre

The Queen's Mercy: Gender and Judgment in Representations of Elizabeth I
By Mary Villeponteaux

Titled Elizabethans: A Directory of Elizabethan Court, State, and Church Officers, 1558–1603
Edited by Arthur F. Kinney and Jane A. Lawson

Elizabeth I's Foreign Correspondence: Letters, Rhetoric, and Politics
Edited by Carlo M. Bajetta, Guillaume Coatalen, and Jonathan Gibson

The Man behind the Queen: Male Consorts in History
Edited by Charles Beem and Miles Taylor

THE MAN BEHIND THE QUEEN

MALE CONSORTS IN HISTORY

Edited by

Charles Beem and Miles Taylor

THE MAN BEHIND THE QUEEN

Copyright © Charles Beem and Miles Taylor, 2014.

All rights reserved.

First published in 2014 by
PALGRAVE MACMILLAN®
in the United States—a division of St. Martin's Press LLC,
175 Fifth Avenue, New York, NY 10010.

Where this book is distributed in the UK, Europe and the rest of the world,
this is by Palgrave Macmillan, a division of Macmillan Publishers Limited,
registered in England, company number 785998, of Houndmills,
Basingstoke, Hampshire RG21 6XS.

Palgrave Macmillan is the global academic imprint of the above companies
and has companies and representatives throughout the world.

Palgrave® and Macmillan® are registered trademarks in the United States,
the United Kingdom, Europe and other countries.

ISBN: 978–1–137–44834–7

Library of Congress Cataloging-in-Publication Data

    The man behind the queen : male consorts in history / Charles Beem
and Miles Taylor, editors.
    pages cm.—(Queenship and power)
    ISBN 978–1–137-44834–7 (hardback)
     1. Queens—Family relationships—Europe—History.
2. Royal couples—Europe—History. 3. Kings and rulers—
Europe—History. 4. Princes—Europe—History.
5. Monarchy—Europe—History. 6. Sex role—Europe—History.
7. Man-woman relationships—Europe—History.
8. Power (Social sciences)—Europe—History.
9. Europe—Kings and rulers—History. 10. Europe—Social conditions.
I. Beem, Charles. II. Taylor, Miles.

D110.M26 2014
940.09′9—dc23   2014026010

A catalogue record of the book is available from the British Library.

Design by Newgen Knowledge Works (P) Ltd., Chennai, India.

First edition: December 2014

10 9 8 7 6 5 4 3 2 1

Other Titles By Charles Beem

The Name of a Queen: William Fleetwood's Itinerarium ad Windsor (2013) (coedited with Dennis Moore)

The Foreign Relations of Elizabeth I (2011)

The Royal Minorities of Medieval and Early Modern England (2008)

The Lioness Roared: The Problems of Female Rule in English History (2006)

Other Titles By Miles Taylor

The Decline of British Radicalism, 1847–1860 (1995)

Ernest Jones, Chartism and the Romance of Politics, 1819–69 (2003) (coedited with Michael Wolff)

The Victorians since 1901: Histories, Representations and Revisions (2004)

The Victorian Empire and Britain's Maritime World: The Sea and Global History, 1837–1901 (2013) (ed.)

The Age of Asa: Lord Briggs, Public Life and History in Britain since 1945 (Palgrave, 2014) (ed.)

CONTENTS

Acknowledgments

The editors wish to thank the staff of the Institute of Historical Research in London, who helped make the original conference in 2011 possible, especially Manjeet Sambi and Elaine Walters; Clarissa Campbell Orr, Janet Dickinson, and Karina Urbach, who advised on the conference program; and the Society for Court Studies for cohosting the event. We would also like to thank Luc Duerloo and Hugo Vickers, who spoke at the conference, and all of our contributors, who kindly donated their time and expertise for the essays included in this volume. Finally, we are grateful for the assistance shown by our editorial team at Palgrave USA; Chris Chappell, Mike Aperauch, and Brigitte Shull.

CONTRIBUTORS

David Abulafia is Professor of Mediterranean History at Cambridge University and a Fellow of Gonville and Caius College. He is a Fellow of the British Academy and Member of the Academia Europaea. His interests embrace the economic, social, and political history of the Mediterranean lands in the Middle Ages and Renaissance, especially southern Italy, the Italian 'despotisms' and the Italian islands (viewing Italian history from an unconventionally southern perspective); and also the trade and society of the Spanish lands of the Crown of Aragon. More generally, he is interested in the interaction of the three religions in medieval Spain and Sicily. A major interest is the opening of the eastern and western Atlantic in the fifteenth and early sixteenth century, with particular emphasis on the encounter of Europeans with native people, the subject of his book *The Discovery of Mankind* (2008). He has now written a history of the Mediterranean from 22,000 BC to AD 2010 for Penguin Books, entitled *The Great Sea* (2011).

Daniel Alves is Auxiliary Professor at the History Department in Faculdade de Ciências Sociais e Humanas, Universidade NOVA de Lisboa, and researcher in the Institute of Contemporary History (IHC). He has a PhD in Economic and Social Contemporary History, and MA degree in nineteenth-century history. He collaborated in several research projects funded by the Portuguese Science and Technology Foundation and by ESF, and has a special interest in the study of the lower middle classes, between 1870 and 1914, Urban History, Historical GIS, and Biography. He published a few articles in Portuguese and international peer reviewed journals, namely a recent one in the *Journal of Interdisciplinary History* regarding railways and population distribution in Portugal between the nineteenth and twentieth century (2011). He also collaborated in the *Portuguese Parliamentary Biographical Dictionary* (2004), elaborating nearly 60 biographies, and has published a small biography of an important Lisbon merchant from early nineteenth century (2008).

Roderick Barman is a leading expert in the history of Brazil during the nineteenth century. A graduate of King's College, Cambridge and the University of California at Berkeley, he has published widely, including three books: *Brazil: The Forging of a Nation, 1798–1852; Citizen Emperor: Pedro II and the Making of Brazil, 1825–1891;* and *Princess Isabel of Brazil: Gender and*

Power in the Nineteenth Century. He is currently writing *Brazil: The Burdens of Nationhood, 1852–1910*. He is Professor Emeritus of the Department of History, University of British Columbia.

Derek Beales has been a Fellow of Sidney Sussex College, Cambridge since 1955. He was elected Professor of Modern History in 1980 (Emeritus since 1997). He is a Fellow of the British Academy and was its representative on the Humanities Committee of the European Science Foundation in the 1980s. He has published *England and Italy, 1859–60* (1961); *From Castlereagh to Gladstone* (1969); *The Risorgimento and the Unification of Italy* (1971, 2nd edition with E.F. Biagini, 2001); *Prosperity and Plunder: European Monasteries in the Age of Revolution* (2003); *Enlightenment and Reform in Eighteenth-Century Europe* (2005); and a biography of Joseph II in two volumes (1987, 2009).

Charles Beem is Professor of History at the University of North Carolina, Pembroke. With Carole Levin he is the coeditor of Palgrave Macmillan's "Queenship and Power" series, and the author of *The Lioness Roared: The Problems of Female Rule in English History* (2006); and the editor of *The Royal Minorities of Medieval and Early Modern England* (2008); *The Foreign Relations of Elizabeth I* (2011); and *The Name of a Queen: William Fleetwood's Itinerarium ad Windsor* (2013). He is currently at work on a monograph entitled *Queenship in Early Modern Europe*.

Michael Bitter is Associate Professor of History at the University of Hawaii at Hilo, where he teaches European and World History. His research focuses on Anglo-Russian relations and interactions during the 1730s, an important period of consolidation of the westernizing reforms of Peter the Great in Russia. He has written on several aspects of Russia, the Russian court, and St. Petersburg during this period. He is currently working on a history of the diplomatic mission of George, Lord Forbes, to St. Petersburg as Envoy and Minister Plenipotentiary of George II of Great Britain

Sarah Duncan is an Associate Professor of History at Spring Hill College, Mobile, Alabama. Her book *Mary I: Gender, Power and Ceremony in the Reign of England's First Queen* (2012) appears in the "Queenship and Power" series. Her essays on queenship in the reigns of Mary I and Elizabeth I have appeared in *Queens and Power in Medieval and Early Modern England*, (2009); *Elizabeth I and the "Sovereign Arts": Essays in Literature, History, and Culture* (2011); and *The Name of a Queen: William Fleetwood's Itinerarium ad Windsor* (2013).

Maria Grever is Professor of Theory and Methodology of History, and director of the Centre for Historical Culture at Erasmus University Rotterdam, the Netherlands (www.eshcc.eur.nl/chc). She has been a research leader in several projects, such as Paradoxes of De-Canonization; New Forms of Cultural Transmission in History, funded by the Netherlands Organization for Scientific Research (NWO); and is currently program leader of the NWO program Heritage Education, Plurality of Narratives, and Shared Historical Knowledge. She has published widely on the construction and canonization of historical knowledge; collective memory, heritage, and plural identities; monarchy and gender.

Trond Norén Isaksen is a historian and author with an MA degree from the University of Oslo, which he obtained with a dissertation about the Bernadottes and the Norwegian succession issue c. 1850–1905. His first book was a dual biography of King Olav V and Crown Princess Märtha of Norway, followed by a biography of their daughter, Princess Astrid, Norway's former first lady. He is currently writing a history of Norwegian coronations. He is also the coauthor of a book on the Norwegian Royal Collections, has published more than 100 articles in several countries and has commented on royal ceremonial events on Norwegian state television.

Caroline Keen holds a PhD from the School of Oriental and African Studies, University of London. Her thesis involved a detailed analysis of British policy towards the Indian states during the period 1870–1909 and she has since published *Princely India and the British: Political Development and the Operation of Empire* (2012), dealing with the late nineteenth-century period of transition for Indian rulers from traditional to modern rule, during which British ideological motives for westernization and civilization, coupled with the need to curb costs and promote efficient government, resulted in a significant loss of princely power. Moving from a wide coverage of the subject to an individual example of British involvement in the Indian princely states, she is currently finalising an account of an anti-British revolt which occurred in 1891 in the small northeastern state of Manipur.

Simin Patel is a PhD candidate at Balliol College, University of Oxford. Her thesis traces the role the Parsi community played in the shaping of the public, particularly social sphere of colonial Bombay from the 1860s, a decade of significant change in city structure and fortune to 1918, the end of the First World War and the onset of Gandhian nationalism. While the community's long history as commercial interlocutors is well acknowledged, her interest is in the Parsis' later and informal role as cultural intermediaries. She holds MA degrees from the Jawaharlal Nehru University, New Delhi and the School of Oriental and African Studies, London. At Oxford she is a recipient of the Clarendon Fund Scholarship and the Hilla Ginwala Scholarship.

Fabian Persson is a Senior Lecturer in History at Linnaeus University in Sweden. His expertise lies in the history of the seventeenth and early eighteenth-century Swedish court, both domestically and internationally. His publications in English include contributions to the *Court Historian* and to John Adamson (ed.), *The Princely Courts of Europe* (1999).

Miles Taylor has been the Director of the Institute of Historical Research, University of London since 2008. Amongst his books are *The Decline of British Radicalism, 1847–60* (Oxford, 1995); *Ernest Jones, Chartism and the Romance of Chartism, 1819–69* (Oxford, 2003); *The Victorians since 1901: Histories, Representations and Revisions* (co-edited with Michael Wolff, Manchester, 2004); and (ed.) *The Victorian Empire and Britain's Maritime World: The Sea and Global History* (Basingstoke, 2013). He is currently completing a study of Queen Victoria and India.

Karina Urbach read Modern European History at the University of Munich. As a Kurt Hahn scholar at the University of Cambridge, she took an MPhil in International Relations and a PhD in history (later published as "Bismarck's Favourite Englishman. Lord Odo Russell's Mission to Berlin"). She was an Assistant Professor of History at the University of Bayreuth (1996–2001), won the Habilitationsprize of the Bavarian Ministry of Culture (2001–2004) and became a Research Fellow at the German Historical Institute London (2004–2009). Since 2009 she has been a Senior Research Fellow at the Institute of Historical Research, University of London. In July 2009, she was awarded a second doctorate (Habilitation) for her monograph: "Go-Betweens. German Aristocratic Families in Europe 1900 to 1939." In 2011 her biography of Queen Victoria was published for the German Publishing House C. H. Beck and went into a second edition within a year. Dr. Urbach has organised several international conferences covering subjects from family networks to espionage. She has reviewed regularly on German and British history for the Frankfurter Allgemeine Zeitung and has participated in history documentaries for the BBC and the German TV channel ZDF.

Jeroen van Zanten earned his PhD from the university of Leiden in 2004. Since 2006, he lectures on Modern European History at the University of Amsterdam. Zanten has written articles and books on parliamentary history, monarchy, revolution, and political culture in Europe during "the long nineteenth century," 1789–1914. In 2013, he published a biography of the Dutch king William II (1792–1849). Currently he is working on a book on "Waterloo and its Nachleben."

Elena Crislyn Woodacre is a specialist in medieval and early modern queenship and a Lecturer in Early Modern European History at the University of Winchester (UK). Her doctoral research was based on the queens regnant of Navarre in the late medieval period, focusing particularly on issues of female succession, matrimonial diplomacy, and the power sharing dynamic between the queens and their kings consort and has recently published a monograph derived from this research (*The Queens Regnant of Navarre; Succession, Politics and Partnership*; 2013). In addition to presenting her research at a number of international conferences, Elena is the primary organizer of the 'Kings and Queens' conference series and is currently developing an open-access academic journal on Royal Studies. She is also the founder of the Royal Studies Network (www.royalstudies-network.org), a resource which aims to bring together scholars who work on monarchical topics to enable them to collaborate and share information on their research.

Ina Zweiniger-Bargielowska is Professor of modern British history in the Department of History, University of Illinois, Chicago. Her research focuses on the relationship between the state and society in the twentieth century and, specifically, the interplay between politics, gender, and consumption. *Austerity in Britain: Rationing, Controls and Consumption, 1939–1955* (Oxford University Press) was published in 2000 and she has published several edited collections including *The Conservatives and British Society, 1880–1990* (University of Wales Press: Cardiff, 1996); *Women in Twentieth Century Britain* (Pearson Education: Harlow, 2001); and *Food and War in Twentieth Century Europe* (Ashgate: Farnham, 2011). Her latest monograph, *Managing the Body: Beauty, Health and Fitness in Britain, 1880s–1939* was published by Oxford University Press in 2010. She is currently working on a study entitled, *The Monarchy, Youth and Fitness in Twentieth-Century Britain*.

Introduction: The Man behind the Queen

Charles Beem and Miles Taylor

On April 23, 1702, Queen Anne, the last of the Stuart monarchs of England and Scotland, was crowned with regal solemnity in Westminster Abbey. As a queen regnant, Anne had inherited the office and estate of king, and was crowned in a manner similar to that of her kingly progenitors. There was, however, one important difference. In a clear break with previous English precedent, Anne was crowned alone, even though she had a husband, Prince George of Denmark, who did not become a king of England as did the wives of kings, who enjoy the title of queen. Prince George nonetheless enjoyed precedence over all the other peers of the realm as he watched the ceremony from inside the Abbey. Noted for his joviality, he did not appear to be in any way emasculated by the fact that he did not share his wife's royal status as a king consort, as Philip of Spain had during his marriage to the sixteenth-century Tudor queen regnant Mary I.[1]

While Mary and Philip's marriage occurred a century and a half previously, it was considered a salient precedent during a series of momentous constitutional events in 1688–89 that were known popularly as the Glorious Revolution. On this occasion another husband of a Stuart heiress, Prince William of Orange, insisted that he share his wife's throne, an outcome reflective of the widespread legal dictum that what a wife brought into a marriage besides her dower or jointure properly belonged to her husband. In the resulting "joint" reign of William III and Mary II, William held full regal power while Mary reigned serenely as a glorified consort who happily surrendered her own political inheritance into her husband's hands, as a good wife should.

But Anne was not like her sister, nor did George of Denmark in any way resemble William of Orange. In fact, George of Denmark is a unique figure in the history of male consorts in that he had no desire to share in his wife's authority, as this anecdote from the coronation festivities illustrates:

> She [Queen Anne] arrived in her sedan chair at St. James's
> Palace in the evening, greatly exhausted. Prince George of
> Denmark, who was in high spirits, was in no mood for retiring.
> At length the Lord Chamberlain ventured to draw attention to

Her Majesty's weariness, and hinted that it might be as well if
he proposed retirement. "I propose!" exclaimed the Prince.
"I cannot; I am her Majesty's subject, and have sworn homage
to her today.
I shall do naught but what she commands me."
The Queen was equal to the occasion, and replied, with a smile,
"Then, as that is the case, and I am very tired, I do command
you, George, to come to bed.[2]

The Stuart era brothers-in-law William of Orange and George of
Denmark were polar opposites in their attitude toward the role of male
consort. Yet these two examples remind us of the presence of the man
behind the throne at two very critical periods of European history. It
is remarkable that for all the influential historical work that now exists
on queens and queenship in history, little attention has been focused on
the partners of female sovereigns.[3] Female rule held sway in the British
Isles for much of the sixteenth, early eighteenth and nineteenth centuries, and of course for the second half of the twentieth century. Empresses
dominated eighteenth-century Russia, and an empress presided over the
Austro-Hungarian realms at the same time. The history of the Spanish and
Portuguese monarchies of the nineteenth century makes no sense unless
female rule is considered, and the modern Netherlands invites similar
consideration. Outside of Europe, in Tang China (Wu Zetian, 624–705)
and in fifteenth-century Burma (Shin Sawbu, 1394–1471) there were well-
documented eras of women on the throne, and in imperial Japan down to
1771 no less than eight empresses enjoyed rule. Such a swathe of women in
power suggests that a deeper study of the male consort is needed, and this
book is intended to commence that enquiry. The volume is by no means
comprehensive, as to time or place. However, as well as charting the lives
and influence of some of the more prominent consorts, it does signal inter-
pretive themes that future scholars may wish to pursue at more length.
The introduction that follows sets out these themes and introduces the
chapters in the volume.

The Role of the Consort

A consort is properly defined as the husband or the wife of a reigning monarch. Monarchy, in its practical application, is widely recognized as a dual
position; of a king and his consort, who went by the title of queen, who
jointly reign and reproduce a hereditary succession. Over time this dual
position has been defined in different ways. The feudal concept of *jure
uxoris* –"by right of his wife" was often deployed to empower male consorts in medieval Europe. In imperial Japan, the separate term for the
male consort, "josei-tenno," was only prohibited in 1889. And although
the literal phrase has been common in the political culture of modern
Europe—prince consort in English, Prinzgemal in German—in only two

instances (Prince Albert, the husband of Queen Victoria, in 1857; and Prince Henrik, husband of Queen Margrethe II, currently the sovereign of Denmark, in 1967) has there been separate legislation introduced to formalize the title. Where the law has proved reluctant to venture, convention and culture have taken root. During the reign of a queen regnant most aspects of the male gendered role of king were played by a woman, while the female gendered role of consort, or queenship, was played by a man. Historically, the job of consort was always a much better fit for a woman, whose primary job was to be a good wife and bear the heirs that perpetuate the dynasty. But queen consorts also played quasi-public roles as sharers of their husband's thrones, a sort of medieval and early modern equivalent to the contemporary position in republics of *first lady*, serving as the official hostess of court functions and using her prestige for noble or religious causes. While kings in history possessed specific male gendered military, judicial, legislative, and sacerdotal functions, queens performed many crucial tasks that also reinforced the power of monarchy, such as creating a reputation for piety and charity, serving as intercessor between a king and his subjects, and negotiating marriage contracts.

Yet, as Clarissa Campbell Orr has argued, consorts also played more overtly political roles. As the wife of a king, they had their husband's ear, especially in the royal bedchamber, away from the constraining influence of male advisors and the public and formal institutions of royal government. Consorts also possessed the ability to influence the distribution of patronage, an integral facet of royal power. But the most talented and politically adept consorts shared their husband's royal power in various capacities and degrees, serving as regents for their husbands when they were temporarily out of their kingdoms, usually to fight wars, or when there were multiple dominions under one crown. Additionally queens occasionally filled the political vacuum created when their husbands were either ill or incapacitated. But queen consorts also faced considerable obstacles in performing their designated roles. They were quite often foreigners, often suspected of favoring their native country's interests or fomenting intrigue and rivalries at court. The most successful queens strove to identify with their adoptive kingdoms in a variety of ways, such as learning the language. The production of heirs, especially male heirs, always served as a reliable bolster to a queen consort's domestic prestige.

Male consorts did perform many of these same tasks and faced many of the same challenges, but not all aspects of the role of consort were appropriate for the male gender, such as serving as intercessor or creating reputations for piety. While kingship is a public role inherently gendered male, [4] it was the exact opposite for the male consort, who struggled to inhabit a female gendered position while maintaining a public role commensurate with their status as the husband of a reigning monarch. Unlike the role of queen consort, which functions as a recognized and integral facet of monarchy, the male consort has been a much more ambiguous, contested, and *de facto* form of male public role. In contrast to the rather standardized title of queen, male consorts were known variously as king consorts, prince consorts, or sometimes by no formal title at all, with the specific position and title dependent upon the particular circumstances surrounding the accession of a queen regnant. Over time, and especially in the case of Britain, it has been argued that the presence of a female monarchy, and the attendant ambiguity surrounding the place of the male consort, has led to the "emasculation" of the monarchy, and deprived it of its chief roles, now restricted to ceremony and philanthropy.[5] Some of the chapters in this collection support this thesis across a longer period, others challenge it with counterexamples.

In the chapters that follow, personality, ambition, and geopolitics play a big role in determining what role a male consort will play. Often, male consorts fulfilled some of the more overtly masculine aspects of the kingly office for their wives. For instance, male consorts could perform military obligations that queens were unable or unwilling to perform, as Ferdinand of Aragon and Gaston d'Orleans did for their wives. Equally, in the case of queens unable or unwilling to rule in their own right, they assumed, either formally, or informally, the prerogatives of kingship, as did William of Orange, Frederick of Hesse, Siddiq Hasan, and a parade of medieval Navarrese king consorts. But just a female inclusive system of primogeniture remained a default mechanism for hereditary monarchies, the political and constitutional arrangements made for the husbands of queens regnant remained equally *ad hoc* in nature. In modern times it has perhaps been the male consort who has done most to cement the idea of a royal family or dynasty on the throne, for better or for worse.

The Male Consort in History

This book discusses male consorts over a long period of history, from the European High Middle Ages to the twenty-first century. In the opening chapter, Elena Woodacre recounts the remarkable history of the medieval kingdom of Navarre's series of five regnant queens and their husbands, all of whom enjoyed the status of king. This chapter graphically illustrates the essentially *ad hoc* nature of the position of male consort in an Iberian kingdom whose fortunes were inextricably tied to those of the larger and more powerful kingdoms of France, Castile, and Aragon. In each succeeding reign, the relationship between the queen and her consort and the power shared between them was renegotiated because of a revolving set of circumstances, most importantly the power the male consort wielded as the hereditary ruler of another state. In widely varying degrees, these queens and their male consorts negotiated personal and political relationships subject to pressures from the larger and more powerful states that surrounded Navarre on both sides of the Pyrenees.

The fourth of these Navarrese kings consort was Juan II of Aragon, the father of Ferdinand II, the male consort of the regnant queen Isabella of Castile. In the chapter, "Ferdinand the Catholic: King and Consort," David Abulafia deconstructs that monolithic historical entity known as "Ferdinand and Isabella," reflected in the intertwined F and Y that appears on so many of their monuments. While Ferdinand and Isabella were highly successful in creating the perception that they acted jointly in all their policies and decrees as symbolized by the motto, "Tanto monta, monta tanto" ("It's one and the same, Isabella the same as Ferdinand"), Abulafia focuses on Ferdinand's actions outside the scope of Castile, the largest and most powerful of the various Iberian kingdoms, where he enjoyed the position of king consort. In this chapter, a much more autonomous Ferdinand emerges, crafting policies geared toward the interests of the Crown of Aragon and its dependencies in the West Mediterranean, and a more pragmatic one as well, in his relative tolerance of both Islam and Judaism, whose foreign policy reflected the traditional Aragonese-French rivalry.

This very same rivalry survived the unification of the Castilian and Aragonese crowns during the reign of Ferdinand and Isabella's grandson, the Hapsburg Holy Roman Emperor Charles V, whose son and heir Philip became the consort of Queen Mary I of England (r. 1553–58). In the chapter, "He to be entituled kinge: King Philip and the Anglo-Spanish Court," Sarah Duncan seeks to dispel some traditional assumptions concerning Philip's tenure as an English king consort. Duncan questions the notion that Philip and Mary's royal court was marred by mistrust and violence between the two nationalities and lacking in ceremonies and entertainments. Instead, she argues that Philip made the most out of a severely circumscribed role of king consort during the time he spent in England, smoothing relations between the two nations and working hard to amalgamate the two courts into a functioning whole while building personal relationships with a number of English courtiers through various court ceremonies.

As we have already seen, the precedent for an English king consort survived the Glorious Revolution only to be discarded during the reign of Queen Anne (1702–1714). In the chapter, "Why Prince George of Denmark Did Not Become a King of England," Charles Beem weaves together the various motivations that served to deny Prince George the position of king consort. In Beem's analysis, George of Denmark's failure was as much due to his personality and lack of ambition as it was to political and constitutional realities that hardened into a durable precedent that prevented both the nineteenth-century Prince Albert and the twentieth-century Prince Philip from sharing their wives' thrones as king consorts.

Both William of Orange and George of Denmark served as salient precedents during the career of Frederick of Hesse, who demonstrated the art of the possible for a more ambitious and forceful male consort. In the chapter, "Frederick of Hesse, Prince Consort of Sweden," Fabian Persson recounts a story of a male consort much more reflective of the gendered realties of eighteenth-century Europe, in which Sweden's regnant queen, Ulrika Eleonora (the second Swedish reigning queen, after the unmarried Christina who was on the throne 1632–54) , abdicated her throne in 1720 after two years on the throne, after failing to get her husband recognized as king consort, so that he could succeed her as a king reigning in his own right. Ironically, while Frederick was a resourceful and active powerbroker behind the throne as consort, while he was king he resigned himself to be a proverbial *roi fainéant*.

If George of Denmark and Frederick of Hesse represent the opposite poles of male consortship, the career of Francis Stephen, the consort of Maria Theresa, represents a more balanced and mutually beneficial relationship between monarch and consort. In the chapter, "Francis Stephen: Duke, Regent and Emperor," Derek Beales describes a partnership reminiscent of that of Isabella and Ferdinand in both the mutual respect and affection that they successfully projected and the near seamless division of authority they deployed within the nexus of the Hapsburg monarchy. Duke of Lorraine from 1729 to 1736, then Grand-Duke of Tuscany from 1737 and Holy Roman Emperor from 1745 until his death in 1765, Francis Stephen's most important role was as the consort of Maria Theresa. As Beales notes, in all these positions he showed good sense, tolerance, and a special skill in financial matters.

While the role of Maria Theresa was an anomaly in the history of the Holy Roman Empire, which only elected men to the imperial throne, Russia was ruled by a series of powerful women (Sophia, Catherine I, Anna, Elizabeth, and Catherine II) over the course of the eighteenth century. Mostly they ruled without their husbands, enjoying their titles due to their partner's demise. In the case of Anna Ioannovna, her husband, the Duke of Courland died immediately after their wedding, and so in his case study in this collection Michael Bitter looks instead at Count von Bühren, her advisor. In so doing, he introduces another theme worthy of wider investigation—the role of the court favorite in a royal household with a female ruler at its centre.

In contrast to von Buhren, who took risks in his unofficial role, Prince Albert, consort of Queen Victoria (r. 1837–1901), reflects the pragmatism of both Philip of Spain and Francis Stephen. In the chapter, "Prince Albert: The Creative Consort," Karina Urbach examines the ways in which Albert responded to the particular challenges of male consortship that nineteenth-century Britain posed. Urbach does what no historian has done before, subjecting Albert to a rigorous gender analysis as she casts fresh light upon Albert's tenure as consort. Urbach describes how Albert successfully negotiated the chasm between perceptions of a "want of manliness" and a desire for "absolute power," overcoming both native xenophobia to his German origins and public emasculation by appealing to the newly emergent middle-class values, and harnessing the power of political theatre in his creation of the royal family as a national model for bourgeois respectability. As Urbach wryly notes, for a man who had no power, Prince Albert used it brilliantly.

In the chapter, "Commemorating the Consort in Colonial Bombay," Simin Patel demonstrates Albert's wide-ranging fame as an imperial icon. Patel considers the competing forces that shaped the logic of indigenous forms of commemoration in the colonial port city as he describes a hitherto unexplored aspect of a complicated imperial relationship, so recently disrupted by the trauma of the sepoy rebellion in 1857–8 , which created a sense of belonging to and partaking of royal domesticity, demonstrating the long imperial reach of Albert's singular domestic accomplishment. Patel explains how commemorative practices reflected the cosmopolitanism of Bombay's civil society, as the needs of each facet of the community supplemented the citywide royal commemoration with their own specific offerings of sympathy, joy, and loyalty to create a relationship with the imperial metropolis.

Prince Albert's first cousin, King Ferdinand II of Portugal (r. 1837–1853), consort of Queen Maria II, reflects the wide variance at play in nineteenth-century European responses to male consortship. In the chapter, "Ferdinand II of Portugal: A Conciliator King in a Turmoil Kingdom," Daniel Alves gives us the example of a kingdom that made ample legal provision for a male consort, which only recognized the husband of a reigning queen as king until after the birth of an heir. Ferdinand was the second major male consort in the history of the Portuguese monarchy, as Pedro III reigned alongside his wife (and niece) Maria I (reigned 1777–1816), Portugal's first queen regnant. Alves analyzes Ferdinand's career through the reports and correspondence of European diplomats and politicians as well as the interconnected royal families of nineteenth- century Europe, arguing that it was Portugal's peculiar political and military situation in the first half of the nineteenth century that determined the political role played by the king, whose conciliatory character was integral in the process of transforming Portuguese's politics in the mid-nineteenth century.

Frederick's nephew by marriage, Gaston d'Orleans, served as a male consort in waiting for his wife, Princess Isabel of Brazil, during the final years of the reign of her father, Emperor Pedro II of Brazil. In the chapter, "Gaston d'Orléans, Comte d'Eu: Prince Consort to D. Isabel of Brazil," Roderick Barman describes the career of a man who possessed a number of advantages, including descent from the French royal family as well as great intelligence and military ability, to create a body of support for himself and his wife during the reign of his father-in-law. In Barman's analysis, Gaston's overarching influence over his wife, combined with his social ineptitude and various health issues, served to undermine his ability to adapt to the role of male consort.

While Gaston and Isabel never made it to the throne, as the Brazilian monarchy was abolished prior to the death of Pedro II, they remained personally devoted to one another despite their unpopularity. Caroline Keen describes a similar couple in the chapter, "The Rise and Fall of Siddiq Hasan, Male Consort of Shah Jahan of Bhopal." Keen describes the improbable end to a series of remarkable female shahs in nineteenth-century Bhopal, the second largest Muslim state in India after Hyderabad, where women were not only allowed to succeed, but expected to rule regardless of who they were married to. The third of these, Sultan Shah Jahan Begam (r. 1868–1901) was dominated by her second marriage to Siddiq Hasan Khan in 1871. Keen uncovers highly conflicting contemporary historical accounts of Shah Jahan's consort. To the royal family Siddiq Hasan was an evil force causing a deep schism among its members over the right to rule of the descendants of Bhopal's Afghan founder, Dost Mohammad Khan. To the British he was a scheming adventurer who, having seduced the begam, was responsible for gross corruption and maladministration in attempting to control all areas of state government. More disturbingly, he was suspected of seditious activities through the propagation of anti-British Wahhabi material that called for jihad against the ruling "infidels." In contrast to these views, Keen describes a Siddiq Hasan who was a brilliant scholar, intent upon using his influence as consort to promote an international movement advocating a return to Islamic roots.

As the volume moves into the twentieth century, the story of a trio of Dutch male consorts once again illustrates the powerful role of personality in determining their public role. In the chapter, "Royalty, Rank, and Masculinity: The Dutch Princes Consorts of the Twentieth Century," Maria Grever and Jeroen van Zanten break new historical ground to offer the first historical assessment of a century of male consortship. Like nineteenth-century Bhopal, the Netherlands also experienced a series of queens regnant, Wilhelmina (r. 1890–1948), Juliana (r. 1948–1980), and Beatrix (r. 1980–2013), while their respective husbands, Prince Hendrik, duke of Mecklenburg-Schwerin, Prince Bernhard zur Lippe Biesterfeld, and Prince Claus von Amsberg, received the title of prince consort. Grevers and van Zanten discuss how these princes, all from Germany, differed significantly in rank, wealth, personality, and political views, and explore how they negotiated their gender both publicly and in the royal family in the long twentieth century.

Perhaps the most visibly famous male consort to contemporary readers is Prince Philip, the Duke of Edinburgh, husband of Queen Elizabeth II of Great Britain. In the chapter, "Prince Philip: Sportsman and Youth Leader, " Ina Zweininger-Bargielowska examines how Prince Philip defined his role as consort by establishing himself as a sportsman and youth leader following his marriage to Princess Elizabeth in 1947. Before and after his wife's 1952 accession, the prince became an indefatigable activist in the sporting world, serving as president or patron of numerous organizations, and carving out a public role that complemented, rather than challenged, his own sense of manhood as he encouraged young men to cultivate a physically fit, tough, and rugged masculinity. Zweininger-Barielowska draws on a range of neglected sources, including reports and publications of the National Playing Fields Association, the Duke of Edinburgh's Award Scheme, Department of Education files, and materials held at the Royal Archives.

In the final chapter, "The Prince Who Would Be King: Henrik of Denmark's Struggle for Recognition," Trond Noren Isaksen illustrates some of the problems of male consortship that seemingly defy time and space. The first male consort in the long history of the Danish monarchy as the husband of Queen Margrethe II (r. 1972–), Isaksen discusses a misunderstood and unrecognized prince, never fully accepted by the Danes, many of whom persist in considering him a foreigner, frustrated by the lack of a clearly defined role. Like William of Orange and Frederick of Hesse, Hendrik wanted to be king, presaging the publication of this volume in his own study of the history of male consortship. What brings this chapter full circle for this volume, as Isaksen wryly notes, is that Hendrik's family were native to Navarre, the land of male consorts, where the husbands of ruling queens always became kings!

Notes

1. See Sarah Duncan's chapter on Philip.
2. Stuart J. Reid, *John and Sarah Duke and Duchess of Marlborough: Based upon Unpublished Letters and Documents of Blenheim Palace* (London: John Murray, 1915), 106. This anecdote is also cited in Agnes Strickland, The Lives of the Queens of England VIII, 157.
3. Anne J. Duggan (ed.), *Queens and Queenship in Medieval Europe* (Woodbridge: Boydell, 2002); Clarissa Campbell Orr (ed.), *Queenship in Britain, 1660–1837: Royal Patronage, Court Culture and Dynastic Politics* (Manchester: Manchester University Press, 2002); idem., *Queenship in Europe, 1660–1815: The Role of the Consort* (Cambridge: Cambridge University Press, 2004); Natalie Mears, *Queenship and Political Discourse in the Elizabethan Realms* (Cambridge: Cambridge University Press, 2005); Carole Levin and Robert O. Bucholz (eds.), *Queens and Power in Medieval and Early Modern England* (Lincoln: University of Nebraska Press, 2009); Theresa Earenfight, *Queenship and Power* (Basingstoke: Palgrave Macmillan, 2013); Elena Woodacre (ed.), *Queenship in the Mediterranean: Negotiating the Role of the Queen in the Medieval and Early Modern Eras* (New York: Palgrave Macmillan, 2013).
4. For an excellent discussion of this in a medieval English context, see: W. Mark Ormrod, "Monarchy, martyrdom and masculinity: England in the later middle ages," in Patricia H. Callum and Katherine J. Lewis (eds.), *Holiness and Masculinity in Medieval Europe* (Cardiff: University of Wales Press, 2004), pp. 174–91.
5. David Cannadine, "From biography to history: Writing the history of the modern British monarchy," *Historical Research*, 77 (2004), 289–312. But compare Clarissa Campbell Orr, "The feminisation of the monarchy, 1780–1910: Royal masculinity and female empowerment," in Andrzej Olechnowicz (ed.), *The Monarchy and the British Nation, 1780 to the Present* (Cambridge: Cambridge University Press, 2007), pp. 76–107.

CHAPTER 1

The Kings Consort of Navarre: 1284–1512

Elena Crislyn Woodacre

Between 1274 and 1512, five women ruled the Pyrenean kingdom of Navarre in their own right. These female sovereigns and their husbands form the largest group of reigning queens and consort kings in Europe during the Middle Ages. This sizable cohort presents a unique opportunity to research the impact of these unusual monarchal pairs and to study the way in which these couples functioned as rulers. An examination of the careers of the kings consort of Navarre demonstrates three distinctly different types of power-sharing dynamics between the ruling pairs. It also provides specific examples of how these men coped with the unusual and challenging role of king consort and the positive and negative impact of their joint rule.

Surprisingly, in spite of the wealth of research in the fields of queenship and wider monarchal studies in recent years, neither the reigning queens of Navarre nor their consorts have been subject to a great deal of academic study. While two of the kings consort, Philip IV of France and Juan II of Aragon have been thoroughly investigated as reigning sovereigns in their own right, very little attention has been paid to their role as consort kings.[1] In her groundbreaking article, "Without the Persona of the Prince: Kings, Queens and the idea of Monarchy in Late Medieval Europe," Theresa Earenfight made a case for the joint or corporate nature of monarchy. She argued that instead of investigating kings and queens separately, it would be more fruitful to examine ruling pairs together and evaluate their partnership:

> To examine both kingship and queenship together is to discern not only their distinct shape, but also the shape that they take on together. It exposes more clearly the dynamic relationship of kingship and queenship and permits a better understanding of how theory and agency—coupled with economy, geography, warfare or demography—affect rulership.[2]

This concept of monarchical partnership is even more central to the study of queens regnant and their kings consort, as it was assumed that a man would take an active role in the rule of his wife's kingdom, given the medieval understanding of a man's dominant position in a married couple. This understanding of the superiority of the male spouse was clearly based in Biblical verse and as Margaret Sommerville rightly noted, "Saints Peter and Paul had not inserted exemption clauses for the case of married queens."[3]

Just as in Kantorwicz's notion of the king's two bodies, a queen regnant could successfully combine the roles of wife and sovereign.[4] However, this required a different approach from her spouse in his joint roles of king consort and husband in that "a queen regnant's consort had to obey her in political matters even as he ruled her in domestic ones."[5] Although this unusual combination of sovereign and spousal authority was possible given the cooperation of the consort, not all medieval writers or modern historians have agreed that it was a viable proposition. The sixteenth century annalist Jeronimo Zurita claimed that "in the old days whenever the succession of the realm fell to a woman, the government was always done by the husband."[6] The Annaliste historian Georges Duby claimed that even when a woman had inherited lands and titles, "the fact remains that it was he who exercised power, not she. She was merely at his side when he exercised it. She had to be there, in token of assent, of association."[7] Moreover, there was a key aspect of rulership which was considered to be exclusively masculine; military leadership. As it was considered wholly inappropriate for women to lead an army, this was an element of the royal role which a reigning queen was entirely dependent on her consort king to fulfill.[8] Indeed in 1343, Elizabeth of Hungary argued that her daughter-in-law Giovanna I of Naples needed her husband to rule as some tasks, such as curbing enemy incursions, were better left to a man.[9]

However, if the king, or even prince consort ruled as "king," this made him a fairly unusual monarch, for he owed his position to those who selected him as a worthy consort for their heiress instead of having the throne as his birthright. His authority therefore was somewhat weakened by his indebtedness to others for his position as an appointed or selected ruler, without the justification of genuine electoral process. The king consort also had to cope with the potentially emasculating fact that his wife was the true or "natural" sovereign of the realm and as such he had to acknowledge both her authority and the reality that his own position was entirely dependent on his marriage to the queen.

The propensity to label a reigning queen's husband with the explicit title of "consort" shows both the ambiguity and uncertainty regarding the relative position of both spouses and the weight given to the word "king." It is normally unnecessary to label the wife of a king as "queen consort" or "princess" so that there is no confusion or ambiguity over who has the right to rule. Theresa Earenfight explores the difficulty in nomenclature with these nonstandard monarchal partnerships. "A queen rarely stands alone," Earenfight declares, "She needs an adjective."[10] A woman who inherits the throne can be designated in a variety of ways, as a "queen regnant," a "sole queen," a "female monarch," or even a "female king." Again it is this last definition which illustrates the gendered understanding of the exercise of power in the Middle Ages and the underlying assumption is that a king is the one who rules the realm.

In contrast to the arguments of Zurita and Duby, all of the Navarrese queens regnant were involved in the exercise of power and the administration of the lands that they inherited. Although the queens' rights as the legitimate sovereign of the realm was consistently acknowledged, their husbands all played a visible and significant role in the governance of the realm. Each of these unusual royal couples determined the way in which they divided up duties and functioned as a personal and political partnership. In terms of the particular pairs profiled in this study, three distinct forms of power-sharing dynamics developed in order to cope with the demands of ruling both the kingdom of Navarre and the patrimony of the king consort. This study examines each of these power-sharing strategies, evaluates the effectiveness of each personal and political partnership and surveys the legacy that each of the kings consort of Navarre left on the realm.

The kingdom of Navarre was strategically located in the Pyrenean region, controlling several key routes between the Iberian peninsula and the rest of the continent. As a small kingdom, it was imperative to build strong alliances in order to protect the realm's sovereignty, particularly in the face of neighbors who were keen to control or annex the realm. The marriages of the queens regnant offered a key opportunity in this regard and each of the queens were married to foreigners who could provide a vital alliance. Each consort also brought significant territory to expand the borders of the kingdom. However, there was a price to pay for both the alliances and the expansion. The influence of the king consort could have a pronounced effect on the foreign policy of the realm and the resulting expansion created unwieldy territorial amalgamations which proved difficult to govern effectively.

The first Navarrese queen regnant, Juana I, was married to Philip IV of France. This marriage brought the crown of Navarre into a personal union with the throne of France, which lasted from the couple's accession to the French throne in 1285 until 1328 when the last of the couple's three sons, who ruled both realms in turn, died. This union was decidedly unfavorable to Navarre, as the smaller and less powerful realm. While it afforded the Pyrenean kingdom protection against the aggressive attempts of Castile and Aragon to absorb it, the years of Capetian administration were unpopular with the Navarrese as the realm was governed *in absentia* by a series of governors and edicts from Paris, first from Philip III of France as the young queen's guardian and later from her husband, Philip IV as king consort.[11] Although, Juana was recognized as the rightful heir to Navarre, Champagne, and Brie, and her consent was always given for official acts, it appears that she was not closely involved with the administration of her

Iberian kingdom while Philip IV exercised considerable authority as king consort.[12]

The Capetian governors exercised power much more tightly than previous kings and introduced a range of reforms to the administration and organization of the realm along French lines.[13] This new system of government triggered a series of protests from the Navarrese in the 1290s. In 1294, the *Buenas Villas* lodged a complaint about the current governor, Hugh de Conflans, who paid little attention to the *Fueros* or customs and laws of the realm.[14] In 1297, both the *infanzones* (or lower nobility) and the *Buenas villas* protested in an attempt to defend their privileges which they felt were being trampled under French rule.[15] However, the royal couple did not respond favorably to the protest of their Navarrese subjects and overt criticism of the king consort in particular was not tolerated; one man who dared to do so in 1304 had his tongue mutilated.[16]

It is important to note however, that Philip handled the county of Champagne in a notably different manner to how he administered the kingdom of Navarre. John F. Benton argues that both Philip and his father were "sensitive about usurping the authority" of the Jours de Troyes assembly.[17] Philip carefully emphasized the role of his wife, the rightful countess, through the couple's nearly annual visits to Champagne and her more visible participation in its governance masked the fact that Philip was simultaneously tightening royal control of the county.[18] If Philip had taken the same care of the sensibilities of the Navarrese, he would have been a far more popular king consort.

The second king consort of Navarre, Philip, count of Evreux, had a decidedly more positive reign with his wife Juana II. However, Philip encountered considerable resistance at the onset of their reign due to the negative experience of a king consort which the Navarrese had previously endured. This manifested itself in an attempt to prevent the new consort from taking part in the coronation of his wife in 1329. The first queen regnant and her husband did not have a formal coronation in Navarre, so there was no precedent for the participation of a king consort in the ceremony.

The plan put forward by the Navarrese was for the queen to be elevated alone on the shield of estate as per their traditional coronation ceremony. The justification for Philip's exclusion from the ritual was that, "my lady will be raised up…as she is the natural lady and no one can be raised up if they are not the natural lord."[19] However, the Navarrese acknowledged that Philip could still participate in the administration and rule of the realm as her spouse.[20] Philip's envoy, Henri de Sully, negotiated for Philip's right to share fully in both the coronation ceremony and the government of the realm, arguing that "as husband and head (of their family) he should have the rights of his wife and companion."[21] Sully's persuasive arguments, coupled with the support of the queen herself for her husband's full participation, swayed the Navarrese and ultimately, both husband and wife were anointed and raised up on the ceremonial shield together in the Cathedral of Pamplona on March 5, 1329.[22]

While Juana II and Philip d'Evreux were able to reside in Navarre far more than their Capetian predecessors, they were still required to spend a considerable amount of time in Northern France to administer Philip's patrimony and the lands granted to them in exchange for her grandmother's Champenois holdings in 1328. Although they left the realm to officials during their absences, they ensured that their French governor had a team of Navarrese administrators to ensure that local law and custom was respected and that the citizens were more directly involved in governance.[23]

Despite their frequent absences from Navarre, the couple were directly involved with the rule of the kingdom and prioritized the political and administrative needs of their new realm. Although Marianne Mahn-Lot claimed that Philip preferred to remain at the French court and had "no personal ambition and no taste for governance," evidence from his reign with Juana II demonstrates that Philip showed a deep interest in the administration of the realm. He is particularly credited with the vital *amejoramiento* or recompilation and restructuring of the *Fueros*.[24] He also worked in concert with his wife on the improvement and construction of cathedrals, monasteries, and royal palaces.[25] The couple were also actively involved in delivering justice, an important royal prerogative. At the beginning of their reign they demonstrated their authority in this area by addressing several pressing problems including cracking down on a spate of anti-Semitic violence and curbing the issue of banditry.[26] They also set up a special commission in 1340 in order to reform the justice process and undo the corruption that had plagued the system under Capetian rule.[27]

This record of service, which was a considerable improvement of the reign of the previous Capetian sovereigns, ensured the popularity of the ruling pair. The contemporary chronicle of Garci Lopez de Roncevalles claims "they were a good king and queen and well loved by all in their kingdom."[28] The chronicle of the Principe de Viana also praised the couple and referred to Philip in particular as *"este bienaventurado rey,"* or "that blessed king."[29] Philip d'Evreux ultimately renovated the tarnished reputation of the king consort in the Navarre and was rewarded with the popular sobriquets *"el noble,"* *"el bueno,"* or *"el prudente."* When Philip was ultimately killed while participating in an Iberian crusade in 1343, he was significantly accorded the honor of burial in the Cathedral of Pamplona as a true Navarrese monarch.

In contrast, the third king consort of Navarre, Juan of Aragon, had a devastating effect on Navarre, both during his reign alongside his wife, Blanca I and during his controversial widowhood. Shortly after their marriage in 1420, Juan became involved in a political conflict in Castile, which ultimately drew Navarre into a destructive war with its Iberian neighbor.[30] Blanca was left to marshal the defense of the realm while simultaneously working to broker a peace accord to put an end to the crisis.

During his wife's lifetime, Juan had little involvement in the governance of Navarre.[31] This was due to several factors: his involvement in Castilian affairs, his role as a lieutenant in Aragon during his brother's frequent absences and finally his wife's capable and experienced governance meant that his own presence was not necessarily required in Navarre.[32] In fact, Juan spent very little of his lengthy time as king of Navarre on the day-to-day management of the realm, leaving that task to his wife and later to a series of lieutenants, including his second wife and two of his children.[33]

After Blanca's death in 1441, Juan refused to cede the title of king to his fully grown son and heir, Carlos, by exploiting a codicil in Blanca's will which asked Carlos to refrain from using the royal title until his father was ready to relinquish it. Initially, there was a period of compromise as Carlos was allowed to effectively govern Navarre, albeit as his father's lieutenant instead of as king. However, when Juan remarried in 1445 any pretext that Juan had to the title of king consort was eliminated and both Carlos and his formidable group of supporters were unwilling to allow Juan to continue to control the realm. This resulted in a prolonged civil war between Juan's supporters, the Agramonts and Carlos and his proponents, the Beaumonts. The conflict continued long after Carlos' death in September 1461 and the protracted unrest had a ruinous effect on the realm, ultimately creating the instability which left it vulnerable to annexation by Castile in 1512. Boissonade summarized the situation for Navarre at Juan's death in 1479, "a state ruined by civil war, disabled by anarchy, that is the heritage that Juan II left."[34]

Gaston IV of Foix, husband of Blanca and Juan's daughter Leonor, spent years trying to achieve the position of king consort, only to be denied by his untimely death. Leonor was the youngest child, and though her place in the line of succession was assured, she was third in line after her brother Carlos and elder sister Blanca.[35] However, Juan disinherited Carlos during their struggle for the crown and the Princess Blanca was also ousted from the succession for supporting her brother's claim. This meant that Leonor was promoted to heir apparent and she and her husband were given the lieutenancy of the realm to exercise on Juan's behalf. Leonor took up the administration of the realm while Gaston provided key military, political, and financial support.

The incorporation of the Navarrese crown into the holdings of the House of Foix-Béarn was an ambition that Gaston's father had cherished but failed to achieve. Gaston's father, Jean I of Foix, was married to another Navarrese heiress, Juana, eldest daughter of Carlos III of Navarre. Although they were confirmed as the future queen regnant and king consort of the kingdom by the Cortes of Navarre in 1402, Juana's untimely death in July 1413 nullified the plan and Jean's suit for Juana's sister Blanca, the new heiress, was rejected.[36] Gaston and Leonor worked tirelessly to bring that dream to fruition and unite Navarre, Foix, Béarn, and Gaston's considerable subsidiary territories, turning the small Iberian kingdom into a sizable trans-Pyrenean block. Unfortunately Gaston died in 1472 while he was en route to Navarre to give support to Leonor and their partisans.[37] Although Leonor ultimately became queen of Navarre, her triumph was short-lived as she died only a few weeks after her father in early 1479.

The last king consort of Navarre was another lord from the French *Midi*, Jean d'Albret, husband of Leonor and Gaston's granddaughter Catalina. The couple's Navarrese coronation was delayed for ten long years as continuing political instability in Navarre and the efforts of Catalina's uncle to unseat her had forced them to remain in their Béarnaise capital of Pau. However, thanks to the precedent set by Philip d'Evreux, both spouses participated fully and equally in their coronation in 1494, with two crowns and sets of regalia although there was only one sword, which was borne by Jean.[38] However, the wording of the coronation documents clearly stresses Jean's position as a foreigner and that the right to rule ultimately derived from the queen, by stating that Jean "has come to this kingdom of Navarre in the right and cause of the Queen Catalina, our wife."[39]

Although Jean's right to rule the kingdom alongside his wife had been confirmed through the process of coronation, this did not guarantee the consort a smooth and successful reign. Jean and Catalina struggled to administer their unwieldy territorial amalgamation, comprised of the Iberian kingdom and the considerable territories of the House of Foix-Béarn north of the Pyrenees. After their long delayed coronation in Navarre in 1494, the couple began to strategically separate for periods of time. This allowed them to maintain the physical presence of the sovereign on both sides of the Pyrenees and achieve particular diplomatic goals. In October 1496, Catalina left Jean with the administration of Navarre while she returned to her French territories but it appears that the Navarrese were not content with the king consort as a substitute. Catalina was forced to defend her absence and respond to the suggestion that they might refute their allegiance to her if she was not physically present in the realm in a missive to the *Cortes* in mid-December 1496; "To this I respond that I am continuing the great and arduous business in this our domain of Béarn and in our other domains and our lands...and this requires...our Royal presence here."[40] Indeed, Catalina was working to achieve a permanent settlement to the lengthy and damaging succession battle with Jean de Narbonne, which resulted in the Treaty of Tarbes, signed in September 1497.[41] Catalina aimed to reassure the *Cortes* that she was working as quickly as possible and that she hoped to return to Navarre shortly "to comfort them with our royal presence."

Despite the protest from the *Cortes,* Catalina continued to use Jean as her surrogate in Navarre for discrete periods of time, particularly during the latter years of their reign. She also dispatched Jean on diplomatic missions to the courts of Spain and France. However, the couple spent the bulk of their reign together, alternating between their French and Iberian territory and moving frequently between different towns and cities in order to bring the royal body to as many places as possible.

The Navarrese complaints to their queen about their dissatisfaction about Jean's performance as her representative may have stemmed from his background as a French lord. Indeed, several early modern writers noted how Jean's Iberian subjects felt that his comportment and behavior were unsuitable for a Navarrese king. Andre Favyn claims Jean's informal tendencies were in keeping with a more French style of rule, which was at odds with his Navarrese subjects:

> governance in the French style is completely opposite to the Spanish. In France the familiar presence of our monarchs delights the French and gives them the love and the reverence [of their subjects]. In Spain if their kings showed themselves every day they would be despised by their people.[42]

Esteban de Garibay claimed that many of the Navarrese "despised [Jean] and held him in little esteem because his subjects looked for honest gravity, moderation and restraint before giving their approval which is very good in all men, especially princes and above all kings."[43]

The comment of the Navarrese chronicler Jose de Moret mirror those of Garibay and Favyn, noting that:

> the decorum of his royal person…was too simple, which greatly reduced his authority, speaking to his vassals and others familiarly as if he was not a king but a certain knight, so much so that he did not mend matters by going to common parties…And it is true to say that it greatly displeased sane and upright men these French manners, where their kings are too familiar with the vassals.[44]

Although Jean's behavior did not directly lead to the annexation of the realm by Ferdinand of Aragon in 1512, the disaffection caused by his actions and foreign style of rule did little to ensure Navarrese loyalty to the king and queen in the face of incursion from their Iberian neighbors.

Three different modes of power sharing between the king consort and queen regnant can be seen though an examination of the reigns of these monarchical pairs. There is an interesting correlation between the couple's power-sharing dynamic and the amount of time each pair spent in Navarre as opposed to their other territories. The first pair, Juana I and Philip IV of France, functioned in a mode which can be termed as "His Way." Philip maintained supremacy in their political partnership, taking on the bulk of administration and governance for both kingdoms. The strength of their personal partnership was noted by contemporary chroniclers and later biographers, however Philip's affection for his wife and his hesitancy to separate from her may have been a key factor which prevented her return to Navarre, even for a short visit.[45] Consequently, the couple were based nearly permanently in the Ile de France firmly favoring his own center of power to the detriment of Navarre.

Another, more equal mode of power sharing can be seen in the partnerships of Juana II and Philip d'Evreux and Catalina and Jean d'Albret. This mode, termed "Team Players" reflects the couples' ability to work together to manage their territorial holdings effectively. Both couples participated jointly and fairly equitably in the administration of the realm, either by working together or by separating when necessary in order to maintain the presence of a sovereign in different areas of their domains. While this mode of power sharing greatly increased the amount of time that the sovereigns were present in Navarre from the "His Way" mode, there were still periods where both couples ruled the realm via governors *in absentia* while they were travelling through their joint dominions.

Juana II and Philip d'Evreux divided their time between Navarre, his patrimony in Northern France and their impressive residence in Paris, the Hôtel de Navarre. They generally remained together, although Philip did return to Navarre alone en route to his participation in the Aragonese Crusade. During Philip's absence, Juana administered Philip's patrimony in Northern France. This flexibility in their partnership, to literally swap roles with Juana governing his territory while Philip went south to visit Navarre and work with their Iberian allies, shows the strengths of their relationship and this mode of power sharing.

Catalina and Jean d'Albret travelled widely within and around their Navarrese and French territories.[46] Pamplona was not their permanent or even preeminent capital, but they both made prolonged stays there. Although they spent the majority of their time together, Catalina and Jean also separated periodically in order to govern and maintain the presence of a sovereign in different provincial capitals. However, as noted previously, Jean was not always accepted as a substitute sovereign in Navarre in place of his wife, the rightful sovereign. Jean was arguably more successful as his wife's diplomatic envoy, conducting diplomatic missions to the courts of Spain and France.

Finally a third mode, "Divide & Conquer" can be seen in the reigns of Blanca and Juan of Aragon and that of Leonor and Gaston of Foix. This mode dealt with the demands of administering multiple, widespread territories by assigning each partner to the governance of one particular area. While this required the couples to physically separate for lengthy periods, it had the positive benefit of ensuring that the (female) sovereign's presence remained nearly permanently in Navarre. Although both couples could and did work together when possible, generally each partner functioned in a separate and fairly equal sphere. This style of governance functioned best when the ambitions and objectives of both partners were in line. For example, Leonor remained in Navarre to exercise the lieutenancy of the realm while Gaston was based in his own territories on the northern side of the Pyrenees. Their mutual ambition to gain the throne of Navarre for themselves and their offspring formed the core of their policy and their military, financial, and political resources were all focused to achieve this goal. Blanca also remained in Navarre to govern the realm, leaving Juan free to pursue his own interests in Castile and serve as his brother's lieutenant in Aragon. However, Blanca and Juan were often working political cross-purposes. While Blanca was focused on administering Navarre and preserving its sovereignty, Juan's ambitions and goals were focused on the preservation of his Castilian territory and ultimately Iberian hegemony.

The marriages made for the children of these ruling pairs is connected to the power-sharing dynamic of each of the queens and their consorts. Navarre's changing foreign policy during their reigns, which are reflected in these marriages, were driven by a combination of external political factors and the interests and ambitions of the king consorts. Indeed, many of these marriages reflect the policy goals of the king consort and his homeland as much as or more than the needs of Navarre. The more powerful the king consort, the more clearly his influence on foreign policy and marital alliances can be seen.

The marriages of the children of Juana I generally reflect the "His Way" dynamic of their marriage, prioritizing alliances beneficial to France. However during Juana's lifetime, there were attempts to make Iberian alliances which may have ameliorated Navarre's relations with their immediate neighbors. In 1294, two marriages were contracted for their children which would have been beneficial to France, Juana's Champenois territory and Navarre; their second son Philip was betrothed to the eldest daughter of Otto IV, Count Palatine of Burgundy and their daughter, Marguerite was contracted to marry the young Ferdinand IV of Castile.[47] However, while Philip's Burgundian marriage was successfully made in 1307, the plans for the Castilian marriage was scuppered by the death of Marguerite and later her sister Blanche who had been offered as an alternative bride.[48] After this succession of untimely deaths, no further attempts appear to have been made to contract a marriage with Castile; perhaps in lieu of a matrimonial connection Philip signed a treaty of alliance with Ferdinand on March 31, 1306.[49] In the same year, another attempt to contract an Iberian alliance was made; their son Robert was promised to Constance, daughter of Frederick III of Aragon, king of Sicily.[50] Just as in the case of the Castilian marriage, this betrothal was also ended by the untimely demise of one of Philip and Juana's children, and Robert's death seems to mark the last effort to contract a Southern marriage.

The marriages which were successfully contracted were those with a northern focus, which had strategic benefits for France and Juana's counties of Champagne and Brie. The importance of building alliances with both the Duchy and County of Burgundy is demonstrated by the fact that all three of their surviving sons, Louis, Philip, and Charles made Burgundian marriages. In addition to Philip's previously mentioned marriage to Jeanne of Burgundy, their eldest son Louis married Marguerite, the daughter of Robert II, duke of Burgundy in 1299 and Charles married Blanche of Burgundy in 1307.[51] Their only surviving daughter Isabella was betrothed to Edward, Prince of Wales (later Edward II of England) in 1303.[52]

Although it could be argued that the imbalance of Northern versus Iberian alliances were due merely to the untimely deaths of three of their children, it would not have been difficult to salvage the matches with

Castile and Aragon, if Philip had desired to do so. Isabella could have married Ferdinand IV of Castile instead of Edward II of England and her brother Charles could have taken Robert's place and married Constance of Sicily. However, France's priority appears to have been binding Burgundy closely through three marriages and improving relations with England rather than Iberia. Once again, Paris was prioritized over Pamplona, reflecting the "His Way" dynamic of Philip and Juana's partnership.

The marriages for the ruling pairs who employed the "Divide and Conquer" dynamic reflect the political ambitions of both partners. The marriages made for Blanca I's children suited the foreign policy goals of Navarre but they were also very much in line with the ambitions of her husband, Juan. The marriage of their son and heir Carlos to Agnes of Cleves, the niece of the duke of Burgundy, reflected the traditional alliance between Burgundy and Aragon.[53] The match with Cleves was also an advantageous marriage for Navarre, bringing not only Agnes' sizable dowry but also the pledge that Agnes and Carlos would succeed to the duchy of Burgundy if Philip le Bon died without heirs.[54] Their daughter Blanca's marriage to Enrique (later IV) of Castile was a key element of the Treaty of Toledo in 1436 that ended the war Juan had precipitated between Castile and Navarre. Blanca had worked tirelessly to broker a peace treaty with their neighbors and repair the damage caused by this destructive conflict.[55] The treaty allowed Navarre to regain some of the territory which had been lost along the Castilian frontier during the conflict and allowed Juan to continue to administer his Castilian inheritance, even though it was ultimately pledged as his daughter's dowry.[56] Finally, their youngest daughter Leonor's marriage to the count of Foix suited both Navarre and Aragon equally as the county bordered both kingdoms.[57]

The marriages of Gaston and Leonor's children were all aimed at furthering Gaston's ambition to create a Pyrenean block and gaining support for Leonor's claim to the Navarrese throne. Leonor and Gaston had ten children and deployed them very successfully to create alliances; one daughter became duchess of Brittany while another became the marquesa of Montferrat.[58] Only one child, Pierre or Pedro, was dedicated to the church and he rose to become an influential and powerful cardinal.[59] The majority of these marriages were made with French houses, strengthening bonds with Gaston's overlord, the king of France or with Foix's neighbors in the *Midi*, including the Counts of Armagnac and Candale.[60] Options for an Iberian marriage may have been limited by consanguinity as the king of Aragon was Leonor's father and she was closely related to the Kings of Castile through both blood and marriage. The success of their strategy also bore fruit in the following generation, as four of their granddaughters became queens.[61]

However, the marriage of their son and heir was their greatest success in matrimonial politics and strengthened both Gaston's position with his French overlord and Leonor's claim to the throne of Navarre. In an effort to neutralize Louis XI of France's support for the claim of Leonor's sister

Blanca to the Navarrese throne, Gaston visited the French court in the winter of 1461–2 and offered the king a matrimonial alliance between Gaston's son and heir and the king's sister Magdalena. The proposal was accepted with alacrity in February 1462 and the wedding took place a few weeks later on March 7, 1462; the bride received a dowry of 100,000 *escudos de oro* and the groom was formally designated as his father's heir to the Foix-Béarn holdings as well as the heir to Navarre after his mother.[62] This marriage brought prestige to the House of Foix-Béarn and improved relations between Gaston and his liege lord and it also served to strengthen Leonor's position as heiress; shortly afterward, Juan II reconfirmed Leonor as his successor in Navarre and Leonor's sister and rival Blanca was incarcerated in Gaston's stronghold of Orthez without hope of a reprieve from her father or her former supporter, the king of France.[63]

The weakest connection to the interests of the king consorts or conversely the strongest connections to Navarre's needs can be seen in the marriages made for the children of Catalina and Juana II. These two couples both employed the "Team Players" mode of power sharing. The emphasis on the Navarrese foreign policy objectives in the marriages made for the offspring of these particular couples may also be due to the fact that both husbands, Jean d'Albret and Philip d'Evreux, held less powerful titles and territory than their wives. Therefore, the interests of the Pyrenean kingdom would necessarily be paramount.

One of the key policy objectives of Juana II and Philip d'Evreux was improving relations with Navarre's Iberian and Pyrenean neighbors. They attempted to use their daughters' marriages to build alliances with three of the most important powers in the region; Aragon, Castile, and Foix. The couple initiated talks for a marriage between their eldest daughter, Juana and Pedro, the heir of Aragon shortly after their arrival in Navarre in 1329. However, the negotiations were quite protracted and an agreement was not signed until April 1333 by which time their second daughter Maria had been substituted for Juana who professed a desire to become a nun instead of being queen of Aragon.[64] Maria and Pedro were finally wed on July 25, 1338 and although there was some residual tension over the late payment of dowry installments, the marriage did serve to draw the two realms closer together.[65]

In addition to the Aragonese alliance, Juana II and Philip d'Evreux also attempted to build marriages in Northern France that would secure Philip's patrimony there. They aimed to create a match between their son and heir Carlos with Jeanne de Penthièvre, the heiress presumptive of Brittany but the match was blocked by the king of France.[66] Philip de Valois was more positive about a marriage for their daughter Blanche with Louis, the son and heir of the count of Flanders and a marital agreement was signed in Paris on March 15, 1340.[67] However, the French king changed his mind following the outbreak of the Hundred Years War and decided to support a marriage between Margaret of Brabant and the Flemish heir instead.

Philip d'Evreux died on an Iberian Crusade in 1343, leaving Juana II with the responsibility of crafting marital alliances for their children. Juana emphasized the strategy of building alliances with Navarre's neighbors in the South. After the failed Flemish match, an attempt was made to secure a marital alliance with Castile for Blanche to repeat their success with Maria's Aragonese wedding. An accord was signed on July 1, 1345 which set the dowry at 300,000 florins and appears to have had papal approval but the match failed to materialize.[68] However, Juana and Philip's daughter Agnes successfully made a strategic marriage to their Pyrenean neighbor Gaston Phébus of Foix in 1349.[69] However, Juana's death from the Plague in October of the same year meant that the dowry was not fully paid, causing disastrous problems in the couple's marriage which undermined the alliance which Juana had attempted to build.[70]

After both Juana II and Philip d'Evreux's death, their children reversed Juana's policy of focusing on Navarrese alliances to focus on marriages in Northern France. After two failed betrothals, Blanche eventually married Philip VI de Valois in January 1350 and her brother Carlos II married the French Princess Jeanne de Valois in 1352.[71] Philip was able to fulfill his parents' ambitions to contract a Flemish alliance when he married Yolande of Flanders in 1353. In 1366, Luis countered this trend with a marriage to Jeanne of Durazzo, a potential heiress of the Kingdom of Naples who brought connections to the Angevin dynasty and their wide-ranging territories in Italy, Hungary, and Provence.[72]

The marriages that Catalina and Jean d'Albret made, or attempted to make for their children, reflect their changing foreign policy direction and their desire to secure the sovereignty of Navarre in an increasingly hostile political climate. In the early years of their reign, they were dependent on the goodwill of Isabel and Ferdinand and accordingly contracted a series of Spanish betrothals for their children in 1494, 1500, and 1504.[73] However, none of these projected marriages came to fruition. Later, when relations with Spain deteriorated and the Navarrese monarchs eventually turned to the king of France for protection, attempts were made to marry Catalina's heir to Renée of France and construct Italian alliances for her daughters.[74] Unfortunately, due to untimely deaths and the reluctance of some marital candidates to get involved in the complicated political situation surrounding Navarre after the Annexation of 1512, many of Catalina's children struggled to marry. Out of their eight children that survived to adulthood, only two were eventually married. Their son and heir, Enrique, eventually married Marguerite d'Angoulême, sister of François I of France in 1527. The only daughter who managed to wed was the youngest, Isabel, who married Rene I, viscount of Rohan in 1534.

Each of the kings consort of Navarre had a huge impact on the realm, both with regard to their territorial holdings as mentioned and their personalities, priorities, and ambition. Ultimately, whether a consort had a positive or negative effect on the realm was largely due to the extent of their ambition and their interest in Navarrese concerns. The consort with the most beneficial impact on the realm, Philip d'Evreux, was content with the rule of the Pyrenean kingdom and his French patrimony. Given that he was raised with the expectation of becoming a count, his promotion to king consort in 1329 would have been a major elevation in status. As discussed previously, he took kingship seriously and worked on projects such as the *amejoramiento* of the law code which had a long-term benefit for the kingdom.

Jean d'Albret and Gaston of Foix both prioritized Navarre to a fair extent, but both ultimately failed to have a positive impact on the realm for different reasons. Jean d'Albret, like Philip d'Evreux, was the son of a French lord. Having reached the top of the feudal ladder by his elevation to king consort, he did not have major territorial or political ambitions. However, the fact that he had been raised as a French lord showed in his deportment and conduct which was at odds with the expectations of kingly behavior by his Iberian subjects. Jean was also distracted by the extensive number of territories held by his family and his wife, although he did generally put the needs of Navarre first after his coronation in Pamplona in 1494. Unlike Philip d'Evreux, he did not engage in any major programs to benefit the kingdom, but this was largely due to the lack of stability in the realm and the difficulties presented by Navarre's tenuous position as a buffer state between two great rival powers.

Gaston of Foix was utterly focused on the acquisition of the Navarrese crown for his wife and their descendants. His marriage to Leonor and the radical changes to the Navarrese succession after the death of Blanca I in 1441 gave him the opportunity to achieve his ambition. However, being promoted to joint heir and lieutenant with his wife did not mark the end of the effort needed to gain the crown itself. His wife remained in Navarre to administer the realm while Gaston divided his time between fighting Navarrese rebels, making diplomatic trips to further his political ambitions and governing his own substantial territories. He was focused on Navarre because the realm itself was the centerpiece of his political objectives but, like Jean d'Albret, he was too busy trying to contain the rebels and administer his other holdings to engage in any beneficial projects for the kingdom.

Both Philip IV of France and Juan of Aragon were destructive consorts, due primarily to the fact that their political focus was elsewhere. Navarre was only important to them as a means to achieve other political ambitions. For Philip IV of France, Navarre was a distant and troublesome realm which gave him a strategic Iberian toehold but was unimportant in comparison to French concerns and interests. He was far more interested in his wife's county of Champagne, which was wealthy, powerful, and strategically located near his own capital. Juan of Aragon appreciated the title of king of Navarre but the realm itself had little value for him except for being as his biographer Vicens Vives termed "the principal front of his premeditated attack on Castile" and later as a means to thwart the ambitions of his rival, the king of France.[75]

In conclusion, the careers of the kings consort of Navarre demonstrate the inherent difficulties of the position. All of these men were foreigners who impacted the realm in both positive and negative ways. They brought key alliances and territorial expansion that benefited the small and somewhat vulnerable Pyrenean realm. However, the territories of the kings consort had a profound effect on foreign policy and the governance of the realm, as the couples were forced to divide their time between Navarre and their wider territorial holdings. Navarre's experience of kings consort was decidedly mixed, from the absent yet heavy hand of Philip of France, men such as Juan of Aragon who manipulated the fate of the realm to achieve his own political goals to the keen interest and diligent efforts of Philip d'Evreux who was ultimately cherished as a true Navarrese monarch.

Notes

1. Examples of well-known biographies of these two men include Joseph R. Strayer, *The Reign of Philip the Fair* (Princeton NJ, 1980); and Jaime Vicens Vives, *Juan II de Aragon (1398–1479): Monarquia y revolución en la España del siglo XV* (Barcelona, 1953).
2. Theresa Earenfight, "Without the Persona of the Prince: Kings, Queens and the Idea of Monarchy in Late Medieval Europe," *Gender and History*, 19.1 (2007), 10.
3. The Bible (Latin Vulgate version), I Peter 3:1. For Paul see Colossians 3:18, "*mulieres subditae estote viris sicut oportet in Domino*" or "wives be subject to your husbands as it behoveth in the Lord." Also Ephesians 5:22–3 "*mulieres viris suis subditae sint sicut Domino quoniam vir caput est mulieris sicut Christus caput est ecclesiae ipse salvator corporis*" or "let women be subject to their husbands, as to the Lord because the husband is the head of the wife as Christ is the head of the church. He is the saviour of the body." Margaret R. Sommerville, *Sex and Subjection: Attitudes to Women in Early Modern Society* (London, 1995), 57.
4. Ernst H. Kantorowicz, *The King's Two Bodies: A Study in Mediaeval Political Theology* (Princeton NJ, 1957).
5. Sommerville, *Sex and Subjection*, 59.
6. Jerónimo Zurita, *Anales de la Corona de Aragon*, ed. Ángel Canellas Lopez, 9 vols., (Zaragoza, 1980–90), vol. 8, 74. Original text is "*aunque la sucesión del reino recayese en mujer, el gobierno siempre fue del marido.*" Note: all translations in the text are my own unless otherwise stated.
7. Georges Duby, "Women and Power" in *Cultures of Power: Lordship, Status and Process in Twelfth Century Europe*, ed. by Thomas N. Bisson (Philadelphia, 1995), 74.
8. For further discussion of the military role of consort kings, see Elena Woodacre, "Questionable Authority: Female Sovereigns and Their Consorts in Medieval and Renaissance Chronicles" in Juliana Dresvina and Nicholas Sparks (eds.), *Authority and Gender in Medieval and Renaissance Chronicles* (Newcastle-upon-Tyne, 2012), 379–80.
9. Full text of this letter included as *Pieces Justificatives* IX in Emile G. Léonard, *La jeunesse de Jeanne I: Reine de Naples, Comtesse de Provence* (Paris:

Librarie Auguste, 1932), 409–10. See also page 265 for more discussion of the letter's contents.

10. Earenfight, "Without the Persona of the Prince," 1.

11. Juana's engagement to Philip III's son and his designation as her guardian is contained in the Treaty of Orleans (1275). Translated text of the treaty printed in Theodore Evergates, "Aristocratic Women in the County of Champagne," in *Aristocratic Women in Medieval France*, ed. by Theodore Evergates (Philadelphia, 1999), 87.

12. It is important to note that Philip's overall style of government was intensely bureaucratic, see Joseph R. Strayer, "Philip the Fair-A 'Constitutional' King," *American Historical Review*, 62.1 (Oct 1956), 18–32.

13. Eloísa Ramírez Vaquero, "Los resortes del poder en la Navarra bajomedieval (siglos XII-XV)," *Anuario de Estudios Medievales*, 25.2 (1995), 430–40.

14. Archivo Géneral de Navarra (hereafter AGN) Comptos, Caj. 4, no.98 dated May 29, 1294.

15. Alfonso Espinet and Juan Manuel Gouzá lez-Cremona, *Diccionario de los Reyes de España* (Barcelona, 1989), 222–3; and Eloísa Ramírez Vaquero, *Historia de Navarra: La Baja Edad Media, Colección Temas de Navarra, vol. II* (Pamplona, 1993), 39.

16. Félix Segura Urra, *Fazer Justicia; Fuero, poder público y delito en Navarra (siglos XIII-XIV)* (Pamplona, 2005), 266. The episode is documented in AGN Reg. 8, fol. 10v. (1304).

17. John F. Benton, "Philip the Fair and the Jours de Troyes," in *Culture, Power and Personality in Medieval France*, ed. by Thomas N. Bisson (London, 1991), 196; and Robert Fawtier, *The Capetian Kings of France: Monarchy and Nation (987–1328)* (London, 1960), 128–9.

18. Elisabeth Lalou, "Le gouvernement de la reine Jeanne 1285–1305," *Cahiers Haut-Marnais* 167 (1986), 16–30.

19. AGN Comptos, Caj. 41, no.37, 2 dated November 30, 1328 at Pamplona, original text is *"madame fust levee…pour ce que elle est dame naturele et nulz ne doit estre levez si il n'est seignor naturel."*

20. Ibid.

21. A portion of the original document reprinted in Javier Zabalo Zabalegui, *La administración del Reino de Navarra en el siglo XIV* (Pamplona, 1973), 53. The provenance of the document is AGN Comptos, Caj. 6, no. 60. Original text is *"assi como marido et cabeça deve aver de los bienes de su muyller et comaynnera."* Note that Sully is clearly drawing on biblical authority, the assertion of Paul that "the head of woman is man" (1 Corinthians, 11.3). Further evidence of the ongoing negotiation between the Cortes and Henri de Sully as the Evreux's representative can be found in AGN Comptos, Caj. 31, no. 7, 7 (2) dated January 12, 1329 at Estella.

22. The coronation documents are AGN Comptos, Caj. 6, no. 60 dated March 5, 1329 at Pamplona. See also Jose Maria Lacarra, *El juramento de los reyes de Navarra (1234–1329)* (Madrid, 1972), 62.

23. Béatice Leroy comments that "progressively, Navarre was governed by the Navarrese" (*progressivement, la Navarre est gouvernée par les Navarrais);* Béatrice Leroy, "Les débuts de la dynastie d'Evreux en Navarre: des experiences mutuelles, de nouvelles situations," *En la España Medieval* 17 (1994), 23. Miranda Garcia also noted the "exquisite respect and tact" (*exquisito res-*

peto y tacto) shown to the Navarrese by Jeanne and Philip; Fermín Miranda García, *Felipe III y Juana II de Evreux* (Pamplona, 2003), 52.

24. Marianne Mahn-Lot, "Philip d'Evreux, Roi de Navarre et un projet de Croisade contre le Royaume de Grenade (1329–1331)," *Bulletin Hispanique* 46 (1944), 227. Original text is *"aucune ambition personnelle, aucun goût de gouverner."* On the *amejoramiento* of the *Fueros* see Miranda Garcia, *Felipe III y Juana II*, 102–07.

25. For their architectural legacy an excellent source is Javier Martinez de Aguirre, *Arte y Monarquia en Navarra (1328–1425)* (Pamplona, 1987).

26. For the anti-Semitic violence see Nadia Marin, "La matanza de 1328, témoin des solidarités de la Navarre chrétienne," *Principe de Viana* 59.213 (1998), 147–70. For a more wider examination of their exercise of justice see Marcelino Beroiz Lazcano, *Crimen y castigo en Navarra bajo el reinado de los primeros Evreux (1328–1349)*, Colección Historia (Pamplona, 2005); and Félix Segura Urra, *Fazer Justicia. Fuero, poder público y delito en Navarra (siglos XIII-XIV)* (Pamplona, 2005).

27. Maria Isabel Ostolaza Elizondo, "El tribunal de la Cort de Navarra durante el siglo XIV (1329–1387)," *Principe de Viana* 47.178 (1986), 504.

28. Garci Lopez de Roncevalles, *Cronica de Garci Lopez de Roncevalles*, ed. Carmen Orcastequi Gros and Ángel J. Martin Duque (Pamplona, 1977), 76.

29. Carlos, Principe de Viana, *Cronica de los Reyes de Navarra*, ed. by Jose Yanguas y Miranda and Antonio Ubieto Arteta (Pamplona, 1843), 168.

30. Although Juan was a younger son of the king of Aragon, he had inherited the sizable Castilian territories of his mother, Leonor de Alberquerque.

31. Joseph O'Callaghan aptly summed up Juan's attitude to the Navarrese crown, "While pleased to have the royal title, Juan was little interested in Navarre and was content to leave its administration to the queen." Joseph F. O'Callaghan, *A History of Medieval Spain* (Ithaca, NY, 1975), 554.

32. Eloísa Ramírez Vaquero, "La reina Blanca y Navarra," *Principe de Viana* 60 (1999), 323–40. Ramírez Vaquero notes Blanca had "considerable experience on her shoulders." See also Maria Isabel Ostolaza Elizando, "D. Juan de Aragón y Navarra, un verdadero príncipe Trastámara," *Aragón en la Edad Media* 16 (2000), 596. Ostolaza Elizando also notes that Navarra continued to be under the adminstration of the queen during Juan's lieutenancy in Aragon.

33. Theresa Earenfight states that "it is fascinating to note how easily Juan delegated authority to his second wife, Juana Enríquez." She believes that the long-standing tradition of lieutenancy in Aragon gave Juan a "habit of corulership." See her work *The King's Other Body: Maria of Castile and the Crown of Aragon* (Philadelphia, 2010), 138–9 for a discussion of Juan's corulership with his second wife.

34. Pierre Boissonade, *Histoire de la Réunion de la Navarre a la Castille (Essai sur les Relations de prince de Foix-Albret avec la France et l'Espagne)* (Geneva, 1975), 8. Original text is *"Un état ruiné par la guerre civile, affaibli par l'anarchie, voilà l'heritage que Juan II laissa."*

35. AGN Comptos, Caj. 104, no. 23, 1 dated August 9, 1427 at Pamplona. Also copied in Yanguas y Miranda, Leg.1, Carp.17.

36. AGN Comptos, Caj. 87, no. 52, dated December 3, 1402. Juana and Jean of Foix were married in October of the same year.

37. J. Reglá Campistol, "La cuestion de los Pirineos a commienzos de la edad moderna: El intento imperialista de Gaston de Foix," in *Relaciones Internacionales de España con Francia e Italia*, ed. Jaime Vicens Vives, Estudios de Historia Moderna (Barcelona, 1951), 30. Gaston died on July 10, 1472 in the Pyrenean town of Roncevalles.

38. Andre Favyn, *Histoire de Navarre; contenant l'Origine, les Vies et conquests de ses Rois, depuis leur commencement jusques a present* (Paris, 1612), 615–16.

39. The only surviving version of these documents are a certified copy from 1544, although the original document dates to January 12, 1494; AGN Papeles Sueltos (PS), 1st series, Leg. 1, no. 7 at Pamplona.

40. AGN Comptos, Caj. 166, no. 25, dated December 15, 1496 at Pau. Original text is *"seguir los grandes y arduos negosios…en este nuestro Senorio de Bearne y en los otros Senorios y tierra nuestras…y sobrebiene se requeriria…de aquellos nuestra presencia Real."*

41. AGN Comptos, Caj. 177, no. 20, dated September 7, 1497 at Tarbes.

42. Favyn, *Histoire de Navarre*, 677. Original text is *"gouuernant à la mode françoise du tout contraire à l'Espagnole. Car en France la presence familiere de nos Monarques resiouit [rejouit] les François et leur accroist d'avantage l'amour et la reuerence qu'ils leur portent. En Espagne si leurs Roys se monstroient à tous les iours, ils seroient mesprisez de leur people"*

43. From the excerpt in Álvaro Adot Lerga, *Juan d'Albret y Catalina de Foix o la Defensa del Estado Navarro* (Pamplona, 2005), 335. Original text is *"otros le menospreciauan, estimandole en poco, por su excessiua blandura, la qual eredó en Francia, donde los Principes son muy manuales y agenos de la sobrada altiuez de algunos caualleros d'España, aunque la honesta grauedad, mesura y templança, antes se deue aprobar y parece muy bien en todos los hombres, especialmente Principes, y sobre todo en los Reyes, que en justo sean reuerenciados y acatados como personas constituydas por la mano de Dios en tan altro trono y magestad, para juzgar y gouernar al mundo."* Note: the word I would like to suggest for *manuales* is "hands on" or "touchy feely"; although both words are arguably slang, I believe they convey Garibay's sentiment that the French princes are excessively tactile with or physically close to their subjects.

44. Jose de Moret, *Anales del Reino de Navarra*, vols. 5–7 (Tolosa, 1891), vol. 7, 157–8. Original text is *"Aún era más insoportable su inconsecuencia en el decoro de su Real persona; porque gastaba tanta llaneza, que desdecia mucho la autoridad, conversando con sus vasallos y con otros extraños familiarmente como si no fuera rey sino un caballero particular, tanto, que no reparaba en ir á los festines vulgares y su regocijo era danzar con las damas y las doncellas…Y á la verdad: desgradaban mucho á los hombres cuerdos y de punto estos aires de Francia, donde sus reyes solian familiarizarse demasiado con los vasallos."*

45. For further discussion of their personal partnership, see Elena Woodacre, *The Queens Regnant of Navarre: Succession, Politics and Partnership 1274–1512* (New York, 2013), 43–4.

46. Álvaro Adot Lerga, "Itinerario de los reyes privativos de Navarra: Juan III de Albret-Catalina I de Foix," *Principe de Viana* 60.217 (1999), 401–58.

47. M. le cher de Courcelles, *Notices Historiques et Généalogiques sur les Maisons Souveraines* (Paris, 1828), 76; and P. Anselme de Sainte Marie and Honoré du Fourny, *Histoire Genealogique et Chronologique de la Maison Royale de France*, 3rd ed. (Paris, 1726), 91.

48. César González Mínguez, "La Minoria de Ferdinando IV de Castilla (1295–1301)," *Revista da Faculdade de Letras. História (Porto)* Ser. 2, Bd. 15 (1998), 1073 (68) and *Histoire Genealogique et Chronologique de la Maison Royale de France*, 91. González Mínguez only mentions the bethrothal of Blanche, not her substitution for her elder sister, Marguerite.

49. This treaty is Archives Nationales (France) J601/40 bis, "Traité d'alliance entre Philip le Bel, roi de France et Ferdinand IV, roi de Castille et de Léon réalisé à Valladolid le 31 mars 1306."

50. *Histoire Genealogique et Chronologique de la Maison Royale de France*, 90.

51. Charles Cawley, *Medieval Lands: A Prospography of Medieval and European Noble and Royal Families*, Foundation for Medieval Genealogy (http://fmg.ac/Projects/MedLands/CAPET.htm#), citing *Continuatio Chronici Guillelmi de Nangiaco*, 592. See also *Notices Historiques et Généalogiques sur les Maisons Souveraines*, 76.

52. Juana I's presence is specifically noted in a betrothal ceremony in Paris in "*Sponsalia inter Edvardum filium Regis & Isabellam Regis Franciae filiam*" dated May 20, 1303 in Thomas Rymer, *Foedera, conventiones, literae, et cujuscunque generis acta publica, inter reges Angliae et alios quosvis imperatores, reges, pontifices, principes, vel communitates, ab ineunte saeculo duodecimo, viz. ab anno 1101, ad nostra usque tempora, habita aut tractata : ex autographis, infra secretiores archivorum regiorum thesaurarias per multa saecula reconditis, fideliter exscripta : in lucem missa de mandato Reginae.* Tomus II (London, 1705), 928. Ironically perhaps, Juana had originally been contracted to marry Henry, another son of Edward I of England in 1273; see AGN Comptos, Caj. 3, no. 65 dated November 30, 1273 at Bonloc. Also printed in Rymer (ed.), *Foedera*, "Conventio Cyrographata inter Regem Angliae, and H. Regem Navarrrae, Super matrimonio contrabendo inter Henr. Filium Regis Angliae, and Johannam filiam Regis Navarrae," 18. On the pope's role in promoting this alliances see Elizabeth A. R. Brown, "The Political Repercussions of Family Ties in the Early Fourteenth Century: The Marriage of Edward II of England and Isabelle of France," *Speculum* 63. 3 (1988), 574.

53. Eloisa Ramírez Vaquero and Pascual Tamburri, *El Príncipe de Viana* (Pamplona, 2001), 23.

54. C. A. J. Armstrong, "La politique matrimoniale des ducs de Bourgogne de la maison de Valois," in *England, France and Burgundy in the Fifteenth Century*, ed. C. A. J. Armstrong (London, 1983), 252. Armstrong does note however, that this pledge of succession went against the Treaty of Arras of 1435, which limited the succession to male heirs. Agnes' dowry is listed as 200,000 francs, 32 *gros monnaie de Flandre* (331).

55. Documentary evidence shows Blanca's peacemaking efforts particularly in 1430: Simón de Leoz, Blanca's secretary was compensated for trips to Castile in August and December 1430; AGN Comptos, Caj. III, no. 3, 4 dated August 17, 1430 and Caj. III, no. 12, 36 dated December 22, 1430. Blanca's confessor Pedro Beraiz, Archbishop of Tiro was compensated for similar trips in February and August of 1430; AGN Comptos, Caj. III, no. 3, 33 dated February 8, 1430 and Caj. III, no. 3, 5 dated August 22, 1430. There is also a messenger compensated for delivering "secret letters" to the king of Castile; AGN Comptos, Caj. III, no. 3, 2 dated September 8, 1430.

56. W. D. J. Phillips, *Enrique IV and the Crisis of Fifteenth Century Castile* (Cambridge, Mass., 1978), 35.

57. Leonor and Gaston's marriage contract is AGN Comptos, Caj. 146, no. 32, dated September 22, 1434 and Caj. 104, no. 41 dated October 12, 1434 at Olite.

58. Marguerite was married to Francis II of Brittany in April 1471. Marie married William X, marquis of Montferrat in January 1465.

59. Cardinal Pierre (or Pedro) of Foix (1449–90).

60. Their daughter Jeanne was married to Jean V, count of Armagnac in August 1469 at Lectoure. Catherine also married Gaston, viscount de Castillon, heir of the county of Candale in 1469.

61. The Navarrese chronicler Moret commented on this unusual situation: "It could be seen at the same time in Christendom four queens, who were all first cousins and Leonor's grandchildren, that is: Lady Catalina, queen of Navarre, Lady Germana of Aragon, Anne repeatedly (twice) of France and another Anne of Bohemia and Hungary. What a great oddity and rarely seen in the world, and without doubt a great honour and glory for Navarre!" Moret, *Anales del Reino de Navarra*, vol. 7, 49. Original text is, *"haberse visto á un mismo tiempo en la cristiandad cuartro reinas, todas primas hermanas y nietas suyas, es á saber: Doña Catalina, Reina de Navarra, Doña Germana de Aragon, Ana, repetidamente de Francia, y otra Ana de Boemia y Hungría. Cosa bien singular y pocas veces vista en el mundo; y sin duda de grande honor y gloria de Navarra!"*

62. Eloísa Ramírez Vaquero, *Leonor de Navarra*, Reyes de Navarra; Reyes Pirenáicos (Pamplona, 2002), 110; and Reglá Campistol, "La cuestion de los Pirineos," 22.

63. Joseph Calmette, *La question des Pyrénées et la marche d'Espagne au moyen-âge* (Paris, 1947), 75.

64. AGN Comptos, Caj. 7, no. 35. Other related documents are AGN Comptos, Caj. 7, no. 36–7 and 47 dated between April 28, 1332 and April 29, 1333. The text of the agreement is also printed in full in José Ramón Castro Alava, "El Matrimonio de Pedro IV de Aragon y María de Navarra," in *Estudios de Edad Media de la Corona de Aragon* III (Zaragoza, 1947), 121–44. Castro Alava discusses the fates of the two sisters, Juana and Maria, in "El Matrimonio," 61–2. He notes Zurita's suggestion that Maria pleased Pedro better and cites the stories of the Early Modern chroniclers Moret and Arnaldo de Oyenhart who confirm Juana's decision to take the veil with evidence of her burial at Longchamps.

65. The marriage capitulations for the couple can be found in AGN Comptos, Caj. 7, no. 58, 1 dated January 6, 1337 at Castillo de Cineto and Pedro's approval of the agreement is in Caj. 7, no. 58, 12 dated April 22, 1337 at Zaragoza. Attached to Castro Alava, "El Matrimonio" is a transcript of a document issued by Maria as queen of Aragon, only days after her marriage, confirming the terms of her marital contract. Original provenance, AGN Comptos, Caj. 7, no. 107.

66. Marie-Laure Surget, "Mariage et pouvoir : réflexion sur le rôle de l'alliance dans les relations entre les Evreux-Navarre et les Valois au XIV siècle (1325–1376)" *Annales de Normandie*, 2008, 58.1–2, 37. It is worth noting that later Navarrese sovereigns continued to persue alliances with Brittany, resulting in the marriages of Juana of Navarre (daughter of Carlos II) and Jean V in

1386 and Marguerite of Navarre (daughter of Leonor and Gaston of Foix) and François II in 1474.

67. Paris, Sainte Geneviève ms 898, f. 3–5 dated March 15, 1340, cited in Surget, "Mariage et pouvoir," 37. See also Jose Maria Lacarra, *Historia Politica del Reino de Navarra: desde sus orígenes hasta su incorporación a Castilla,* vol.3 (Pamplona, 1972), 46. The Foundation for Medieval Geneaology suggests that an earlier betrothal was made for Blanche in 1335 with Andre de Viennois, heir to Humbert, Dauphin of Viennois. However, there appears to be no surviving documentary evidence of this match in the AGN to support this claim. Andre also died in 1335, so even if the betrothal was made this would account for Blanche's freedom to contract another marriage.

68. Lacarra, *Historia Politica del Reino de Navarra,* 46. Lacarra lists the original document's provenance as Arch. Nat de Paris, J602, no.43. See also Georges Daumet, "Etude sur les rélations d'Innocent VI avec Don Pedro 1er Roi de Castille au sujet de Blanche de Bourbon," *Mélanges d'archéologie et d'histoire* 17.17 (1897), 153–98. For an interesting discussion of an attempt of Clement VI to reinvigorate the betrothal between Blanche and Pedro after the death of Philip de Valois, see G. Mollat, "Clement VI et Blanche de Navarre, reine de France," *Mélanges d'archéologie et d'histoire* 71.1 (1959), 377–80.

69. The marriage contract for the couple was signed at Pontigny on July 4, 1349; AGN Comptos, Caj. 3, no.119–20.

70. One of the early documents in this dispute notes the groom's receipt of only 1,000 livres of the 20,000 promised; AGN Comptos, Caj. 9, 122–3 dated August 12, 1349 at Conflans. Another 1,000 appeared to arrive via the executors of Juana's will later that year; AGN Comptos, Caj. 9, no. 126 dated December 2, 1349.

71. More background on Blanche's period as queen and queen dowager of France can be found in Brigitte Buettner, "Le Système des Objets dans le Testament de Blanche de Navarre," *Clio* 19 (2004), 37–62.

72. For the Neopolitan marriage see Nancy Goldstone, *The Lady Queen: The Notorious Reign of Joanna I, Queen of Naples, Jerusalem and Sicily* (New York, 2009), 228–9 and 233. See also a discussion of how this marriage enabled Juana's son to organize an expedition to Greece; Ramirez Vaquero, *Historia de Navarra,* 71.

73. The first of these marital agreements was for a betrothal between Catalina's eldest child and current heiress, Ana and the Infante Juan or one of his cousins in 1494 (AGS, Patronato Real, leg. 12, fol. 58, signed at Medina del Campo on April 19, 1494). Ana was also the intended bride for a second projected alliance in 1500, to marry one of Isabel and Ferdinand's grandsons (AGS, Patronato Real, Leg. 2, fol. 14, signed May 14, 1500). The third treaty brokered a match between Catalina's son Enrique and Isabel of Flanders (ADPA E 550, signed at Medina del Campo, March 17, 1504).

74. Attempts were made to marry Catalina's daughters into the great Italian houses of Medici, Sforza and Este, however none of these negotiations were successful. See Amada Lopez de Meneses, "Magdalena y Catalina de Albret-Foix, Infantas de Navarra," *Hispania* 97 (1965), 5–42.

75. Vicens Vives, *Juan II de Aragon*, 138. Original text is, "*el centro principal de la premeditada ofensiva contra Castilla.*"

CHAPTER 2

Ferdinand the Catholic: King and Consort

David Abulafia

The subject of this essay is one that presents special methodological difficulties. To write about Ferdinand without Isabella until recently seemed unthinkable. The tendency to treat the two *Reyes Católicos* as a single unit is expressed not merely in the grant of that title by Pope Alexander VI in 1496, but also in the titles of two of the most recent books on their rule over Spain, Miguel Ángel Ladero Quesada's *La España de los Reyes Católicos*, and John Edwards' identically titled *The Spain of the Catholic Monarchs*.[1] It is fair to state that these books are assessments of the state of the Spanish kingdoms rather than attempts to delineate the life of either ruler, and that they are firmly based in traditional interpretations of the two rulers; it is therefore only to be expected that they deal rather briefly with Ferdinand's projects in Italy, the New World, and other lands beyond Iberia, even though these were developments with quite enormous consequences in the Mediterranean and in the wider world.

In fact, the literature shows a heavy imbalance since most studies of the reign of Ferdinand have concentrated heavily on the period up to 1492. First he was occupied helping his wife to assert her authority in Castile, and then he was busily occupied with the conquest of Muslim Granada. Thus, José Angel Sesma Muñoz' study of *Fernando de Aragón, Hispaniarum Rex* never in fact goes beyond 1492.[2] The next 12 years of Ferdinand's life have been passed over rather more rapidly, while the 12 years during which he outlived Isabella have been treated as no more than a codicil, as can be seen, for example, from the brief last chapter of John Edwards' book, a mere eight pages summarily entitled "Crisis, Death and Legacy" in a work of 300 pages.[3] This period might appear to be of minor interest at a colloquium on royal consorts, but it is important to take into account Ferdinand's handling of Isabella's legacy, and the changes of direction that were already apparent toward the end of her life, when he perhaps took advantage of her increasing ill-health. He in a sense resumed his role as royal consort not when he remarried—his second wife Germaine de Foix was not royal, though she brought him a firmer claim to the kingdom of Navarre—but as partner in government in Castile with his mentally unstable daughter Juana la Loca, who long outlived him, following the early death of her own Flemish consort Philip the Handsome.[4]

Modern trends in historical writing have ensured that interest in the career of Ferdinand's first wife Isabella has, however, burgeoned. Catholic writers, notably Tarsicio de Azcona, had already lauded Isabella's monarchy as a fine example of Christian rulership, with an eye on her elevation to sainthood.[5] Then in 1991, Peggy Liss published *Isabel the Queen* in the United States (a similar book by Nancy Rubin appeared almost identical in format and organisation). Liss was intent on demonstrating the role of a strong woman in government, though she did rather less to explain the constitutional niceties of female rule than one might have hoped.[6] Yet the predictable criticism of Liss' book was that she found it well-nigh impossible to show which decisions were made by Isabella and which by Ferdinand. Indeed, if we assume a certain amount of mutual delegation of responsibility, we cannot even draw firm conclusions from the name that appears on a particular document in Castile, though the constitutional arrangements in Aragon-Catalonia largely excluded Isabella from decision-making there.

Isabella granted her husband extensive powers within Castile, for which he showed himself greedy from the start. He even tentatively advanced his own claim to the Castilian throne on the death of her brother King Henry IV, in competition with his own wife. It is clear that there were areas of policy that he saw as his own. Yet, even there Isabella might sometimes appear to express herself very decisively, perhaps applying conscience rather more than her husband. She allowed him considerable freedom in the affairs of the Caribbean lands newly discovered by Columbus, but she did intervene to protect the American Indians from excessive exploitation, and was anxious to ensure they were not actually enslaved.[7] This intervention occurred when Ferdinand, greedy for new sources of money, was actively planning the seizure of the kingdom of Naples. That the conquest of Naples held far more attraction for Ferdinand than for his dying queen is abundantly clear. In any case, it was achieved on the basis of traditional Aragonese claims. The role of Castile was confined to the provision of valuable resources and manpower, notably the commander of the Spanish armies, the brilliant general Gonzalo Fernández de Córdoba.[8] But sometimes the attribution of a primary role to either king or queen becomes far more difficult. Was Ferdinand or Isabella keener to expel the Jews from Spain? This is a good example of a problem where historians have jumped to conclusions without necessarily reviewing all the evidence. They simply assume that the queen possessed the religious fervour that would sanction such an act, and that Ferdinand was more dispassionate and mercenary in his dealings with his non-Christian subjects.

The aim here is to see whether we can arrive at a judgment about the political role of Ferdinand, not Ferdinand and Isabella. The subject is Ferdinand *without* Isabella. First, I attempt to ascribe certain specific initiatives to Ferdinand rather than Isabella. Second, I attempt to show that the interests of Ferdinand as king of Aragon have been underestimated during the lifetime of Isabella, greatly affecting our understanding (or misunderstanding) of the direction the policy of the Catholic Monarchs took. The emphasis in the approach I adopt is thus policy rather than personality, though this was an age in which personality often determined policy. If at times I appear to be talking more about the "Aragonese" direction of policy than about Ferdinand himself, this is because I obstinately insist that the hand of Ferdinand can be detected in the wider direction of policy, which in my view was geared more to the interests of Ferdinand in Aragon and its dependencies than has generally been assumed. Clearly it is not possible here to examine all aspects of the many reigns of Ferdinand, and it has seemed best to make a ruthless selection of linked topics, connected to the treatment of religious minorities in Spain and further afield. This way we see Ferdinand at work in not just Aragon, Valencia, and Catalonia, but Sicily, Sardinia, and Naples, and exercising strong influence in both Portugal and Navarre, as well as in the newly discovered islands of the Caribbean. It is also an aspect of the reigns of Ferdinand and Isabella that has dominated discussion of the period in recent years.

This geographical range is itself unusual, for another feature of the books by Ladero, Edwards and Liss is their emphasis on the affairs specifically of Spain, more especially Castile. This reflects, once again, traditional preoccupations. It is the legacy of a long-standing centralist view of Spanish history that maintained its dominance under Franco. As well as an emphasis on the formation of a Spanish state, we find an emphasis in some works on the Christian identity of that state, reaffirmed when the Catholic Monarchs dealt harshly, though rather differently, with their Jewish and Muslim subjects. In the years around 1940, the idea of the Christian mission of Castile was forcefully expressed in the works of José-Maria Doussinagué on the foreign policies of Ferdinand the Catholic, one of the few works on the reign which concentrates heavily on the early sixteenth century. The learned Carlist historian of law and political ideas, Elías de Tejada, saw the Spanish occupation of the kingdom of Naples as beneficial to southern Italy precisely because it drew the area into the unique world of Christian Spanish civilisation, which was, he passionately argued, neither European nor African. The views of these historians might easily be dismissed as irrelevant and outdated, were it not for the fact that Elías de Tejada still has his enthusiasts in contemporary Naples, where one of his books has recently appeared in Italian (admittedly under the imprint of a far Right publishing house), and that Doussinagué and his contemporaries exposed to view a rich documentation which makes their works essential places of reference.[9]

Against this centralising tradition, it should be stressed that there has been a general shift in recent years in the writing of fifteenth and early sixteenth-century Spanish history, away from a view that revolved around the royal court of Castile toward one that takes into account the existence of all five Iberian states: Portugal, Navarre, Castile, Aragon, and Granada. Aragon itself was a medley of political entities, consisting of no less than five kingdoms and one principality, Catalonia. Several of these Aragonese kingdoms lay outside the Iberian peninsula: Majorca, Sardinia, and Sicily, and also the kingdom of Naples that was ruled by the king of Aragon from 1442 to 1458 and from 1503 onward. Even within these units we can see a tendency toward particularism and the defence of local rights, expressed in meetings of the *Corts* or *Cortes* of the various entities, and in the principle that the king must rule by consent. The theory of monarchy in the lands of the Crown of Aragon stood poles apart from the Roman law traditions that dominated Castile. This has led to the assumption that Aragon was inherently weak and hard to govern, by comparison with a supposedly unitary Castile. But when you start to look at Spain as a whole in the age of Ferdinand, and at Aragon as a whole with interests that extended beyond Spain, you develop a different perspective on the era in which, according to traditional historiography, Spain was, or began to be, "united." Even Castile was far from being a unity; great noble estates challenged royal power in the late fifteenth century, while the Basque country had particular privileges which established the region as a *señorio* in some respects free from direct government interference. Seen from the centre, these regional exceptions and differences were a matter of concern. Governments like homogeneity. The Aragonese kings too, given the chance, would willingly have imposed tighter control from the centre. Ferdinand knew that he could only gain a following within the Crown of Aragon by balancing the interests of the grandees and the cities, and as the *Sentencia de Guadelupe* of 1486 shows, he was also prepared to take the part of peasants seeking emancipation against the landlords.[10]

It can be seen at a glance that the reigns of Ferdinand and Isabella have given rise to many contrary judgments; his Catalan biographer Ernest Belenguer has pointed out, indeed, that there is a Francoist Ferdinand, a socialist Ferdinand, a liberal Ferdinand, to be found just within the Spanish historiography.[11] The rich historical writing on this era in English should be remembered as well, beginning with the classic studies of the nineteenth-century American writers William H. Prescott and Washington Irving. The latter was captivated by the Moorish legacy of southern Spain, and the former, though almost blinded as a young man in a bun fight at Yale University, wrote a series of elegant books about this period, several of which have remained in print to this day. His book on the reign of Ferdinand and Isabella is still worth attention for its fresh insights about such matters as military affairs. Prescott was ready to criticise the Catholic Monarchs for their acts of intolerance, such as the expulsion of the Jews, but he had a high regard for their achievements as nation builders.[12]

Yet, if there is one that still seems to stand the test of time, it is the view that the marriage of the two rulers gave Castile a genuine lead in Spanish affairs, and that it launched Spain on to the stage of European politics—the latter is an assumption that is hard to contradict. There is certainly plenty of evidence that the reign of Isabella saw the imposition of much tighter control by the Crown over the affairs of Castile, notably over its burgeoning towns. However, if one looks at other aspects of the reign of the two monarchs, different emphases seem to emerge. Under King Ferdinand, the south of Italy that had earlier been ruled by Ferdinand's uncle Alfonso V of Aragon, and then by Alfonso's bastard Ferrante, fell under the rule of the king of Aragon yet again. Just as Alfonso had made it the centrepiece of his policies, Ferdinand also took a keen interest in the Neapolitan kingdom, seeing it as a base for further victories in the Mediterranean which would, he hoped, bring him to the walls of Jerusalem over which he also possessed a title: Columbus recorded the prophecy of Joachim of Fiore that a Spanish king would recover "Zion." Under Ferdinand the Catholic, interests were pursued along the north coast of Africa which had long been high on the agenda of the kings of Aragon and their subjects the merchants of Barcelona and Valencia, culminating in the capture of Oran and Tripoli; Melilla, taken in 1497, remains to this day politically part of Spain.[13] This, once again, was a Castilian expedition; but it clearly was part of a series of African raids that served traditional Aragonese ends. In many ways, the reign of Ferdinand saw the revival of the fortunes of Aragon, at least as much as the restoration of the fortunes of Castile. It certainly saw the revival of traditional Aragonese policies, not to mention a degree of commercial recovery. Moreover, it was far easier to see how the conquest of Naples in 1503 strengthened Ferdinand's immediate position than it was to predict what the consequences of discovering the vaguely delineated edges of the Americas might be. In the lifetime of Isabella, only Hispaniola was colonised among the lands discovered to the west, and this was with difficulty. The conquest (as opposed to discovery) of Cuba took place only in the last years of Ferdinand, in 1511–12, at a time when the promised tons of American gold had still not materialised.

Of course it would be foolish to assume that royal policy was uniform throughout Ferdinand's long reign (or rather reigns). Since Ferdinand survived his wife by 12 years, the directions taken in royal policy between 1504 and 1516, culminating in the acquisition of Navarre, with its strategic importance to kings of Aragon anxious to control the Pyrenees and hold back the French, need to be considered in a full account of his multiple career. However, it is not difficult to show that the interest Ferdinand maintained in southern Italy predated Isabella's death (the conquest of Naples was achieved in the months before the queen died), and in any case Naples was a long-standing concern of Ferdinand, a territory in whose affairs he had intervened several times in the past, in support of his cousins who ruled there. It is possible, indeed, that he never really accepted the claims of these relatives, the Neapolitan house of Aragon, to rule in Naples, though he did send his sister to be consort to the strong-willed King Ferrante (Ferdinand I) of Naples, who was already his first cousin. Moreover, his many kingdoms, embraced under the general label of the

"Crown of Aragon," included two very large Italian islands, Sicily and Sardinia, even before he acquired Naples in 1502–3. He thus had a substantial interest in the waters of the western and central Mediterranean, and was bound to be as worried by north African piracy and by Turkish naval advances in the Mediterranean as was his cousin Ferrante. Indeed, his very first kingdom was that of the island of Sicily, granted to him by his father John II of Aragon in 1468, partly so that he would be a more impressive suitor for the hand of Princess Isabella of Castile, and partly to distract the Sicilians from other hostile claimants to the same throne, who were of French origin. In Sicily, his reign saw the continuing reassertion of royal authority by way of his viceroys. This was most definitely not a period when government from afar meant weak and ineffective government.[14] Much the same is true of the assertion of royal authority in Sardinia, in the face of local rebellions.[15] The federal character of the Crown of Aragon meant that the various kingdoms were already long accustomed to rule by viceroys; this was particularly the case under Ferdinand's uncle Alfonso of Aragon, who stayed in Italy from 1432 to his death in 1458, and after his conquest of Naples in 1442 had no wish to return to his ancestral lands in Iberia.

Underlying the argument that the reign of Ferdinand in Aragon saw the beginning of a process whereby Castile gained the ascendancy in Spain. It is the notion that the economy of the Crown of Aragon was experiencing a severe crisis at the end of the fifteenth century, from which Castile largely escaped. The argument seems to suggest that Aragon was so debilitated that it could not provide a power base for the Catholic Monarchs. It is essential to address this issue in the light of 30 or so years of critical research. In the first place, the argument for the economic decline of Aragon-Catalonia has very much depended on the single case of Barcelona. There has been a tendency to argue outward from Barcelona to Catalonia and from Catalonia to all the lands, Spanish and Italian, of the Crown of Aragon. This gloomy assessment was based on the judgment of two distinguished economic historians, Pierre Vilar and Jaume Vicens Vives. It had a great influence on John Elliott's brilliant synthesis of Spanish history in this period, but it was also a generalisation too far.[16] In 1972 the Italian historian Mario del Treppo demonstrated how rapidly the merchants of Barcelona responded to new commercial opportunities created by the Aragonese conquest of Naples in 1442. It was in any case well established that another major city of the Crown of Aragon, Valencia, enjoyed considerable prosperity in the late fifteenth century.[17] King Ferdinand acknowledged this in a rather perverse way, by increasing the tax burden on Valencia and setting off serious tensions between crown and city.[18] Elsewhere, certainly, the picture was uneven: signs of crisis in Majorca, increasing buoyancy in the economy of Sicily and southern Italy. The trade of Barcelona recovered significantly after the end of the Catalan civil war, as Manuel Peláez has demonstrated in his study of Catalonia between 1472 and 1479. He avers that *no es pot afirmar rotundament que com a conseqüència de la guerra civil arribà la polvoritzaciò del comerç exterior català,* "one cannot assert that the civil war caused the collapse of Catalan foreign trade."[19] In fact, Catalan consuls were being nominated in many trade centres of the central Mediterranean: in Palermo, Alghero, Syracuse, Malta, Reggio di Calabria, Dubrovnik, Aigues-Mortes, Genoa, Syracuse, Trapani, Manfredonia, and Venice—hardly evidence of serious decline, any more than the building of magnificent loggias (*llotjas*) in the major cities of the Catalan-speaking world in the late fifteenth century. The publication in 1494 of a printed text of the maritime law code known as the *Consulate of the Sea* also served to affirm the continuing standing of the Catalans among the traders of the Mediterranean world. Ferdinand did not inherit in Catalonia-Aragon a decadent congeries of states, but lands which had shown remarkable resilience during the crisis of civil war and French invasion under his father.

While Castile began to develop its major interest in the Atlantic, the great cities of the Crown of Aragon might again function as the nodal points of a lucrative trading network that linked Naples, Sicily, Sardinia, Mallorca, Barcelona, and Valencia. Under Ferdinand, the crown took a direct interest in the commercial recovery of the Catalan-Aragonese world, and it is a fallacy to suppose that the lack of encouragement to Catalans to trade in the New World signified a lack of sympathy for their commercial interests. Rather, the monarchy aimed to foster Catalan trade in the traditional commercial arena in which the Catalans had operated, as a complement to the trading activities of the Castilians in the Atlantic. Ferdinand thought of a division of function between Catalan and Castilian merchants, between Atlantic and Mediterranean. Thus, the policy appears to have worked well in his own lifetime.

Like his uncle, Ferdinand was a conqueror: Granada, Navarre, Naples were only some of his prizes. And his first prize was indeed Castile and its claimant, Isabella, a usurper of the legitimate rights of the daughter of Henry IV, called Henry the Impotent by his many foes. There is no reason to doubt that the Infanta Juana la Beltraneja was the legitimate daughter of King Henry, whether or not he was a homosexual. It is possible that the emphasis on moral reform under Isabella represented an attempt to justify by her actions her shaky claim to the throne.[20] However, Henry had acknowledged Isabella as his successor at one point; and, more importantly, she defeated la Beltraneja's champion the king of Portugal and secured Portuguese and rebel recognition as queen of Castile in 1479. It had taken five years, during which Ferdinand's support had been crucial. It was a period that culminated in the death of Ferdinand's unhappy father, King John II of Aragon. It was also a period in which the Aragonese crown had recovered politically from civil insurrection and foreign invasion, at the high price of losing the lands now known as French Catalonia (Roussillon and Cerdagne) to King Louis XI of France, ruler of a kingdom traditionally antagonistic to Aragon and favourable to Castile.[21] Another loss, whose recovery took well over thirty years, was the kingdom of Navarre,

strategically positioned to allow the French entry into the Iberian peninsula, if they could bring it within their orbit. John II of Aragon had ruled
this territory before his brother Alfonso bequeathed him Aragon in 1458,
but his attempts to hold on to Navarre were undermined by deep factionalism within the mountain kingdom, with his elder son, Charles of Viana,
opposing him until his suspiciously premature death. Ferdinand had no
intention of playing off Navarrese nobles against his father in the same
way as his elder half brother had done; but he proved capable of harnessing
the factionalism between Beaumonts and Agramonts to his own political interests. By means, in part of the Inquisition, Ferdinand eventually
proved capable of drawing Navarre into his net, several years before the
death of Isabella and many years before his formal annexation of the territory in 1512.[22]

II

It is now time to home in on certain aspects of Ferdinand's conduct,
beginning with his policy toward the Muslims of Nasrid Granada and of
the territories that had long been under Christian rule. During the war
against Granada, Ferdinand took charge of the day-to-day conduct of
policy toward the Nasrid sultanate. Of course, there is no denying that
he was fighting the Granadans with Castilian priorities in mind. A victory against the Nasrids would secure the respect of the Castilian nobility
and of the *Cortes* for the king and queen. It would lay to rest the image of
a monarchy which made bold proclamations and showy assaults against
Muslim territory, without achieving much, as had been the case under
Henry IV. Victory would reconcile the Castilian nobility to the presence
of an Aragonese king as coruler of Castile, and reaffirm Isabella's claim to
authority.[23] Ferdinand was able to seize a golden opportunity: the kingdom of Granada was divided between rival factions, and the Catholic
Monarchs as deftly exploited the rivalries in Granada as it would later do in
Navarre. The situation, already favourable to Castilian interest, improved
further when the Nasrid Prince Boabdil was captured in 1483 on a fool-
hardy raid into Christian territory. Ferdinand let him go back to his native
land, and did not even consent to Boabdil's offer to kiss his hands, which
might have been seen as an act of abject submission. What this reveals,
of course, is that Ferdinand had set his mind not on the restoration of
Castilian influence in Granada, long exercised through the levy of tribute,
but on the eventual conquest of Granada. Ferdinand's prominent role in
the Granadan war would reconcile the Castilian aristocracy to the fact
that an Aragonese king who was Isabella's consort now exercised enormous influence in their country's affairs. Above all, the final extinction
of Muslim rule in the Iberian peninsula would bring everlasting glory to
the king who led the campaign. But all these calculations that must have
been prominent in the thinking of Ferdinand and Isabella, must be set
alongside another fervent desire that both of them held: they were Christ's

champions, and Ferdinand was cast in the role of an almost Messianic leader, who would bring salvation to the people not merely of Spain but of the Mediterranean world, culminating in the recovery of Jerusalem itself, and the beginning of mankind's final redemption. Such an image of monarchy may seem far removed from Machiavelli's idea of Ferdinand as a scheming Renaissance prince who showed extraordinary political skills and a high degree of pragmatism in his Italian policies. But Ferdinand's messianism was also part of the common vocabulary of rulership in the fifteenth-century Iberian peninsula. The badge of the bat, worn also by his uncle Alfonso V of Aragon, had been the signal that this king was the secret agent of redemption. Prophecies abounded, the "concealed king," *el Rey encubierto*, was the subject of speculation. Ferdinand was determined to fulfil what the prophets foretold.

A few events in the campaign have a special place in this argument. On the occasion of the fall of the mountain city of Ronda, in May 1485, Ferdinand spelled out clearly, in the surrender treaty, the rights of the Muslim population. Most of the inhabitants of Ronda itself paid the price of their resistance and were ordered to leave for Africa with whatever they could take along with themselves. But more interesting is what happened to the Muslims who lived in the newly conquered countryside. In guaranteeing the right of the Muslims to reside in the towns and villages around Ronda and to practise their religion, Ferdinand deliberately adopted an approach which was more Aragonese than Castilian: not the expulsion of Muslims from conquered lands, as had happened in significant areas of thirteenth-century Andalucía, but the conservation of the Muslim communities, and the creation of a large dependent population of subject Muslims, *mudéjares*, under the ruler's direct protection. They were described as *sierbos mudejares* of the king and queen. In other words, they acquired the status of the king's Muslims throughout Aragon and Castile, as "servants of the royal chamber" and part of the royal treasure.[24] The *mudéjares* of Ronda would be subject to their own judges, who would dispense the law in accordance with the *xaraçuna*, that is, the Islamic *shari'a* and *sunna*. In this sense we can say that even in his Granadan policy Ferdinand revealed himself as an Aragonese king.

A similar Aragonese framework determined the arrangements for the cession of Granada itself on January 2, 1492.[25] The terms of the cession made by Boabdil of his crown and kingdom were generous to the conquered. The king and queen emphatically promised that all, "great and small," would have the freedom to follow their own religion, retaining use of their mosques, *para siempre jamás*, "for ever after." Islamic law would be applied by Muslim judges. The Granadan Muslims could retain their arms, apart from the cannon. Those who wished to leave because they could not stomach Christian rule were free to go, without having to pay any special tax, during the three years after the conquest, and in fact 10 great vessels stood ready during the next 70 days to transport them to the Maghrib free of charge. If they decided to travel there later, they could book a ship, again at no cost, by giving 50 days' notice. Those who did not wish to emigrate permanently were still free to go to North Africa for trade. Muslims were solemnly assured that the king, the queen, and their heir the Infante Juan, and all future rulers, would never demand that the Muslims of Granada wear a special badge. The forced conversion of Moors was also not to be countenanced. Indeed, only the Jews were required to convert to Christianity or leave. The Nasrid sultan Boabdil himself was promised a substantial estate nearby, though he soon left to live in Africa. Of course, all this was conditional on the observance of the surrender terms by the vanquished Muslims.

There was little that was unusual in these provisions, especially from an Aragonese viewpoint: around 1400 perhaps 20 percent of the population of the kingdom of Aragon proper were *mudéjares*, with a particularly dense concentration in Valencia, though in Castile the Muslims tended to be scattered in tiny groups. It is therefore possible to insist on the importance at this stage of the Aragonese-Valencian model for the treatment of the Granadan Muslim population. Ferdinand was already well accustomed to ruling over communities in which Christian inhabitants were rare or even nonexistent. He knew from his Valencian and Aragonese experiences that it was possible to benefit from the economic skills of a subject Muslim population, quite apart from the income that would accrue from the levy of a poll tax in the longer term. He was also quite prepared to tolerate the continued practice of Islam, despite his growing hostility to the practice of Judaism. Dislike of the one religion did not automatically mean dislike of the other.

It was a revolt against the Catholic Monarchs from 1499 to 1500 that prompted the new rulers to set aside the recent guarantees, and to insist that all Granadan Muslims must become Christians. The revolt itself had been sparked by a more aggressive policy toward toleration of Islam under the great ecclesiastic Cisneros. Although the suppression of Islam in Granada may appear to be a breach of the surrender terms by Ferdinand and Isabella, the view from Valladolid (as it were) was that the Muslims had shattered the agreement by daring to rebel against the crown that was then entitled to move from the soft approach sanctioned by one tradition, to a hard approach sanctioned by another tradition. Moreover, the suppression of Granadan Islam was followed within a couple of years by the suppression of Islam throughout Isabella's domains, that is, in Castile alone.

In Castile alone, the Muslims of Valencia and Aragon, Ferdinand's possessions (I mean both the Muslims and the kingdoms were his possessions) were not touched. Mark Meyerson has distinguished between the outlook of Isabella (advised by Cisneros), always more fanatical on the question of religious uniformity, and the more pragmatic Ferdinand II, who saw the Muslims, and indeed the Jews, as financial assets in the same way as his predecessors on the Aragonese throne had done (later, in examining the fate of the Jews, we see that the distinction may not work as well as Meyerson supposes).[26] For the areas that did retain a Muslim population, such as the countryside around Valencia, were highly prized by the fifteenth century for the exceptional range of specialised foodstuffs and artisan products that were available there to foreign merchants: sugar, rice, raisins, almonds, fine ceramics, silk, dyestuffs, and a catalogue of goods not dissimilar to those available also from mid-fifteenth-century Granada. We can thus understand why King Ferdinand was anxious to keep the Muslim population of Granada in place.[27] Demand for Moorish ceramics had never been so strong. The royal tables of Europe groaned under the weight of fine pottery from Granada and Valencia, and newcomers to high society such as the Medici of Florence had dinner services made in southern Spain which carried their coats of arms. In most of Spain these communities were formally organised as an *aljama*, a self-governing corporation which was given the authority to collect taxes and to treat with the crown, and King Ferdinand took great interest in the *aljamas*, even to the extent of encouraging the foundation of brand new ones. Ferdinand seems to have had little compunction about luring Muslims who had previously lived on noble lands to the royal *morerías* which he patronised.

Ferdinand's response to the *mudéjar* question in Aragon and Valencia reveals how certain he was that he wanted to hold on to this population. In Borja, for example, the Jewish quarter was vacated in 1492 following the expulsion of the Jews, and Ferdinand tried to lure Muslim settlers into the Jewish houses by freeing them from the head tax known as the *morabetí* for one year. "Nature abhors a vacuum," or rather King Ferdinand abhorred a hole in his income from the deserted Jewish quarter. Such exemptions could be taken much further: in Xàtiva (Játiva), a notable town in the kingdom of Valencia, new Moorish settlers were promised exemption from the hearth tax for ten full years. The Moors whom the king hoped to attract also included Granadan migrants, so that in the late 1480s we can see Ferdinand bringing captives from Málaga, who were allowed to be ransomed by local landlords in search of manpower on their estates. Such was the awareness of the benefits of having Moors in one's midst that several cities actually petitioned the crown so that Moorish quarters, *morerías*, could be established. Thus, Ferdinand could quite honestly inform a worried Egyptian sultan that he guaranteed the rights of his Muslim subjects, and it is hard to argue that he intended to subject the *mudéjares* of Valencia and Aragon to the same fate as the Jews, or as the Muslims of Castile. He was no doubt relieved that only a few Valencian radicals joined the rebellion of the Granadan Muslims in 1499; this seemed to be proof that tolerance paid dividends. It was only nine years after Ferdinand's death that Charles V initiated a policy of forced conversion among the *mudéjares* of Aragon and Valencia.

III

We can thus see a clear line between the policies adopted by Ferdinand and Isabella toward their Muslim subjects in Castile and in Aragon. But there is no reason to doubt that Ferdinand shared with his wife the formulation of the policies that resulted in the emergence of the Spanish Inquisition and the expulsion of the Jews from Spain. Ferdinand of Aragon appears to have given his enthusiastic support to the Inquisition. Indeed, had he not done so, it is hard to see how its authority could have extended across the two Crowns of Castile and Aragon, uniquely among the institutions of the combined monarchies.[28] According to some accounts it was Isabella who at first had more reservations about the extension of the Inquisition's powers. The role of the Inquisition as a means to impose royal authority should not be underestimated. Not just religion, but the power of the monarchy was at stake here, even, as will be seen, in the nominally independent kingdom of Navarre. This is apparent from the contests that took place in the Aragonese town of Teruel, traditionally subject to its own local statutes or *fueros*, to the extent that there was some doubt whether it was an integral part of the kingdom of Aragon, or a sort of autonomous city republic loosely subject to a lord who was also the king of Aragon. John Edwards has shown that the coming of the Inquisition to Teruel changed decisively the political balance, enhancing Ferdinand's authority in Teruel. What was true for Teruel was true more widely still. So too in Zaragoza (Saragossa), the Aragonese capital, tensions boiled over when the inquisitor Pedro Arbués was struck down by local *conversos* as he prayed in the cathedral one night during September 1486. Once again it seems that local politics was as great an issue as the question whether the converts were sincere Christians. The presence of the Inquisition was understood to be a means by which Ferdinand could strengthen his control over the city. Moreover, the assassination of Arbués strengthened Ferdinand's conviction that the *conversos* must be held in check; and one means to do this proved to be the expulsion not of the *conversos* but of professing Jews.

Ferdinand was alive to the political implications of the Inquisition, but was also devoted to its religious aims. Only 11 days before the decrees expelling all Jews from Spain were issued (March 31, 1492), Tomás de Torquemada, the Inquisitor General, was writing to the bishop of Girona, in Catalonia, ordering the expulsion of all Jews from what had once been, but certainly was no longer, a major centre of Jewish scholarship and kabbalah in the Iberian peninsula. The language of the order is at some points strikingly similar to that used in the decree of expulsion of March 31. On the other hand, it is hard to understand what legal validity this document possessed, since the Inquisition had only limited rights over unconverted Jews. Local solutions were seen, however, as inadequate. The Catholic Monarchs viewed the decree of expulsion as a means to secure a further wave of conversions. A general policy was enunciated throughout Spain, Sicily, and Sardinia, offering the Jews the choice among conversion, expulsion, and execution. The conversion of the Jews would itself be a sign that the End of Time was nigh and that *el Rey Encubierto* was ready to emerge and defend Christendom against Antichrist. The aims are abundantly clear from the edicts of expulsion, of which only Queen Isabella's for Castile has been closely studied. It was issued in Aragon and its many dependencies by King Ferdinand was in fact first published in print only 499 years after its proclamation.[29] The decree of expulsion issued by Ferdinand in the Aragonese territories is far more aggressive in tone, particularly in its lurid description of Jewish practices. While it owes much to Torquemada, it also reveals that Ferdinand was second to none in his visceral hatred for the religion of Israel. He was not following where Isabella led.

The Aragonese version lays emphasis on the crimes committed by the Jews in blaspheming Christ, as well as condemning the Jews for the bad influence of their "usury," which was undermining Christian society. This is a puzzle, for the remaining Jews of the Crown of Aragon do not appear in the records as significant moneylenders (the Sicilian parliament protested to Ferdinand that the Jews were not usurers at all but useful artisans). We can thus conclude that the reference to usury owes more to hostile stereotypes of the materialistic Jew than to reality. Another distinctive feature of the Aragonese decree is the reference to the idea that "the bodies of all the Jews... are ours, concerning which we can... order and dispose according to our wish." This of course refers to the well-established concept that the Jews were "possessed" by the king, an idea which can first be traced in Aragonese and Castilian urban statutes of the twelfth century. It meant that the king protected "his" Jews, but it also meant that they were subject to his will, and if they acted against the interests of crown and commonwealth, the king could dispense with their presence. The inclusion of the non-Iberian lands in the decision to expel the Jews is significant. The expulsion was to be complete, in a way that the suppression of Islam in Castile after 1502 was not absolutely quite complete. The infection of Judaism was seen as a source of heresy and corruption in a way that did not apply to Islam. Not for nothing did Ferdinand's Aragonese decree compare Judaism to "leprosy." And the aim was totally to purify the lands under the rule of King Ferdinand by expelling all professing Jews from each of his kingdoms.

Ferdinand's Aragonese decree describes how the Jews summoned the *conversos* to meetings where they taught them Jewish beliefs, arranged the circumcision of male *conversos* and their children, gave them prayer books, and instructed them in the fasts and feasts of the Jewish religion. According to the decree, the practices to which they succumbed included the eating of unleavened bread during the festival of Passover, the consumption of kosher meat slaughtered according to Jewish law, and avoidance of those foods (such as pork) which are forbidden by "the law of Moses." It was therefore essential to make contact between Jews and Christians impossible by exiling the Jews for all time: "if the chance to err has gone, then the error goes," as Ferdinand's decree argued. In the last analysis, to cite the Aragonese decree, the Jews were "incorrigible" and they could not be made any better, except of course by baptism. And how did the king know that this was happening? The answer was that many of the confessions which had been collected by the Inquisition pointed in this direction. The Castilian expulsion decree insisted that it had tried to adopt a more lenient approach, concentrating on the areas of Spain which were most "infected." The Jews had been expelled from the towns and villages of Andalucía, "where it seemed they had done the most damage," in the hope that this example would put fear into the hearts of the Jews and *conversos* elsewhere in the Spanish kingdoms. The Aragonese decree, by contrast, seems to reveal resentment at the resistance the Inquisition was experiencing in the cities, from Barcelona to Zaragoza.

The decrees did not state that all Jews were guilty of the crime of infecting *conversos* with Jewish beliefs and practices. The rulers cited the exemplary punishment which might be meted out to an institution such as a university college where some members had been guilty of a detestable crime, and it was deemed necessary to close down that institution, so that even those who carry less guilt suffer for the errors of the more guilty. For the point is that the errors of the most guilty "may be a danger to the republic," that is to say, the fabric of society is threatened by the actions even of a few. Indeed, Ferdinand was aware that the expulsion was a root and branch treatment which would bring financial harm to the monarchy, but he insisted that he was taking this course of action at the prompting of the Inquisition itself:

> The Holy Office of the Inquisition, seeing how some Christians are endangered by contact and communication with the Jews, has provided that the Jews be expelled from all our realms and territories, and persuaded us to give our support and argument to this, which we now do, because of our debts and obligations to the said Holy Office: and we do so despite the great harm to ourselves, seeking and preferring the salvation of souls above our own profit and that of individuals.

It is abundantly clear that neither Ferdinand nor Isabella disliked *conversos* on racial grounds. By keeping close to them at court a good number of *conversos*, such as the chronicler Pulgar, the bishop of Segovia Juan Arias d'Avila, and the financier Santangel, demonstrated their support for those *conversos* who accepted wholeheartedly their new faith and even campaigned against Judaism and crypto-Judaism. Contrary to the badly misconceived arguments of Benzion Netanyahu, the royal campaign against Jews and secret Jews was not racist in tone, though in parts of their kingdoms views concerning those with Jewish blood in their veins were expressed which certainly had a racist dimension.[30] It was, of course, the Jews who were expelled, that is, those who continued to refuse baptism. But those Jews who entered the community of Christ were another matter. The expulsion decrees have to be read not so much as attempts to encourage the Jews to leave, as attempts to encourage them to stay, if only they would convert. The Catholic Monarchs probably expected most Jews to remain in Spain, as Christian converts. Although there was a danger that these converts would be halfhearted, they would all fall under the control of the Inquisition; they would no longer be subject to the influence of Jewish kin or neighbours, and they would no longer have access to synagogues, kosher butchers, and other Jewish institutions.

In traditional historiography, Ferdinand was almost swayed by the pleas of his eminent Jewish courtiers Abraham Seneor and Isaac Abravanel. It is likely that both these figures promised Ferdinand and Isabella a large sum of money if they would revoke the order of expulsion. This was enshrined in mythology when a nineteenth-century Spanish painter illustrated this scene, and even a modern collection of first-class articles by scholars from Israel, Spain, and elsewhere, published in Israel, takes this as its cover design. If the event occurred, this was not, as often described, a last minute bribe. It was a standard way in which medieval monarchs had raised money from the Jews. It was hard for the Spanish Jews to believe that the threat of expulsion was not yet another excuse to raise some money. Ferdinand, true to character, is said to have seen the advantages of accepting the offer, but Isabella was fortified in her resolve by the tempestuous Torquemada. However, years later Ferdinand was keen to claim the initiative for the expulsion, and the Aragonese decree suggests that he was indeed stronger in his convictions than Isabella. Moreover, we find Ferdinand insisting, with some justice, that the expulsion will hurt his pocket.

The persistence of the Catholic Monarchs' campaign against Judaism can be measured from the way that it was continued across the borders of Castile and Aragon as part of the diplomatic initiatives which Ferdinand actively pursued with his neighbours. In 1496–7 Portugal was under strong diplomatic pressure from Spain. The new king, Manuel, was anxious to seal a marriage alliance with the Catholic Monarchs, and proposed to take as his wife their daughter Isabella. One view is that she inherited her parents' hatred for Judaism and insisted that the marriage could not take place until the Jews and crypto-Jews had been expelled from Portugal. Recent research points inward to the conviction of the Portuguese king that the time had come to put an end to Jewish (and also Muslim) practice in his kingdom, perhaps with the hope of speeding the return of Christ to earth. Manuel's messianism was even more marked than that of the Aragonese dynasty. His solution was forced mass conversion, but he did resist the imposition of an Inquisition on the crypto-Jews.[31]

Even more revealing is the case of the kingdom of Navarre, which seemed more welcoming to Jewish refugees at first. However, Castilian influence was growing in this mountain state, not least by way of interference by the Inquisition.[32] This can already be seen in the bullying attitude of Ferdinand following the murder of the Aragonese inquisitor Pedro Arbués by *conversos* in Saragossa in 1485. The suspects fled to Tudela, just across the Navarrese border, and Ferdinand, with the help of the pope, then demanded that the Inquisition be admitted to Tudela, backing up his demands with the seizure of several stronghold and the threat of armed intervention on a much larger scale. Needless to say, the Navarrese gave way to such relentless demands, though by the time an agreement with Ferdinand had been reached, the suspects had fled yet again, and they were found guilty *in absentia* at an auto-da-fé. Pressure from the Catholic Monarchs is easy to trace. By 1488 the king and queen of Navarre were issuing orders that Jews and Christians must be segregated. For a time the situation appeared to stabilise: the king and queen of Navarre were quite successful in asserting their much contested authority, and they even recognised the Jewish immigrants from Castile and Aragon as a separate *aljama* or community, probably in the hope of maximising their revenue from the Jewish population. But the survival of an independent dynasty in Navarre was only rendered possible by Ferdinand's fear that his full-scale intervention would trigger a French counterinvasion. By 1497 Ferdinand was better able to ensure that Navarre stayed within his sphere of influence, countering French pretensions in the Pyrenees. He effectively guaranteed the nominal independence of Navarre in return for promises that Judaism in Navarre would be suppressed. Thus, in 1498 the Navarrese Jews were given the choice of exile or conversion, and, for lack of an escape route, almost all converted. With the fall of Navarre's Jewries, Judaism came to an end, officially at least, in the Iberian peninsula. No less significantly, Navarre was revealed as a client state of Aragon-Catalonia. After Isabella died, Ferdinand's pressure on Navarre became intolerable as a result of the king of Aragon's marriage to his second wife, Germaine de Foix, which produced an additional claim to the little kingdom, given that he already had a relatively weak claim through his father John II of Navarre and Aragon. The persecution of the Jews of Navarre should thus be seen as an important stage toward the final conquest of Navarre by Ferdinand of Aragon in 1512. And this itself was the completion of a policy deeply rooted in Aragonese history.

The hounding of the Jews by Ferdinand was also continued across the seas, but with revealing variations. Very many Spanish and Sicilian Jews had taken refuge in 1492–3 in the south Italian kingdom, ruled by Ferdinand's namesake and cousin, Ferrante or Ferdinand I of Naples. Yet, as has been seen, this was a kingdom to which Ferdinand would shortly articulate his own claim. The conquest of the kingdom of Naples by Ferdinand the Catholic, completed by 1503, introduced new uncertainties. Ferdinand rapidly resolved to expel the south Italian Jews, and yet within a few months his order had been suspended. Ferdinand had the clearest of motives:

> Indeed you know that many years ago we ordered the expulsion from all our realms of all the Jews to be found in them, because of their offences against the Lord which result from their being there; thus we request that there should be Jews in none of our kingdoms, and least of all in that kingdom, where we are working to purify it of all the things that offend our Lord, and we order that, when the appropriate time comes, we shall try to expel all the Jews from the said kingdom [Barcelona, July 11, 1503].

It is noticeable that even this very stern letter allowed the Viceroy to decide when the right moment had come for the expulsion of the Jews. This was essentially the policy which was followed for a long time, since expulsion decrees were repeatedly deferred or modified by Viceroys with their own local priorities that were not necessarily those of religious purification after the style of King Ferdinand. In fact, the first Viceroy, *El Gran Capitán*, Don Gonzalo Fernández de Córdoba, had acquired the reputation of being quite partial to the Jews. So long as they had such a formidably powerful patron as the commander of the Spanish armies in southern Italy, the Jews were in less danger of expulsion. Writing to Ferdinand, the Viceroy insisted that the expulsion of the Jews would have a detrimental effect on the economy, all the more so since many of the Jews could be expected to settle in Venetian territory, thereby handing to Venice a handsome benefit (Don Gonzalo rather contradicted himself by also denying that the numbers of Jews were significant at all). The natural result of Don Gonzalo's action was that Ferdinand suspended the decree of expulsion of the Jews. Indeed, following representations from the Neapolitan elite, the decision was made to confirm the privileges conferred on the Jews of southern Italy by Ferrante and his successors. In December 1508 the crown's protection was conferred once again on native and Spanish Jews resident in the Neapolitan kingdom, an extraordinary event given the ferocity of the 1492 decrees in Spain. Ferdinand was, like any ruler, content to confirm ancient privileges handed down from his predecessors in the kingdom of Naples. But the problem remained because of the almost fanatical insistence of Ferdinand that his lands should be free of Jews. Even so Ferdinand allowed himself to be swayed by financial considerations, though not nearly as generously as he had allowed such considerations to determine his policy toward the Muslims of Valencia. Thus, he was also prepared to allow twenty prosperous Jewish families to linger in his newly conquered *presidio* of Oran in north Africa, though his policy in north Africa was, as usual, distinctly more favourable to Muslims than to Jews.[33]

Ferdinand's pragmatism reemerged when the Jews were ordered out of southern Italy in 1510. While this decision clearly reflected Ferdinand's wish not to permit Jews to live in his dominions, so long as they practised Judaism, the policy was permitted important exceptions. Two hundred families were in fact allowed to stay by Ferdinand, subject to payment of a 3,000 ducat annual tribute. In the last analysis, Ferdinand did not insist on the principle that southern Italy must at once be *Judenfrei*, but it does appear that this was one of his long-term aims. The *conversos* too were expelled from southern Italy in 1514–15, an act which was never undertaken in Spain itself, where the Inquisition preferred to take them closely in charge. Ferdinand appears to have suspected that many of them were renegade *conversos* from Spain who were escaping the attentions of the Inquisition. A final expulsion of all Jews from Naples did not occur until 1541, under Charles V, which was in fact 16 years after the Valencian Muslims had been forced to convert or leave.

IV

The year 1492 saw victory against Islam and the expulsion of the Jews, also, of course, it saw Ferdinand and Isabella acquire plenty of new subjects who were not Christian. Early observers of the New World noted that the inhabitants of Hispaniola and neighbouring islands were not "idolaters" and had "no religion," meaning that they were not Hindus, Buddhists, or Muslims. From the start, the discovery of new peoples, unashamedly naked, in some cases apparently cannibalistic, raised problems about their standing in God's creation. Ferdinand's interest in these peoples was as much in their gold as in their conversion, and this is not the place in which to examine his intentions toward them closely. It has been seen that by the end of her life, Queen Isabella actively sought to ensure that Indians were not enslaved, yet though the development of the *encomienda* system left the Indians legally free, the burden placed upon them was intolerable. Some attention does however need to be paid to the introduction in 1512–13 of *El Requerimento*, the requirement that Spanish conquerors should literally read their rights to the Indians before presuming to wage war against them. This was the result of the deliberations on the status of the Indians authorised by Ferdinand that produced the so-called *Leyes de Burgos*. The Indians were not required to convert but they must show respect to Christianity, listen to preachers, and they must not take up arms against the Spaniards. Patricia Seed has suggested that the model for *El Requerimento* can be found in the Islamic *aman*, the Surrender Treaty offered to those who fell under Muslim rule, which itself, in Christian form, survived, particularly in Aragon-Catalonia, as the preferred model for subduing Spanish Muslims. We have already seen such Surrender Treaties in operation as Ferdinand swallowed the remnants of the Nasrid kingdom of Granada. Although the formal reading of this document to uncomprehending natives of the Caribbean, at great speed and from a safe distance, such as the deck of a ship, made a mockery of the whole exercise, it can be seen as an interesting by-product of the Aragonese heritage of Ferdinand the Catholic, along with institutions such as the Catalan system of consulates that spread through the New World, and the Catalan preachers who first, in the tradition of Ramon Llull, tried to bring the word of Christ to the Indians. One of them, Ramon Pané, the author of the first book in a western language to be written in the New World, appears to have encountered Ferdinand and Isabella along with Columbus at Badalona in 1493, before being sent off to learn Indian languages and customs. In other words, the impact of Ferdinand and his Aragonese territories could be felt in the Atlantic as well as the Mediterranean, affecting Taíno Indians in the Caribbean as well as Jews and Muslims. And indeed the fact of the American discoveries only underlined the sense that Ferdinand was destined to perform a special role in human history.[34]

Ferdinand's treatment of the Jews had an apocalyptic element too. If he was *el Rey encubierto*, whose mission was the redemption of Jerusalem, and thereby of mankind, then the conversion of the Jews was a step toward the realisation of God's aims. His victories over the Muslims in Granada and Africa were also a stage in the unfolding of Christian history, but the focus of attention in prophetic literature had always been the conversion of Jews rather than Muslims. Besides, he combined with his sense of mission a pragmatism that very often guided him in quite different directions. He was prepared to tolerate Islam in his Aragonese dominions, where the economic value of his Muslim subjects was rather greater than was the case in Castile. His plans for Naples were predicated on the assumption that expulsion would occur. He and his successor Charles V saw no difficulty in using taxes on the Jews of southern Italy to finance the urgent war against the Turks. Ferdinand's approach to religious questions was also influenced by his predecessors. He showed an inherited willingness to tolerate the practice of Islam, within certain constraints that were themselves, it is clear, imitated from early Islamic practice toward non-Muslims. This had been the policy of generations of great Aragonese kings, such as James the Conqueror, Peter the Great, and Alfonso the Magnanimous. Where he diverged was in failing to maintain their conditional tolerance of the Jews that was founded on the Augustinian principle of allowing Jews to live under Christian protection within Christian society. Yet even here we see paradoxes. Up to 1492, he used Jewish advisers in much the same way as Peter the Great two hundred years before. Peter, indeed, had been forced by Church and *Corts* to dismiss his Jewish courtiers. It was a Jew, Samuel Abulafia, who organised the supplies for Ferdinand's Granada campaign. Up to the moment of expulsion, the king forbade violence against Jews and protected them as his subjects or indeed as possessions, and yet he admitted that the expulsion greatly harmed his pocket.

Ferdinand appears, then, as a man of contradictions. Or rather, like any ruler, he was torn between his principles and pragmatism. Alongside his attachment to the image of *el Rey encubierto*, the king remained relentless in pursuit of his dynastic rights and legal titles, determined to win Navarre, Naples, the Catalan counties across the Pyrenees, towns in north Africa long targeted by his predecessors on the throne of Aragon, and even Castile after Isabella's death in 1504, despite the claims of his eccentric daughter and her Flemish husband. The pursuit of Aragonese-Catalan interests was single-minded. His Neapolitan war of conquest was complete before Isabella died. His foreign policy, which sought to isolate France by alliances with England, Brittany, the Holy Roman Empire, stands in a long tradition of Aragonese-French rivalry. Even after Isabella died, he continued to take a very active role in planning New World exploration, including the settlement of Cuba and the expedition of Ponce de León to Florida. It is clear that his actions decisively altered the political and religious map of the Mediterranean and of the rest of the world. In achieving such spectacular results, he continuously played the Aragonese card.

Notes

1. M. A. Ladero Quesada, *La España de los Reyes Católicos* (Madrid, 1999); J. Edwards, *The Spain of the Catholic Monarchs, 1474–1520* (Oxford, 2000).
2. J. A. Sesma Muñoz, *Fernando de Aragón, Hispaniarum Rex* (Zaragoza, 1992).
3. As also in J. Edwards, *Ferdinand and Isabella* (Harlow, 2005), following the early death of her own Flemish consort Philip the Handsome.
4. R. Ríos Lloret, *Germana de Foix: una mujer, una reina, una corte* (Valencia, 2003); B. Aram, *Juana the Mad: Sovereignty and Dynasty in Renaissance Europe* (Baltimore MD, 2005); M. Fernández Álvarez, *Juana la Loca: la cautiva de Tordesillas* (Madrid, 2000); J. M. Cauchies, *Philippe le Beau: le dernier duc de Bourgogne* (Turnhout, 2003).
5. T. De Azcona, *Isabel la Católica: estudio critico de su vida y reinado* (Madrid, 1964; 3rd ed., Madrid, 1993).
6. P. Liss, *Isabel the Queen* (New York, 1991; 2nd ed., Philadelphia, 2004); N. Rubin, *Isabella of Castile, the First Renaissance Queen* (New York, 1991).
7. D. Abulafia, *The Discovery of Mankind: Atlantic Encounters in the Age of Columbus* (New Haven CT, 2008).
8. C. J. Hernando Sánchez, *El reino de Nápoles en el imperio de Carlos V: la consolidación de la conquista* (Madrid, 2001), which despite its title has rich material on Ferdinand the Catholic; J. E. Ruíz Domènec, *El Gran Capitán: retrato de un época* (Barcelona, 2002).
9. J. M. Doussinagué, *La política internacional de Ferdinando el Católico* (Madrid, 1944); F. Elías de Tejada, *Napoli spagnola: la tappa aragonese (1442–1503)* (Naples, 1999), and subsequent volumes translated from the five-volume original.
10. P. Freedman, *The Origins of Peasant Servitude in Medieval Catalonia* (Cambridge, 1991).
11. E. Belenguer Cebrià, *Fernando el Católico* (Barcelona, 1999).
12. W. H. Prescott, *History of the Reign of Ferdinand and Isabella the Catholic of Spain* (Bentley, 1838); part of the work has been reedited as *The Art of War in Spain: The Conquest of Granada 1481–1492* (London, 1995).
13. R. Gutiérrez Cruz, *Los presidios españoles del Norte de África en tiempo de los Reyes Católicos* (Melilla, 1999).
14. J. Vicens Vives, *Fernando el Católico príncipe de Aragón, rey de Sicilia, 1458–1478: Sicilia en la política de Juan II de Aragón* (Madrid, 1972).
15. A. M. Oliva and O. Schena, *Acta Curiarum Regni Sardiniae: i documenti dei Viceré Giovanni Dusay e Ferdinando Girón de Rebolledo (1495, 1497, 1500, 1504–1511)* (Cagliari, 1998).
16. J. H. Elliott, *Imperial Spain, 1469–1716* (London, 1963); Pierre Vilar's views on the economic decline of late medieval Catalonia can now be read conveniently in a collection of his articles: *Crecimiento y desarollo: economia e historia, reflexiones sobre el caso español* (Barcelona, 2001), pp. 212–79; see also J. Vicens Vives, *Approaches to the History of Spain* (2nd ed., Berkeley CA, 1970).
17. M. del Treppo, *I mercanti catalani e l'espansione della Corona d'Aragona nel secolo XV* (Naples, 1972).
18. E. Belenguer Cebrià, *Fernando el Católico e la ciudad de Valencia* (Valencia, 2012; Castilian rev. ed. of his classic *València en la crisi del segle XV*, 1976).

19. M. Peláez, *Catalunya després de la Guerra Civil del segle XV: institucions, forms de govern i relacions socials i econòmiques (1472–1479)* (Barcelona, 1981).
20. A. I. Carrasco Manchado, *Isabel I de Castilla y la sombre de la ilegitimidad: propaganda y representación en el conflict sucesorio (1471–1482)* (Madrid, 2006); T. de Azcona, *Juana de Castilla, mal llamada la Beltraneja: vida de la hija de Enrique IV de Castilla y su exilio en Portugal (1462–1530)* (Madrid, 2007).
21. J. Calmette, *La question des Pyrénées et de la Marche d'Espagne au moyen âge* (Paris, 1947).
22. B. Gampel, *The Last Jews on Iberian Soil: Navarrese Jewry 1479 to 1498* (Berkeley CA, 1989).
23. See M. A. Ladero Quesada, *La Guerra de Granada (1482–1491)* (Granada, 2001).
24. J. Boswell, *The Royal Treasure: Muslim Communities Under the Crown of Aragon in the Fourteenth Century* (New Haven CT, 1977).
25. See L. P. Harvey, *Islamic Spain 1250–1500* (Chicago IL, 1991) for a full discussion of the surrender arrangements.
26. M. Meyerson, *The Muslims of Valencia in the Age of Fernando and Isabel: Between Co-existence and Crusade* (Berkeley CA, 1991).
27. J. A. Vilar Sánchez, *1492–1502: una década fraudulenta. Historia del reino cristiano de Granda desde su fundación, hasta el muerte de la reina Isabel la Católica* (Granada, 2004); also D. Coleman, *Creating Christian Granada: Society and Religious Culture in an Old-World Frontier City* (Ithaca NY, 2003); A. K. Harris, *From Muslim to Christian Granada: Inventing a City's Past in Early Modern Spain* (Baltimore MD, 2007).
28. There is a vast literature on the expulsion of the Jews, with historians such as Haim Beinart, Benzion Netanyahu, Norman Roth, John Edwards, Angus Mackay, and Henry Kamen taking very different positions—just to mention those writing in English.
29. Rafael Conde y Delgado de Molina, *La Expulsión de los Judíos de la Corona de Aragón. Documentos para su studio* (Zaragoza, Institución Fernando el Católico, 1991), doc. §1, pp. 41–4.
30. B. Netanyahu, *The Origins of the Inquisition in Fifteenth-Century Spain* (Ithaca NY, 1995).
31. F. Soyer, *The Persecution of the Jews and Muslims of Portugal: King Manuel I and the End of Religious Tolerance (1496–7)* (Leiden, 2007).
32. Gampel, *Last Jews on Iberian Soil*.
33. D. Abulafia, "Insediamenti, diaspora e tradizione ebraica: gli Ebrei del Regno di Napoli da Ferdinando il Cattolico a Carlo V," in *Carlo V, Napoli e il Mediterraneo: Archivio storico per le province napoletane*, eds. G. Galasso and A. Musi (Napoli, 2001); also Hernando Sánchez, *Reino de Nápoles* for continuities from earlier reigns.
34. For a fuller discussion see my *Discovery of Mankind*.

CHAPTER 3

"He to Be Intituled Kinge": King Philip of England and the Anglo-Spanish Court

Sarah Duncan

T he Anglo-Spanish court of Philip, king consort of England, and his wife Queen Mary I has traditionally been depicted as one that was characterized by mistrust and violence between the two nationalities as well as lacking in ceremonies and entertainments. This negative image of the court, and Philip's role in it, is not entirely accurate, however, and more recently has begun to be challenged. From his arrival in England, Philip made attempts to smooth relations between the two nations, worked to amalgamate the two courts into a functioning whole, and presided over ceremonies that allowed him to both forge ties with the English courtiers while establishing himself in a position of leadership. From the fall of 1554 through spring 1555 by all indications the Anglo-Spanish marriage was a resounding success. Philip had taken a leading role in the return of Catholicism to England, succeeded in providing the realm with an heir (although unbeknownst to everyone at the time, Mary's pregnancy would later be confirmed to be false), and started to define his unprecedented role as king consort to a ruling queen. In particular, his assumption of the ceremonial role of king in a number of court revels, including a series of tournaments and martial sports that were staged during this time period, helped to highlight his prowess in matters of religion, matrimony, and dynasty-building, as well as to establish his ability to rule.

Co-monarchy

The short-lived reign of Queen Mary I of England and her marriage to Prince Philip of Spain have received increasing attention in the last decade. Consequently, Mary's role as a queen with the powers of a king has been reevaluated by a number of historians, including Judith Richards, Anna Whitelock, Linda Porter, and Charles Beem, among many others.[1] Together they have produced a revised and much more sympathetic portrait of the queen, arguing that Mary was more competent, rational, intelligent, and successful than she has traditionally been depicted, and therefore, in Richards' words, a "less bloody, less reactionary, less tyranni-cal monarch than popular mythology—and rather too much history—still has her."[2] Similarly, as the reevaluation of Mary's role as queen has begun, historians have also started to reassess Philip in his role as king consort. The question of how much power Philip had in his unprecedented posi-tion and to what extent he wielded it has long been debated, and although a recent publication has focused on Philip's role as king of England, those questions remain unresolved.[3] From the outset of the marriage, as hus-band to England's first regnant queen, Philip's role was defined not by the authority he would hold as king consort, but by the powers he was forbid-den to exercise. Months prior to the wedding, steps were taken in England to ensure that all royal authority would remain in Mary's hands even after her marriage. In March 1554, Parliament passed the Act Concerning Regal Power which stated that Mary, as queen, would enjoy "All Regall Power...in as full large and ample maner" as any of her predecessors, all male rulers; a second act passed at the same time ensured that the queen would remain "solye and a sole quene." The marriage contract, signed by Philip and Mary and also passed into law by Parliament in April 1554, cir-cumscribed Philip's position to that of helpmeet to the queen to "ayde" her in the administration of her government.[4] Impeded by the contract that he had secretly repudiated before leaving Spain, from changing the laws or customs of the country, or disposing of benefices and offices among other restrictions, Philip seemed limited in his role.[5] In fact, an abstract of the marriage treaty summed up the respective positions the couple would play, stating: "(1) First he to be intituled kinge duringe the matrimony. (2) But she to have the disposicion of all benefices etc."[6] Moreover, in spite of holding the title of king for the duration of his marriage to Mary, Philip would never be crowned king of England.[7]

Although, on paper, the marriage contract upheld Mary's autonomy as sovereign while limiting her husband's constitutional role, questions remained about what kind of power over the government, and influence over the queen, Philip might wield in person; this was in part because Mary, herself, took actions that seemed to relax the constraints upon his involvement in the government. After his arrival in England, Mary ordered the Lord Privy Seal, the earl of Bedford, "Furste to tell the kyng the whole state of the Realme, with all thynges appartaynnyng to the same, as myche as ye knowe to be trewe. Seconde to obey hys comand-ment in all thynges."[8] In addition, the Privy Council ordered that "a note of all such matters of estate as should pass from hence should be made in Latin or Spanish from henceforth, and the same to be delivered to such as it should please the king's highness to appoint to receive it."[9] The extent to which Mary wanted Philip to "ayde" her in ruling remains unresolved, and historians have differed—to the point of being diametrically opposed—in their estimations of how powerful Philip was as Mary's consort, from

David Loades' assessment that, as king, "there is no doubt that Philip was a failure" because "he did not seriously try to succeed" in establishing a role for himself as English king, to Glyn Redworth's argument that Philip's "position as Mary's husband belied all limitations. Whenever he so wished, Philip was politically the dominant partner."[10] More recently, however, several historians have convincingly begun to argue that Philip and Mary established a "co-monarchy" in which they shared power, countering the views that Philip was either a complete failure or all powerful, and providing a more nuanced picture of the relationship between the queen and her consort: one in which Philip played an important part without fully subsuming Mary's authority.[11] The Philip that has emerged is one who "cultivated an image for himself as king of England" and was more successful in defining the unprecedented role of a male consort.[12]

Philippus Rex

Once he had committed himself to the union Philip took steps to ensure its success, in spite of his unhappiness with the terms agreed to in the marriage negotiations concluded on his behalf by his father Emperor Charles V and the imperial ambassadors. Even prior to his arrival in England, Philip worked to create good relations with English courtiers and to establish himself in the role of English king.[13] In March 1554 Mary sent ambassadors to Spain, led by John Russell, earl of Bedford, to present the marriage contract for Philip's formal ratification. These men were subsequently joined by Sir John Mason and another 40 young Englishmen in April. Philip thus had an opportunity to make a first impression on members of the English court including some of those, such as lord Fitzwalter, son of the earl of Sussex, who would be part of his English household.[14] Courtly ceremonies and festivities would be used not only to entertain the English courtiers but also to facilitate good relations between them, the Spaniards, and Philip himself, just as they would be utilized in England in the fall of 1554 to bring English and Spanish courtiers together. Having arrived in Galicia, what one Englishman termed "the rudest country of all Spain," the English ambassadors made their way to Valladolid where they gave "report of the gentle entertainment that all the Queen's Majesty lords and gentlemen have had there."[15] Feasts and tournaments, including the Spanish *juego de cañas*, were held in honor of the English courtiers. A banquet was given on April 30 by the duke of Albuquerque who "as hartto-lie [heartily] did interteyne the yerll of warcestor and allso all the roest of the inglishe gentillmen in as mache as he cold devise."[16] One Englishman, George Everett, reported that he had been "very well entertained" and that he did "well perceive that all the whole realm of Spain doth much rejoice at the marriage of their prince with our Queen's Highness and in my opinion they all bear her Majesty as much good will as their own prince."[17] He hoped that these feelings might be reciprocated, writing to Mary's council,

"I pray God the people of England may also bear the like good will to the prince that perfect amity may be had on both parties according to the Queen's Majesty desire and all your Honors."[18] Philip had made a good impression even on those Englishmen who spoke no Spanish. Edward Lord Dudley reported that Philip had apologized to him for not speaking much with him "partly for that he was informed I could not speak the Spanish tongue" but nevertheless the prince "gave me thanks more than I am worthy," and promised "that at his coming into England...he would speak with me and do me all the good he could."[19] With these personal connections Philip was thus able to establish his commitment to his new role as English king, a commitment he underlined the following month by sending letters to several members of Mary's council signed Philippus Rex.[20] Although Habsburg ambassador Simon Renard refused to allow these letters to be delivered, believing that the prince's assumption of a title he did not yet hold might convey the wrong impression to the English, Philip was successful in making an initial overture in establishing good relations with the English courtiers prior to his marriage.[21]

Philip contrived to continue this impression once he arrived in England in July for the marriage ceremony on the twenty-fifth of the month, proceeding to charm his new bride and the English court not only with gifts and pensions but also by his courteous behavior and his adoption of English customs, clothing, and even a few words of English.[22] He succeeded so well that in the early days of August one man declared himself "right gladd to heare" that "the kings highnesse useth hymself so gentlelye and lovinglye to all mene." He behaved so circumspectly in England immediately after the marriage that Dr. Nicholas Wotton, resident ambassador in France, stated that "from hence furthe the rebells shalbe fayne to seeke some other coulour to grownd their rebellion upon, then the terrible and fearefull oppression of the Spaynards."[23] Philip's ability to make himself personally agreeable to the English, in particular the English courtiers, however, did not completely eradicate the difficulties of amalgamating the English and Spanish courts and establishing cordial relations between the two nationalities during and after the wedding ceremony. Both sides acknowledged prior to the wedding that it was possible for hostilities to break out between the two groups. Fearing that there would be hostility toward Philip and the Spaniards who accompanied him, Mary, therefore, had issued a proclamation before their arrival requiring that in order not "to break the good and friendly agreement that ought to be nourished and continued between the subjects of this realm and such as shall come in with the said most noble prince," Englishmen should "use all such strangers...with courteous, friendly, and gentle entertainment." The proclamation informed the Queen's subjects that the Spaniards had already received their own orders to behave properly, and in addition commanded all noblemen and gentlemen of the realm to control their servants' behavior.[24]

Competition and Cooperation

These concerns were well founded. Once Philip had arrived in England, the difficulties attendant upon creating a combined Anglo-Spanish court became apparent and the two nationalities, from the first, did not always see eye to eye. Alexander Samson has recently explored the history of sixteenth-century Anglo-Spanish relations, including how the earlier adoption of Burgundian court ritual was held in common by both courts, as well as examining the way in which "Burgundian influences encouraged a rapprochement between English and Spanish courtly cultures, especially the matrix of chivalry, the *libros de caballerías*, that provided a defining point of contact," and through which Spanish courtiers, in particular, understood their first impressions of England. Samson has argued that Anglo-Spanish relations were a "complexity of diplomatic and cultural exchange, assimilation, competition, and cooperation."[25] Those aspects of competition and cooperation were present from the initial encounters between the two nationalities and even during the very festivities—the "triumphing, bankating, singing, masking, and daunsing, as was never in England heretofore, by the reports of all men,"—that celebrated the Anglo-Spanish union.[26]

The Spaniards were initially impressed, describing the banquet after the wedding ceremony as "very magnificent" and admitting that "the King, Queen and Bishop dined most sumptuously together to the strains of music," while ambassadors, grandees, English and Spanish gentlemen and the ladies of the court who filled the places at four more tables were "admirably served, in perfect order and silence."[27] When the dancing commenced, however, the spirit of competition between individuals of each nationality immediately emerged in their descriptions of the festivities. John Elder's published account of the marriage was one of the few that refrained from such comparisons, instead conforming to the ideal of chivalric romances by attesting that at "dansing time," to see "the dukes and noblemen of Spain daunse with the faire ladyes and the moste beutifull nimphes of England, it should seme to him that never see such, to be an other worlde."[28] Although many Spaniards were willing to admit that "there are more sights to be seen here in England than are described in any book of chivalry: country-houses, river-banks, woods, forests, delicious meadows, strong and beautiful castles, and everywhere fresh springs," they did not, however, see the English themselves in the same light.[29] Certainly the English style of dance did not impress them, which to their eyes "only consist in strutting or trotting about," nor did the English ladies, of whom one Spanish courtier stated, "They are neither beautiful nor graceful when dancing," and additionally, "not a single Spanish gentleman has fallen in love with one of them nor takes any interest in them, and their feelings for us are the same."[30] In contrast, Edward Underhill, one of the Queen's gentlemen pensioners who witnessed the events of the day while participating as a chief server, believed that it was the king and the Spanish courtiers who were lacking. He wrote:

> I wyll not take uppon me to wryte the maner off the maryage, off the feaste, nor off the daunssyngs of the Spanyards thatt daye, who weare greately owte off countenaunce, specyally kynge Phelip dauncesynge, when they dide se me lorde Braye, Mr. Carowe, and others so farre excede them; butt wyll leve it unto the learned, as it behovithe hym to be thatt shalle wryte a story off so greate a tryoumffe.[31]

It was left to Philip to find a way to compromise: when he led his new wife to the dance floor, the royal couple danced neither in the English style nor in the Spanish, but "after the German fashion."[32] This was a dance obviously known to both of them, but it was Philip who devised and demonstrated a way for the two nationalities to come together in harmony and for Anglo-Spanish relations to progress forward in a spirit of cooperation rather than competition.

The Dual Household

The need for cooperation would become clear in the months following the wedding ceremony as Philip tried to resolve a number of complications resulting from the need to combine his Spanish household that he had brought with him, with the English one provided for him upon his arrival. Initially it was the Spanish courtiers who were unhappy, when it became apparent shortly after Philip landed on English shores that his new English servants did not want his Spanish attendants to serve him.[33] The novel situation created by the arrival of Philip's retinue, thus swelling the size of the royal court, additionally led to problems with housing and also an increase in the numbers of hangers-on who followed the court, and it was reported that "over two thousand artisans have entered London, in defiance of the city's privileges, since the King arrived."[34] Contributing greatly to the feeling of unrest in the city it was believed that these men:

> under the name of serving men...do lurk about the court and the cities of London and Westminster and the suburbs and other places adjoining to the same, who being none otherwise occupied do spend their time in quarreling, gaming, and other like disorders to the evil example of others and great trouble and disquiet of their highness' good and loving subjects.[35]

By August, according to one report, there were "so many Spanyerdes in London that a man should have mett in the stretes for one Inglisheman above iiij [4] Spanyerdes, to the great discomfort of the Inglishe nation."[36] Over the next few months, however, solutions were found to these problems. In late August over 80 Spanish courtiers had requested and been given permission by Philip to leave England, thus alleviating the housing issue which was itself being resolved by a joint Anglo-Spanish commission that had largely completed its work by mid-October.[37] Additionally, on September 15, 1554, a proclamation was issued to address the influx of artisans ordering that vagabonds and "other loitering, idle persons, as well Englishmen as strangers of whatever nation, being masterless and having none entertainment" to depart the city of London, Westminster, and the "suburbs and places adjoining."[38]

Philip, meanwhile, found an answer to the problem of his dual household by resolving to be served by his Spanish attendants privately, within his privy chamber, and by his English courtiers in public. This compromise gave rise to English jealousies and rivalries among the noblemen and their servants. By September, it was observed by Renard that "very few Englishmen are to be seen in his Highness's apartments" and he also reported that "several lords' servants are already murmuring against them, calling them 'knavish Spaniards': words likely to breed violence."[39] Subsequent changes that occurred in the royal household provided an occasion for malcontent Englishmen to lay the blame on the foreigners: when, for example, the "Earl of Arundel put a stop to the serving of certain dishes which some English servants were in the habit of eating in the Queen's kitchen," this unwelcome alteration was "put down to the Spaniards with the object of making them unpopular."[40] Lord Fitzwalter, one of Philip's Gentlemen of the Chamber, complained that he was losing what little Spanish he had learned due to the lack of intermingling within the court.[41] Philip's dismissal of his English Master of the Horse, Sir Anthony Browne, resulted in yet another point of contention that had to be smoothed over by Browne's creation as Viscount Montague in early September.[42] Rising antagonism between the two nationalities would ultimately lead to violence as evidenced by the oft-quoted observation by one Spaniard the following month that "not a day passes without some knife-work in the palace."[43]

"There is often dancing at Court"

By October, however, the same month that violent outbreaks at court were being reported, opportunities for more peaceful interactions began to occur. This was due in part to the fact that Philip and Mary returned to London in late September from Hampton Court, after a series of short progresses to a number of Mary's palaces.[44] Their arrival immediately set into motion the resumption of courtly festivities, with the anticipation of "rejoicing and tournaments on that occasion," that had largely been in abeyance since the wedding celebrations, Philip's installation in the Order of the Garter at Windsor, and the royal entry into London in late August.[45] As a result Renard believed that the "nobility are now mixing a little with the Spaniards and are greatly impressed by the King's humanity and kindness."[46] Philip's *sumiller de corps* Ruy Gómez de Silva also credited Philip's return with having a quieting affect on the populace of London:

"His Highness has come to London, and a good thing too; for the longer he put it off the more disorderly people became, but now that he is here they are quieting down."[47]

The chief entertainment provided by the court in early October that afforded more pleasant opportunities in which the two nationalities could find common ground was dancing. The Spaniards had already noted, soon after their arrival, that dancing was a popular activity among the Queen's ladies, who "spend their afternoons and nights dancing, and well they may with so many young English and Spanish gentlemen to entertain."[48] Philip once again took the leading role in the festivities when on the first day of October he "went to the ladies' hall and danced with the Admiral's wife, and the Admiral with the Queen. Afterwards there was a torch-dance, and the King took out the Queen as a partner."[49] That the increased revelries seemed to be improving the atmosphere at court is borne out by a letter written over a week later by Francis Yaxley, who commented that he had observed Philip and Mary to be "in helth and mery, whom I did see dance together uppon Sunday at nyght at the court where was a brave maskery of cloth of gold and sylver, apparailed in maryners garments."[50] Philip's leadership provided an example for both nationalities to follow, and subsequently the envoy from the duke of Savoy, Count Giovanni di Stroppiana, observed that by early October the Spanish gentlemen, in spite of fears of violence directed toward them, "are making friends." He had also offered his judgment the previous month that:

> foreigners are not treated as badly as has been said. The Spaniards, in truth, are not generally liked, but the hatred against them is dying down gradually, and matters are smoothing out little by little. Things have never been in reality as bad as they were painted to me when I first arrived here. The worst ill-treatment is directed against purses and I bear my share of it. The rest all honor and consideration are shown to us.[51]

By mid-October Renard agreed that "things are going rather better with the help of winter's approach and the fact that there is often dancing at Court where Spaniards and Englishmen are beginning to mingle."[52] Clearly, initial impressions had undergone a change, and the dancing that at least one Spaniard had initially found objectionable had become acceptable and an important component in bringing the two groups together.

"All is on the right road"

The increase in festivities within the court allowed for the subsequent improvement in civility between the two nationalities, and in addition to the dancing and masks, other activities in the court and in the city of London had also been planned for the month of October in which both Englishmen and Spaniards could participate. Immediately after the king and queen's return to London at the end of September, rumors began circulating about "some celebrations organized by the Spaniards, who have got up a very fine bout at cane-play," or *juego de cañas*, and further, that "certain Englishmen are taking part."[53] Just as soon as the plans became known, however, word spread that they had been postponed "from day to day, or rather from one holiday to the next."[54] Undismayed, the Spaniards began planning for another specifically Spanish pastime and it was reported that:

> from the 10 day of Octobar vntyll the xvj day a greate preparacion was made in Smythefylde for the spanyards to bayte the bull after the maner of Spayne, called Juga de Tauro, vpon sainte Lukes day, & a great frame for an house newe sett vp ther.

On the eve of that day, however, "beynge the xvij day of Octobar, it was knowen that the same pastyme shulde be put of, so that all the preparacion for this tyme was voyde."[55] The bullbaiting, unlike the *juego de cañas* which took place later in November, never took place at all.

In spite of the apparent failure, at least for the time being, by the Spaniards to make any headway in introducing some cultural elements of their own into England, they did take part in a traditional English celebration at the end of October, the festivities surrounding the election of a new Lord Mayor of London. Extensive revelries took place within the city of London when the new mayor, "master Lyons," took his oath of office on October 29, 1554.[56] Traditionally the Lord Mayor's election was followed by a ceremony in which he traveled in procession to the Thames and took a barge to Westminster, accompanied by "alle the craftes of London in ther barges, and with stremars," with "gones and drumes and trumpetes, rohyng to Westmynster up and don," at which point he took his oath of office and was presented to the sovereign. After the return journey the mayor and the other participants landed at Paul's wharf, and proceeded to Paul's churchyard where they saw pageants performed in honor of the occasion.[57] The revelries officially came to an end at the Guildhall where a great banquet was served to the prominent citizens of London, the lords of the privy council and foreigners of distinction. The Spanish courtiers therefore had an opportunity not only to witness the spectacle of a traditional London ceremony, they also participated in the revelries at the feast, "for ther dynyd my lord chanseler and all the nobuls, and the Spaneardes, and the juges and lernyd men."[58] Aside from this banquet, some of the Spanish nobility likely dined with the mayor on other occasions, as it was his responsibility during the course of his tenure to receive and entertain visiting foreign notables as well as English dignitaries who happened to be in London.[59]

It is perhaps not a coincidence that the increased festivities at court and the subsequent easing of tensions between English and Spanish courtiers came at the same time that rumors began to circulate that the queen might be expecting a child: if all went well, Philip would soon be father to the heir to the English throne. Ruy Gómez de Silva was one of the first to mention this possibility in his letter dated October 2. This news may not have been common knowledge within the court; Ruy Gómez may have been initially privy to the news by virtue of his position in Philip's household but the information soon became more widespread. Belief in a viable pregnancy and the male heir that such a pregnancy would surely produce, not only answered the hopes of all who had worked to bring about the marriage, it also created an opportunity within the court. The knowledge that Mary expected a child enhanced Philip's popularity and his position as king consort, giving rise to speculation about his possible coronation as king.[60] In addition, it gave both nationalities more of a stake in making the alliance work, promoted a more festive atmosphere in court life, and created hopes for a more long-lasting union. Thus, the combination of relief and satisfaction contained in Ruy Gómez's final comment in his letter, "All is on the right road."[61]

Tournaments: The Historical Debate

The month of November brought more revelries within the court, including at least two masks, a Mask of Mariners, worked on between 17 to 21 October and produced November 1, 1554, and a Mask of Hercules, or "men of war comynge from the sea," as well as the long-awaited Spanish cane-play on the twenty-fifth of November.[62] The oft-postponed event marked an increased number of court revels that would extend into April of 1555, and included various masks with the assorted themes of mariners, Venetians, Turks, Moors, Alemains, Amazons, and goddesses, as well as dancing, the production of a play, and the *juego de cañas* and tournaments in which Philip played a leading role.[63] Historians have traditionally viewed the tournaments devised by Philip and the Spaniards as a failed attempt to engender goodwill within the court between themselves and the English courtiers. Alan Young ascribed the motive for the tournaments to "the somewhat naive hope of creating a healthy spirit of bonhomie among English and Spanish through their joint participation," which he concluded was a "hopeless task."[64] In particular, the *juego de cañas* has been singled out as a particular failure, after which "the Spanish attempted to redeem the situation immediately" by offering a more conventional sport.[65] Richard C. McCoy's account of the "abortive cane-game" came to a similar conclusion, and he argued that: "the exotic novelty of [the Spaniards'] own martial sports having failed to impress, they decided to meet the English on their own terms in a more traditional English contest."[66] More recently, however, David Loades has argued that the tournaments were Philip's main contribution to court life, the intent of which was "to build bridges to the English aristocracy, partly by giving them a chance to show off their martial skills, and partly to win their respect by demonstrating his own." John Edwards, similarly, has agreed that Philip "would use the organization of chivalric contests... to display his royal prowess and form bonds with the English aristocracy."[67]

It has thus been acknowledged that Philip's participation in the tournaments helped to establish his leadership abilities, albeit in a ceremonial setting, allowed him to forge ties with English courtiers, and demonstrated how, as consort, Philip assumed the masculine role of king by engaging in the male-gendered sphere of martial arts where Mary could not. Seen in conjunction with the other revelries devised from November of 1554 to April of 1555, however, the tournaments were part of a larger story, particularly when the timing of the *juego de cañas* and jousts are considered. These martial entertainments also defined and fêted Philip in his role as king because they were at the heart of planned celebrations to acknowledge the imminent birth of an heir to the English throne and the return of England to the Catholic Church—two important achievements in which Philip had played a leading role, just as he did in the tournaments. In addition, the tournaments not only helped Philip establish stronger relations with English courtiers, they strengthened the goodwill between the Spanish and English courtiers of the dual court by allowing them to act cooperatively in competitive martial sports, thus mitigating tensions at court through the use of sanctioned violence.

The first of these displays of contained and competitive martial entertainments was the *juego de cañas*, originally planned to take place in October but then "deferred so as to be held just at the opening of Parliament, in order that it may give pleasure to a greater number of spectators."[68] It was delayed once again, however, and the cane-play, a martial sport that emphasized equestrian skill, speed, and agility rather than strength, did not take place until almost two weeks later on November 25. On that date, according to the diarist Henry Machyn, six bands of men "dyd ryd in dyvers colars, the Kyng in red, and som [in] yellow, sum in gren, sum in whyt, sum in bluw, and with targets and canes in ther hand, herlyng of rods on at a-noder," banners flying, to the accompanying sounds of trumpets and drums.[69] Don Pedro de Cordoba described the event in even more detail: "There were ten gentlemen in each band, all dressed in silk and gold...Don Juan de Benavides and his band, ten in all, were in white and gold, Luis Vanegas's in green and silver; Don Diego de Córdova's, in which the king rode, purple and silver...On the other side were Ruy Gómez in gold and blue, the Duke (of Alva) with his band of eleven in yellow and silver, and Don Diego de Acevedo in black and silver." He concluded, "They made a brave display when they appeared, and the play passed off without accidents." Yet another English account merely recorded the brief information that the contestants had "their targettes on their sholderes; and thankys be to God that there was no harme done there."[70] Much has been made of the idea that the greatly anticipated display of Spanish sport was continually put off from day to day, and that once executed it "left the spectators cold."[71] This comment, made by Giovanni di Stroppiana, who added "the English made fun of it," may have been true of the English observers but Philip and the court clearly did not see it as a failure, as it did not stop the performance of another *juego de cañas* the following spring. In fact, as

a planned court entertainment accompanied by additional festivities held
that same day, and as the first of many celebrations to come over the next
few months, it was a noteworthy success given its timing.

"Her belly laid out"

By late November the fact that Mary was believed to be pregnant was
now becoming widely acknowledged. At the opening of Parliament on
November 12, it was noted that Mary appeared with "her belly laid out,
that all men might see that she was with child." Not only had Philip
apparently satisfied the English desire for a (presumably male) heir to the
throne, but the royal couple's aim to bring about the return of Catholicism
had also borne fruit and on November 24, Cardinal Reginald Pole arrived
at Westminster, having journeyed to England as the pope's legate for
England's return to the papal fold; there he was ushered in by Philip to see
Mary who "felt her child move."[72] The following day, November 25, Philip
took a leading role in the *juego de cañas*. Performed at the court gate at
Westminster after days of preparations and observed by English commoners as well as members of the court, it was both a public and a court event.[73]
After this spectacle the festivities continued for the members of the court
with a banquet, where the king and queen dined in state, dancing, masks,
and finally, a challenge issued by Don Ferdinando de Toledo, *comendador
mayor*, for a tournament on foot.[74] On November 28, Philip, Mary, and
Cardinal Pole met with both houses of Parliament "for the better understanding of his legation" (and the following day it was agreed that the laws
passed in previous reigns imposing Protestantism would be repealed).
That same day, at a service at St. Paul's Cathedral attended by the mayor
of London and other city dignitaries it was publicly announced that Mary
"was conceived and quick with child."[75] Two days later, November 30,
Cardinal Pole, Mary, and Philip returned to Parliament where Pole pronounced absolution and on December 2, Cardinal Pole, Philip, and members of the nobility and Privy Council attended a celebratory mass at St.
Paul's Cathedral after which Stephen Gardiner, bishop of Winchester, gave
a sermon to the people of London and announcing he had been empowered by Pole to deliver absolution, which he then performed. On his return
to the palace with Cardinal Pole, Philip was cheered by the Londoners,
who "displayed far more joy and loyalty than had ever been expected."[76]
The tournament on foot then took place on December 4, 1554, and was
but one of many tournaments that followed throughout the holiday season
and continued into the spring of 1555.

Christmas Festivities

Yet another "grett tryhumph at the court gatte" took place on December
18 in which "the Kyng and dyvers lordes boyth English-men and
Spaneards" took part in a contest where they "rane on fott with spayrers

and swerds at the tornay."[77] The earliest tournaments, in late November and December, including one on December 29, were followed by other revelries that diverted the court over the Christmas period. They included a mask of Venetian senators with galley slaves as torchbearers and a mask of six Venuses or Amourous Ladies with six Cupids and six torchbearers, as well as at least one play, performed between late December and early January.[78] Other than entertainments designed specifically for the court, courtiers participated in religious ceremonies as well, including the Feast of the Immaculate Conception ("the Conceptyon of owre blessed lady the Vyrgyn") celebrated on December 8, 1554, when there was "a goodly prossessyon at the Save [Savoy] be the Spaneards, the prest carehyng the sacrement ryally be-twyne ys hands, and on deacon carehyng a sonser sensing... and a nombur of frers and prestes syngyng, [and every] man and woman, and knyghts and gentylmen, bayryng a gren tapur bornyng, and viij trumpeters blohyng" after which they attended mass.[79]

Another arena in which the dual court cooperated and the two cultures juxtaposed, was that of the Chapel Royal. When Philip had arrived in England in July with all his retinue, the numbers of Spaniards and others who accompanied him had included his *capilla flamenca*, his own chapel choir. By Christmas they had already performed for him on a number of occasions as he attended public mass.[80] On December 2, the first Sunday of Advent, at the mass at St. Paul's Cathedral celebrating the arrival of Cardinal Pole, the formal absolution of the nation and the return of England to the Roman Church, as well as the official news of Mary's pregnancy, the Spanish and English choirs came together to perform. As mentioned previously, not only were Pole, the king, Gardiner, and members of the court in attendance, but in addition, a large number of clergy and bishops, the mayor of London, and "all the craftes in ther leverey," were also on hand when "Boyth the quen('s) chapell and the kynges and Powlles quer song."[81] The music performed that day and again on December 25, a seven-part Christmas Mass, was *Puer natus est nobis*, by Thomas Tallis. Jeremy Noble, Paul Doe and others have argued, based on internal evidence, that Tallis may have written this mass specifically for the combined English and Spanish choirs on this occasion, and that "the choice of the Introit, 'Puer natus est nobis et filius datus est nobis cuius imperium super humerum eius...,' may not have been wholly unconnected with the then highly topical news that Mary was expecting an heir."[82]

The Role of Martial Sports

Seen in this light, the cane-play that took place in England on November 25 was not a failed attempt to introduce a Spanish event that had to be quickly corrected by substituting a martial sport more familiar to the English. It was, instead, the initial program in a larger scheme for festivities surrounding the return of Catholicism and the rejoicing over an expected heir to the throne, while celebrating the figure standing at the center of these achievements, Philip himself. The idea of combining a purely Spanish entertainment with others more familiar to the English was not a new one: Philip and members of his court had participated in such diverse tournaments before, on Philip's extensive tour in 1549 of the territories belonging to his father, the Emperor Charles V. In fact, the tournaments in England followed a similar pattern to the tournaments that had been devised to fête Philip in his first travels outside of Spain. In his journeys to Italy, Germany, and the Low Countries, Philip and members of his court had taken part in a number of different tournaments, including jousts and tournaments on foot, as well as those of cane-play, at different sites along the way. In addition, the combatants in many of these tournaments included not just Spaniards but nobility of other nationalities.[83] Moreover, the challenge given by the Spaniards the evening of November 25 after the *juego de cañas* for a new tournament on foot had most likely already been planned to take place: there was no need to redeem the situation because the necessity for staging other tournaments to celebrate the season, the religious triumph, and Mary's pregnancy had already been anticipated. Indeed, the same day the *juego de cañas* was performed there was news that, in addition to the aforementioned challenge, "the King is later going to get up a very fine joust."[84] That Philip himself considered the *juego de cañas* to be the initial event in a long season of court revelries is clear. He marked the occasion not only by outfitting at least 30 of the participants in the cane-play in their different costumes, as well as the trumpeters and drummers in white silk, in Spanish style, but also by liberally providing the cloth for the dresses worn by the ladies of the court.[85] Don Pedro de Córdova estimated that over 30 of Mary's gentlewomen were in attendance, all dressed in gowns of gold and silver cloth, as well as crimson and purple velvet, "of which the king had ordered each one of them to be supplied with as much as they asked for."[86]

After Christmas the festivities continued when English and Spanish couriers competed in a tournament, a "ronnyng at the tylt at Westmynster with spayrers" on January 23, 1555, and in February they participated in several sports at the daylong celebration of the wedding of Lord Strange to Lady Cumberland. After dinner there were jousts followed by a "tornay on horsbake with swordes," then after supper another *juego de cañas* was performed. The festivities were rounded out with a mask and a banquet.[87] On March 25, another tournament, "as gret justes as youe have sene at the tylt at Vestmynster," took place in which Philip once again performed, where, according to Machyn, "ther was broken ij hondred stayffes."[88]

As well as the aforementioned tournaments in January, February, and March, including the celebrations surrounding the marriage of Lord Strange, additional masks were devised for performance within the court over Shrovetide, February 24–26, 1555, which included one involving six Turkish magistrates with archers as torchbearers and another mask of eight Goddesses Huntresses with eight women dressed in Turkish costume as torchbearers.[89] In addition, another display of martial arts took place in March, during which "Richard White maister at tenne kynde of weapons" along with four others performed a "challenge played at Westminster before King Philip and Queen Mary," the council, and "all odur that wold come at the court."[90] In April, Mary and Philip and the rest of the court removed to Hampton Court "to kepe Ester ther, and so her grace to her chamber ther," but the withdrawal of the Queen to her private apartments to await the birth of her child did not end court festivities, although they no longer occurred with the same frequency.[91] That same month Philip and other Spanish courtiers also attended two more weddings, those of Henry Lord Maltravers, son of the earl of Arundel, and Lord Fitzwalter, who married Frances Sidney on April 26, 1555.[92] Philip traveled to London "on purpose from Hampton Court with all his chief courtiers," in honor of Lord Maltravers' wedding "which was solemnized in his father's house," and the king "gave the bride a jeweled necklace, said to be worth a thousand ducats." Fitzwalter's wedding took place at the court, a daylong celebration in which "his Majesty in person, as a mark of greater honor, took part in person with many other gentlemen at a tourney on foot, and armed himself and fought like the others."[93]

Ceremonial Ties

The tournaments allowed Philip to take center stage in entertainments that showcased his abilities and celebrated his success. His participation in these martial sports, as well as ceremonies surrounding the Order of the Garter and the creation of knights, also enabled him to construct a kingly persona that would be accepted by the English nobility. It has been more widely acknowledged that they also helped him create personal ties with the English nobility. It has often been noted, for example, that Robert Dudley, the duke of Northumberland's son, who took part in the jousts in March, benefited from Philip's goodwill while he was in England. Both Lord Fitzwalter, and Lord Strange, son of the earl of Derby, in whose wedding celebrations Philip had participated, were members of the king's English household, and by honoring both young gentlemen in this way, according to the Venetian ambassador, "by such demonstrations [the king] from day to day gains the goodwill of all."[94] Lord Maltravers, the earl of Arundel's son and also a member of the king's household, whose wedding Philip had also attended, would later present Philip with a Latin translation of the rules of the Order of the Garter which the king would take with him when he left England.[95] As well as attending these three weddings, Philip would also become godfather, by proxy, to three children, all named after him, born to members of the English court, including Sir Henry Sidney's son Philip; Philip Howard, son of Thomas Howard, duke of Norfolk who had been appointed first gentleman of the chamber in the king's household; and Philip Basset, son of James Basset who served in both Mary and Philip's privy chambers.[96]

While Philip could thus take on the persona of English king in the tournaments and other martial sports, Mary played the traditional role of queen consort, attending at least three of the tournaments, including the initial cane-play on November 25, 1554, when the queen dressed in all her finery watched the event along with all the other gentlewomen of the court.[97] It was Mary who "gave a banquet to the King and his gentlemen" after the *juego de cañas* had ended.[98] Similarly, it was the queen who awarded the prizes to the winners "by the advise of other princesses ladyes and gentlewomen of this noble court" at the tournament on December 4, including a prize for Philip for swordsmanship.[99] She also was present at the tournament of March 25 at Westminster, "the wyche was owre lade [day]" the Feast of the Annunciation to the Blessed Virgin Mary, when after watching Philip participate and worried for his safety she "could not conceal her fear and disquietude about the King, sending to pray him (having done his duty, and run many courses as in truth he did) not to encounter further risk, which request he gratified."[100] No tournaments were staged at Mary's court prior to Philip's arrival, but Mary clearly was willing to let Philip take the initiative in these events after they married; she, therefore, was the chief spectator in the more passive role of consort whereas he was able to demonstrate the military component of kingship while building ties to the English court.

Cooperation at Court

In addition to allowing Philip to establish himself in the ceremonial role of English king, the tournaments also offered the kind of chivalric entertainments in which both English and Spanish courts could find common connections. These martial sports helped to mitigate mutual antagonisms by allowing English and Spanish courtiers to cooperate in competing both with and against each other in condoned acts of aggression. The martial entertainments that began in November 1554 provided opportunities for the courtiers of the dual court to interact in ways that lessened the hostilities that had built up between them by competing both against and with each other: they were cooperative in nature from the beginning. When the Spaniards produced the first cane-play, for example, at least one Englishman, Lord Fitzwalter, took part in that event with the Spaniards.[101] His inclusion in the *juego de cañas* was an obvious attempt by Philip and the other Spaniards to address his unhappiness—it was Fitzwalter, after all, who had complained the previous month of losing what little Spanish he knew. In order to participate, he needed to know something of the sport, knowledge that could either have been gained during his visit to Spain the previous spring, or, more likely, by working with the Spanish courtiers in November before the event took place. Cooperation between everyone involved thus would have been necessary.[102]

That cooperation continued during the tournaments through the winter and spring of 1554 and 1555 in which English and Spanish courtiers took part equally. Englishmen and Spaniards both took part in the challenge for the tournament played on December 4, 1554, and prizes were given afterward to those who had shown themselves most valiant.[103] In addition, the four gentlemen who judged the event included two Englishmen, the earl of Arundel and the Lord Clinton, and two Spaniards, Don Pedro de Cordoba and Gutierre López de Padilla.[104] The judges also roughly divided the prizes between those English and Spanish participants believed to be most worthy in the different events. These included an award given for the best entry, and prizes for prowess with the pike and the sword as well as other contests.[105] The tournaments, therefore, were intended to be joint cooperative events, as is borne out by the fact that on March 25, 1555 Sir George Howard and an unnamed Spaniard together offered a challenge to anyone willing to accept. From the staging of the first *juego de cañas* a compromise had also been reached with the question of language: after the cane-play and banquet following, an English king of arms proclaimed the challenge for the December 4 tournament in both English and Spanish, suggesting that the court had accepted a bilingual approach in order to deal with language difficulties and increase communications on the occasion of formal court events.[106]

"The Queen's safe deliverance"

Another reason for the increased cooperative behavior between the nationalities, however, was not just Philip's efforts but the belief in the queen's pregnancy and the corresponding hope for an Anglo-Spanish heir; it was expected that once Mary gave birth, conditions in England would improve even more. Revels had ceased to occupy the court by May, as English and Spanish courtiers alike began to await signs of the Queen's imminent delivery of her child, a far more anticipated and important occurrence. In early May false rumors of the birth of the baby were circulating not only in England but at continental courts as well, and Mary and Philip apparently also expected the birth at this time: on May 16 four courtiers, including Lord Fitzwalter, "appoynted to beare the newse of the Queenes Majesties good deliverance... to sundrie princes" were issued allowances to pay for their journeys.[107] By the end of May court members still waited for the event, while being assured that it would not be amiss for the birth to be postponed until sometime in June.[108] By the end of June, with that hope slowly dying Renard attested that:

> Everything in this kingdom depends on the Queen's safe deliverance. Her doctors and ladies have proved to be out in their calculations by about two months, and it now appears that she will not be delivered before eight or ten days from now... If God is pleased to grant her a child, things will take a turn for the better. If not, I foresee trouble on so great a scale that the pen can hardly set it down.[109]

Unhappily for Mary, Philip, and the success of the Anglo-Spanish union, the pregnancy proved to be false. Although Mary continued to insist that she was pregnant, Philip began to make arrangements for his long postponed departure from England and he left for Brussels at the end of August, not to return to England again until 1557.

During his residence in England (and in spite of the fact that hopes for a child born of the Anglo-Spanish union were not fulfilled), Philip was successful in defining a role for himself as king consort. From the fall of 1554 to the spring of 1555 Philip established his ability to lead, was instrumental in bringing about the return of Catholicism, and was seemingly successful in fathering an heir to the throne. Within the context of court culture, he established a means by which the nobility of England and Spain could relate through competition and cooperation, as well as celebrate his own triumphal role through the communal activities of court revels, ceremonies, and martial sports. Had the union actually produced a child, it would have been a crowning success. In spite of that disappointment, Philip had used his stay in England to enhance his reputation as a ruler not only within the English court, but also in the continental court of opinion, not an inconsequential feat given that his father, Emperor Charles V, would soon begin to transfer control of his vast empire to Philip within months of his arrival in Brussels. Philip, himself, believed that he had succeeded in building personal relationships with English courtiers, creating a role for himself as king consort, and learning a great deal about England and its governance during his tenure as king. It is perhaps not so surprising that he could claim in 1570 that he could give "better information and advice on that kingdom and on its affairs and people, than anyone else."[110] It is likely that the debate over the extent of Philip's power as king consort will continue to be hotly disputed, and the truth of the matter may never be known conclusively, in part, because so many of the records of his activities during this time period were subsequently lost at sea.[111] The reassessment of how Philip negotiated his unprecedented role is ongoing: it is clear, however, that the definitive reevaluation of Philip as king of England has yet to be written.

Notes

1. See Judith M. Richards, *Mary Tudor* (London and New York, 2008); Anna Whitelock, *Mary Tudor: England's First Queen* (London and New York, 2009); Linda Porter, *The Myth of "Bloody Mary"* (New York, 2007); Charles Beem, *The Lioness Roared: The Problems of Female Rule in English History* (New York, 2006), ch. 2, "Her Kingdom's Wife: Mary I and the Gendering of Royal Power," pp. 63–100. For a discussion of other revisionist works on Mary, see my historiographical essay, "'Bloody Mary'?: Changing Perceptions of England's First Ruling Queen," in *The Name of a Queen: William Fleetwood's Itinerarium ad Windsor*, eds. Charles Beem and Dennis Moore (New York, 2013); see also Susan Doran and Thomas S. Freeman, "Introduction," in

Mary Tudor: Old and New Perspectives, eds. Susan Doran and Thomas S. Freeman (New York, 2011), 1–17.

2. Judith M. Richards, "Reassessing Mary Tudor: Some Concluding Points," *Mary Tudor: Old and New Perspectives*, 206–24, p. 224 for quotation. See also Richards, "Examples and Admonitions: What Mary Demonstrated for Elizabeth," in *Tudor Queenship: The Reigns of Mary and Elizabeth*, eds. Alice Hunt and Anna Whitelock (New York, 2010), 31–45.

3. Harry Kelsey, *Philip of Spain, King of England: The Forgotten King* (London and New York, 2012).

4. 1 Mary, st. 3, c. 2, *Statutes of the Realm, Volume 4, Part 1 [1547–1585]* (London: Record Commission, 1819), 222–6.

5. Andrés Muñoz, *Sumaria y verdadera relación del buen viaje que el…Príncipe…don Felipe hizo a Inglaterra* (Zaragoza, 1554), reprinted in Pascual de Gayangos, ed., *Viaje de Felipe Segundo á Inglaterra, por Andrés Muñoz (impreso en Zaragoza en 1554), y relaciones varias relativas al mismo suceso* (Madrid, 1877), pp. 50–1.

6. State Papers Foreign, Mary, and Philip and Mary, SP 69/3/128.

7. See Sarah Duncan, *Mary I: Gender, Power, and Ceremony in the Reign of England's First Queen* (New York, 2012), esp. ch. 2 for a discussion of how Mary was crowned as both king and queen, and ch. 7, 142–7, for the question of Philip's coronation.

8. British Library, Cotton MS, Vespasian F iii, no. 23.

9. *Acts of the Privy Council of England New Series, 1542–1628* (London: His Majesty's Stationery Office, 1840–1940), 4:53.

10. David Loades, "Philip II and the Government of England," in *Law and Government under the Tudors*, eds. C. Cross, D. Loades, and J. Scarisbrick (Cambridge, 1988), 194; David Loades, *The Reign of Mary Tudor: Politics, Government, and Religion in England, 1553–1558*, 2nd ed. (London, 1991), 397; Glyn Redworth, "'Matters Impertinent to Women': Male and Female Monarchy under Philip and Mary," *English Historical Review* 112 (June 1997), 611.

11. See, for example, Alexander Samson, "Power Sharing: The Co-Monarchy of Philip and Mary," in *Tudor Queenship: The Reigns of Mary and Elizabeth*, eds. Alice Hunt and Anna Whitelock (New York, 2010), 159–72; John Edwards, *Mary I: England's Catholic Queen* (New Haven and London, 2011); Duncan, *Mary I*. A discussion of the degrees to which opinions differ on how, and in what ways Philip and Mary were corulers, is beyond the scope of this essay. David Loades, in his more recent work on the court, *Intrigue and Treason: The Tudor Court 1547–1558* (Harlow, England: Pearson, 2004), has revised his earlier dismissal of Philip as a "failure", see ch. 7, "King Philip." Another debate concerning Philip's role in the government revolves around the question of his establishment of the "Select Council" while he was in England: see Loades, "Philip II and the Government in England;" Glyn Redworth, "'Matters Impertinent to Women;'" D. E. Hoak, "Two Revolutions in Tudor Government: the Formation and Organization of Mary I's Privy Council," in *Revolution Reassessed: Revisions in the History of Tudor Government and Administration*, eds. C. Coleman and D. R. Starkey (Oxford, 1986), 87–115; John Guy, "The Marian Court and Tudor Policy-Making," undergraduate lecture,

www.tudors.org/undergraduate/the-marian-court-and-tudor-policy-making/.

12. Alexander Samson, "Images of Co-Monarchy in the London Entry of Philip and Mary (1554)" in *Writing Royal Entries in Early Modern Europe*, eds. Marie-Claude Canova-Green and Jean Andrews, with Marie-France Wagner (Brepols, 2013), vol. III, 113–27, 113 for quote.

13. In January 1554, although Philip ratified the articles of the marriage treaty and swore to uphold them, at the same time he secretly signed a "writing ad cautelem" in which he refused to consider himself bound by the contract or his own oath to obey it. See *Calendar of Letters, Despatches and State Papers Relating to the Negotiations between England and Spain Preserved in the Archives at Simancas and Elsewhere*, eds. Royall Tyler et al., 13 vols. (London: His Majesty's Stationery Office, 1862–1954), 12:4–5. [Series hereafter cited as *CalStP-Spanish*]. See Duncan, *Mary I*, ch. 4 for a discussion of the reversal of Mary and Philip's traditional gender roles and Philip's subordinate role in the marriage negotiations.

14. *CalStP-Spanish*, 12:149; 177–8.

15. *CalStP-Spanish*, 12:174.

16. SP 69/4/207, Edward Lord Dudley to the Council May 17, 1554. Andrés Muñoz, *Viaje de Felipe Segundo a Inglaterra*, ed. Pascual de Gayangos (Madrid: Sociedad de Bibliófilos Españoles, xv, 1877), 1–12.

17. George Everett to the Council in England, May 12, 1554, SP 69/4/204; Edward Lord Dudley to the Council, May 17, 1554, SP 69/4/207. See also Renard and de Courrieres to Charles, May 22–25, 1554, *CalStP-Spanish*, 12:262.

18. George Everett to the Council, May 12, 1554, SP 69/4/204.

19. They communicated in Latin and Edward Lord Dudley communicated to the Council that "thowghe but rudlie I specke the same yn mas humble mannor as I colld devize I reternd thancks," May 17, 1554, SP 69/4/207.

20. *CalStP-Spanish*, 12:249–50. Although Philip had been awarded the title in the contract by the time he wrote these letters, he did not enjoy the full regal style until after the wedding on July 25, 1554.

21. The imperial ambassadors had previously, in January, had a similar experience when they journeyed to England to conclude the marriage negotiations on Philip's behalf, and were treated to a lavish reception complete with banquets, dancing, and the performances of masques and plays at the English court. See *CalStP-Spanish*, 12:10–11, 14, 22–3, 252–3; John G. Nichols, ed., *The Chronicle of Queen Jane and of Two Years of Queen Mary, and Especially of the Rebellion of Sir Thomas Wyat*, Camden Society Publications 48 (London, 1850), 34; Henry Machyn, *The Diary of Henry Machyn: Citizen and Merchant-Taylor of London from A.D. 1550–1563*, ed. John Gough Nichols (London: Printed for the Camden Society, 1848), 50; John Gough Nichols, ed., *The Chronicle of the Grey Friars of London*, Camden Society Publications 53 (London: Printed for the Camden Society, 1852), 85–6.

22. *CalStP-Spanish*, 12: 315–6.

23. SP 69/5/251.

24. *Tudor Royal Proclamations*, vol. 2, *The Later Tudors II*, ed. Paul Hughes and James F. Larkin (New Haven, CT: Yale University Press, 1969), 33–4. Spanish courtiers had similarly been warned of the importance of keeping their servants under control, "for trouble more often comes from presumptuous

and insolent servants than from masters, and this kind of offence is the hardest for the English to bear." Charles V to Count d'Egmont, February 18, 1554, *CalStP-Spanish*, 12: 116.

25. Alexander Samson, "A Fine Romance: Anglo-Spanish Relations in the Sixteenth Century," *Journal of Medieval and Early Modern Studies,* 39:1 (Winter 2009), 65–94, see pp. 72, 66 for quotes.

26. John Elder, *The Copie of a Letter Sent in to Scotland, of the arivall and landynge, and moste noble marryage of the moste Illustre Prince Philippe*, printed in *Chronicle of Queen Jane and Queen Mary*, 143–4.

27. *CalStP-Spanish*, 12:322; 13:10.

28. Elder, 143.

29. *CalStP-Spanish*, 13, 31.

30. The entertainment "was more after the English than the Spanish fashion," *Chronicle of Queen Jane and Queen Mary*, 170; *CalStP-Spanish*, 13:10, 31. The type of dance referred to as "strutting or trotting about" may have referred to one of the most popular dances in England, the Basse dance, known as the measures, which was "a slow, sedate procession," and "progressed at a deliberate and dignified pace." See Skiles Howard, *The Politics of Courtly Dancing in Early Modern England* (Massachusetts Studies in Early Modern Culture) (Amherst, MA, 1998), 6, 14–5.

31. *Chronicle of Queen Jane and Queen Mary*, 170.

32. *CalStP-Spanish*, vol. XIII, 10.

33. *Colección de documentos inéditos para la historia de España* (Madrid, 1842–95) (hereafter cited as CODOIN), 3:530.

34. Renard to Charles V, September 18, 1554, from London, *CalStP-Spanish*, 13:49.

35. *Tudor Royal Proclamations*, vol. II, 46.

36. *Chronicle of Queen Jane and Queen Mary*, 81.

37. *CalStP-Spanish*, vol. XIII Oct. 13 Renard to Charles V.

38. *Tudor Royal Proclamations*, II, 46–8. See also Machyn, *Diary,* 69.

39. *CalStP-Spanish*, 13: 23, 31. 45.

40. Renard to Charles V, September 3, 1554, *CalStP-Spanish*, 13: 45.

41. *CalStP-Spanish*, 13: 50.

42. See my discussion of this ceremony and Philip's role in it in Duncan, *Mary I*, 102–4.

43. *Viaje de Felipe Segundo á Inglaterra, por Andrés Muñoz (impreso en Zaragoza en 1554, y relaciones varias relativas al mismo suceso*, ed. Pascual de Gayangos (Madrid: Imprenta de Rivadeneyra, 1877), 118: "y ansí hay cada dia en palacio cuchilladas entre ingleses y españoles." Violence did take place within the court but it was the servants rather than the nobility who proved to be the primary aggressors. Ruy Gómez de Silva is the only nobleman to be identified in an episode of Anglo-Spanish hostilities and was the victim rather than perpetrator.

44. *CalStP-Spanish*, 13: 443–5.

45. Machyn, *Diary,* 69. See also *CalStP-Spanish*, 13: 51, Renard to Charles V, September 18, 1554. While the royal couple was at Windsor, "the 7 of August was a general huntinge at Wyndsore forest, where was made a great toyle of 4 or 5 myles longe," William Douglas Hamilton, ed., *A Chronicle of England during the Reigns of the Tudors from A.D. 1485-1559, by Charles Wriothesley's*

(New York, 1965), 2:121. See Duncan, *Mary I*, 99–102 for my discussion of the ceremony inducting Philip into the Order of the Garter.

46. Ambassador Renard to the Emperor Charles V, October 13, 1554, from London, *CalStP-Spanish*, 13:64.

47. *CalStP-Spanish*, 13:60. Renard concurred, stating that "the people of London have ceased to be as insolent as they formerly were," 64.

48. *Viaje de Felipe Segundo*, 100–1; see also *CalStP-Spanish*, 13:13.

49. Ruy Gomez de Silva to Eraso, October 2, 1554, *CalStP-Spanish*, 13:60. The admiral was William Lord Howard of Effingham.

50. He continued, "the cheif doer wherof I thinke was my L. Admiral." BL Lansdowne 3, f. 92. See also W. R. Streitberger, *Court Revels, 1485–1559* (Toronto, 1994), 211.

51. *CalStP-Spanish*, 13: 62; 51.

52. Renard to Charles V, October 13, 1554, from London, *CalStP-Spanish*, 13:64–5. Renard added that "it is a good thing that the King should have decided to keep some English household officials, who will serve him with their Spanish colleagues."

53. *Viaje de Felipe Segundo*, pp. 118–9. The Spanish courtier who spoke of it thought "it will please the Queen and consequently all the English people, whose interest will be keen as the sport is unknown here." See also Langosco di Stroppiano to the Bishop of Arras, October 6, 1554, *CalStP-Spanish*, 13:63.

54. Longosco dei Conti da Stroppiana to the Bishop of Arras, October 22, 1554, *CalStP-Spanish*, 13:75. He continued, "I believe it will be deferred so as to be held just at the opening of Parliament, in order that it may give pleasure to a greater number of spectators. His Majesty is to take part in it, with the Dukes of Alva and Medinaceli, the Count of Feria and all the greatest nobles."

55. Charles L. Kingsford, ed., "Two London Chronicles from the Collection of John Stow," *Camden Miscellany 12*, Camden 3rd Series (London, 1910), 38. This is apparently the only source for the plans for a Spanish bullfight or bullbaiting.

56. Machyn, *Diary*, 73. This was John Lyon who in 1554 replaced the previous mayor, Thomas Whyte. See Valerie Hope, *My Lord Mayor Eight Hundred Years of London's Mayoralty* (London, 1989), 185.

57. On this occasion the "goodly pagant" included "a gryffen with a chyld lyung in harnes, and sant John Baptyst with a lyon." Machyn, *Diary*, 73.

58. Machyn, *Diary*, 73; *A Relation, or Rather a True Account of the Island of England: With Sundry Particulars of the Customs of These People and of the Royal Revenues Under King Henry the Seventh, About the Year 1500*, ed. and tr. Charlotte Augusta Sneyd, Camden Society Publications 37 (London 1847) 44; Margaret R. Kollock, *The Lord Mayor and Aldermen of London during the Tudor Period* (Philadephia, 1906), 30–3.

59. Wriothesley, *Chronicle*, 122–3, 125; Hope, *My Lord Mayor*, 51. Other opportunities to intermingle and associate with England's officials may have also arisen; the Bishop of London entertained some of the Spanish courtiers at a dinner at least once, and it is likely there were other such occasions, although the records are scarce. *Historical Manuscript Commission*, 7th Report, Appendix, W. M. Molyneux (Loseley MSS), p.611: "Warrant, under

the Queen's sign-manual and signet, to Sir Thomas Cawarden; to deliver to the bishop of London, 'in consideracioun he hath the entertaynment of divers nobell menne of Spayne' a buck of the season, out of Nonesuche Park."

60. See Duncan, *Mary I*, 142 – 5 for my discussion of Philip's coronation.

61. *CalStP-Spanish*, 13:60.

62. Albert Feuillerat, ed., *Documents Relating to Revels at Court in the Time of King Edward VI and Queen Mary* (The Loseley Manuscripts) (Louvain, 1914), xiv, 159–79.The mask of Hercules with mariners was probably performed November 30, 1554.

63. Streitberger, 68–9, 99, 129, 159, 288, 294.

64. Alan R. Young, *Tudor and Jacobean Tournaments* (Dobbs Ferry, NY: Sheridan House, 1987), 30.

65. Young, 31.

66. Richard C. McCoy, "Communications. From the Tower to the Tiltyard: Robert Dudley's Return to Glory," *The Historical Journal*, 27, 2 (1984), 429.

67. Loades, *Intrigue and Treason: The Tudor Court*, 190–1; Edwards, *Mary I: England's Catholic Queen*, 210. In contrast, Alexander Samson has not been quite as positive, suggesting that "Philip's attempts to blend distinctive cultural forms such as the joust and Spanish juego de cañas together might have been a failure, giving rise to slighting comments about its unmanliness," "Power Sharing," p. 166. For my discussion of Philip's role in the tournaments see Duncan, *Mary I*, 104–7.

68. *CalStP-Spanish*, 13: 75.

69. Machyn, *Diary*, 76. A brief description of cane-play is provided by J. Deleito y Piñuela in *El rey se divierte* (Madrid, 1955), 182: "The juegos de cañas were an adaptation of the tourney: several teams of horsemen competed [at the gallop], attacking each other with lances of cane or wood, which they hurled as projectiles." See also Kelsey, 105–6.

70. Don Pedro de Cordoba to the king of the Romans, *Traslado de una carta que fue embiada del reyno de Inglaterra*, Biblioteca Nacional R/31746, printed *Viaje de Felipe II a Inglaterra.*; *Chronicle of the Grey Friars*, 93.

71. This was Count Langosco da Stroppiana's judgement, who added that only the clothes of the players pleased the spectators and "the English made fun of it." *CalStP-Spanish*, 13: 105. None of the English accounts of this event describe it as a disappointment. See Machyn, *Diary*, 76, *Chronicle of the Grey Friars*, 93, and "Two London Chronicles," 39–40.

72. *CalStP-Spanish*, 13:104–5; John Gough Nichols, ed., *Narratives of the Days of the Reformation, Chiefly from the Manuscripts of John Foxe* (1859; repr., New York and London, 1968), 289. This was the same parliament at which "they said laboure was made to have the kinge crowned, and some thought that the quene for that cause dyd lay out her belly the more," ibid.

73. *Chronicle of the Grey Friars*, 92, records that "the xix day of November began the pluckynge downe of the postys at the corte gatte at Westmyster by the hyeway syde for the play of the Spanyardes that was callyd the cane."

74. *Viaje de Felipe Segundo*, 137–8; Ambassador Renard to Charles V, *CalStP-Spanish*, 13:108–9.

75. *CalStP-Spanish*, 13:120; *Viaje de Felipe Segundo*, 129–30.Wriothesley, *Chronicle*, 2:124. The priest took his sermon from Luke 1:30: "And the angel said unto her, Fear not, Mary: for thou hast found favor with God."

76. *CalStP-Spanish*, 13:112.

77. Machyn, *Diary*, 79. Of this event Renard wrote to Charles V from London December 21, 1554: "Last Tuesday the foot tournament arranged some time since took place, and was so gallantly carried out that both assailants and defenders reaped high praise. The King very successfully took part in one of the bands," *CalStP-Spanish*, 13:126.

78. Feuillerat, 159–60, 166–71.

79. Machyn, *Diary* , 78. According to Machyn, a bear-baiting took place the following day "on the Banke syde," but no mention is made of this event being attended by anyone from the court. Philip took part in another religious procession in late January 1555, "the Conversione of Sent Paulles day," see *Chronicle of the Grey Friars*, 94.

80. See, for example, Machyn, *Diary*, 72: "The xviij day of October king Philip came down on horseback from Westminster unto Paul's, with many lords, being received under a canopy, at the west end: and the lord Montagu bare the sword afore the king. There he heard mass, and Spaneards song mase; and after masse [he went back to] Westmynster to dener." On another occasion Machyn recorded that the burial of an unnamed Spaniard in November included "boythe Spaneards and Englysmen syngyng," 75.

81. Machyn, *Diary*, 77. After the service, Philip who had attended the mass, "returned through the city to his palace, hailed by a mighty concourse of people, who displayed far more joy and loyalty than had ever been expected." Count G. T. Langosco da Stroppiana to the Bishop of Arras, December 3, 1554, *CalStP-Spanish*, 13:112.

82. "A boy is born for us and a son is given to us whose government will be upon his shoulder," Paul Doe, *Tallis* (Oxford, 1976), 20–9.

83. For examples see Juan Cristóbal Calvete de Estrella, *El Felicísimo Viaje del muy alto y muy poderoso Príncipe Don Felipe* (Madrid, 1930), vol. I, 137, 189, 202, 307–11; vol. II, 404–9. See also Henry Kamen, *Philip of Spain* (New Haven, CT, 1997), 41.

84. *CalStP-Spanish*, 13: 105.

85. *Translado de una carta*, BN R/31746: "Don Diego de Cordova consus diez donde una el rey de recamado y oro, que eran los treynta de un puesto: a aguestos dio el rey de vestir, y a sus trompetos y atabales al modo de España vestidos de seda blanca."

86. *Translado de una carta*, BN R/31746; *Viaje de Felipe II*, 138; *CalStP-Spanish*, 13: 119.

87. Machyn, *Diary*, 80, 82. According to Machyn the activities included a "grett dener, and justes, and after tornay on horsbake with swordes, and after Jube the cane, a play, with torch-lyght and cressett-lyghtes, lx cressets and c. of torchys, and a maske, and a bankett."

88. Machyn, *Diary*, 84. This took place March 25, 1555. One of the companies of men who competed entered the designated arena costumed as Turks and in this guise they certainly provided an image that both Englishmen and Spaniards could target as an enemy. Machyn also records an additional tournament in March in which "the Kyng's grace rune at the tylt a-gaynst odur Spaneards, and brake iiij stayffes by viij of the cloke in the mornyng," 83.

89. Feuillerat, 172–7.

90. B. L. Sloane MS 2530, f. 38. The others are identified as "William Hunt, Thomas Weaver, Roberte Edmonde, and Willyam Hearne." Machyn, *Diary*, 82, recorded the date as being March 5, 1555 and called White "the master of fensse."

91. Machyn, *Diary*, p. 84; *CalStP-Spanish*, vol. 13:166. The fact that there were fewer activities coincides with the fact that Philip desperately needed money, which may have curtailed some of the expenditure on tournaments.

92. Giovanni Michiel to the Doge and Senate, April 29, 1555, *Calendar of State Papers and Manuscripts Relating to English Affairs, Existing in the Archives and Collections of Venice, and in Other Libraries of Northern Italy*, eds. Rawdon Brown, et al., 39 vols. (London, 1864–1947), vol. 6:58. Thomas Radcliffe, styled Lord Fitzwalter, was the son of the earl of Sussex.

93. Michiel, *CalSP-Venetian*, 6: 58. He continued, "By such demonstrations he from day to day gains the good will of all."

94. *CalStP-Venetian*, 6: 58.

95. *CalStP-Spanish*, 13: 442.

96. Philip Howard's mother, Mary Fitzalan Howard, was sister to Henry Lord Maltravers; Philip Basset's mother was Mary Clark, alias Roper, granddaughter of Sir Thomas More. She also served as one of Mary's gentlewomen. The Spanish influence can also perhaps be seen in the fact that Henry Stanley, Lord Strange, named his second son, born in 1559, Ferdinando.

97. BN R/31746: "la reyna de brocado pelo, cota de un nuevo brocado, y ropilla de tercipelo carmesi mozado aforrado en lobos con gran suma de pedreria y perlas y recannado de plata de martillo y oro, y el collarico de diamentes, y en el tocado gran coasa de diamantes y rubies."

98. Renard to Charles V, November 30, 1554, *CalStP-Spanish*, 13: 108.

99. BL, Harleian 69, f. 24v; William Segar, *Honor military, and ciuill, contained in foure bookes* (London: Robert Barker, 1602), 193. Just who provided the jewels for the occasion is in question; Mary, while known for frugality with court expenses, could also be quite generous: in October when Don Fernando Gonzaga departed, she gave him "a ring with a single ruby and a chain with a pendant formed by a diamond and a big pearl, valued 800 or 1,000 crowns, for the princess, his spouse." *CalStP-Spanish*, 13: 75.

100. See *CalStP-Venetian*, 6:32.

101. *Diary of Machyn*, p. 76.

102. Other Englishmen may also have taken part, as was rumored in early October during the preparations for the cane-play, although no others were named as actors in the actual event. See *CalStP-Spanish*, 13: 63.

103. College of Arms, M6, ff. 59–61; BL, Harley 69, ff. 23–5; Harley 6069, f. 26; Segar, 192–3.

104. College of Arms, M6, f. 59v; BL Harley 69, f. 23v; Segar, p. 193.

105. The lists of prizes is given by Segar, 93.

106. Translado de una carta, BN R/31746: "un rey de armas Ingles con su cota leyo el cartel Ingles y Español." Again this suggests that the challenge had already been planned.

107. B. L. Harleian 643, ff.47v-48. These courtiers included the Lord Fitzwalter who was "to be sente to the Frenche kinge."

108. Ruy Gomez de Silva to Erasso, May 8, 1555, Archivo de Simancas, Estado 809, f. 128; same to same, May 22, 1555, Estado 808, f. 128.
109. Renard to Charles V, June 24, 1555, *CalStP-Spanish*, 13: 224.
110. Quoted in Geoffrey Parker, "The Place of Tudor England in the Messianic Vision of Philip II of Spain: The Prothero Lecture," *Transactions of the Royal Historical Society*, Sixth Series, 12 (2002), 167–221, 185 for quotation.
111. Parker, 184, n. 32.

CHAPTER 4

Why Prince George of Denmark Did Not Become a King of England

Charles Beem

It does not seem all that strange to us today that Prince George of Denmark served as an unofficial male consort to his wife Queen Anne, the last of the Stuart monarchs in Britain, during the first decade of the eighteenth century. After all, for nearly 60 years we have grown accustomed to Prince Philip of Greece, the duke of Edinburgh, walking dutifully but not quite so comfortably behind his wife Elizabeth II, a queen who reigns serenely without any apparent need for a king by her side, even though she has a husband whom she clearly loves and cherishes. The duke's role is singular, highly visible, and ultimately essential to the maintenance of the monarchy, but it nonetheless remains an informal one, something akin to an American first lady, or gentleman, should we Americans ever elect a woman as our president.

Philip's role as an informal consort to a regnant queen is based upon precedents derived from the career of his and his wife's joint ancestor, Prince Albert of Saxe-Coburg-Gotha. Prince Albert also served as an informal male consort for 17 of the 21 years he was married to Queen Victoria, although he was formally created prince consort by letters patent in 1857, a status none of the governments of her present majesty, going all the way back to Winston Churchill, has seen fit to bestow upon the duke of Edinburgh.[1] It is a fair assumption that both Prince Albert and Prince Philip would have been much happier with a more formalized role, like say a king consortship, the gendered equivalent to the status enjoyed by British queen consorts, who are anointed, crowned, and share their husband's thrones. In Albert's case, it was Prince George of Denmark's precedent as an informal male consort that Whig Prime Minister Viscount Melbourne gently deployed in order to sway Victoria from her initial desire to have her husband share the royal dignity with her.[2]

However, when Queen Anne came to the throne in 1702, the English precedents surrounding the role of the male consort were markedly different. In fact, if we examine the precedents surrounding the husbands of previous regnant queens, such as Philip of Hapsburg, later King Philip II of Spain, and William of Orange, later King William III of England, then what happened to Prince George of Denmark emerges as a rather striking break with precedent that, in turn, hardened into a more enduring one that served to prevent both Prince Albert and Prince Philip from sharing their wives thrones as king consorts.

As I have argued elsewhere, regnant queenship is in fact a form of kingship that has made it difficult, both in theory and in practice, to recognize the husbands of female kings also as kings.[3] This problem first reared its ugly head during the reign of the mid-sixteenth-century monarch Mary I, England's first regnant queen. Because she had been successively statutorily bastardized and then restored to the succession by parliamentary statute, Mary came to the throne at the age of 37 as an unmarried woman. According to the developing political theory known as the "king's two bodies," Mary's body natural had unmistakably inherited the eternal body politic of kingship in the same fashion as her noble progenitors, the kings of England.[4] But she did so as a queen. For the first year of her reign, Mary performed the dual roles of king and queen simultaneously as England's *first* virgin queen who simultaneously touched for the King's evil, a sacerdotal function previously only performed by kings. Mary's coronation ritual made this perfectly clear, with the queen's long hair hanging free, virgin like, as she was fitted with the spurs of martial kingship; Queen Anne would also be crowned in a remarkably similar fashion a century and a half later.[5] Although Mary fully inhabited the body politic of kingship, it was up to her flesh and blood body natural to propagate the Tudor dynasty through the female line. For this she needed a husband. Philip was drafted primarily for this purpose, although the marriage also revived the old Anglo-Burgundian alliance that dated back to the Yorkist king Edward IV, which made it worth it to Philip's father, Holy Roman Emperor Charles V, even in the short term. But negotiating the marriage was difficult, for the queen and her negotiators were anxious not to part with a shred of the royal prerogative, as the queen informed Charles V:

> She would wholly love and obey him to whom she had given herself, following the divine commandment, and would do nothing against his will; but if he wished to encroach in the government, she would be unable to permit it, nor if he attempted to fill posts and offices with strangers, for the country itself would never stand such interference.[6]

In the final draft of the marriage contract, ratified as statute in the parliamentary session of spring 1554, Philip was specifically barred from undertaking any kind of formal role in his wife's government, nor was he given a farthing for the establishment of his own royal household.[7] Despite these rather emasculating terms, the contract did bow to the dictates of sixteenth-century European patriarchy, as it gave Philip the courtesy title of King as well as precedence over his wife in their official documents and pronouncements. However, at the same time parliament ratified another statute, an Act For the Queen's Regal Power that clearly defined a regnant queen as the same political substance as a king, rendering Philip's English kingship a rather unstable and ill-defined public role.[8] When Mary died childless in 1558, Philip's kingship terminated, as Mary's successor, Elizabeth I, sidestepped the issue of figuring out what the official status and role of any of her prospective husbands might be, leaving Philip and Mary's marriage treaty as the sole statutory pronouncement and precedent regarding this issue.[9]

The issue became salient once again more than a century later during the reign of the Stuart King Charles II (r. 1660–85). Charles had been unable to produce legitimate heirs with his queen Catherine of Braganza, making his younger brother James, duke of York, his heir presumptive. York in turn had two daughters, Mary and Anne, by his first wife Anne Hyde, and thus far no surviving issue from his second wife, Mary of Modena. Despite his private inclinations toward Catholicism, and his clandestine dealings with King Louis XIV of France, Charles II found it politically expedient to find Protestant husbands for his nieces. The elder, Mary, marched down the aisle with her first cousin, the Dutch Stadtholder Prince William of Orange in 1677. Although he was not impressive physically, William was a forceful, dynamic, and capable politician and military leader, a leading figure in the government of the Dutch United Provinces, who spent most of his life trying to rein in the expansionist policies of Louis XIV.

He was, in fact, the polar opposite of his brother-in-law, Prince George of Denmark, a younger brother of Danish King Christian V, who married Anne in 1683.[10] Quite unlike William of Orange, who was obsessed with his and his wife's prospective succession rights in England, Prince George, who came to reside in England with Anne as Mary did for William in Holland, never expressed any interest in the idea of sharing his wife's throne should she become queen one day.[11] Indeed, soon after his marriage, George lamented:

> We talk here of going to tea, of going to Winchester, and everything else except sitting still all summer, which was the height of my ambition. God send me a quiet life some-where.[12]

As the decade of the 1680s progressed it became clear that the childless William and Mary would not be propagating a Protestant line of succession, which made Anne and George the dynastic saviors who would perpetuate the Stuart succession through the female line. Sadly, and despite 17 pregnancies, none of George and Anne's children were able to survive the rigors of childbirth, infancy, and childhood.[13] Nevertheless, over the course of the 1680s, Anne's thoughts continued to wax dynastic, but unlike her sister, who would not consider ascending the throne without her husband, Anne never gave any indication that she might like to share her future throne with her husband.[14]

Nevertheless, George had an important role to play, whether he liked it or not, in the public and all-male spheres of war and government. Following

Charles II's death in 1685 and the accession of the Catholic James II, the Stuart sisters Mary and Anne stood second and third in line to the English and Scottish thrones. But because they were women, they could not enjoy the kind of public roles, offices, and honors that royal male heirs had always enjoyed. So, George played the role of proxy for his wife, becoming a garter knight, obtaining his own military regiment, inspecting military installations with Samuel Pepys, and relaxing with John Churchill, the future duke of Marlborough, whose wife Sarah was Anne's best friend.[15]

What was clear to everyone who knew him was that Prince George possessed serious liabilities as a future consort to a ruling queen. While he was personable and amiable around those he was familiar with, in public he was notoriously if not pathologically shy. William Blathwayt, who had sailed to Denmark to help negotiate the marriage, remarked that George of Denmark was, "a quiet man, which was a very good thing in a young man."[16] The diarist John Evelyn was also willing to give him the benefit of the doubt, describing him as "a young man of few words, spake French ill, seemed somewhat heavy, but reported valiant."[17] While George quickly learned the English language, he never overcame a rather thick Danish accent, which only increased his public shyness.[18] But what was much more disturbing to his contemporaries was his utter lack of ambition or talent; he liked to play cards, drink wine, ale, and brandy, consume prodigious amounts of food, and engage in salacious gossip.[19] John Macky, who later served as an intelligence officer for William III, later described George in these terms: "very fat, loves news, his bottle, and the Queen."[20] George shared many of these same pursuits with his wife, and the couple gave every indication of having enjoyed an affectionate and companionate relationship over the course of their 25-year marriage. Quite unlike the rest of the men in the Stuart royal family, noted philanderers all, there was never the slightest hint of any sexual infidelities on George's part.

In marked contrast to her husband's utter lack of desire for power and influence in any form, Anne was both motivated and vigilant concerning her own dynastic prospects. Anne, in fact, was the dominant partner in their marriage, a situation George never tried to challenge, which perhaps explains the secret behind their two and a half decades of uninterrupted domestic bliss.

In fact, it seems that the women who populated the Stuart court appreciated Prince George much more than men did. Anne esteemed her husband until the day he died, while Sarah Churchill, who rarely had anything nice to say about anybody, had mostly positive comments about George, especially concerning his fierce sense of loyalty to his friends and family.[21] But the men in the Stuart royal family universally despised him, undoubtedly because of his utter lack of either talent or ambition. Charles II once quipped that drunk or sober, George had nothing inside of him, and that was about the nicest thing that any male member of the Stuart royal family had to say about him.[22] Following his 1685 accession, James II had little use for his son-in-law, and tolerated his presence at court grudgingly.

Anne found herself one heartbeat closer to the throne in 1688, when James II disrupted the delicate power relations that existed between himself and his Protestant daughters and sons-in-law, when his wife, Mary of Modena, gave birth to a male child in June 1688. This blessed event forecast a Catholic succession as it sidelined the succession hopes of William and Mary as well as Anne, who absented herself from witnessing the birthing so she could later allege that her stepmother had given birth to a dead child and substituted a warming pan baby, a rather ingenuous if not cynical ploy to deny the infant Prince of Wales his succession rights, and justify a Protestant Succession to follow James on the throne.[23] After the "Immortal Seven," a group of prominent Protestants, invited William to come over to England with a sizeable army to "help" King James resolve his disagreements with his subjects, Prince George was with his father-in-law in Salisbury as the king's army evaporated before his very eyes. George apparently had a habit of exclaiming "est il possible?" whenever he heard something startling; when King James was informed that George had joined the exodus to William that was hemorrhaging his army, he tartly replied, "what- est il possible gone too? After all, a good trooper would have been a greater loss."[24] After James fled to France and exile, effectively vacating his throne, a Convention of Estates considered what to do to resolve this unprecedented constitutional situation.

By the time Mary arrived in England to join her husband in January 1689, the Convention had already decided to disinherit the Prince of Wales, but they were not exactly sure *who* was to succeed to James II's vacant throne. As we have seen, the only relevant precedent was that of Philip and Mary, which had no appeal for the Princess of Orange, who wished to share her throne fully with her husband, as she revealed to the earl of Danby:

> She was the Prince's wife, and would never be other than what she
> should be in conjunction with him; and that she would take it extremely
> unkindly, if any, under a pretence of their care for her, would set up a
> divided interest between her and the Prince.[25]

Privately, William demanded the sole exercise of the royal prerogative for the remainder of his life. In February 1689, the Convention invited William and Mary to take the throne as joint monarchs, after they agreed to a number of limitations upon the royal prerogative as listed in the Declaration of Right, which brought to a conclusion the series of events known popularly as the Glorious Revolution.

One notable nonparticipant in these proceedings was Prince George of Denmark. His singular position as Anne's political proxy certainly should have afforded him access to those high level meetings and debates that shaped the outline of the Revolution settlement, in which, for the second time in early modern English history, England had a regnant queen and a king all at the same time. But George was not there, unable or unwilling to impress upon his contemporaries the obvious analogy between himself and either Philip or William, and obtain acceptance to ascend the throne jointly with his wife, who was now William and Mary's heiress presumptive. Instead, the revolutionary settlement defined Anne's position constitutionally as if she were a single woman, making no provision whatsoever for George of Denmark.

But Anne was never happy with her place in the Stuart succession, and relations between Anne and William and Mary soon soured, to the point that in 1691 Anne and Mary stopped speaking to each other over Anne's refusal to dismiss Sarah Churchill from her household, a situation that remained unresolved upon Mary's untimely death in December of 1694. To William and Mary, Anne was a troublesome female Clarence accompanied by a Falstaff with a thick Danish accent. Nevertheless, she remained their heir, and George continued to serve as Anne's proxy, created duke of Cumberland, attending the House of Lords as well as William's Privy Council, and later serving on the Council of Nine, which assisted Mary in ruling the kingdom while William was periodically fighting the Nine Years War on the continent.[26] These appointments indirectly acknowledged Anne's position as heir, but they were also made under the assumption that George would just sit there, keep his mouth shut, and not do anything to embarrass himself, although William and Mary well knew that George would return home and give a full report of the proceedings, chapter and verse, to his wife.[27]

Indeed, the enmity between William and Mary and Anne provided an additional dimension to George's role as proxy, as he served as his wife's whipping boy. William was particularly brutal to George, refusing to allow him to ride in his coach during the 1690 Irish campaign, and forbidding him to volunteer for service in the navy the following year in an embarrassing episode in which Queen Mary sent the earl of Nottingham to forbid George from serving in the navy, at the very moment he was boarding the ship.[28] These were slights Anne never forgot, and only increased her antipathy toward her brother-in-law. In turn, William despised George for his utter lack of talent or motivation, and, unable to attack Anne directly, his fury fell upon his hapless brother-in-law, who nevertheless did his best to try to heal the breaches within the Stuart royal family.

But the need for George to play the role of political proxy evaporated after William died after being thrown from his horse, in March 1702. It remains a great irony that until the moment they ascend the throne, regnant queens were unable to perform any public roles or hold formal offices or appointments reflective of their status as heirs. As we have seen, George performed such roles and enjoyed such appointments on behalf of his wife, but when Anne's sunshine day finally arrived, she ascended her throne alone.

Why this was the case is not perfectly clear, but a series of events prior to Anne's accession seems to have pointed the way. In 1701, following the tragic death of the 11-year-old duke of Gloucester, Anne and George's only child to survive infancy, Parliament felt compelled to reinforce certain provisions of the Bill of Rights in the Act of Settlement, which settled the crown on the House of Hanover, Protestant descendants of James I, to forestall any attempt by the exiled Catholic Prince of Wales, later known as James, the Old Pretender, to succeed to the English and Scottish thrones.[29] As the Act reiterated Anne's position as William's heir, it also remained silent upon the issue of what status George of Denmark would enjoy upon his wife's accession, reinforcing the Revolution settlement that had taken no constitutional notice of him whatsoever. Indeed, one of the few points that William and Anne probably saw eye to eye on was that George should not be a king, and it had obviously been worked out beforehand that George would be on the sidelines as Anne ascended her throne alone.

When she did, no one seemed to blink an eye. John Sharpe, Archbishop of York, pointed out the gendered realities of the situation in his coronation sermon:

> Her reign alone will let us see, that it is not without great reason, that in my text Queens are joyn'd as equal sharers with kings.[30]

Thus, the only person being recognized as king was Anne. Had George of Denmark possessed even a fraction of the ambition of William of Orange, or the rest of the male aristocrats who stalked the Stuart court, clamoring for their place in the court hierarchy, he might have negotiated for himself some kind of formal recognition as the husband of the monarch. Instead, George of Denmark simply joined the peers in his proper place of precedence, as a devoted and obedient subject, while his wife was crowned England's next sovereign.

Indeed, Anne had no use for the precedents of her sister's reign, which had invested the royal prerogative solely in William's hands. In fact, the Glorious Revolution's settlement of the succession was an anomaly, as Anne's coronation ritual reached back to the sixteenth-century precedents, when both Mary I and Elizabeth I had been crowned as single women. As a contemporary treatise argued, Anne was in fact England's *true* Deborah, which was just one of the identifications linking her to Elizabeth I.[31] But unlike Elizabeth, Anne had to delineate the duality between her position as queen, which rendered her sovereign and beholden to no man, and her role as a wife, in which she was expected to be both devoted and subservient, as her sister Mary had so very publicly behaved toward William III. As she endeavored to create her own representation of good queenship, Anne was also concerned that her subjects perceived her as a good wife. Good wives are always generous to their spouses, so in lieu of a shared crown, Anne heaped a number of honorific offices upon her husband to atone for the fact that George no longer shared her status, but was, as George himself declared, merely her majesty's subject.[32] The irony here is that the only discernible interest George ever displayed was for military affairs, a role denied him by James II and William III. But by the time he became Lord

High Admiral and Generalissimo of all English landed forces, he was too old and sick to play any kind of role in the War of the Spanish Succession that had just commenced.[33]

But even these creations could not completely silence contemporary comment concerning the disparity in status between Anne and her husband, which constituted an exceptional detour from contemporary rules and expectations regarding marital status.[34] In fact, during Anne's first parliament, an anonymous pamphlet circulated urging parliament to make George a king consort for just these reasons, and apparently, there were some closed door discussions between the queen and her ministers regarding taking such a step.[35] But the idea never made it to the floor of Parliament for discussion, for ultimately Anne decided that George should not share her throne with her.[36] But Anne still wanted her subjects to know how much she esteemed her husband, lobbying successfully for a £100,00 annuity for George in case he outlived her, because, as Bishop Gilbert Burnet of Salisbury explained:

> She thought it became her, as a good wife, to have the act passed, in which she might be the more earnest, because it was not thought advisable to move for an act that should take Prince George into the consortship of the royal dignity.[37]

This decision may have represented a sharp break with precedent, but it simply made a lot of sense. Anne possessed the ability to perform the duties of her office, but George did not. He would have been as effective as the Lancastrian Henry VI, a monarch with a decided lack of kingly resolve, and it was this factor that, in all likelihood, overrode the glaring social displacement inherent in the spectacle of a woman enjoying a public role and status not shared by her husband. There is no evidence that George of Denmark objected to any of these decisions that, for most men of his age and class, would be considered a humiliating form of emasculation. Yet George simply pretended that this was not the case at all, and, until his death in 1708, he appeared by the side of his sovereign wife, both cheerful and deferential. It was in the performance of this one public role, that of an informal consort to his wife, that Prince George of Denmark excelled, so much so that the experience hardened into what appears to us today as a curious yet durable precedent.

Notes

1. *London Gazette*, n. 22015, p. 2195, June 26, 1857.
2. Lord Melbourne, Queen Victoria's first prime minister, considered George of Denmark "a very stupid fellow," as he recounted to Victoria the story of James II and "est il possible?" Viscount Esher, ed., *The Training of a Sovereign* (New York: Longmans, Green, and Co.,1912), 129.

3. Charles Beem, *The Lioness Roared: The Problems of Female Rule in English History* (New York, 2006).

4. "Announcing the Accession of Queen Mary I," London, July 19, 1553, *Tudor Royal Proclamations, 1553–1587*, vol. 2, ed. P. L. Hughes and J. F. Larkin (New Haven, 1969), 3, n. 388.

5. See Jayne Laynesmith, *The Last Medieval Queens* (Oxford, 2004), 92–4.

6. *Calendar of State Papers, Spanish*, XI, p. 290.

7. *Statutes of the Realm*, I Marie, sess. 3, cap. II, pp. 222–4

8. *Statutes*, I. Mary st. 3 cap I, 222. A provocative discussion of the passage of this act is found in William Fleetwood's mid-sixteenth-century essay, "Itinerarium ad Windsor." See *The Name of a Queen: William Fleetwood's Itinerarium ad Windsor*, Charles Beem and Dennis Moore, eds (New York, 2013) 33–6.

9. While Elizabeth never married, Mary and Philip's marriage treaty served as a blueprint for her possible marriage to the duke of Anjou, see "Calendar of the Manuscripts of the Most Hon. Marquis of Salisbury," *Reports of the Historical Manuscripts Commission*, IX, pt. 2, pp. 243, 288–93, 543–4.

10. For a larger study on George of Denmark, see Charles Beem, "I Am Her Majesty's Subject: Prince George of Denmark and the Transformation of the English Male Consort," *Canadian Journal of History* vol. 39, no. 3 (December 2004) 457–87.

11. William's belief that his marriage carried a vested interest in the English crown was made explicit in his Declaration of 1688, which stated, "And since our dearest and most entirely beloved consort the Princess, and likewise ourselves, have so great an interest in this matter and such a right, as all the world knows, to the succession of the crown." William III, *The Declaration of His Highness William Henry, By the Grace of God, Prince of Orange, &c. of the Reasons Inducing Him to Appear in Arms in the Kingdom of England, for Preserving of the Protestant Religion, and for Restoring the Laws and Liberties of England, Scotland, and Ireland* (London, 1688).

12. *Reports of the Historical Manuscripts Commission*, vol. 9, part 2 (London, 1884), 458.

13. For a medical reconstruction of Anne's efforts to further the protestant succession and its devastating effects on her health, see H. E. Emson," For the Want of an Heir: The Obstetrical History of Queen Anne," *British Medical Journal*, 304 (May 1992), 66–7.

14. In an often quoted letter from Anne to Sarah Churchill in 1692, Anne clearly looked forward to her own "sunshine day" when she would inherit the throne. In this letter, as in many others between the two, Anne referred to Sarah as "Mrs. Freeman," and herself as "Mrs. Morley," so they could correspond as social Equals. See *The Letters and Diplomatic Instructions of Queen Anne*, ed. Beatrice Curtis Brown (New York, 1935), 60–1.

15. Narcissus Luttrell, *A Brief Historical Relation of State Affairs from September 1678 to April 1714* (5 vols) (Oxford, 1857), I, 287, 312. Luttrell's political diary briefly recorded many of Prince George's public appearances and political tasks from 1683 until his death in 1708.

16. *Calendar of State Papers, Domestic Series- Charles II, 1683*, 244.

17. John Evelyn, *The Diary of John Evelyn*, vol. 3, intro. and notes by Austin Dobson (London: Macmillan, 1906), p. 107. John Evelyn (1620–1706), a

royalist supporter of Charles II who enjoyed royal patronage during the Restoration, kept a lively diary from 1640 until his death, recording his impressions of the major figures of his day, including this brief mention of Prince George.

18. Burnet, *Bishop Burnet's History of his Own Time* (5 vols., Oxford, 1858) V, 351. Burnet observed that George, "knew more than he could well express, for he spake acquired languages ill and ungracefully."

19. Sarah Churchill, who knew him quite well, commented that, "the Prince used to employ himself agreeably all day either standing upon a stairhead or looking out a window, making malicious remarks upon the passerby," concluding that, "Anne grew uneasy at the figure his highness cut in that princely amusement." Stuart J. Reid, *John and Sarah Duke and Duchess of Marlborough: Based upon Unpublished Letters and Documents of Blenheim Palace* (London, 1915), 141.

20. John Macky, *Memoirs of the Secret Services of John Macky, esq., during the Reigns of King William, Queen Anne, and George I* (London, 1733), b3.

21. See Sarah Churchill, duchess of Marlborough, *An Account of the Conduct of the Dowager Duchess of Marlborough* (London, 1742), 86.

22. Gilbert Burnet, *History*, III, 49.

23. See Lois G. Schwoerer, "Women and the Glorious Revolution," *Albion*, 18, 2 (Summer 1986) 195–218. In his declaration to the convention parliament, William of Orange reiterated his suspicion that "the pretended prince of Wales was *not* born by the Queen – many both doubted of the Queen's bigness and the birth of the child." *Journal of the House of Commons*, X, December 26, 1688-October 26, 1693, 4.

24. From the earl of Clarendon's diary, November 26, 1688, cited in Thomas Babington Macaulay, *The History of England from the Reign of James II* (3 vols.) (New York, 1880), II, 81.

25. *The Parliamentary History of England*, V, 1688–1702 (London, 1809), p. 63. In her political journal, Mary of Orange clearly stated her total identification with a conventional social women's role, accepting of a secondary, domestic role within her marriage. See Mary II, *Memoirs of Mary, Queen of England 1689–1693* R. Doebner, ed. (London, 1886), passim.

26. Luttrell, II, p. 391, *Journal of the House of Commons*, XI, 566–7.

27. Mary II recorded in her journal her belief that the impetus for George to serve in the military under William lay with her sister, and not with George. Mary II, *Memoirs*, 38.

28. The episode is described in Churchill, *Conduct*, 39, and Luttrell, II, 225.

29. See *Sources of English Constitutional History*, (2 vols.), eds. Carl Stephenson and George Marcham (New York, 1972), II, 610–2.

30. John Sharp, Archbishop of York, *A Sermon Preached at the Coronation of Queen Anne* (London, 1702).

31. Sir Thomas Craig, *The Right of Succession to the Kingdom of England in Two Books*, trans. James Gatherer (London, 1703), 83. Craig originally wrote the work in Latin prior to James I's 1603 English accession, to bolster James's legitimacy through female descent. Gatherer's 1703 translation was a timely bolster to Anne's position as a married monarch.

32. An anecdote from Anne's coronation described George of Denmark's public admission that he was his wife's obedient subject. Reid, 106.

33. *Calendar of State Papers, Domestic, Anne, vol. 1, 1702–1703,* ed. Robert Pentland McNaffy (London, 1916), 85, 466.

34. In his 1743 biography of Marlborough, Thomas Lediard recorded that news of a possible scheme to make George king was circulating in the "Protestant Courts of Germany, esp. Hanover, that Anne had design of proposing to Parliament the royal dignity [for her husband]." Thomas Lediard, *The Life of John, Duke of Marlborough,* (2 vols.), (London, 1743), II, 136.

35. *A Letter to a Member of Parliament in Reference to his Royal Highness Prince George of Denmark,* British Library, misc. 85/1865 c.19 (100).

36. Lediard, II, 137.

37. Burnet, *History,* V, 55.

CHAPTER 5

From Ruler in the Shadows to Shadow King: Frederick I of Sweden

Fabian Persson

"Potz Donner haben wir das alles getan?" This is what Frederick I of Sweden (r. 1720–51) is said to have exclaimed on one occasion when confronted by a sycophantic flatterer with a list of all the recent beneficial and wise decisions made by His Majesty the king of Sweden.[1] That is also how Frederick I is remembered,—as the *roi fainéant* par excellence of Swedish history. The reality, however, is far more complicated.

Defining power is always difficult and defining the role of prince consorts in an age of personal royal power is even more of a challenge. Early modern prince consorts were characterized by being curtailed. Their role clashed with existing gender expectations. As a man, a prince consort was expected to have power over his wife, but as a prince consort, he was subjected to her will. This was a balancing act that could easily go wrong. In Sweden, this became even more difficult by the transition from absolute royal power to parliamentary power in just a few years following 1718.

The Path to Becoming a Prince Consort

When analysing the career of Frederick of Hesse, Prince Consort of Sweden, it is clear that he went through several stages. First as suitor to Princess Ulrika Eleonora (1710–15), later as husband to the princess (1715–18), then as prince consort to Queen Ulrika Eleonora (1718–20) and finally as king (1720–51). The potential to become a king through his wife was something that marked a number of prince consorts. This was gendered as it was rare for a queen consort to step up to become queen regnant—Catherine the Great of Russia was truly exceptional. For Frederick, the great prize of becoming king was present on the horizon from the very start in 1710.

To understand what happened, we must begin in 1710, when Sweden was still an absolute monarchy ruled by Charles XII (r. 1697–1718). The king had been campaigning against the enemies of the realm for a decade and remained unmarried. If peace was concluded, he would be likely to marry, but in the meantime anything could happen and Charles XII had only two potential successors: either his sister Ulrika Eleonora or his ten-year-old nephew Charles Frederick, son of King Charles's late sister Hedvig Sophia and the duke of Holstein. A Swedish princess who married forfeited her right to the throne, so strictly speaking the little Duke had no legal right and Princess Ulrika Eleonora was only heir apparent as long as she remained unmarried. Under normal circumstances, things would have been sorted out by the king marrying and begetting heirs, but the 1710s were anything but normal for Sweden. After the disastrous defeat against Russia at Poltava in 1709, Sweden was surrounded by ever more enemies: Russia, Poland, Saxony, Hanover, Denmark, and Prussia, all of them eager to dismember the failing state. On top of this, the King's absence for several years in Turkey made decision-making slow and cumbersome.

The parlous state of the realm had to be addressed. In 1713, the council at last called for a parliament, using the king's sister Ulrika Eleonora as figurehead and stand-in for the monarch. The parliament barely had time to convene when a package of letters from the king arrived. They had been delayed as the skipper on the vessel thought they were gingerbread because they were kept in a gingerbread jar.[2] When the royal letters fragrant with gingerbread were opened, the king's wishes were clear: under no circumstances would he tolerate a parliament. So, the parliament was dissolved in confusion. The king agreed, however, that his sister Ulrika Eleonora would attend the council as his representative, because, in the king's words, "we two who are one cannot have but one will."

The princess would soon lose her position as the foremost heir apparent: she was being courted for several years by a rather unknown German princeling, Frederick, Prince Hereditary of Hesse-Kassel. In 1710, he had tried to become ruler of Luxembourg but failed. Instead, his interest focussed on Sweden from 1710 onward. His emissary Conrad Ranck made contact with Emerentia von Düben, the great favourite of Ulrika Eleonora. In May 1710, a formal letter of proposal of marriage arrived in Stockholm. This letter received no reply, but the Prince Hereditary continued his quest. Contacts assured him that the very plain princess was "as appetizing" in body as in mind. Valuable presents were also made to the favourite of the princess. In 1711, the princess at last asked her brother the king about her suitor, with their grandmother acting as middleman. The princess later sent a letter of her own, making her desire to marry clear. Prince Frederick was also said to be "almost the only one among all the German princes who led a good and virtuous life with his [former] wife."[3] More than a year later, the king gave his assent. At the same time the princess sought the advice of various people. The Chief Marshal, Nicodemus Tessin, wrote a memorandum to prove that the princess would not lose her right to the throne by marrying. The General Gustaf Adam Taube also urged the princess to marry, because Prince Frederick was a proven soldier and anything could happen to the king.

Prince Frederick, at the same time, avoided broaching the thorny question of the succession. In reality, he and his advisors were frantically working to ensure a Hessian succession.[4] The king wanted the princess to stay in Sweden and any possible heirs raised as Lutherans. This was highly promising, but as to the right to the throne, nothing was said explicitly. The princess's favourite von Düben, however, assured Prince Frederick's Swedish go-between Ranck in 1714 that if the princess ever inherited the throne she would happily hand over the governing to Frederick.[5] In 1715, the prince came to Sweden for the marriage and was received with great pomp. At the banquet, drums and trumpets were heard for the first time in many years at court. The Prince Hereditary brought his own court to Sweden where there was already an abundance of courts: the campaigning court with the king in Lund, the court in Stockholm, the queen dowager's court, the Holstein court, and the Polish court in exile.

Now two different factions were in waiting for a struggle for the succession. The king's powerful advisor Baron Georg Heinrich von Görtz was a supporter of the teenaged duke of Holstein while the princess had her adherents. For years, the Holstein faction had been working for the king to declare his nephew as the heir.[6] In September 1715, Prince Frederick had been made Generalissimus of the Swedish army and that strengthened his position.[7] The Holstein faction was still dangerous, and in 1718 Prince Frederick complained that the Holsteiners had outflanked the Hessians completely. Baron Görtz was all-powerful and ran peace negotiations with Russia. Especially threatening were marriage negotiations between the duke of Holstein and a daughter of Tsar Peter. In May 1718, Prince Frederick let his courtier David von Hein put together a memorandum on what to do if the king died.[8] This was sent to Ulrika Eleonora so she would know how to act if the prince was absent on such an occasion.

From Prince to Prince Consort

In November 1718, King Charles XII was shot campaigning in Norway. At last the moment had come. Prince Frederick sent a courier to his wife in Stockholm, while simultaneously arresting Görtz.[9] Other Holsteiners were arrested in Stockholm by the princess. She now claimed to have the army behind her and proclaimed herself queen. The council, however, would not play ball. Queen Ulrika Eleonora was not recognized and the matter was deferred to parliament. Supporters of the Holstein Duke began offering the renunciation of absolutism as his price for the crown (along with possible help from Russia). Even though Prince Frederick resisted, he realised that absolutism had to go, otherwise the duke might still win the crown.

The crucial council discussion about the queen's right to inherit the crown took place in January 1719.[10] The councillors denied that the queen had any right to inherit the throne. They even interpreted the law of 1604, giving a place in the succession to princesses, as being limited to daughters only of the king at that time. It was claimed that if Charles XII had left any daughters, they would have had no right to the throne. Still, all the council assured they only wanted Ulrika Eleonora as queen, but just one councillor, a former courtier, supported her claim to inherit the crown. She, in vain, implored: "I would wish that no one argued against my right to inherit."

Thus the council effected a *coup d'état*. The parliament of 1719 would formalize the overthrow of royal absolutism, by thrashing out how Sweden was to be ruled henceforth. From the very start, Queen Ulrika Eleonora wanted a co-regency with Prince Frederick along the lines of William and Mary. Already in December 1718, she wrote to the prince: "I am ready to share the crown with you whenever it pleases you, so I call you my King and my Sovereign."[11] A little later, the self-proclaimed queen wrote again to her husband stating that: "I have against my own will become mistress over my dearly beloved in matters of state."[12] However, the queen's plan to make Prince Frederick king and co-regent met violent opposition in parliament and had to be abandoned. In February 1719, an anonymous letter was handed to the speaker of the nobility urging for Prince Frederick to be made king. A sharp note signed by about half the nobility present in parliament denounced this effort as "the destroyer of public tranquility."[13] The queen did not give up her favourite plan to rule in tandem like William and Mary in England. She called speakers from all the estates to an audience. Ulrika Eleonora pleaded for support for herself and the prince as joint monarchs ruling together. The burghers were positive but the nobility was adamant in its resistance.[14]

In March 1719, Queen Ulrika Eleonora was crowned in Uppsala. She was declared to be "Queen Ulrika Eleonora crowned king of Sweden and its provinces and no one else." By crowning her king, her status as reigning queen was emphasized, and possibly the scope for making Frederick king, further restricted. The new constitution severely restricted royal power. It was still rather vague, though. The queen was not ready to submit to the will of the leader of the council, Arvid Horn, and forced his resignation. In all, she took the advice of Prince Frederick, to the great displeasure of many. The suspicions against him also took the form of changing his plan to the organizing of the higher echelons of the army. His strong adherent Taube was replaced by someone who said it was his duty to look after what the prince did. When the new leader of the council quarrelled with Prince Frederick, he was ordered by the queen to stay away from the council.

Queen Ulrika Eleonora never abandoned her firm belief in her birthright to the Swedish crown and the superiority of royal succession by inheritance. In a book, she marked a section emphasizing the excellence of "la royauté héréditaire" and wrote "nota bene" in the margin.[15] The ironic tone of the text was lost on the queen, who saw this as a defence of absolute monarchy by the grace of God.[16] These were views totally opposite to the council's.

It was an old court hobbling around the new royal couple of Queen Ulrika Eleonora and her husband, the Prince Hereditary Frederick of Hesse, in 1719. What had once been the starting point for fresh-faced, youthful aristocrats now appeared as some kind of elephant churchyard. Decrepitude and illness was everywhere to be seen. Later a courtier noted that "among our court adventures in Sweden can be reckoned that at the same time the Court Stable Master had no hands, the Court Painter was blind, the Master of the King's music was deaf, and the Dancing Master had a limp."[17] To this can be added that the fencing master was lame.

The Hope for a Swedish William and Mary

It was obvious that the new constitution of 1719 left the queen considerable power over many issues and that she was primarily advised not by the council but by the Prince Consort Frederick. In 1719, the speaker for the peasant estate said that the prince consort could just as well rule openly as secretly in the name of the queen.[18] When in 1720 a new parliament was convened, the opposition against the queen's rule saw their chance. The 1720 parliament could result in the queen continuing as queen regnant, a co-regency with the queen and Prince Frederick as king or with the queen abdicating and Prince Frederick becoming sole regent as king. For the opposition against the queen, this was both a threat and an opportunity. The energetic and driven prince consort as co-regent or as continued power behind the throne was a problem for the opposition. During the last year the royal couple had used the 1719 constitution to exert as much royal power as possible. The queen and the prince consort had used that time to build more support for their cause by a liberal use of ennoblement, promotions, and bribes.[19] To use a constitutional revision as a bargaining chip in exchange of making the prince sole regent was a strategy that the opposition to absolute power would deploy. The issue of succession could also be used to put pressure on the royal couple, who detested the thought of the duke of Holstein as their possible heir.

It was well-known that both the queen and the prince wanted the latter to be made co-regent and king. For this cause, the French and Dutch ambassadors also acted. The queen herself still had her heart set on a co-regency. Her closest circle also advised her to work for a co-regency, rather than abdicating in favour of the prince. A French diplomat said that she "feared that the Prince, once king, will push her aside and take mistresses." In February 1720 she submitted a request that the prince "becomes equal with me and as King takes part in government."[20] The house of nobility discussed the queen's demand on February 27, but decided against it. The following day, the queen, in a letter to the speaker of the nobility, Arvid Horn, once again reiterated her wish to rule like "King William and his Queen."[21] The explicit comparison to England and William and

Mary is illuminating. Ulrika Eleonora had few international parallels to use. The gender expectations could also be used to support her plea for a co-regency. According to the speaker of the burghers, the present system with the reigning queen did not work well. She had said that the prince consort "possesses her heart and can make her do what he wants." Thus a co-regency was better because as it was the prince who "anyway rules secretly through Her Majesty." Opponents of the requests countered the William and Mary analogy with the example of Queen Anne and Prince George, where the latter remained prince consort. The council and the parliament both, however, refused the queen's wish. Handwritten political pamphlets warned that a co-regency was a step toward rebuilding absolute royal power.[22] In these pamphlets the comparison with William and Mary was rebutted by the argument that Queen Mary had no "use of Her Majesty but depended in all on Her Master."

The queen had to back down and changed her wish in another letter, a few days after her first, to a co-regency with the real power resting with her husband. She also indicated that she was prepared to abdicate in order to see Prince Frederick made king. The queen's fundamental opposition toward the new limitations on royal power in the constitution of 1719 had created a lot of conflict between her and the council. Thus, there were many politicians willing to see her abdicate if the constitution could be changed so the new monarch would have even less power. To make the prince king, the demand from the majority in parliament was for the queen to abdicate as queen regnant. The request for an abdication was also used by the opposition against stronger royal power to rewrite the constitution of 1719, which led to the remaining royal power being much curtailed. During the last year, the opposition against the queen had been made aware of the loopholes she could use, according to the quickly written constitution of 1719. These were now closed off and the council was left all the important decisions with the monarch having just two votes in council. The queen was deeply unsympathetic to the new constitution of 1720. In a copy she has scribbled in the margin "Mischief" when the constitution states that all major decisions should be made in council. At the paragraphs where the king promises to rule together with the council, she has written "As with little children."[23] Another paragraph the queen wanted to change was the one restricting the succession. If the queen had children, they would inherit the throne, but not children of Frederick alone. Legitimacy remained with the queen rather than with the king. If the king died or was absent, the queen would reassume the throne. All efforts to make the duke of Holstein heir apparent were, however, blocked by King Frederick. He would in the coming year try to use the issue of succession for his own purposes.

The abdication of the queen was signed in March 1720 and in May the same year, King Frederick was crowned. This ceremony posed problems of its own. As a former ruling queen, Ulrika Eleonora insisted to use all five regalia, while the council only wanted her to use the three of a queen consort. In this, the queen got her wish, even though the council made clear that this was to be seen as "pure ceremony and decoration." The powerful secret committee in parliament agreed despite "great fear and worry" to this manifestation of royal authority.[24]

The Prince Consort as King

The prince consort turned king worked hard on rebuilding royal power and the peace negotiations offered an opportunity.[25] In the autumn of 1720, Sweden was still fighting a losing war with Russia after having signed treaties with Denmark, Hanover, and Prussia. By linking the peace negotiations to the Swedish succession, political aims could be achieved. It was by now generally admitted that King Frederick and Queen Ulrika Eleonora would not have any children. Thus it was an open question as to who would succeed them eventually. One possibility was the queen's nephew Duke Charles Frederick of Holstein. English support in the final stages of war was hotly sought after, and it carried more weight when the seasoned English diplomat Earl Stanhope thought the royal couple should push for this solution and work together with the Duke for increased royal power "outside the narrow limits, to which it had been curtailed."[26] Still, the Holstein option was unthinkable to the royal couple.

Another possibility was someone from the house of Hesse. By securing the succession for a Hessian prince, the royal family would be strengthened and if this could be linked to the peace negotiations, it was even better. By marrying a Hessian prince to the daughter of the tsar, the succession could be made a part of the Russian demands during the negotiations. The nightmare scenario was that the Holstein Duke would marry a Russian princess and be inserted into the Swedish succession against the will of King Frederick. In the end, the Hessian plans were foiled and the Holstein Duke indeed married the tsar's daughter.

Despite this setback in the peace negotiations in 1720–1, King Frederick had no intention of being a king without power. He continued trying to claw back royal authority. One method was to travel around the realm, not unlike an American presidential candidate, in an effort to garner support. At the parliament in 1723, royal power would take back what it had lost.[27] The Austrian envoy in Stockholm reported in February 1723 about "Frederick's plans for absolute power."[28] A secret plan for increased royal power was hatched during nightly meetings in the king's chamber between Frederick and representatives of the peasants.[29] The peasants supported the king, but the nobility absolutely refused.[30] The clergy and the burghers followed the nobility. Thus the great plan failed. The king's Hessian secretary Gehebe was arrested for the crime of having circulated a plan for a revised constitution. Peasants who insisted on a new constitution were also imprisoned. The king realized he had lost and, rather dramatically, burned the peasants' written plea for a new constitution in council, thus making it clear that "His Majesty will never submit such plans again."

He said that the parliament was to decide on the laws and asked for forgiveness and letting bygones be bygones. The duke of Holstein was made Royal Highness—a sign that he belonged to the Swedish royal family and might succeed to the throne. The surrender was utter and complete. New regulations for parliament also prohibited any proposals to increase royal power.[31]

The King Accepting Defeat

The disaster of the parliament of 1723 would set its seal on the next 28 years of the king's reign. He would no more try to rule, but instead devoted himself to pleasure. This consisted mainly in hunting and in hunting young girls. He would also retell the same anecdotes again and again from his campaigning days with Prince Eugene. He was surrounded by German body servants and never learnt Swedish. A number of these along with some Swedes acted as favourites and channelled money and minor appointments.

The English diplomat Stephen Poyntz clearly described the defeat of royal power in the mid-1720s. Even what power was left to him was not used: "Another misfortune of the King of Sweden is, that though he be a Prince of the greatest personal Bravery, yet partly through indolence and love of pleasure, partly through want of what may be calld Political Courage and Constancy, He dares not exert in the manner he safely and fairly might the little power that is left Him, by preferring his friends according to their merit and the justice of their pretensions, even when He has the opportunity; but suffers himself, tho' with reluctancy and an ill grace and out of season, to be teasd from his promises and resolutions, and often to bestow his favours on his greatest Enemys."[32]

A few months later, Poyntz yet again gives the image of a royal couple that has given up hope. "He [the King] is so uneasy in his private circumstances, and so destitute of all assistance from his own Father, that I verily believe if the Landgrave were dead and he had but a sure retreat at Cassel, he would accept the first terms that should be offerd him from Muscovy & Holstein for abdication. The Queen has certainly more bravery and resolution, but her personal fondness for the King would make it almost as great a heartbreaking to her, to part from him as from the Kingdom. Besides that Her Spirit is a good deal broken by the late compliances & submissions he has forced her to. A Lady who has a good share in Her confidence has lately told me that She is often in tears in private."[33]

Foreign ambassadors continued to report mainly of the king's bear hunts, sometimes dangerously close, and his amorous liaisons. In 1730, he made the 16-year-old Hedvig Taube his mistress. After her death, the now 70-year-old king pursued new young girls even more vigorously. The new Crown Princess, Lovisa Ulrika, found it all rather distasteful and called King Frederick "Old Pan" or "Saturn." She wrote to her brother that he would smile at the sight of King Frederick, "A marvellous wig and the head on his knees, running after all the girls in the world with no other enjoyment than changing wigs and chairs. Between ourselves, and keep for God's sake quiet about it, in one word: an old annoying man."

Carl Gustaf Tessin liked the king personally, but found him badly lacking as regent. He later wrote that "During Frederick I's reign the sciences flourished—he never read a single book. Industries have been founded and trade increased. He has never given a daler in encouragement or even bought a fire shade to his rooms. The palace has been built. He has never even been curious to have a look." During the 1740s, the council began using a stamp so the king did not have to sign his name. This has been seen as the nadir of royal authority.

In conclusion, Prince Frederick chose Princess Ulrika Eleonora already in 1710 as a means to establish himself on the Swedish throne. For several years he negotiated for the princess to be made heir to her brother King Charles XII, but at the marriage in 1715, this great matter was still unresolved. Once he was married to the princess this manoeuvring continued over the next years. He acted decisively in 1718 to make his wife queen and himself, thereby, prince consort. In this process the royal couple gave up absolute royal power but still retained a considerable leeway to influence decisions. This was then put to use, when Frederick, as prince consort, wielded considerable power in 1718 to 1720 through the queen. Nevertheless, such a state of affairs created opposition from council and parliament. The gender expectations meant that a prince consort was seen as a constant threat as he might influence his wife, who would normally be subordinated to him. This contrasts sharply to the expectations of queen consorts. They could be seen as unduly influencing royal power, but normal gender expectations would be that queen consorts as women were subordinated to the king. The fluid power situation after 1718 meant that Prince Consort Frederick could exert power but had to bargain it away to become king in 1720. The price for attaining the crown was the severe curtailing of royal authority. Frederick intended this to be temporary only but failed in his effort to claw back royal power in 1723. From being a highly active prince and then a powerful prince consort he now resigned himself to be the great *roi fainéant*.

Notes

1. Lennart Josephson, "Från Kungshuset till slott" in Gösta Berg et al. (eds.) *Det glada Sverige. Våra fester och högtider genom tiderna, Vol 2*. (Stockholm, 1947), 1038.

2. Walfrid Holst, *Ulrika Eleonora d.y. Karl XII:s syster* (Stockholm, 1956), 100.

3. For a brief outline of Prince Frederick's first wife, the Prussian Princess Luise Dorothea, see Sabine Köttelwesch, "Luise Dorothea von Hessen-Kassel," in Helmut Burmeister (ed.) *Friedrich. König von Schweden, Landgraf von Hessen-Kassel* (Hofgeismar, 2003), 49–58.

4. Stig Jägerskiöld, "Den hessiska politiken och den svenska tronföljdsfrågan 1713–1718," *Karolinska Förbundets Årsbok* (Stokholm, 1934), 111–43.
5. Holst, 180.
6. Jägerskiöld, 1934, p. 114. K. J., Hartman *Karl XII och hessarna* (Åbo, 1935), 25.
7. Holst, 129.
8. Lennart Thanner, (ed.), *Handlingar angående revolutionen i Sverige 1718–1719* (Stockholm, 1954).
9. Lennart Thanner, *Revolutionen i Sverige efter Karl XII:s död. Revolutionen i Sverige efter Karl XII:s död. Den inrikespolitiska maktkampen under tidigare delen av Ulrika Eleonora d.y:s regering* (Uppsala, 1953), 61.
10. Thanner, 14–45.
11. Holst, 166.
12. Ibid., 167.
13. *Sveriges ridderskaps och adels riksdags-protokoll,* vol.1, 1719 (Stockholm, 1875), 25.
14. Ibid., 31, Holst, 182.
15. Hans Wieselgren, "Taflor från krigs- och olycksåren efter Carl XII:s död, 1719–21. Tecknade af Justus van Effen och Carl Adlerfelt," *Historisk Tidskrift,* 1893, 168.
16. Thanner, 423.
17. KB L 82:1:4 Åkerödagbok fol.615, May 31, 1758.
18. E. G. Geijer, *Teckning af Sveriges tillstånd och af de förnämsta handlande personer* (Stockholm, 1839), 36.
19. Thanner, 238.
20. *Sveriges ridderskaps och adels riksdags-protokoll,* vol.1, 1720 (Stockholm, 1875), 54–5.
21. RA Arvid Horns arkiv E4279, Ulrika Eleonora to Arvid Horn, February 28, 1720.
22. Karin Tegenborg Falkdalen, *Kungen är en kvinna. Retorik och praktik kring kvinnliga monarker under tidigmodern tid* (Umeå, 2003), 159.
23. Holst, 229.
24. Geijer, 36.
25. Einar Carlsson, "Fredrik I och den hessiska successionen," *Historisk Tidskrift,* vol.59, 1949, 337–68.
26. Geijer, 34.
27. Birger Sallnäs, "En kraftmätning mellan konung och råd 1723," *Historisk Tidskrift,* vol.60, 1950.
28. Anders Fryxell, *Berättelser ur svenska historien,* vol.31 (Stockholm, 1863), 65.
29. Geijer, 59.
30. Sten Landahl, (ed.), *Bondeståndets riksdagsprotokoll,* vol.1, 1720 (Uppsala, 1939), 258–9.
31. Geijer, 59–60.
32. PRO SP 95 35, Stephen Poyntz, Stockholm November 4, 1724.
33. PRO SP 95 36, Stephen Poyntz, Stockholm February 2, 1725.

CHAPTER 6

Count Ernst Johann Bühren and the Russian Court of Anna Ioannovna

Michael Bitter

I n the early modern period of Russian history, the phenomenon of the male consort, or favorite, of a ruling empress was most common in the years immediately following the reign of Peter the Great and continuing until the end of the eighteenth century.[1] After the end of that century, no woman ruled Russia in her own name, and, consequently, the role of the male consort of a female ruler disappeared. One of the things that makes the male favorites of this post-Petrine period stand out is, in the words of historian John Alexander, "their presumed role in the politics and policy-making of the newly mighty Russian empire."[2] This study takes a close and focused look at the actual, rather than presumed, role of the first, and most infamous, of these eighteenth-century favorites, Count Ernst Johann Bühren, or Biron, as he called himself, the favorite of Tsaritsa and Empress Anna Ioannovna, who ruled the Russian empire for a decade, from 1730 until 1740.

Midway through this reign, the British diplomatic mission of King George II's envoy to St. Petersburg, George, Lord Forbes, and the political, military, and commercial issues surrounding his mission, provided a unique perspective from which to view the inner workings of the Russian court in this period. Close, sometimes daily, contact with Count Biron gave the British ministers a rare opportunity to observe and document his statements and activities. Forbes, assisted by Claudius Rondeau, the British Resident at St. Petersburg, had a vested interest in observing and understanding both the extent and limits of Count Biron's effect on the empress and Russian policy. It was to Great Britain's advantage for Forbes and Rondeau to know precisely how to influence the Russian court's decisions. As a contemporary observer of Anna Ioannovna's court, George, Lord Forbes, highlighted Count Biron's influence with the empress, the resentment it created, and the insecurity of his position in Russia, in a description of the favorite he presented to Queen Caroline of Great Britain in 1734. Of Biron he wrote, "His great Power with the Sovereign and Her great favour to him draws the Envy of the Russ, and the Nation upon him, as it will certainly their resentments in case any change should happen in the Sovereign or the favour of the Sovereign"[3] A close examination of the most important foreign policy issues over this limited and very well-documented period provides valuable evidence of the influence Count Biron was able to exert. The experience of British representatives at the Russian court demonstrates that Biron's sometimes decisive influence with the empress was far more informal and personal than official, and was often limited. In addition, it shows that Biron exercised his influence with the caution of a German favorite who understood the precariousness of his own position at the Russian court.

Anna Ioannovna was the niece of Peter the Great and ascended the throne only five years after her uncle's sudden death. Her reign consolidated both the reforms of Peter within Russia and Russia's position in the European political and diplomatic system of the time. During this reign, Ernst Johann Biron was considered the most influential man at the Russian court. Historians of the nineteenth and early twentieth centuries portrayed him as an evil foreigner (he was a Baltic German), who ruthlessly exploited Russia and the Russians in the interests of his own personal power, wealth, and glory. His reputation was so dark that the entire reign of the Empress Anna Ioannovna was known as the *Bironovshchina*, the era of Biron.

Count Biron's German origins played a key role in the creation of his reputation, both during the time he was at court and in the subsequent historiography of the period. The immediate post-Petrine period in Russia was a time when a number of prominent Germans filled the highest military and court positions. Although Biron owed his position and influence to his personal relationship with the reigning empress, other Germans, most prominently the *de facto* head of the College of Foreign Affairs, Count Andrei Osterman, a Field Marshal of the Russian army, Count B. C. von Münnich, and one of the most influential military and diplomatic figures of the period, Karl Gustav von Loewenwolde, had previously served Peter the Great and, by the 1730s, had reached the top of their respective professions. During Anna Ioannovna's reign, Karl Gustav von Loewenwolde, became an indispensable general and diplomat, as well as a considerable and stabilizing influence on Count Biron himself, a role that was also noted by Lord Forbes. The prominence of these loyal and talented, yet foreign, officials allowed later Russian monarchs, most notably the daughter of Peter the Great, Empress Elizabeth Petrovna, to condemn the 1730s as a period of foreign (particularly German) domination of Russia and her people. This xenophobic characterization dominated the Russian view of the era, as well as its historiography, until the twentieth century. Although he gained his position at court through personal, rather than bureaucratic, means, Biron was viewed as the leading member of the supposed "German faction" during the reign of Empress Anna Ioannovna.

A century later, in 1835, the famous Russian author Alexander Pushkin wrote of Biron that "He had the misfortune to be a German."[4]

Questioning this overwhelmingly negative assessment, some historians have successfully reassessed Count Biron's role at the Russian court.[5] In its various forms, this revision has emphasized the absence of coordinated action by prominent German ministers and courtiers in Russia, as well as the lack of evidence that Biron, himself, had the type of strong, personal role in politics and policy making that has been attributed to him.[6] In effect, much of what has been written about Biron in recent decades, rather than highlighting his actual influence and activities, demonstrates what he could not or did not do in Russia, emphasizing that he was not responsible for many of the negative aspects of Anna's reign. Even Pushkin, in admitting the xenophobia of the era, insisted that the "horror of Anna's reign" had been "dumped" on the favorite unfairly. As an afterthought in a letter to a friend, the great poet, without elaborating, went so far as to describe Biron as having "great intelligence and great talents," an uncharacteristically positive assessment even today.[7]

The approach in this current analysis is different, focusing on well-documented events of a very limited period to show how Count Biron actually functioned at the Russian court. Rather than an emphasis on the "evil" he did or did not do, the focus here is on his actions and accomplishments within the parameters of his role as the favorite of the empress. The goal is to present Ernst Johann Biron, not from the perspective of his angry rivals, or even of his later apologists, but rather through the eyes of contemporary, and perhaps slightly less biased, observers who witnessed and recorded his activities on a regular basis and over a limited but very important period.

Analyzing Count Biron's role in key diplomatic and military decisions made during the period from 1733 to 1734, this study demonstrates that, while he had a significant influence on court dynamics, treaty negotiations, and political events, he was reluctant to become involved in formal policy-making and clearly understood both his lack of a ministerial role and his precarious position in Russia. This cautious self-awareness did not prevent him from acting, yet it significantly circumscribed his activities and reputed power. In short, Biron appears as a cautious male favorite, whose influence on Empress Anna Ioannovna was both unique and considerable, though ultimately limited in matters relating to diplomatic and military policy.

Ernst Johann Biron's Rise to Prominence

Ernst Johann Biron was born in Courland (in modern Latvia) in 1690, to a noble family in the service of Poland. He attended the University of Königsberg for some time and, in 1718, was admitted to the court of Duchess Anna of Courland in Mitau (modern Jelgava).[8] His appearance at the Mitau court was to change the course of his life. The 25-year-old Duchess Anna had been widowed very shortly after her marriage to Duke Frederick William of Courland in 1710, yet, as the niece of Peter the Great, she was obligated to take her place as duchess of Courland in order to consolidate Russia's control over the Baltic state.[9] In 1723, Biron married a lady in waiting at Anna's court, Benigta Gottlieb von Trotha, reportedly at the instigation of the duchess in order to conceal her own relationship with him. By 1725, he seems to have publically gained Anna's favor, since she had given him the rank of chamberlain and selected him to represent her in St. Petersburg at the funeral of her uncle, Peter the Great. Within two years, at the time of Catherine's death, Biron's position as Anna's favorite was secure, and he accompanied the duchess to Moscow to attend the coronation of her young cousin, Peter II, in February of 1728.

In 1730, as a result of the sudden death of Peter the Great's grandson, Tsar Peter II, Anna Ioannovna was chosen to be the next ruler of Russia by the Supreme Privy Council, made up largely of members of the aristocratic Golitsyn and Dolgoruki families. Several historians have speculated that Anna's selection as a "weak" female choice as the next Russian monarch may have contributed to even greater resentment toward Biron as a stronger "male" influence on her reign.[10] Although initially prevented from traveling to Russia, Biron arrived in Moscow in time for the coronation ceremony. At the same time, he received the rank of Great Chamberlain (chief gentleman in waiting, or *ober kamerger*), as well as the title of Count of the Empire. His status was now that of imperial favorite (*sluchainyi chelovek*). This rank, title, and status he retained throughout the ten-year reign of Empress Anna Ioannovna.

Rather than distancing him from the duchess, Biron's marriage created a sort of court "family" for Anna that endured for the rest of her life. Her biographer reports that, in 1730, when she traveled to Moscow to accept the Russian throne, she took with her Biron's wife and children as traveling companions.[11] Much later, when she was empress in St. Petersburg, she customarily dined at noon with Count Biron, his wife, and their children, and, according to one biographer, treated the Birons' ten year old, Hedwig, "like a daughter."[12] Although, this arrangement may appear somewhat unusual, it seems that not only Biron, but his entire nuclear family, played an important role in the monarch's personal life.

Hints of the close bond between the empress and Count Biron were evident from the beginning of Anna Ioannovna's reign, though the reports of the British minister in Russia, Claudius Rondeau, were slow to emphasize Biron's special relationship with the empress. Rondeau served as the King's representative to the Russian court for several years, yet the sudden death of Tsar Peter II, and the arrival of the new empress from Mitau, in Courland, where she had spent much of her time during the previous 13 years, left him unfamiliar with the individuals now coming into power.

Still, the overwhelmingly foreign nature of the new court was already a source of discontent. Only four months after Anna's arrival in Moscow, Rondeau wrote in a letter to London dated May 11, 1730:

> The nobility seem very much dissatisfied that Her Majesty employs so many foreigners about her person. Mr Biron, a courlander, who came with her from Mitaw, is made great-chamberlain, and several other of that country are in great favour, at which the old russ, who did expect she would have preferred them before those gentlemen, are displeased.[13]

A month later, Rondeau restated his observation that the "old russ... begin to murmur very much, that Her Majesty has so many courlanders and germans about her person."[14] These are the earliest beginnings of the accusations that would plague the reign of Anna Ioannovna, and the reputation of Ernst Johann Biron, for many years to come. Yet, the British Resident still seemed unaware of the power and influence that Biron wielded with the empress. Still early in the reign, Rondeau wrote:

> If I was permitted to give my opinion, I believe count Biron will not be able to maintain himself long, for I am inclined to think baron Osterman has consented that all sort of honours and riches should be heaped on that gentleman to render him odious to the russ and by that means be able in time to ruin him, as he has done all the other favourites[15]

Clearly, Rondeau understood the cunning and talent Baron Osterman had used in the past to maintain his control over a variety of domestic and foreign issues, yet, early on, he did not grasp the power and influence Count Biron would possess under the new regime. Biron would become "odious" to the Russians at court, but Osterman would not be able to remove him from his position as favorite during the reign of Anna Ioannovna. His influence with the empress remained too great.

This realization came slowly, but by early 1731, Rondeau reported that the empress "is wholly and absolutely governed by her favourite, count Biron, the two counts Levenwolde, Paul Iwanitsch Jaguginsky and baron Osterman"[16] By this point, Biron was listed first in a group consisting of one Russian and four Germans, including Count Osterman. In the same letter, Rondeau expressed the opinion that the empress thought of "nothing else" but masquerades, comedies, and "to heap up riches and honour on count Biron"[17] In addition to recording Biron's growing public prominence, Claudius Rondeau began to relate more intimate displays of the monarch's attachment to her favorite. On January 11, Rondeau reported that both Anna and Biron had been bled by doctors due to illness, and that the empress had taken her meals in Biron's chamber during his last sickness. By April, Rondeau's letters included the detail that Anna had presented Biron with a miniature portrait of herself set with "very fine" diamonds, and, as he reported, "that gentleman advances daily in favour."[18]

While these early observations provide a sense of the close relationship between Count Biron and Empress Anna Ioannovna, the correspondence of Rondeau, and later Lord Forbes, also documents Biron's increasing influence and involvement in Russian policy issues, particularly those involving foreign affairs.

Recognition among the European representatives in Russia of Count Biron's ability to influence foreign relations developed gradually, while the extent of this ability, and his willingness to use it, remained uncertain. One of the first indications given by Claudius Rondeau that Count Biron played a role in diplomatic decisions, involved the secret negotiations of the king of Poland to arrange a marriage between himself and Anna Ioannovna. Rondeau assured his superiors in London that the tsaritsa would never take such a proposal seriously, observing that "her great-chamberlain count Biron is too much in her good graces to consent to any such thing."[19] Only a year after coming to Russia, Biron's influence on Russian policy was already attracting attention in the reports of the British diplomat.

Count Biron and the Diplomatic Mission of George, Lord Forbes

Less than two years later, in the spring of 1733, George, Lord Forbes, was sent from London to St. Petersburg as George II's, Envoy Extraordinary and Minister Plenipotentiary to the Russian court, with instructions to negotiate and conclude the first formal commercial treaty between Great Britain and Russia. Forbes arrived in St. Petersburg by ship on June 9, 1733. Rondeau's knowledge of Russian and German (Forbes spoke French), as well as his acquaintance with the leading figures within the Russian administration, most importantly Counts Biron and Osterman, made him indispensible to the newly appointed envoy. Over the course of the next year, Forbes and Rondeau met regularly with Count Osterman, and even more frequently with Count Biron, to discuss trade and other diplomatic concerns. These meetings resulted in the signing of the Anglo-Russian Commercial Treaty of 1734, which helped to guide political and commercial relations between Great Britain and Russia for the remainder of the eighteenth century. During the same period, Russia became involved in the military conflict known as the War of Polish Succession. The record of the intense negotiations and discussions surrounding Forbes's mission provides insight into the dynamics of the Russian court, as well as a unique view of the extent and limits of Count Biron's influence on diplomatic and military policy. Forbes and Rondeau were keen observers of the dynamics of the Russian court and its most important members. Their weekly reports to London, as well as the diary Forbes kept and the "Account of Russia" he completed after his return to Great Britain, provide a unique and detailed perspective on Russian people and events in the mid-1730s.[20]

By the time of Forbes's mission, Claudius Rondeau had lived in Russia for five years. He had already developed a close, working relationship with both Count Biron and Count Osterman.

The goal of the Russian court was to engage Great Britain not only in a commercial treaty but in a defensive alliance as well. This Forbes had been strictly forbidden to discuss by George II. Britain was not interested in any agreement that included an obligation to defend the vast territories under Russian control. Although Biron and Osterman both hoped to convince Forbes to negotiate a more formal alliance, they approached the British envoy in very different ways. This difference in approach toward the British ministers provides a unique view of Count Biron's ability to influence the empress and, through her, Russian foreign policy.

Count Biron saw the satisfaction of British commercial desires, in the form of an advantageous Anglo-Russian commercial agreement, as a first step toward the Russian desire of a more comprehensive political and defensive alliance. Therefore, he assured Forbes that the British would receive an advantageous commercial agreement, providing help when he could, but always emphasizing that he held no ministerial post and, therefore, was unable to intervene directly in diplomatic affairs. His lack of an official ministerial position was often an excuse the favorite used to avoid personal risk. Count Osterman, on the other hand, insisted that he could not discuss a commercial agreement, except as part of the negotiations for a larger defensive alliance. For Osterman, the only way that Russia could justify commercial concessions to British merchants was if they were part of the defensive agreement that St. Petersburg wished to conclude with London. In the absence of a defensive alliance, Osterman refused to discuss commercial issues. This stance, taken by Osterman in his capacity as the vice chancellor of the Russian College of Foreign Affairs, was particularly frustrating for Lord Forbes.

As time went by and Anglo-Russian commercial talks ground to a halt (largely as a result of Count Osterman's intransigence), Forbes saw informal discussions with Count Biron as his only chance to move things forward. Adding to the diplomatic confusion of the period was the fact that the Polish throne had recently become vacant, and it was feared at many European courts that the struggle to fill that vacancy had the potential to lead to a major European war. In fact, the War of Polish Succession was fought from 1733 until 1735, and placed Russia and its ally Austria in opposition to France, with battles fought mostly around the Polish city of Danzig. For St. Petersburg, the military and political implications of this war were important to Russia's status and control in Eastern Europe. From the viewpoint of some, the legacy of Peter the Great was at stake in this conflict.

Two months after the death of the king of Poland, and before Lord Forbes arrived in St. Petersburg, Count Biron had taken Rondeau aside to inform him privately, but at the express order of the empress that she would support the selection of the Elector of Saxony, the son of the deceased king, as the next king of Poland. Rondeau wrote:

> At present I take the liberty to acquaint your lordship that last Wednesday count Biron took me into his closet to inform me in great confidence, that Her Imperial Majesty, his mistress, had ordered him to tell me, that she should be glad to favor the elector of Saxony's being chosen king of Poland, in case His Majesty approves of it…Count Biron added, that Her Majesty would be glad the king, my master, would insinuate this affair to the court of Vienna.[21]

This is Ernst Johann Biron in his most common role—private, secret, and completely unofficial, yet communicating issues of the utmost diplomatic and political importance. He was relating a message directly from the empress of Russia to the king of Great Britain, through the king's resident, Rondeau, entirely outside of the customary Russian diplomatic and ministerial channels. Confirming Biron's role as the unofficial channel of Russian foreign policy at the highest level, Rondeau concluded his description of the meeting:

> and his excellency [Biron] made me promise, that I would mention nothing of what he had told me to anybody here, not even to baron Osterman, and he desires your lordship will not mention it to Prince Cantemir, for, as he was a young man, they could not well depend on his accounts.[22]

Anna Ioannovna had initiated this alternate channel of communication through her favorite for her own diplomatic purposes, and, if Rondeau's interpretation is correct, even her foreign minister in St. Petersburg and her envoy in London had no knowledge of the message she was communicating to King George II. For Rondeau, and later for Forbes, Anna Ioannovna's favorite represented a direct channel to the highest level of decision making at the Russian court, an avenue through which, if necessary, they could communicate discreetly with the empress. Of course, this gave Biron a great deal of control as well, since his interpretations of events and issues were the versions communicated directly to and from the empress. For the British ministers at the Russian court, Count Biron provided a way around the official obstacles they would encounter, political, commercial, diplomatic, or military.

In London, unofficial communication between Biron and Claudius Rondeau was welcomed. George II was "extremely pleased" with the information provided by Biron regarding the empress's preference in the Polish election. Rondeau was instructed to compliment the count on his "friendly communication," and reply, through him, with several additional details concerning Britain's actions in support of the election of the Elector of Saxony.[23] Due to the sensitive nature of its contents, the letter from London containing this information was written almost entirely in code to avoid the possibility that it might be read by the Russian officials. Even the British Northern Department, the precursor to the Foreign Office, understood the value of encouraging and protecting this unofficial channel of communication with the empress through Count Biron.

George, Lord Forbes's arrival in St. Petersburg on June 9, 1733, began a year of the highest level of diplomatic representation between Britain and Russia in almost 15 years, that is, since the reign of Peter the Great. The combination of commercial treaty negotiations and the impending conflict over the succession to the Polish throne enabled Forbes to observe the Russian ministers and courtiers closely. His experience, recorded in his reports, letters, and journal, confirm the always unofficial and hesitant, yet significant role of Count Biron in matters of foreign policy. They also demonstrate the limits of the favorite's influence and control in a period of crisis.

From the start, Forbes understood the value of the British relationship with the favorite. Two days after his arrival in St. Petersburg, Lord Forbes made his first official visits to members of the Russian court. On that day, the first person he visited in Russia was Count Biron. Only after this meeting with the favorite did he meet with the chancellor, Count Golovkin, and then the vice chancellor, Count Osterman, to whom he delivered his official letter of credence from King George II to the empress. A ceremonial dispute over the kissing of the empress's hands kept Forbes from regular attendance at the Russian court for almost two months, but it did not prevent him from joining Rondeau in meetings with counts Biron, Osterman, and others to discuss commercial and diplomatic affairs.

The succession crisis in Poland dominated European diplomacy at this time, and it also created a rift between the minister, Osterman, and the favorite, Biron. Count Osterman was seen as a proponent of the Prussian cause in central Europe, whereas Count Biron favored the Imperial court at Vienna and the choice of the elector of Saxony as the next king of Poland. Rondeau suggested to London that Biron's dislike for the Prussian cause may have had a personal element as well. He wrote to Lord Harrington, head of the Northern Department in London:

> One of the great reasons of it, which, I believe, few are acquainted with, is that some time ago the king of Prussia, having drunk, spoke at table slightingly of his excellency [Biron], and Paul Iwanitsch Jagouginsky, who does not love the prussians, has informed him of what the king had said.[24]

This personal slight against the favorite, given his influence with the empress, is likely to have contributed to the strained relations between the Russian and the Prussian courts, driving the two even further apart as the situation in Poland deteriorated. By mid-July, 1733, Rondeau reported that these diplomatic concerns had "occasioned a great dispute between count Biron and baron Osterman, and Her Majesty is displeased with baron Osterman for espousing with so much zeal the interest of the king of Prussia."²⁵ Forbes added that Count Osterman had raised suspicions regarding the Elector of Saxony at the court of Vienna, but that "count Biron had reproached baron Osterman before Her Majesty with the intrigue and it is thought it may go worst with baron Osterman."²⁶ By the end of the month, it appeared to Lord Forbes that Count Biron and the cause of the Elector of Saxony had officially carried the day, leaving Osterman worried about the possibility of war with France, whose candidate for the Polish throne, Stanislas Leszczynski, was the father-in-law of the French king. Confirming both the direction of Russian policy and the power of Biron's influence, Forbes wrote, "I believe baron Osterman is very uneasy, that things are like to come to a rupture; he has done all he could to hinder their engaging too far, but count Biron's counsels have prevailed."²⁷ At this juncture, the influence of Count Biron with regard to Russia's foreign policy seemed stronger than that of Count Osterman, the minister officially in charge of Russia's foreign affairs. Count Biron was at the heart of events that culminated in the War of the Polish Succession. On a regular and ongoing basis, he met with the British ministers and others to inform them of Russia's diplomatic actions and troop movements, at the same time denying any ministerial authority, particularly when military and political outcomes seemed uncertain. In a time of military crisis, the favorite's influence seemed stronger than ever, yet his apparent confidence included periods of uncertainty and doubt.

Count Biron and the War of the Polish Succession

At the end of July, 1733, it was Count Biron who informed the Saxon minister in St. Petersburg that the empress had ordered Russian troops to march into Poland. A concern immediately developed over whether the troops promised by Russia's ally, Austria, would enter Poland at the same time. Though Vienna had agreed to support Russia in Poland, the emperor was now more concerned about an attack from France on his German territories. The Austrian ministers in Russia begged Forbes and Rondeau, as representatives of George II, ally to the emperor, to intervene. Because Forbes had been instructed to help the Austrian minister at St. Petersburg whenever possible, he travelled to the empress's summer residence at Peterhof to discuss the matter of the Austrian troops, and, as he reported, "took mr Rondeau to assist me with the great-chamberlain."²⁸ Without hesitation, Forbes decided to address his arguments over troop movements and Austrian treaty obligations to Count Biron, the favorite, rather than through any other more official ministerial channels. Forbes reported that "Count Biron was difficult on the point," but promised that he would consider what the British ministers had said. After dinner, Forbes "stood in his [Biron's] way as he came from Her Majesty," and received a reply that he interpreted as a concession by the Russian court to excuse the Austrian troops from entering Poland.

Count Biron, who had the greatest share in encouraging Russia's military involvement in the Polish election, was clearly hesitant to agree that Russia should invade Poland alone, without the military assistance of her ally in Vienna. Having involved himself in political affairs that now threatened to burden Russia with the entire military responsibility in Poland, the favorite temporarily abandoned his customary role by suggesting that Forbes present his concerns through official channels, by addressing his arguments to Count Osterman. "He told me," wrote Forbes, "that I should say the same things to count Osterman that I had said to him, but that I should not mention his sentiments to anybody, for that he talked freely to us, as friends but that he was no minister."[29] Forbes, having no alternative, met with Count Osterman, but reported "I could not move him at all."[30] The minister was unwilling to release Vienna from its treaty obligations. The following day, Forbes reported, "everybody went as usual to the great-chamberlain's," and the British ministers related their lack of success with Count Osterman. Biron stated that "though what I [Forbes] had said to him had inclined him to be of our side, yet that he would not take an affair of so great consequence on himself if he could not bring the council of state to his opinion, which he would endeavour."[31]

In his continuing effort to avoid unilaterally endorsing an unpopular decision, Count Biron agreed to attempt to influence not only the empress, who was already leaning toward compromise, but the council of state as well.[32] Throughout the period of the Anglo-Russian negotiations, it was rare for Biron to admit that he would attempt to influence the tsaritsa's council of state. In this instance, his willingness to work through official channels can be seen as evidence of his hesitation and uncertainty in dealing with matters of the greatest importance to Russia's international standing. When it came to issues of war, the favorite was more concerned with the risk posed to his own position than with his control over Russian policy. In the end, he informed Rondeau that the empress had agreed to excuse Austrian troops from entering Poland, as requested by the British, "in deference to the opinion of the king." Not missing the opportunity to ingratiate himself with the British court, particularly now that the danger to his position had passed, Count Biron added "that he himself would lay hold of all occasions to show his great respect for His Majesty and his interest, as far as it was consistent with his duty to his sovereign."[33]

With events moving rapidly toward war, Count Biron was increasingly outspoken in his criticism of the Prussian court and its king. Rondeau reported that the Russian opinion of the Prussian court was very low. Expanding on this anti-Prussian theme, he wrote:

> count Biron told me some days ago that the king of Prussia was very angry with him, because he had overset the measures that were concerted by some of this court and that of Vienna to get a prince of Brandenburgh elected duke of Courland after the death of the present duke, and because he had persuaded Her Imperial Majesty not to give her niece, the princess of

Mecklenburgh, to a prince of Brandenburgh, which baron Mardefeld [the Prussian minister at St. Petersburg] had long tried to bring about.[34]

The crisis over the Polish succession had exacerbated the strained relations between the two courts, and, it seems, between the Russian favorite and the Prussian king. Biron threatened that Russia would not forget the actions of the Prussian king, if he later required Russian assistance. At this point, the animosity between the Prussian and the Russian courts had become something of a personal feud between the favorite and the Prussian king. Once again, Count Biron's actions and statements show him to be intimately involved in European diplomatic and military affairs at the highest level.

As the Polish crisis deepened, the British ministers at St. Petersburg continued to rely on the assistance and influence of Count Biron in their negotiations with the Russian court, yet they also began to discern the more subtle strengths and weaknesses of the leading advisors to Anna Ioannovna. In September, 1733, Forbes reported that the animosity between counts Biron and Osterman was more evident than ever. In comparing the two, he wrote that, "[t]he first of these [Biron] is all powerful by favour, the second [Osterman] all necessary from his experience and capacity; the first has all the good qualities of the heart, the second all those of the head with some of the vices of the heart."[35] Forbes maintained this positive opinion of Biron and even included it in the description of the favorite he later presented to Queen Caroline.[36] Both Forbes and Rondeau continued to rely on Biron as a direct channel to the empress.

The value of Count Biron's friendship toward the British was also recognized in London. George II himself instructed Forbes and Rondeau to compliment Biron and to continue to improve their relationship with the favorite. Lord Harrington relayed the king's message in October:

> The king was extremely pleased with the account you sent of count Biron's obliging conduct towards you, and you may, if you think it proper, make that gentleman a suitable compliment in His Majesty's name thereupon; and, as you have found by experience the great influence he has upon all the counsels of that court, it is unnecessary to recommend to you cultivating as much as possible his good dispositions and friendship.[37]

Though other portions of this letter were written in code, this compliment to Count Biron and royal recognition of his influence at court was not. Needless to say, the British king's official recognition of Biron's value and importance in military and political decision making at the Russian court was well received by the favorite, who, Forbes wrote shortly thereafter, "is without doubt all powerful here."[38]

Late in October, 1733, the influence and power of Count Biron in military affairs appeared, once again, with regard to issues surrounding Austrian involvement in the Polish succession crisis. Biron informed Rondeau that the empress had decided to make 45 thousand regular troops available to the emperor in Vienna if they were necessary to protect his German territories from a French attack. The favorite added that the empress had not yet informed her council of this decision, but that he had told Rondeau "in confidence" so that the British court could be notified. However, when the emperor finally requested the assistance of these troops in late November, Biron's attitude had changed considerably. It seems that the court in Vienna had credited Count Osterman with the earlier assistance in excusing Austrian troops from entering Poland. Biron explained that "he had singly, and in opposition to all the rest, brought that about, but that the court of Vienna had never taken the least notice of this to him, but had owned the obligation to baron Osterman," who had been most against it.[39] Now, he suggested to the emperor's minister that, since Count Osterman was to get the credit for the upcoming troop movements, "he [Biron] would leave the trouble of asking them to him." Once again, the British ministers attempted to help the beleaguered Austrians. They discovered that, although the Austrian ministers in St. Petersburg had asked Vienna to acknowledge the favorite's assistance on several occasions, the emperor had not done so. Emphasizing Biron's growing influence, Forbes and Rondeau warned that "if count Biron should be disobliged so as to be capable to go over to any other measures, he can certainly alter those of this court."[40] The Austrian representatives to the Russian court were in danger of losing the support of Anna Ioannovna's favorite. The difficulties of the Austrians demonstrated Count Biron's potential to influence political and military policy, as well as the importance of his assistance at the Russian court.

Later in the Polish conflict, when the Russian armies had actually engaged those supporting Stanislas Leszczynski around the city of Danzig, Count Biron once again seemed to lose his nerve. To the British ministers, he complained of having to support the Saxon cause and the policy of Russian military intervention alone at the Russian court. Forbes reported that "Count Biron is very uneasy, and says, that he stands as much alone in keeping Her Majesty steady in what she has undertaken, as the emperor does against the attacks that are made on him in so many places."[41] A few weeks later, Forbes and Rondeau notified London that the Russians were "very uneasy about their affairs in Poland and dissatisfied with king Augustus' [the Saxon candidate's] conduct." They reported:

> Count Biron, who is the chief friend king Augustus has at this court, says, that he shall not be able alone to bear up against the insinuations that are made to Her Majesty, that she does all, and the Saxons do nothing, that the affair is buthensome to them, and that, if king Augustus will neither lay out money to gain the people, nor join his troops with theirs...they shall be obliged to quit the party...and leave the poles to do as they will.[42]

Having espoused an interventionist Russian policy in favor of the Saxon candidate for the Polish throne, Count Biron doubted his ability to maintain that policy in the face of continued, and potentially expanding, warfare due to a new threat of French intervention by sea. At this point, the limits of Count Biron's influence and political courage appear to have been reached. In the end, however, Russian forces defeated the Polish supporters of Stanislas Leszczynski, as well as the invading French, and the Saxon candidate became the king of Poland with the military assistance of the Russian empress and the influence of her favorite.

Count Biron's Influence on Anglo-Russian Commercial Negotiations

Though the succession crisis in Poland dominated the attention of the Russian court throughout 1733 and 1734, Forbes had originally traveled to St. Petersburg to negotiate an Anglo-Russian commercial agreement. Not surprisingly, the two issues became closely connected, yet whenever possible, Forbes pressed Count Osterman, the minister in charge of treaty negotiations, for progress in Anglo-Russian commercial discussions. In this realm, too, Osterman and Biron differed in their approach, though they shared the common goal of a closer relationship between Great Britain and Russia. Count Osterman informed Forbes that Russia could not consider the negotiation of a trade treaty except within the context of a broader Anglo-Russian political alliance. In short, Osterman was unwilling to discuss a commercial agreement apart from a treaty of alliance. Count Biron, on the other hand, encouraged Forbes to expect that Russia would, in fact, sign a commercial agreement acceptable to the British crown and its merchants, without demanding a formal alliance that included a British guaranty of Russian territory. The instructions Forbes had received from George II contained a strict prohibition against negotiating any treaty of alliance that would obligate Great Britain to defend Russia's vast borders. Therefore, Forbes could discuss only a commercial treaty, not a defensive alliance. Understandably, this situation made Forbes prefer his discussions with the favorite over his talks with the vice chancellor, though official negotiations of any kind were the exclusive prerogative of Count Osterman's ministry.

In addition, a difference in personality and style between the two members of the Russian court added to the preference Forbes felt for dealing with Anna's favorite. After only six weeks in St Petersburg, Forbes wrote to Lord Harrington, "I apprehend a hard bargain from count Osterman, who seems to marchandise [sic] very much, and wished I could explain myself to count Biron, who deals openly and soundly."[43] In September, 1733, when France was attempting to lure Russia away from its commitments to the election of the Saxon candidate for the Polish throne, Forbes related yet another example of the difference in style between the favorite and the vice chancellor. To Lord Harrington he wrote:

Your lordship will please to observe that the great-chamberlain [Biron] communicated this affair to us fully and clearly, as if he intended only to cultivate a mutual confidence; the other [Osterman] communicated it partially and darkly, as if it were intended to alarm.[44]

This preference for interaction and discussions with Count Biron is found throughout the reports of the British ministers, and it eventually benefitted the British cause.

In November, Forbes and Rondeau used the opportunity of Austrian troop discussions with Count Biron to raise the issue of their treaty of commerce, draft articles of which had been under consideration by Count Osterman's ministry since August. Osterman had a reputation for falling ill whenever he encountered diplomatic issues with which he did not want to deal. This was apparently the situation at the end of 1733, as the British ministers were pressing ever more insistently for a commercial treaty. With regard to the negotiation of the Anglo-Russian commercial treaty, Count Biron "said that and some other things made baron Osterman sick, for that Her Majesty had often ordered him to dispatch that treaty."[45] This was the first time Count Biron confirmed that the empress had ordered the vice chancellor to conclude the Anglo-Russian commercial agreement Forbes came to Russia to negotiate. Though the commercial negotiations were at a standstill, the favorite continued to encourage the British representatives. Shortly before the end of the year, Forbes reported that "Count Biron gives us all imaginable assurances that this treaty shall be concluded to our satisfaction, and now and then says very hard things of baron Osterman, and, I believe, would procure some other to treat this affair, if we desired it."[46] After debating the merits of such a request with Claudius Rondeau, Forbes decided against asking the favorite to intervene to remove the treaty negotiations from the vice chancellor's control. Although Osterman was clearly obstructing the negotiation of an Anglo-Russian commercial treaty, something that was, according to Biron, in violation of a direct order from the empress, the British ministers felt it was simply too dangerous to offend the vice chancellor by relying entirely on the assistance of the favorite. Despite the support of Count Biron for their commercial requests, Forbes and Rondeau were unwilling to ignore the power wielded by Count Osterman by virtue of his superior knowledge of foreign affairs, his long experience at the Russian court, and his exemplary service to the Russian throne.

The beginning of the new year, 1734, brought little change to the situation of Britain's commercial treaty negotiations, though the interaction between counts Biron and Osterman with regard to those negotiations and the events in Poland continued to demonstrate the extent and limits of each man's power and influence. Forbes complained to London that "[w]e are forced to wait the dilatory resolutions of baron Osterman, and the more dilatory methods he has put it [the treaty] into...and, as count Biron is the only person we can do any business by, we can only lay hold of some of his moments, when he is not pleased to cut us short by saying that he is no minister."[47] Osterman's delaying tactics and Biron's denial of ministerial authority in the face of difficult decisions left the British representatives with little hope. It appears, however, that they were becoming more adept at negotiating a path between these two powerful individuals.

In January, Forbes and Rondeau reported that they had the opportunity to remark to Count Biron that the endless delay and unreasonable demands of the Russians seemed "designed to break off this treaty."[48] This observation resulted in a response, not from the favorite, but from Count Osterman, to the effect that the Russian court was, in fact, willing to address the demands that the British merchants viewed as unreasonable. For the first time, a comment regarding the commercial negotiations made to the empress's favorite had been answered by a concession on the part of the ministry in charge. Although the British negotiators could not have known it at the time, this incident signaled the start of a shift away from the delaying tactics of Count Osterman, and toward a greater disposition on the part of the Russian court to conclude the commercial agreement desired by the British, just as Count Biron had promised. Unfortunately, it was also at this moment that the outbreak of hostilities in Poland began to interfere most dramatically with the Anglo-Russian negotiations.

By February, 1734, Count Osterman increased his demands on Lord Forbes to discuss an Anglo-Russian defensive alliance. This renewed interest in an alliance resulted from Russian concerns over the outbreak of fighting around the Polish city of Danzig, the lack of success, in general, in Polish affairs, and the duration and expense of the Russian intervention. In addition, with the spring thaw in the Baltic Sea came the specter of a French naval squadron entering the conflict in Poland to support the claim of Stanislas Leszczynski to the Polish throne. These concerns seemed to alarm the Russian court and, in the opinion of the British ministers, put the future of an Anglo-Russian commercial treaty at risk. Under the circumstances, Count Osterman pressed his demands for an Anglo-Russian defensive alliance with renewed vigor. The Russians hoped an alliance would result in the arrival of a British fleet in the Baltic to defend Russian ports from French naval attack. This was exactly the sort of scenario Forbes was forbidden to discuss, yet, with events deteriorating in Poland, Count Osterman insisted that a commercial agreement could not be negotiated without first signing a defensive alliance. Forbes reported that "we are in great doubt now, as to the success of this affair," and the reason for this doubt was closely linked to the position and confidence of Count Biron in the current state of affairs. He explained that,

> count Biron, whom we chiefly relied upon, begins to be impatient, and to be troubled at the appearance of the difficulties and delay in Poland and with the consequences; so that, as baron Osterman is the only man of resource among them; the other seems, as if he would give up the helm, as the weather grows rough.[49]

As events in the Polish war threatened Russia with greater danger than ever before, Biron appeared to Forbes and Rondeau to relinquish his power and influence to others. Military crisis appeared to force the favorite to abandon his optimistic view of commercial negotiations in order to preserve his position, and this gave Count Osterman the upper hand. Forbes and Rondeau wrote to Harrington, "Your lordship will judge from this how difficult it is for us to act between these two great men, on whom all favours and business of this court roll."[50] As discouraging as the situation now appeared, a change in Lord Forbes's status as Great Britain's Envoy Extraordinary and Minister Plenipotentiary completely transformed the circumstances of the commercial negotiations, and Count Biron, the empress's favorite, took a leading role in communicating the new decision.

In a letter dated March 1, 1734, Lord Harrington informed Forbes that the king would recall him from his mission to Russia. This recall motivated the Russian court to attempt to conclude a formal commercial treaty with Great Britain before Forbes left St. Petersburg. Given Russia's situation in Poland, a treaty of commerce that necessarily implied close Anglo-Russian political ties as well, would be preferable to no treaty at all. Forbes and Rondeau described how Count Biron gave them the news:

> Yesterday being at count Biron's, he took count Levenvolde and us apart, and told us that Her Majesty...had ordered that our treaty of commerce should be concluded before my (Forbes) departure.[51]

Once again, the empress's favorite related a very significant Russian policy decision privately, at his residence, and completely outside of official ministerial channels. When the British ministers mentioned the specific difficulties they had encountered up to that time with respect to their commercial treaty negotiations, Biron blamed Count Osterman for everything. As an indication of just how "unofficial" and devoid of ceremony Count Birion's announcement was, Forbes reported that the empress herself was "standing in a door behind a curtain all the time," listening to the discussion between her favorite and the British ministers.[52]

Triggered by the recall of Lord Forbes, Anglo-Russian commercial negotiations rushed forward. The negotiations were immediately removed from Count Osterman's hands, and a new group of Russian negotiators made rapid progress toward an agreement, conceding to British demands in almost every case. With a few additional delays over ceremonial details, Claudius Rondeau and Count Osterman signed the Anglo-Russian Commercial Treaty of 1734 to the great satisfaction of Great Britain and her merchants, much as Ernst Johann Biron, the favorite of Empress Anna Ioannovna, had promised more than a year before.

According to his original instructions, Lord Forbes, upon his return from St. Petersburg, was to write an account of Russia that included details of the country, as well as the Russian court and its major figures.[53]

After a year of frequent interaction with Count Biron, Forbes had a number of interesting observations to share about his character and role at the Russian court. Given the experience of his mission to St. Petersburg, his description of the favorite is worth quoting in its entirety, with all of its original spellings and punctuation:

> Count Biron has the greatest share in her Majestys favour and Confidence he is a Gentleman of Courland about 35 Years old[54], a good Person and Face, Noble, Generous Open and polite in his manner & behavour but the Little knowlege that he has in Home and Foreign Affairs makes him diffident and uncertain in Business and apt to trouble, at Events thô the warmth of his Temper Sometimes Engages him in things that in his cooler thoughts he would not have undertaken. His great Power with the Sovereign and Her great favour to him draws the Envy of the Russ, and the Nation upon him, as it will certainly their resentments in case any change should happen in the Sovereign or the favour of the Sovereign, which makes him desirous of the Protection of some Foreign Power, and made him for a while Court and favour the Interest of Prussia at the Russian Court, but the Interessedness and changableness of that Princes Temper or Councils, not suting with the Generous and open Temper of the Count Biron, the Breach is now greater, that ever the Friendship seems to have been, since which Count Biron has thrown himself Intirely into the Emperours Interest, which he Espouses on all Occasions as farr as it is consistent with his Duty to his Sovereign. But as the Count, his Lady, and Family are Lutherans he seems rather to wish for the Protection of some Protestant Power, and often Expresses himself dissatisfied with the Emperours little Regard for the Protestant Interest. He seems faulty in choosing his Instruments & Creatures, nor indeed has he much Choice, he depends chiefly on (the Elder) Count Lewenwolde and is most stedy when he is at his Elbow, and yet is it thought he willingly lets him be Employ'd abroad least by too constant a Residence at Court he should take deeper root there than he desires.[55]

In light of the preceding analysis of Ernst Johann Biron's role as the favorite of Russian Empress Anna Ioannovna in the mid-1730s, much of what Forbes wrote is understandable, perhaps even insightful. It is not surprising that Lord Forbes presented a significantly more sympathetic portrait of the favorite than can be found in most other sources, either contemporary or historiographic. At key points during the Anglo-Russian negotiations, Count Biron related information and influenced decisions that contributed directly to the success of the British diplomatic mission to Russia. The reports and observations of the British ministers at the Russian court highlight Biron's strengths and weaknesses. He was a favorite with considerable influence over his empress and, at times, her policies, yet he also understood the limits of his control and was often unwilling to risk his position in moments of crisis. As one of the most prominent Germans at the Russian court of the 1730s, his favor with the empress and the power it provided did, in fact, draw "the Envy of the Russ, and the Nation upon him," and, perhaps unfairly, this reaction darkened his own reputation and the history of the era of Anna Ioannovna for centuries.

Notes

1. Though not unique to the eighteenth century in Russia, the phenomenon of the "male consort" was most common in the post-Petrine period, more specifically, from 1725 to the end of the reign of Catherine the Great, whose attraction to male favorites throughout her reign is well known. Still one of the best discussions of the phenomenon of favorites and favoritism in Russia is John T. Alexander, "Favorites, Favoritism, and Female Rule in Russia, 1725–1796," in *Russia in the Age of the Enlightenment*, eds. Roger Bartlett and Janet Hartley (New York, 1990).
2. Alexander, "Favorites, Favoritism, and Female Rule in Russia," 109.
3. George, Lord Forbes, "Account of Russia in 1734 By George 3rd Earl of Granard." The original manuscript of this account is held in Castle Forbes, County Longford, Republic of Ireland. Photocopies of this manuscript are in the collection of the Public Record Office of Northern Ireland (PRONI) in Belfast. The PRONI reference number for the document is T3765/H/6/11/6.
4. Alexander Pushkin, *The Letters of Alexander Pushkin*, trans. Thomas Shaw (Madison, 1967), 731.
5. The revision of Biron's role began as early as 1873 and continues until today. See especially V. Stroev, *Bironovshchina i kabinet ministrov. Ocherki vnutrennei politiki imperatritsy Anny* (Moscow-St. Petersburg, 1909–10); as well as A. Lipski, "A Re-examination of the 'Dark Era' of Anna Ioannovna," *Slavic Review* XV, no. 4 (1956), 477–88.
6. See especially A. Lipski, "A Re-examination of the 'Dark Era' of Anna Ioannovna," and "Biron, Ernst Johann (1690–1772)," by David M. Griffiths in *The Modern Encyclopedia of Russian and Soviet History* (MERSH), IV (Gulf Breeze, Florida, 1977), 178–82.
7. Pushkin, *Letters,* 731; and Mina Curtiss, *A Forgotten Empress: Anna Ivanovna and Her Era* (New York, 1974), 84.
8. For a short reference biography of Biron in English, see Griffiths, "Biron, Ernst Johann (1690–1772)," 178–82.
9. For a more detailed account of Anna's marriage and the death of her husband, see Lyndsey Hughes, *Russia in the Age of Peter the Great* (New Haven and London, 1998), 412–3.
10. See Alexander, "Favorites, Favoritism, and Female Rule in Russia," 110; and Mina Curtiss, *Forgotten Empress: Anna Ivanovna and Her Era,* 58.
11. Biron himself was forbidden from accompanying Anna Ioannovna to Moscow by the Supreme Privy Council of State that selected her to be Empress. Later, Biron was believed to have been involved in the public condemnation and imprisonment of Vasili Dolgoruki, a leading member of the Supreme Privy Council, for his part in preventing Anna's favorite from traveling to Moscow with the future empress.
12. Curtiss, 236.
13. This and subsequent quotations are from letters and reports of the British representatives in Russia to the ministers in charge of the Northern

Department (one of precursors to the Foreign Office) in London. These reports are bound and archived at the British National Archives in Kew. This letter is from Claudius Rondeau to Viscount Townshend, then in charge of the Northern Department, dated May 11, 1730, and found in The National Archives (hereafter, TNA), State Papers collection (hereafter, SP), volume 19, item number 11 (or TNA, SP 19/11)

14. Rondeau to Townshend, June 22, 1730, TNA, SP 19/11.

15. Ibid.

16. Rondeau to Townshend, January 4, 1730, TNA, SP 19/12. The Loewenwolde brothers, Count Karl Gustav Loewenwolde and Count Reinhold Loewenwolde, were from Latvia. The elder started his career during the reign of Peter the Great, and reached his greatest influence as a general major and diplomat during the reign of Anna Ioannovna. According to Lord Forbes and Claudius Rondeau, the elder Count Loewenwolde had significant influence over Count Biron. Pavel Ivanovich Iaguzhinsky rose to prominence by serving as one of Peter the Great's permanent attendants. In 1722, Peter made Iaguzhinsky procurator-general with considerable powers.

17. Rondeau to Townshend, January 4, 1730, TNA, SP 19/12.

18. Rondeau to Harrington, April 5, 1731, TNA, SP 19/12.

19. Rondeau to Harrington, April 19, 1731, TNA, SP 19/12.

20. George, Lord Forbes, "Account of Russia in 1734 By George 3rd Earl of Granard," T3765/H/6/11/6.

21. Rondeau to Lord Harrington, April 7, 173, TNA, SP 91/14.

22. Rondeau to Lord Harrington, April 7, 173, TNA, SP 91/14. Prince Antiokh Kantemir was the Russian representative to the court of George II in London. At the time he was appointed, he was 23 years old, yet Count Osterman insisted to Claudius Rondeau that he was 28 years old.

23. Harrington to Rondeau, May 4, 1733, TNA, SP 91/14.

24. Rondeau to Harrington, July 21, 1733, TNA, SP 91/14.

25. Rondeau to Harrington, July 14, 1733, TNA, SP 91/14.

26. Forbes to Harrington, July 14, 1733, TNA, SP 91/14.

27. Forbes to Harrington, July 28, 1733, TNA, SP 91/14.

28. Forbes to Harrington, August 14, 1733, TNA, SP 91/14.

29. Ibid.

30. Ibid,

31. Forbes and Rondeau to Harrington, August 18, 1733, TNA, SP 91/14.

32. According to Forbes, this council consisted of only three individuals: Count Golovkin, Count Osterman, and Prince Cherkassky.

33. Forbes and Rondeau to Harrington, August 18, 1733, TNA, SP 91/14.

34. Forbes and Rondeau to Harrington, August 25, 1733, TNA, SP 91/15.

35. Forbes to Harrington, September 12, 1733, TNA, SP 91/15.

36. See this description in its entirety (below), as it is found in Forbes's "Account of Russia."

37. Harrington to Forbes and Rondeau, October 2, 1733, TNA, SP 91/15.

38. Forbes to Harrington, October 6, 1733, TNA, SP 91/15.

39. Forbes and Rondeau to Harrington, November 24, 1733, TNA, SP 91/15.

40. Ibid.

41. Forbes and Rondeau to Harrington, April 20, 1734, TNA, SP 91/16.

42. Forbes and Rondeau to Harrington, May 4, 1734, TNA, SP 91/17.

43. Forbes to Harrington, July 21, 1733, TNA, SP 91/14.

44. Forbes and Rondeau to Lord Harrington, September 8, 1733, TNA, SP 91/15.

45. Forbes and Rondeau to Harrington, November 24, 1733, TNA, SP 91/15.

46. Forbes to Harrington, December 15, 1733, TNA, SP 91/15.

47. Forbes and Rondeau to Harrington, January 12, 1734, TNA, SP 91/16.

48. Ibid.

49. Forbes and Rondeau to Harrington, February 16, 1734, TNA, SP 91/16.

50. Forbes and Rondeau to Harrington, February 23, 1734, TNA, SP 91/16.

51. Forbes and Rondeau to Harrington, March 30, 1734, TNA, SP 91/16.

52. Ibid.

53. These instructions can be found in the British National Archives, dated April 9, 1733, TNA, SP 91/14.

54. Biron was born in 1690, so at the time of Lord Forbes's mission to Russia, he was about 44 years old, rather than 35 years, as Forbes states. At the time of his mission, Forbes was 49 years old and Empress Anna Ioannovna was 41 years old.

55. Lord Forbes, "Account of Russia in 1734 By George 3rd Earl of Granard," T3765/H/6/11/6.

CHAPTER 7

Francis Stephen of Lorraine (Emperor Francis I, 1745–65), Consort of Maria Theresa, Ruler of the Austrian Monarchy from 1740

Derek Beales

Introduction

Francis Stephen was born in 1708, the second son of the ruling duke of Lorraine. Lorraine in the early eighteenth century was a small though virtually independent state, bordering France but within the Holy Roman Empire. Despite this rather unpromising start, Francis was in 1745 elected Holy Roman Emperor, thus becoming the senior sovereign in Europe. His twenty-year reign as emperor, previously undervalued, has been reappraised positively by recent historians. But he is most famous as the consort from 1736 of Archduchess Maria Theresa of Austria. She was the daughter of Charles VI, emperor and ruler of the Austrian Monarchy (1711–40), and his acknowledged heiress in the latter role. Immediately after she succeeded her father in 1740, she nominated her husband to the entirely new position and title of her co-regent and coadministrator. This nomination was endorsed by the authorities of her provinces. Francis retained this position after becoming emperor in 1745.[1]

In addition, Francis had a number of hereditary roles and titles in his own right. Of these the most important were: duke of Lorraine (where he actually ruled only from 1729 to 1736) and grand-duke of Tuscany, where he ruled from 1737 to 1765. Until he became emperor, however, his highest rank was that of king of Jerusalem, a title dating back to the Crusades which was flaunted by more than one European dynasty, although no such kingdom had existed for many centuries.[2]

The relationship between the Holy Roman Empire and the Austrian Monarchy causes much confusion. This is hardly surprising since, from the fifteenth century until the empire was abolished in 1806, the ruler of the two entities was the same—except during the years with which this article is concerned, 1740–65. Moreover, the territories of empire and monarchy substantially overlapped: the Austrian duchies, the kingdom of Bohemia and most of the Belgian provinces formed part of both empire and monarchy. On the other hand, nearly all of Germany was part of the empire but not of the monarchy; and large parts of the monarchy were outside the empire, most prominently the then vast kingdom of Hungary. Informed contemporaries were well aware of the distinction between empire and monarchy. The state that was to become the Austrian Empire in 1804 and lasted until 1918 was in the eighteenth century never officially described as an empire, precisely because that term was reserved for the Holy Roman Empire, generally known simply as "the empire" headed by the emperor. So the great collection of provinces that were effectively ruled by the Habsburgs as sovereigns in the eighteenth century was known not as an empire but as the Austrian Monarchy. The empire and the monarchy had distinct bureaucracies, though both were normally based in Vienna.[3]

There were two fundamental differences between the two entities. First, the emperor was not in the ordinary sense sovereign: he cannot be said to have ruled any significant part of the empire. The emperor's main function was to try to preserve a degree of uniformity in law and custom across the literally hundreds of political units into which Germany was divided, and to try to defend the interests of the smaller units—cities and monasteries for example—against the bullying of the great states. The emperor, his law courts, and his bureaucracy worked to settle disputes about such matters as the boundaries, inheritance, and religious position of these units, and to facilitate or control trade, travel, and publishing within the empire as a whole. However, the larger political units within the empire, especially the Austrian duchies and the states of those rulers who were electors to the office of emperor, had won exemption from imperial interference in most of their internal affairs. The most tangible benefit that the ruler of the Austrian Monarchy derived from also being emperor was that he thus became entitled to recruit soldiers throughout Germany and to call his army "imperial and royal." On rare occasions, as in 1756, the emperor was actually empowered by the empire to raise and lead an army to defend it.[4]

Second, it was a crucial difference between the two polities, empire and monarchy, whereas the rule of most of the numerous constituent parts of the Austrian Monarchy was *hereditary*, the Holy Roman Emperor had to be *elected* by the nine princely Electors—and had also to be male. Maria Theresa was known as empress after 1745, but that was simply because her husband had been elected emperor. In this context *she* was *his* consort.[5]

Francis's progress from his relatively modest origins to marriage with the heiress to the Austrian Monarchy, and then to the glory of the imperial throne, was a very complicated story, and all its stages were significant not only in his advancement but also in forming his outlook. In the early part of the story Charles VI (1711–40), who was both the emperor and the ruler of the Austrian Monarchy, was the prime mover. He had no sons or any close male relatives, only daughters and nieces. But in many (though by no means all) of the kingdoms, duchies, counties, and so on that made up the monarchy, women had hitherto been excluded from the succession. So Charles put together in 1713 a document tiresomely known as the Pragmatic Sanction, in which it was declared, first, that the lands of the monarchy should be indivisible, and, second, that his daughter Maria Theresa—and, failing her, his younger daughter Maria Anna—should succeed him as their sovereign. He then set about securing the agreement to these terms of all major foreign powers and of all his provinces. On paper he had more or less achieved this aim by the time he died in 1740, though Bavaria stood out: its ruler was married to a daughter of Charles's elder brother, emperor Joseph I (1705–11), and hence a princess who arguably had a better claim than Maria Theresa to succeed as ruler of the monarchy.[6]

Charles, however, could certainly not bequeath the rule of the elective empire. Still, he considered it natural and also advantageous to Austria that, as had been the case for 300 years, the sovereign of Austria should be elected emperor; and, since women did not qualify, he thought that a suitable husband for Maria Theresa should be found who could reasonably be put forward as emperor instead. There were few obvious candidates, but one was the duke of Lorraine. His duchy was an outer bulwark of the Holy Roman Empire. Its ruling dynasty had supplied a number of generals to the Austrian Habsburgs, especially in their wars against the Turks, but also against the French; and several princes of Lorraine had been brought up and educated in Vienna. At first Charles naturally fixed on Francis's elder brother, but he died in 1723 and so Francis became the heir to the duchy. He was soon invited by Charles to Vienna, where he stayed for eight years, being educated (at least after a fashion) and getting to know the imperial family, especially Maria Theresa. Charles treated him like a son—they were in fact distant cousins—and the prospective bride and groom got on well together. But in 1723 Francis was fifteen and Maria Theresa only six.[7]

The next twist in the story was that Francis's father died suddenly in 1729, and so Francis succeeded as duke of Lorraine at the age of 21. But he did not leave Vienna to assume the rule of his duchy for nearly a year after his accession, during which time his mother acted as his regent. When he did get to Lorraine, though, he proved rather effective, giving the first example of what became his trademark skill, financial sense. His father had lavished money on his mistress and built a huge palace at Lunéville. According to Voltaire, you could go from Versailles to Lunéville without realizing you had moved.[8] Francis found ways of rescuing and stabilizing the duchy's finances. While based in Lorraine, he got to know Louis XV of France when doing homage to him for his second duchy of Bar.[9] In 1731 he embarked on a lengthy tour that took in the Dutch Republic, Austria's Belgian provinces, Britain, and Germany. He met and impressed George

II, he stayed with Walpole and went to Newmarket. In Germany he was able to talk with the future Frederick the Great, temporarily released from prison for the occasion by his tyrannical father. Incidentally, Francis became the first royal prince to be inducted as a Freemason.[10]

Returning to Austria in 1732, he was made by the emperor a Knight of the Golden Fleece and viceroy or Statthalter in Hungary. He had to reside in the Hungarian capital, Pressburg, or Pozsony, and chair the country's chief council of government. This post carried a decent salary with it, and he took the opportunity to buy the first two properties in what was to become a vast portfolio. And he exploited them in original and characteristic ways. In Holics he established a manufacture of majolica, and in Sassin a cotton factory, believed to be the very first operations of their kind in Hungary.[11]

Charles VI did not finally commit himself to the marriage of Francis and Maria Theresa until 1735, and even then the duke was made to submit to a last-minute condition. Austria had become involved in the War of the Polish Succession from 1733, in which its armies performed particularly badly. In order to extricate himself, Charles had to agree to a peace under which the duchy of Lorraine was assigned to the failed candidate for the Polish throne—as a first stage on its way to becoming, at last, part of France. So, before Charles allowed the marriage to go forward, he had to get Francis to agree to surrender his right to rule his native duchy. This Francis did, but with extreme reluctance.[12] The deal led to a considerable exodus of officials and intellectuals from Lorraine, many of whom Francis later employed or helped. The most important was his younger brother Charles, who was regarded by the emperor as a potential ruler of a province, commander of an army and husband of his younger daughter—all of which plans came to fruition. In 1744 Charles was made viceroy of the Austrian Netherlands, which included the monarchy's richest provinces. He held the office until his death in 1780 and played a role in promoting some of Maria Theresa's reforms—and fending off some of Joseph II's.[13] The wider group of exiled Lorrainers was to form an important element in Austrian society, contributing to its Frenchification under Maria Theresa and to its scientific and artistic development.[14]

Francis as Grand-Duke of Tuscany, 1737–65

As compensation for the loss of Lorraine, Francis was awarded the grand-duchy of Tuscany to rule, but he was not to get possession of it until the last male of the Medici line, its current grand-duke, died. In this as in other dynastic matters, Francis was lucky. The last Medici died little more than a year after Francis's marriage, and so in 1737 he became grand-duke of Tuscany and his wife grand-duchess, as his consort.[15]

In the winter of 1739–40, when her father still appeared to be in good health, Francis and his wife paid a ceremonial visit to Florence as grand-duke and grand-duchess. Some suggested that this was "a kind of exile," imposed because Charles was displeased at Francis's attitudes and military performance; and Hungarians were said to feel the same. But the visit was a success, though the winter travel was difficult, especially for Maria Theresa, who was pregnant. On the pompous commemorative arch that was erected in Florence to mark the occasion, Francis is described, rather optimistically, as "Francis III, duke of Lorraine and Bar, and grand duke of Etruria, king of Jerusalem, pious, famous, merciful, promoter and enhancer of the noble arts."[16]

Neither Francis nor Maria Theresa ever visited Tuscany again. It had been laid down by treaty that the grand duchy must remain independent of the Austrian Monarchy, and it was genuinely Francis who ruled it. One of the ministers he put in charge, marquis Botta-Adorno, declared that "the grand duke of Tuscany is more despotic than the Grand Turk at Constantinople."[17] Francis succeeded in partially reforming the duchy's hopelessly outdated tax system; and, since he kept Tuscany neutral during all the wars of Maria Theresa's reign, he built up a substantial surplus, including a considerable personal fortune. When he died, leaving nearly all his property to his eldest son and successor as emperor, Joseph II, most of this fortune, together with the considerable sums he had amassed from his properties and other sources, ended up in the monarchy's coffers. The total was perhaps 31 million florins. Part of it Maria Theresa and Joseph agreed to use to create a family fund of eight million florins, which formed the basis of the private wealth of the Habsburg-Lorraine dynasty thereafter.[18]

In case that result makes it seem as though Francis ripped off the Tuscans for Vienna's benefit, what he did during the terrible Italian famine of 1764 should be recorded. Botta-Adorno proposed to him to deal with the situation by various new controls and exactions. Francis replied:

> We do not wish to hear argumentation, we do not seek to impose [new] taxes…we desire all our funds to be made available to relieve our subjects, and grain to be purchased regardless of expense…Finally we wish these sentiments of ours to be known to all our very faithful subjects.

It became commonplace that these orders "had made Tuscany flourish while [the rest of] Italy was impoverished." Only Francis's prudent management could have made possible this massive expenditure by the Tuscan state.[19] This episode surely shows that Francis was a capable ruler in his own right, especially where economic issues were concerned. It could be questioned whether this was *Enlightened* Absolutism, but it was indubitably *Benevolent* Absolutism.

That Francis had run this show almost without reference to his wife is confirmed by two remarks that she made in letters to Botta-Adorno. In 1763 she wrote to him: "Although I am not at all involved in the arrangements that are being made in Tuscany, I could not conceal from you my desire to be informed about them from time to time." A little later, after

Francis's death and hence when his son (Peter) Leopold had become the grand-duke, she wrote to Botta: "I must express to you my astonishment that at this moment we are better informed about America than we are about Tuscany."[20]

One reason why she was ignorant of Tuscan affairs was that Francis conducted them from a house (or palace) that he had bought for himself in the Wallnerstrasse in central Vienna, where he worked and amused himself, surrounded by Lorrainers, especially some who had knowledge of alchemy, astronomy, and zoology, in all of which fields he took an informed interest and made significant collections. If he practised freemasonry anywhere, which is uncertain, it must have been there.[21]

Francis as Co-Regent of the Austrian Monarchy, to 1745

Now for Francis's specific role as consort to his wife as ruler of the monarchy, after she succeeded her father in this capacity, by inheritance, under the terms of the Pragmatic Sanction, in October 1740. Francis became the very prince of consorts. By 1743 he had become consort to the queen of Hungary and the queen of Bohemia—although, as we shall see, in both these cases she had actually been crowned "king"—and to the queen of Croatia, to the queen of Dalmatia, to the queen of Slavonia, to the ruling archduchess of several Austrian duchies, to the great princess of Transylvania, to the duchess of Milan and of Mantua, and to the holder of various titles under which she governed the greater part of what are now Belgium and Luxemburg—and that is not a complete list of Maria Theresa's titles and territories.[22] I must emphasise that all these titles, unlike that of Holy Roman Emperor, conveyed real sovereignty. On the other hand, these lands had mostly not been governed despotically, or as one, or as "a Totum," which Charles VI had been urged to aim at.[23]

What happened immediately after Maria Theresa succeeded her father is of crucial importance. By this time, as I've explained, Francis had been playing a major role in the government of Hungary for eight years; he had governed Tuscany for three years; he had got to know the rulers of France, Britain, and Prussia and had travelled extensively; he had taken part in several military campaigns and commanded armies; and he had become in effect the deputy chairman of the Privy Conference on foreign affairs in Vienna, officiating when the emperor himself was not present. Maria Theresa, on the other hand, was still totally without any such experience. She was also four months pregnant with her fourth child. The eldest of her three daughters had recently died; the second, though lively and intelligent, had some deformity that was to preclude her being offered as a bride; and the third was nine months old and may well have been ailing already since she died two months later. The Pragmatic Sanction declared that Maria Theresa was to inherit the lands, but it did not specify how they were to be ruled. Apparently, on the day Charles VI died, his daughter was debarred from seeing him on health grounds because she was pregnant, while Francis spent two hours with him. It certainly looks as though Charles expected Francis, rather than Maria Theresa, to be his effective successor as ruler of the monarchy.[24]

On the evening of the day Charles died, officials came to see her to find out whether she would confirm their appointments. She agreed. This was unsurprising. But what she did on the following day seems simply astonishing. The Privy Conference met then to deal with the consequences of Charles's sudden death. Maria Theresa turned up with her husband, and it was she who now took the chair. The historiography does not seem to find this action as remarkable as it seems to me. So far as we know, she had never been in the slightest degree involved in anything of the kind before.[25] No doubt she believed that she had been given by God the duty to rule the monarchy and, despite some misgivings, was determined to do the job. But this was an extraordinary assertion of her unparalleled position.

There were, however, particular reasons why she and others may have thought that she needed to preside over this and subsequent meetings. She intended to make Francis her co-regent, an idea put forward by some of her ministers—something that he could hardly have proposed himself. She sought by this means to enable her husband to act for her during her lifetime as "co-regent and co-administrator" whenever she wished— though not otherwise, because it was imperative that she should not formally abandon the sovereignty accorded to her by the Pragmatic Sanction. She also wanted him to be able to act as regent if she died before him and before her direct heir attained the age of majority. She certainly needed a stand-in during her pregnancy, and she must have expected that there would be more pregnancies to come. In fact she was to have altogether 16 children with Francis. But in 1740, with only a sister and two sickly baby girls to ensure the succession, some arrangement had to be made in case she died young.[26]

There was an additional, equally powerful reason for establishing the co-regency that she and some of her advisers wanted, to procure for Francis election as emperor in succession to her father. They rightly believed that the connection was advantageous to the monarchy and that the election as emperor of another prince coming from a different state would be highly damaging. But one of the acknowledged qualifications to be emperor was to be in a position to defend his subjects from attack, especially from the Turks. Hence he had to have an army at his disposal. He also had to maintain an imperial court. As a mere consort Francis would seem unable to do these things, while as co-regent of the monarchy it was plausible to say that he could. In fact, since Tuscany was not part of the empire, he would otherwise have had no legal authority in any part of the empire or monarchy—except in two small territories that he possessed as a remnant of his Lorraine inheritance, namely, the duchy of Teschen on the border of Silesia and the county of Falkenstein close to Lorraine. So, right from the start of her reign, as in the calculations of Charles VI before her marriage, the desire to obtain the imperial title for Austria both greatly influenced her policy and made Francis's position crucial.[27]

Both she and Francis, but especially she, went in for writing documents explaining and justifying themselves, for their successors and children or for posterity. The most important of these pieces is what is known as her "Political Testament," written probably in 1749.[28] At her accession, she declared in this document, she found herself "without money, without credit, without army, without experience and knowledge of my own, and finally without any advice." The fact was that her father, partly because he had been concentrating on securing the succession for his daughter by treaties, had neglected other aspects of policy and, above all, the army. During the 1730s roughly a third of Charles's territory had been lost through war. When his daughter succeeded, other powers knew how relatively weak her position and Austria's army were. Furthermore, King Frederick II of Prussia and the other electors to the office of Emperor knew that Austria would try hard to obtain that position for Francis. Even if they failed to prevent his election, the procedure would give them an opportunity to demand concessions from the monarchy in return for their support or acquiescence.[29]

A month after the death of her father, Frederick invaded her province of Silesia, to part of which he produced dubious historical claims. Of all the central provinces of the monarchy this was the richest. Maria Theresa's elderly and princely ministers advised concessions. But she held out against them, giving in her Political Testament the chief credit for supporting her to the rather younger and much less aristocratic minister Baron Bartenstein.[30] Maria Theresa was determined, if she could, to retain her whole inheritance.

In her desperate situation, however, some of her provinces seized the chance to assert themselves. Since in many of them law and custom required that she be either crowned or formally inducted, their representatives sought to extract new conditions from her, most conspicuously in the case of Hungary. In Bohemia the position was even worse: there was no possibility of her being crowned there at first because Charles Albert of Bavaria, who himself aimed to become Emperor and supported his wife's claim to Maria Theresa's thrones, seized the opportunity to invade the kingdom and was elected and crowned king there. Some of the monarchy's other provinces made serious difficulties about agreeing to the co-regency, but the great majority had done so by the end of 1741. It was one of Maria Theresa's greatest achievements to win Hungarian support by a brilliant performance at her coronation in Pressburg in that year—where she was crowned king, not queen—and again when she appeared at the Diet with her newly born baby heir Joseph in her arms. Francis's experience as governor of the country had made him more sympathetic to it than most of Vienna's appointees had been, and his approach evidently influenced his wife's attitude.

We have only a limited knowledge of Francis's role as co-regent during her reign because his written contributions to the debates in the central councils have mostly disappeared. It is believed that after his death, Maria Theresa, for unknown reasons, had his papers removed from the monarchy's central archives and destroyed.[31] The documents relating to Tuscany are extant because they were kept in the Wallnerstrasse house. But one significant document of Francis's that concerns war and foreign policy in 1742 has survived—because it too was kept in that house. France had joined in the War of the Austrian Succession from 1740 onward in order to diminish the power of her long-standing rival, Austria. She was best placed to do so in the southern Netherlands, much of which were to be occupied by French troops in the mid-forties. In this document Francis suggests that Austria should agree to Frederick's demand that she should cede him a portion of Silesia, after which Frederick claimed to be willing to join a coalition against France. In every paper of Francis's the spelling almost defies belief and comprehension, but the substance is well-argued and well-informed.[32] This document bears out the view that, though Maria Theresa saw Prussia as the chief enemy, Francis still had the Lorrainer's perspective in which France was the bugbear. He always retained this stance: he was to disagree with Kaunitz's successful advocacy of a French alliance in the mid-fifties.[33]

After 1742 the war in Central Europe turned in Maria Theresa's favour and Charles Albert was chased out of Bohemia, so that in the following year she could be crowned king in Prague in his stead.[34] But earlier, at the summit of his military success, Charles Albert of Bavaria had been elected emperor and had been crowned as Charles VII in Frankfurt early in 1742. This was a severe blow to Austria, and it had long-lasting effects. It meant that the administration of the empire and that of the monarchy had to be strictly separated, which they had not previously been: the imperial bureaucracy and its archives left Vienna. But Charles Albert's position was weak and steadily deteriorated: Bavaria's resources did not compare with the monarchy's as a foundation for imperial rule. When he died unexpectedly, early in 1745, there was no serious opposition to the election of Francis Stephen to succeed him. This was a triumph for Maria Theresa. But, intriguingly, she would not agree to be crowned with her husband. She declared variously that she was pregnant, that she had not the necessary money and that she did not choose to change sex in her coronations. She did, though, attend the coronation ceremony, where she was much amused by the antique robes and observances.[35]

One of Francis's more surprising attitudes, expressed in a long paper he wrote called *The Hermit in the World*, was a Jansenist, almost Protestant concern with his personal religious beliefs and behaviour, distancing himself from the grandeur and pageantry of official Roman Catholicism, so oppressive at the Court of Vienna. He attended many more of the customary Church services than his wife, who regularly made excuses on grounds of health or pregnancy. The limited reduction during her reign in the number of mandatory royal appearances at church ceremonies is attributed to his influence, and his attitude is assumed to have encouraged his children,

Joseph II and Leopold II, to make their much more radical reforms of similar tendency in Austria and Tuscany.[36]

Francis as Emperor

Francis's election as emperor meant that Maria Theresa's court was turned upside down. Now her husband counted as the senior figure, the one to whom all visitors had to pay their respects first. This fact, the relative success of her armies in the later stages of the War of the Austrian Succession, and the steady increase in the number of her children, led her and the emperor to plan and execute considerable changes to their summer palace of Schönbrunn outside the city. The Hofburg in central Vienna remained the seat of their government and their winter residence. They abandoned the Favorita palace that Charles VI had preferred to Schönbrunn. When not engaged in ceremonial duties, they liked to live as simply as possible. They even devised a mechanical table that was intended to enable them to receive and eat their family meals without servants present, though this experiment was short-lived. A theatre was opened in the grounds in 1747. Francis was particularly interested in creating a menagerie or zoo in the park, which was designed by one of his Lorrainer companions, Nicholas Jadot, and was ready to be visited by 1752. The imperial family would take breakfast there, and Francis would show it off to his guests.[37]

What he achieved as emperor was considerable. His election caused the imperial archives and bureaucracy to return to Vienna. He succeeded in reviving the influence of the imperial law courts, in having imperial armies raised to fight against Prussia, and in settling some of the numerous outstanding disputes in German states between Protestant subjects and Catholic rulers, and vice versa. Jo Whaley, in his just published monumental study of the Holy Roman Empire, reckons that Francis restored the status of the empire to the point that it was again respected as the focus of German feeling and aspirations. In 1764 he achieved the unusual feat of procuring the election of his eldest son Joseph as king of the Romans, which qualified him to succeed as emperor without an interregnum. The best justification of Francis's reign—and perhaps the best single description of the empire in this period—was written by his youngest son, Max Franz, Elector-Archbishop of Cologne, when he contrasted in 1790 the provocative conduct of Joseph II as emperor after 1765 with that of their father:

> Germany was useful to Francis I, useless and even dangerous to Joseph II … [Francis] easy, polite, affable, reigned over all hearts. The empress, gracious and generous, supported him marvellously. The princes of the Empire were attracted to Vienna, were amused, flattered, manipulated, and were full of it when they got back home. The ecclesiastical princes were treated with the greatest consideration, and the canons found ample satisfaction for their interests and ambition in the chapters and bishoprics of the hereditary

lands, in the abbeys of Hungary, in the invariably effective recommendations made by the Imperial Court to the Pope. Not even the smallest election took place without the influence of the Imperial Court preponderating, and its creatures, finding themselves looked after, remained devoted to the House of Austria. The lesser princes and counts were honoured with places in the army... [or] the Civil Service. The Theresianum and the Savoy College [educational establishments in Vienna] attracted many noblemen from the Empire who then dispersed to all parts of Germany, regarding Vienna as their second home, imbued with its principles and keeping up their connexions there. It was by all these means that Francis I caused the Empire to act [on Austria's behalf] in the Seven Years War even against its own interests.[38]

This was a rather too rosy account, too ecclesiastically focused, but it is that of an eye-witness of the work of both emperors and of a player in imperial politics as archbishop-elector of Cologne after 1784. It is substantially borne out by the work of Whaley and other scholars who have recently rehabilitated the role of the empire in this period. Moreover, it gives the lie to Ranke's mot: "In reality Maria Theresa was the emperor."[39] It was in 1761 that Voltaire published his immortal joke, dismissing the imperial institution as "neither Holy, Roman, nor an Empire."[40] Of course he was right on all three counts. But under Francis it was at least useful, pan-German, and a working federation.

Francis as Co-Regent after 1745

What Francis contributed to his wife's government as co-regent was equally important. The first time she mentioned him in her Political Testament was as the person who recommended to her count Haugwitz, the minister who masterminded the great administrative and financial reform of 1749. The story has been brilliantly told by Peter Dickson in his *Finance and Government under Maria Theresa*.[41] Essentially with a view to reconquering Silesia, but also for general security, she needed a standing army, and so her provinces had to be persuaded to provide permanent funds to maintain such a body. The number of troops eventually agreed on by the central lands was 108,000 regulars. Haugwitz, like Bartenstein a convert from Protestantism born outside her territories, first came to Francis's notice as an official in his duchy of Teschen. He then moved to the remnant of Silesia still retained by Austria. He showed a grasp of the needs of the central government which few provincial bigwigs shared. Promoted to take charge of the operation for all the Austrian hereditary lands, Haugwitz, strongly backed by emperor and empress, put through his reform against tremendous opposition both central and local. The independence of the provincial Estates was greatly reduced, the government's debt diminished, and the role of the Vienna bank enhanced. It is plain that Francis was involved throughout. This was his single most important contribution to the work of Maria Theresa. It did not in the event lead to the recovery of Silesia, but it certainly amounted to a modernization and centralization of the monarchy's government. It placed the state's finances on a footing much more secure than previously and more than what most states boasted at the time.[42] As shown earlier, Francis was responsible too for providing in his will a vast windfall to the Austrian Monarchy and the dynasty of Habsburg-Lorraine, chiefly derived from Tuscany. He also achieved a famous reform of the coinage, establishing the Austrian thaler as a reliable currency, used in much of Germany and later in the Middle East.[43]

The state of the archives does not allow us many glimpses into the personal or governmental relationship between Francis and Maria Theresa. In 1757, however, one of her most trusted and judicious ministers, count Khevenhüller-Metsch, wrote in his diary:

> We have two masters, the Emperor and the Empress. Both wish to rule; and, although the Emperor directs military matters, and up to a point the finances—or at least in both these branches of government nothing of importance is lightly undertaken without his knowledge and involvement—he is too easy-going to be able to cope with such a great task. The Empress, for her part, is too fiery in her opposition, cannot bear delay and so sticks to no system.[44]

Maria Theresa was in thrall to Kaunitz' intelligence, flattery, and eloquence.

In 1760, after four years of war, with still no recovery of Silesia, the state of the finances and the army were again spoken of in desperate terms. Kaunitz now "entered domestic politics" and proposed the establishment of a new central government agency, the Staatsrat or Council of State, charged with looking at ways in which the monarchy could be reformed, especially with a view to making it more effective in war.[45] It is obvious that the empress was going to have to tread warily with her husband over this proposal. She was relieved that, when Francis first got to hear of it, he approved: "the ice is broken," she wrote to a confidant.[46] In November 1762, it became a question whether the bankrupt monarchy should seek to make peace now that her ally, Russia, had changed sides. When the empress learned that the emperor welcomed the idea, she wrote to Kaunitz: "We must take advantage of the favourable views of the master, which can still change, but today he seems to desire the end, as I do, and my son too."[47] The war was soon brought to an end.

Not only had the political relationship between husband and wife become less close, but their personal rapport was damaged by the emperor's sexual liaisons. The imperial couple's last child, Max Franz, had been born in 1756, and by the end of the decade gossip had it that Princess Maria Auersperg was Francis's mistress. The attitudes of emperor and empress to extramarital affairs mirrored those of the society around them. Just before his death Francis gave written advice to his son Leopold on behaviour toward the wife he was about to marry. He spoke warmly of the happiness of his marriage, but he said nothing at all about faithfulness, though he repeatedly recommended treating a wife with "douceur." When in 1766 the empress in her turn gave advice to her daughter Marie Christine on how to behave toward the husband she was about to marry, Prince Albert of Saxe-Teschen, she stressed the benefits that flowed from a happy union, but urged Marie Christine to allow him maximum freedom and never to show suspicion of his relationships with other women.[48]

It is well-known that, when Maria Theresa encountered Princess Auersperg after Francis's death, the empress commiserated with the mistress on their joint loss. Less well-known is the very circumstantial account of the affair in the memoirs of the English diplomat and traveller, (Sir Nathaniel) William Wraxall, which I quote at some length because it has been ignored by the emperor's biographers. The author during his long spell in Vienna had access to many notable ministers and courtiers who had personal knowledge of these matters. He wrote:

> In [the princess's] society, and that of a select company of both sexes, [Francis] used to pass many of his evenings. A supper of ten or twelve covers was provided, where the Princess presided, and from which all form or etiquette were banished. In public, whether at the theatre, or elsewhere, Francis observed towards the empress every mark of deference and attention; but, when she was not present at the performance, he always repaired to the princess's box. At the opera he usually stood behind her, concealed from view; and the box was locked ... [But] a cough, to which he was subject, generally betrayed his retreat, and divulged his secret to the world.
>
> It is a fact, that on the evening before his dissolution [in Innsbruck], which was sudden and unexpected, he had presented [the princess] an order on his treasurer, for no less a sum than two hundred thousand florins, or near twenty thousand pounds... In a secret council, held after Francis's death, it was debated whether a pecuniary donation of such a nature, to so great an amount, should or ought to be fulfilled. More than one voice declared against it; but Maria Theresa, superior to every consideration except what she thought her own and her husband's honour demanded, issued orders punctually to discharge this sum.[49]

It was in October 1762, that Mozart, at the age of six, was taken, at the court's invitation, to visit the imperial family at Schönbrunn. The boy's father, Leopold, widely known as the author of the first German primer on violin playing, reported:

> Their Majesties received us with such extraordinary graciousness that, when I shall tell people of it, they will swear I have made it up... Woferl jumped up on the empress's lap, put his arms round her neck and kissed her

heartily. In short, we were there from three to six o'clock and the Emperor himself came out of the next room and made me go in there to hear the Infanta [Joseph's wife] play the violin…On the 15th the Empress sent us by the Privy Paymaster, who drove up to our house in state, two dresses, one for the boy and one for the girl.

The boy's dress had been made for archduke Max Franz, the girl's for an archduchess. "Woferl" got ill but, when he recovered, the family was invited to come and observe a state dinner, and the empress called out to Mozart's father asking how the boy was.[50]

These reports bring out that in private the imperial family genuinely led something like a bourgeois life. But this encounter is significant for other reasons too. Notoriously, music was immensely important to the Austrian Court and to Viennese society. All the royal family were musicians of one kind or another. Maria Theresa was a good singer, Joseph played cello and keyboard, his brother Leopold played keyboard, and so on. We do not know what instrument Francis played, but he had certainly had music lessons, had some appreciation of the art, and attended countless opera performances.[51] Nearly every year some special entertainment, usually an opera, was mounted both for his birthday and his nameday, so long as they did not fall on a Friday. The entertainment for his nameday on October 5, 1762 was a completely new piece, none other than the opera that was and is taken to mark a musical revolution, Gluck's *Orfeo ed Euridice.* Mozart's father saw it twice; on the second occasion the children too heard it from a box they were lent. It must have been understood by all, from emperor and empress downward, that this was something new, different, and remarkable, with simpler music and more human characters than was usual, especially in a work on a classical theme.[52]

The piece made an astonishing impact on the imperial family. On the day after the first performance, Joseph's clever and characterful wife wrote to her sister-in-law, Archduchess Marie Christine:

I was between the archduke [Joseph] and my brother[-in-law] Leopold. I confess to you I should not have been able to bear anyone else there. For I should have thought all the time: what has become of my dear Eurydice? And I should have wept as much as Orpheus at the very idea that you are mortal.[53]

Maria Theresa apparently attended the extraordinary number of 14 performances of the opera in this first run, and she was particularly anxious to hear what is still its best-known aria, *Che farò senz'Euridice* ? It is tempting to speculate whether the choice of libretto and the empress's fondness for it had anything to do with the fact that, as Joseph's sharp young wife had grasped, the emperor was in thrall to princess Auersperg. But surely none of those involved could have failed to relate the feelings so powerfully expressed in the opera to their current situation.[54]

Three years later, on August 18, 1765, while attending the wedding ceremonies of his son Leopold in Innsbruck, the emperor collapsed and died, without uttering a word. He had had a massive stroke. Observers had been aware that he had put on a lot of weight—so much that embalming his body and transporting it to Vienna for burial presented major problems. But on August 31, he was buried in the Capuchins' vault in the capital under the grandiose double canopy prepared for his wife and himself in the 1750s.[55]

What can be said of him in summary? His career owed almost everything to Charles VI's decision to propose him as the husband of Maria Theresa. He proved to be amiable and unpretentious, prudent, responsible, open-minded, and tolerant, conducting himself with sense and dignity in a unique and difficult position. He revealed a special talent as a manager of money, a rare skill among monarchs. While it was she who made him co-regent of a great state and enabled him to become emperor, his collaboration and his financial expertise were important in making possible her achievements as ruler of the Austrian Monarchy. His and his wife's fecundity ensured that the succession to the Austrian throne was never again in danger from a want of male heirs. There is a serious case that, if his foreign policy had been followed rather than Kaunitz's, it would have served the monarchy better.[56] Probably the most important of his genuinely personal achievements was this: after the disastrous reign of Charles VI, he reinvigorated the empire. But it can be affirmed—and this is no small claim—that he left all his four sovereignties, Lorraine, Tuscany, the Austrian Monarchy, and the Holy Roman Empire, in better shape than he found them.

Notes

1. The modern published lives of Emperor Francis Stephen are: F. Hennings, *Und sitzet zur linken Hand* (Vienna, 1961); and R. Zedinger, *Franz Stephan von Lothringen, 1708–1765* (Vienna, 2008) [henceforth Zedinger]. vol. 23 of the *Jahrbuch der österreichischen Gesellschaft zur Erforschung des 18. Jhdts* 23 (2008), entitled *Franz Stephan von Lothringen und sein Kreis*, eds. R. Zedinger and W. Schmale, is a most useful collection. For other recent reappraisals of Francis's activity as emperor see K. O. von Aretin, *Das alte Reich 1648–1806*, vol. III (Stuttgart, 1997), pp. 19–111, and J. Whaley, *Germany and the Holy Roman Empire* (2 vols., Oxford, 2011), vol. II, esp. sections III and IV, and pp. 347–92. I owe particular thanks to my wife Sally, Prof. T. C. W. Blanning, Prof. P. G. M. Dickson, Prof. R. J. W. Evans, Dr M. Hochedlinger, Prof. Grete Klingenstein, and Prof. H. M. Scott for help, guidance, and stimulus over many years.
2. On C18 Lorraine see Zedinger and J. Charles-Gaffiot, *Lunéville, Fastes du Versailles lorrain* (Paris, 2003). On Tuscany Zedinger, pp. 111–78. Of books in English on Tuscany E. Cochrane, *Florence in the Forgotten Centuries* (Chicago, 1973) shows little interest in Francis's rule; and R. Burr Litchfield, *Emergence of a Bureaucracy: The Florentine Patricians, 1530–1790* (Princeton, 1986) has too narrow a focus to deal properly with Francis.

3. Nothing is more helpful to the understanding of the relationship between Monarchy and Empire than a good historical atlas, esp. a German one like Putzger's. But there are good maps in my *Joseph II, vol. I, In the Shadow of Maria Theresa* (Cambridge, 1987) and in T. C. W. Blanning, *The Pursuit of Glory: Europe, 1648–1815* (London, 2007), which also contains an admirable short account of the Empire, pp. 275–85. The best survey of the Austrian Monarchy in the eighteenth century which is available in English—and probably the best in any language—is M. Hochedlinger, *Austria's Wars of Emergence: War, State and Society in the Habsburg Monarchy, 1683–1797* (London, 2003).

4. See the works on the Empire cited in n. 1, para.2 above. On German armies, and especially imperial armies, see Peter H. Wilson, *German Armies: War and German Politics, 1648–1806* (London, 1998).

5. See on imperial elections, esp. that of 1745, Aretin, *Das alte Reich*, vol. III, esp. pp. 19–28, and more generally, Whaley's book.

6. This story is told in every general work on the period. A particularly good account is to be found in H. L. Mikoletzky, *Oesterreich. Das grosse 18. Jahrhundert* (Vienna, 1967), pp. 124–50. The essence of the Pragmatic Sanction is printed in C. A. Macartney, *The Habsburg and Hohenzollern Dynasties* (London, 1970), pp. 88–91. See in English my *Joseph II*, vol. I, pp. 22–4; and Whaley, *Germany and the Empire*, vol. II, esp. pp. 158–62.

7. On Francis's early life Zedinger, esp. pp. 31–8; and on his time in Vienna ibid. pp. 38–44. As for his education, even by the standards of the period his spelling and punctuation were crazy. Whether he was dyslexic, or had been taught languages almost entirely orally, seems to be unknown. Here is an example of his French, from a letter he wrote in 1745 to Maria Theresa urging her to be crowned with him in Frankfurt: "je vous le repete ille me semble que vous deverie ausi vous faire couronne, care san cela fera hici un tres moues efet, tout le monde contan la desut et cela naret pas 4 joure de plus et et presque nesesere hi ettan presente." [quoted by A. von Arneth, *Geschichte Maria Theresias* [*GMT*] (10 vols., Vienna, 1863–79), vol. III]. In some passages Francis fuses or divides words. A short sample of his German will be found in n. 32.

8. Charles-Gaffiot, *Lunéville*, p. 9 and passim.

9. On Francis' visit to Lorraine as duke, Zedinger, pp. 47–54; on the homage to Louis XV ibid. pp. 50–2.

10. On the European tour Zedinger, pp. 54–61.

11. See H. L. Mikoletzky, "Holics und Sassin, die beiden Mustergüter des Kaisers Franz I. Stephan," *Mitteilungen des österreichsichen Staatsarchivs* (*MÖSA*) 14 (1961), pp. 190–212; S. Serfözö, "Schloss Holitsch und die Wallfahrtskirche Sassin zur Zeit Franz Stephans," in *Franz Stephan von Lothringen und sein Kreis* [see n. 1 above].

12. Hennings, *Und sitzet zur linken Hand*, pp. 174–87; Zedinger, pp. 61–7.

13. On Charles of Lorraine see the splendid Europalia exhibition catalogue *Charles-Alexandre de Lorraine* (2 vols., 1987); Zedinger, pp. 70–5.

14. There is much material on the influence in Austria of the Lorrainers in *Franz Stephan von Lothringen und sein Kreis* [see n. 1 above].

15. Zedinger's two chapters on Tuscany in her *Franz Stephan*, pp. 117–78, are particularly valuable.

16. See G. Pansini, "Franz Stephan von Lothringen und die Reform des Staates des Medici, 1737–1765," in W. Koschatzky (ed.), *Maria Theresia und ihrer Zeit* (Vienna, 2nd edn., 1980), pp. 123–9.

17. Botta-Adorno, quoted in Botta to Pfütschner, April 19, 1760: "Votre Excellence prétend que le grand-duc de Toscane est plus despotique que n'est le grand turc à Constantinople." (J. C. Waquet, "La nomina del marchese Botta-Adorno a capo del governo toscano (1757) e la posizione istituzionale del Granducato nei confronti della monarchia absburgica," in C. Mozzarelli e G. Olmi, *Il Trentino nel Settecento fra Sacro Romano Impero e antichi stati italiani* (Bologna, 1985), p. 276.

18. See my *Joseph II* (2 vols., Cambridge, 1987, 2009), vol. I, pp. 149–53; P. G. M. Dickson, *Finance and Government under Maria Theresa* (2 vols., Oxford, 1987), vol. II, pp. 52–4, 358–9. Prof. Dickson generously gave me a copy of this fundamental pioneering work. On the Habsburg family fortune H. L. Mikoletzky, *Kaiser Franz I. Stephan und der Ursprung des habsburgisch-lothringischen Familienvermögens* (Vienna, 1961).

19. Quoted in F. Venturi, *Settecento riformatore*, vol. V (Turin, 1987), p. 344.

20. Both quotations from Maria Theresa come from the article by Waquet cited in n. 17 above, pp. 274, 282.

21. On the purchase of the Wallnerstrasse house in 1740, explicitly with a view to Tuscan business, see Zedinger, p. 111 and her article in *Franz Stephan und sein Kreis*, pp. 23–40: "Einleitung; Das Palais Wallnerstrasse 3: Kaiserliches Refugium – lothringische Arbeitswelt."

22. A splendid version of her full title is to be found in Koschatzky (ed.), *Maria Theresia und ihre Zeit*, p. 55, but that list includes the dubious queenships of Galicia and Lodomeria acquired by the partition of Poland in 1772. A printed version of her earlier full title can be seen ibid. p. 232.

23. Mikoletzky, *Oesterreich*, p. 143, quotes Prince Eugene urging that the Monarchy be turned into a Totum in a memorandum of 1721. V. L. Tapié, *The Rise and Fall of the Habsburg Monarchy* (London, 1971) gives the date 1726 for this recommendation (p. 164), but calls his whole chapter on the early C18 "The Monarchy as ein Totum."

24. Arneth's full account (*GMT*, vol. I) does not breathe a word of this possibility, but other Powers considered it. On the rather mysterious physical condition of Archduchess Marianne see the references to her in my *Joseph II*.

25. See J. Kallbrunner (ed.), *Kaiserin Maria Theresias Politisches Testament* (Vienna, 1952), p. 29.

26. Zedinger, esp. pp. 82–5. On the co-regency the crucial study is F. Reinöhl, "Die Übertragung der Mitregentschaft durch Maria Theresia an Grossherzog Franz Stephan und Kaiser *Joseph II*," *Mitteilungen des Instituts für österreichische Geschichtsforschung* (*MIÖG*), Erg.Bd. 1929, pp. 650–61. See also my Joseph II, vol. I, ch. 1.

27. In addition to the sources in n. 23 and 24, my *Joseph II*, vol. I, esp. pp. 135–7.

28. The whole document was published by Kallbrunner [see n. 25]. The most significant sections are translated in Macartney, *Habsburg and Hohenzollern Dynasties*, pp. 94–132.

29. The best account of Maria Theresa's campaign to get Francis elected emperor is now Whaley, *Germany and the Holy Roman Empire*, vol. II, pp. 347–56, 366–87.

30. Macartney, *Habsburg and Hohenzollern Dynasties*, pp. 98–101.

31. Zedinger, pp. 17–18.

32. J. Schwedfeger, "Ein Denkschrift des Großherzogs (nachmaligen Kaisers) Franz Stephan…1742," *Archiv für österreichische Geschichte* LVIII (1898), pp. 359–78. See n. 4 above for a sample of Francis's French. Here, from Schwedfeger's article, are a few lines of his German: "das wan der alerhogste Monark Sig mit Seinen glidern wol halt Si inststant Sein uon kain ander Puisance Sich was uor Zuschreiben lasen und ocontrer er in uorschreiben kann."

33. Zedinger, pp. 91–5.

34. See on Bohemian affairs and coronations Tapié, *Rise and Fall*, pp. 180–5.

35. Whaley, *Germany and the Holy Roman Empire*, vol. II, esp. ch. 42.

36. See A. Wandruszka, "Die Religiosität Franz Stephan von Lothringen," *MÖSA* 12 (1959), 17.

37. On the development of Schönbrunn J. Glaser, *Schönbrunner Chronik* (Vienna, 1969) esp. ch. 5 and pp. 40–1, 119–20.

38. Whaley, *Germany and the Holy Roman Empire*, vol. II, esp. ch. 42. The quotation from Max Franz comes from a letter to Leopold II of March 1, 1790, published in W. Lüdtke, "Der Kampf zwischen Österreich und Preußen," *MIÖG* 45 (1931), pp. 70–153. See also the interesting appraisal by C. Gnant, "Franz Stephan von Lothringen als Kaiser," in *Franz Stephan von Lothringen und sein Zeit* [see n. 1 above], pp. 115–29.

39. L. von Ranke, *Die deutschen Mächte und der Fürstenbund* (2 vols., 1871–2), vol. I, p. v.

40. In an edition of that date of the *Essai sur les moeurs*.

41. Dickson, *Finance and government under Maria Theresa*, esp. vol. I, pp. 222–5, 236, 264–6, 341–2 and vol. II, pp. 10–21. See Kallbrunner, *Maria Theresia's Politisches Testament*, p. 53.

42. A convenient and authoritative account of these reforms can be found in Hochedlinger, *Austria's Wars of Emergence*, esp. ch. 13.

43. The reform of the currency is described in the catalogue of a recent exhibition in the National Museum, Prague: *Coins and Medals of the Emperor Francis Stephen of Lorraine* (ed. T. Kleisner and J. Boublik, Prague, 2011). I am most grateful to Dr Kleisner for sending me a copy of this fine catalogue.

44. Khevenhüller-Metsch 7 Schlitter (ed.), *Aus der Zeit Maria Theresias* (8 vols., Vienna, 1907–72), vol. IV, pp. 141–2.

45. F. Walter, "Kaunitz' Eintritt in die innere Politik," *MIÖG* xlvi (1932), pp. 37–79. Extensive recent discussions of Kaunitz's policies are to be found in Hochedlinger's Austria's Wars of Emergence and F. A. J. Szabo, *The Seven Years War in Europe 1756–1763* (Harlow, 2008). See also Blanning, *Pursuit of Glory*, pp. 576–7.

46. Arneth, *GMT*, vol. VI (1875), pp. 495–6.

47. Ibid. pp. 372–3 and 488–9.

48. Francis's memorandum "Sur le mariage" went with "Instruction pour mon fils Leopold," dated January 15, 1765. Both are substantially reproduced, though in German, in A. Wandruszka, *Leopold II* (2 vols., Vienna, 1964–5), vol. I, pp. 81–8. Maria Theresa's instructions to Marie-Christine of April 1766 are in A. Wolf, *Marie-Christine, Erzherzogin von Oesterreich* (2 vols., Vienna, 1863) and, more accessibly, though in German, in W. Koschatzky and S. Krasa, *Herzog Albert von Sachsen-Teschen* (Vienna, 1982), pp. 72–3, and

in French in *Marie Christine van Oosterijk* (*Anciens Pays et Assemblées d'État*, vol. LXXVII (1979)).

49. See Zedinger, pp. 270–2; N. W. Wraxall, *Memoirs of the Courts of Berlin, Dresden, Warsaw, and Vienna in the Years 1777, 1778, and 1779* (3rd ed., 2 vols., 1806), vol. II, pp. 357–75. Wraxall was not in Vienna or Innsbruck in 1765, but he had contacts such as Sir Robert Murray Keith, the British ambassador to Vienna (though not in 1765), and count Hatzfeld, who had worked with the emperor and became president of the Staatsrat in 1771.

50. On the Mozarts' visit to Vienna the numerous letters of Leopold Mozart in E. Anderson (ed.), *The Letters of Mozart and his Family* (3rd ed., London, 1985), pp. 3–15, esp. pp. 6, 8, 11; R. Halliwell, *The Mozart Family* (Oxford, 1998), ch. 3.

51. See, e.g., D. Heartz, *Haydn, Mozart and the Viennese School, 1740–1780* (London, 1995), pp. 80, 85, 121, 134–7, 217. On Francis, D. Brandenburg, "Gluck and Co.: Musik für den Kaiser," in *Franz Stephan und sein Kreis* [see n. 1], pp. 371–81, and the two following lists of works performed for Francis's birthdays and namedays, pp. 383–90.

52. There is a vast literature on the significance and impact of *Orfeo ed Euridice*. See esp. many references in Heartz, *Haydn, Mozart and the Viennese School*; B. A. Brown, *Gluck and the French Theatre in Vienna* (Oxford, 1991); *Letters of Mozart*, pp. 5, 12.

53. Quoted in my *Joseph II*, vol. I, p. 80.

54. Calzabigi to Kaunitz, March 6, 1767, printed on p. 731 of Heartz, *Haydn, Mozart and the Viennese School*, and discussed by Brown, *Gluck and the French Theatre*, p. 374.

55. Zedinger, pp. 289–96. The oversize monument by Moll in the Capuchins' crypt in Vienna is very difficult to photograph satisfactorily as a whole, but Plate XVII in Henning's biography [see n. 1] prints a good detail of the figures of Maria Theresa and Francis.

56. See, e.g., Blanning, *Pursuit of Glory*, pp. 587–8.

CHAPTER 8

Prince Albert: The Creative Consort

Karina Urbach

T hey courted journalists, controlled paintings of themselves, and inspired favourable press articles. They lived a very visible family idyll and propagated the idea of "simplicity, princely thrift, and concern for the common people."[1] The Prussian Crown Princess Vicky and her husband Fritz, were excellent self-publicists. Yet their royal showcasing was a franchise. The methods Vicky employed had been developed by her father Prince Albert. Vicky had been his brightest child and it was certainly not for lack of trying that the Prussian franchise ended badly. The original British version however was an immense success and parts of Prince Albert's presentation are employed by the Royal family to this day.

If one wants to understand how and why the monarchy changed in the nineteenth century, it is therefore essential to understand Albert. Of course monarchs had marketed themselves and their families successfully for centuries. Pomp and Circumstance had usually worked well. But though the pomp was still appreciated, the circumstances had changed. In the nineteenth century the monarchy had lost power and came under pressure to perform more frequently and in a novel way. Prince Albert realised this and as a consequence became a highly creative consort.

The stagecraft in which Albert would excel started with his courting of Victoria. This courtship was sold as a true love story, but primarily it was a well-planned *remake* of the popular marriage between the handsome Leopold of Sachsen-Coburg-Saalfeld and George I V's daughter Princess Charlotte in 1816. For the British people Charlotte had been a national treasure and when she died unexpectedly in childbirth, the public felt cheated. The Coburg family had every reason to share this feeling. They had groomed Leopold as the ideal prince consort in waiting and had lost their prospects overnight. However, they remained determined not to give up their foothold in Britain and commissioned a *remake*. It was an uncertain enterprise, but unlike so many *remakes*, the Victoria and Albert one became much more successful than the original.

That Albert would become an outstanding prince consort would have been hard to predict. The moment he set foot on English soil, he was told what he could *not* do: he could not get involved in his wife's work, he could not choose his own staff and he could not expect an adequate allowance. What he *should* do was father children and be an ornament. He famously ignored the latter and consequently faced endless criticism.[2]

The role of a male consort per se was an abnormality in an age when men were in sole charge of everything. Albert's sheer existence threatened comfortable gender roles. His predecessor as consort, Queen Anne's husband Prince George of Denmark, had been regularly ridiculed.[3] Now it was Albert's turn to be publicly emasculated. To contemporary eyes he showed a "want of manliness." According to rumour he was bad on horseback and generally useless at hunting. Even his German habits irritated the British public. Dining early was one of them. It was also seen as odd that he did not spend time at London clubs but prefered a daily walk with his wife instead (whether walking with one's wife was very German, could not be verified though). That he was in charge of running the family's daily life and actually displayed an interest in his children made him look even more feminine. One caricature showed him, surrounded by his offspring, tugging helplessly at Victoria's petticoats. At the same time he was accused of being the eminence grise behind the throne. Of course it was contradictory that he was seen as both—a feminine, pitiful partner and a dangerous, powerful manipulator.

His Coburg background seemed to be his greatest liability. From the moment of his engagement to Victoria, Albert had been perceived as a weak choice. In the British aristocracy there existed a general snobbishness about a penniless bridegroom: "[The English aristocrat] marries out of love and loves where the money is. He seldom marries to improve his crest."[4] Victoria's uncle William IV had favoured richer and more powerful suitors. The Coburgs were seen as pushy newcomers on the dynastic marriage market, travelling solely on looks and charm. Also their morals seemed doubtful. Albert's father, Duke Ernst I, had not only discarded Albert's mother under a feeble pretext, he was also known for his preference for underage girls. One of them had written an unflattering memoir which was available in most European countries.[5]

There are three factors that can cause the downfall of a dynasty: the biological factor (lack of heirs), outer threats (war and revolution), and inner threats (dysfunctional family dynamics). Albert feared the last the most. In June 1843 he wrote: "no outside enemy can harm a family as much as its own members."[6] At the time he was alluding to his brother Ernst who had money problems and a weakness for prostitutes (later Albert would experience a repetition of this with his son Bertie). In the prince's opinion such "vices in high places" could cause social unrest and therefore had to be suppressed. Albert tried his utmost to restore the honour of the House of Coburg. Because of his marriage to Victoria the Coburg family hierarchy had been turned upside-down. The younger brother Albert was allowed to criticise his older brother Ernst, something he would never have dared to do if circumstances had been different. Since Albert was married to a queen, he could be brutally honest. His letters to Ernst are therefore vacillating between cajoling and threatening. Repeatedly Albert lamented about Ernst's "moral insanity" which was bringing disrepute on the Coburg family: "it is sad for me to say that my brother is ruining his life and does not care about his reputation." And when Ernst protested, Albert retorted: "Perhaps I should just write about the weather then."[7]

Apart from trying to sort out the Coburg family, Albert was also doing his best to get the British royals under control—in particular Victoria's "vicious uncles." In the early 1840s the Hanoverians, that is, the old royal family, were still very visible and therefore potentially harmful. Rehabilitation for them seemed difficult. At the wedding of the duke of Cambridge's daughter in 1843, one of the vicious uncles Ernst August, king of Hanover turned up.[8] Albert had given Hanover the nickname "the Satan King" and indeed Ernst August had a famously violent side. He thought of Albert as a socially inferior person who did not deserve precedence at royal events. Consequently Hanover insisted on walking Victoria in and out of the church. Yet he underestimated his opponent. Prince Albert looked angelic but he was certainly no pushover. He retaliated by elbowing the King down the church steps, grabbed Victoria and signed the marriage register before "Satan." Albert took particular pleasure in hearing that after the cantankerous ceremony, Hanover had fallen over some stones at Kew and damaged his ribs.[9]

The "vicious uncles" were not just a serious threat to Albert but also to his concept of a new royal family. After the Cambridge wedding, Albert and Victoria therefore decided to freeze out the "Satan King" and the duke of Cambridge who had sided with him. Pushing the lesser, and morally ambiguous members of the old royal family to the periphery, meant that a new dynasty could begin. Albert wanted a dynasty with new values. But where did he—a product of his father's court—get these values from?

The prince had a seismographic sensitivity to the new rhythm of his epoch. He recognised the social problems that industrialisation had produced but he also recognised that it had created a new class—the middle class. They symbolised everything he admired. His bourgeois teachers at Coburg had been Florschütz and Stockmar. It was their value system he now copied: a strong work ethic, close-knit family ties, lifelong education, thrift, and self-improvement. Albert and Victoria consciously wanted to appeal with their exemplary family life to the tastes of the upcoming meritocratic middle classes. It was in some ways a PR strategy—of course a royal couple could not live a bourgeois family life. But Albert and Victoria really did believe in this value system. They invented new family rituals, new family homes, and circulated new images of their family. The new rituals changed the court life forever—it became a place that must have looked to aristocratic eyes square and dull. The Royal family staged musical evenings, the children played theatricals, drew pictures, and wrote poems as presents for their parents (when Bertie actually *bought* a present for his mother's birthday, Victoria was shocked about this lack of originality). This was a family that went on outings to the circus, built a snowman, and went to bed at ten.[10]

A new royal family also needed a new stage, that is, new homes. The grandest medium of dynastic display had always been public architecture. Albert, like so many princes, saw himself as a born architect and John Davis has shown in his monograph of the Great Exhibition how instrumental Albert's support for the controversial Crystal Palace was.[11] But apart from public architecture, Albert also created new *private* homes. They were meant to be the opposite of George IVs Brighton Pavilion. In reaction to such loucheness, Balmoral and Osborne House stood as mixtures of aristocratic grandeur and bourgeois cosiness. They were also meant as an educational tool. Balmoral for the outdoor life to toughen the childrens' character and the Swiss Cottage at Osborne to teach them how to cook, fire a cannon, and shop for milk.

To document for the public that this Royal family lived a different life style, Albert used photography, paintings, and prints. By doing this he consciously chose to *sentimentalize* his family. This meant he played with the public's emotions—a risky business if gotten wrong. But Albert was successful at it because being an emotional person himself he understood emotions well. Like Proust's hero in *À la recherche du temps perdu*, he could write in a sensual way about the taste of certain sweets he had eaten in childhood or the feelings for his beloved dog that died prematurely. What some would call an almost feminine sensitivity, was turned by him into an asset. The sentimental staging of his family did not feel fake. It also mirrored the *Zeitgeist* well. The *Saturday Review* believed that all Victorians lived in a thoroughly sentimental age.[12] Albert recognised this mood. He wanted to show a stable, caring family monarchy that offered a moral compass in a world of unprecedented change. Like every good director, Albert needed a gifted set designer to transport the right pictures of his family. The painter Franz Xaver Winterhalter became his favourite. Winterhalter might not have been, as Roy Strong put it, "an El Greco," but he created family portraits that were distinctive.[13] While other Royal families still preferred being painted with regal insignia, the British Royal Family commissioned both: stately and "intimate" paintings, like the one of the five year old Prince of Wales leisurely standing in front of the sea, his hands firmly in his pockets.[14]

Pictures of charming royal children and their good looking parents are an important point if one wants to understand Albert's novel image making. To be successful, the project needed attractive subjects. Royal portraits had always been commissioned to sell one's children on the marriage market, to impress the public and as a reference point for the family. To have a Habsburg jaw was seen as proof of authenticity. Yet more charming chins were increasingly preferred. In the nineteenth century the gaze of the public had become intense and Albert wanted his family "to look the part." As a young man he himself fitted the ideal he propagated: he was handsome and did his best to battle against his greatest enemy—hair loss: "to save my hair from total ruin, I have now started a radical treatment. Mr Mesnakur rubs in rectified spirits on my skin at night and in the morning a very fatty oil. He thinks it will work out very well."[15]

In the nineteenth century, a model aristocrat needed a slim, elegant body for hunting, fencing, and other sports. A haughty, distinguished aristocratic face was of course another ideal (seldom achieved when it came to the offspring of the rather podgy Hanoverians). Karl Marx got it right when he wrote that the aristocracy believed in zoology. Like dogs and horses, aristocratic and royal children had to be a good breed and if that breed was wanting, parents increasingly despaired. The obsession with looks became an important issue in many royal and aristocratic correspondences. One father for example admonished his married daughter that her portrait was problematic: "your eyes are not bright and open as they should be with a friendly expression, your chin is too much of a double one…do have this altered."[16] She was also sent on endless diets. Queen Victoria shared this predicament. Because her husband wanted the family on public display as often as possible, she fretted in long letters to her half sister Feodora about her weight and skin problems.[17] In her quest for beauty she was not only highly critical of herself, but also of her family. The letters between Queen Victoria and her oldest daughter Vicky are full of complaints about little grandson Wilhelm's disappointing appearance. It was not just his withered arm that caused offence, but also his face which looked "too weak and podgy."[18] Wilhelm internalised this criticism and became obsessed with beauty himself. His officers had to be sewn into their tight uniforms and he himself designed his wife's elaborate dresses.[19] When she did not fit into them—after seven pregnancies hardly a surprise—he put her on a strict diet. It was an obsession that Albert would have approved off. He had done his best to present a moral *and* beautiful family to the public. Once the pictures were right, the accompanying newspaper stories had to be flattering too. The media revolution of the time helped. The circulation of newspapers had increased, more people could now read and afford papers. The hunger for stories and pictures of the Royal Family grew. Also the new middle-class readers yearned for role models whose lifestyle could equip them with a moral compass.

Albert was highly aware of the power of the press. He read numerous newspapers (English ones, but also German ones, in one letter he lists "die Deutsche -, die Kölner-, die Berliner-, die Weser- und die Allgemeine Zeitung.")[20] He also saw how cunning politicians cultivated the media. Palmerston, Gladstone, and Disraeli knew what journalists needed and equipped them with the necessary "sound-bites." Albert and Victoria had to be much more careful but they could "inspire" the press in their own way, *indirectly* by delivering the right stories and pictures and *directly* by "encouraging" a pamphlet like "Why is Prince Albert so unpopular"—a pamphlet which, despite its title gave all the reasons for him to be popular.[21] What an old hand Albert became at playing the press, shows a letter he wrote to his brother Ernst. During the revolution of 1848 he advised him to get the German press "inspired": "Encourage your best people to write, no official articles with bureaucratic authority, that patronise the ignorant audience, but arguing in a popular way, talking common sense. This is more important now than any files."[22]

In peacetime Albert "inspired" articles about royal travels, charity work, and military commitment. Travelling was particularly popular with the papers. Before Albert took over the management of Victoria, she had been sent on annual cross-country trips by her mother the duchess of Kent and the despised comptroller of the duchess's household, Sir John Conroy. These enterprises had been successful with the public but made Victoria highly strung. To open parliament or to travel to industrial centres put her into a state of "greatest anxiety." As soon as Albert accompanied her to these functions she overcame her fears. He kept admonishing her not "to retreat into herself"—what he actually meant was that she tended to be self-obsessed. Albert had not only to get his wife's nerves under control, but everyone else's as well. These trips were planned like a military operation—"spontaneity" was organised. When the royal couple travelled to Coburg for example, Albert gave very specific instructions. Dances to amuse Victoria had to be arranged but it was also important to draw in the public. To his brother Albert wrote: "the citizens must be allowed to give (Victoria) a reception which mirrors their feelings."[23]

Because his mental map embraced at least two countries— "Germany" and Britain, it was natural for Albert to think internationally. He therefore also encouraged visits to Ireland and France. They secured excellent press coverage and eventually Albert made this concept global. By developing the idea of sending his sons on trips around the empire (something the royal family does so effectively to this day), he widened the geographical reach of the monarchy. Though he could not know that one day members of his family would even become governors, he was the first to realise that the empire posed new fields of influence for the Crown. India was a particular passion of his, which Victoria inherited. Already in the 1840s Albert was outraged by the East India Company's practices and he did have an impact on the 1858 Government of India Act. Ever the imaginative designer, he also developed a special award system for Indian and British elite: *The Star of India*. After all he knew how effective an extended honours system could be.[24]

Another way of demonstrating the new royal value system was through charity work. Since the medieval period, anecdotes about charitable monarchs had helped to legitimise them. This was never "The Kindness of Strangers" but followed the principle, "do good and talk about it." Charity was propaganda work and also a means of exerting social control. The aristocrat or the monarch decided where to place his charity—who was included and who was excluded.[25] Prince Albert thought along these lines. When his brother Ernst did not equip his wife with money to spend on charities, Albert admonished him: "Alexandrine should have pocket money to do charity work...She needs this to fulfil her role as a mother to the country (Landesmutter). This will support your work as well. She is very popular but in our rotten times powerlessness is not respected."[26]

Albert knew what could happen when such duties were neglected. If the first family of the region was not considered to be generous and "caring," this could be another contributing factor for social unrest. To build trust was decisive. This was easier in the countryside than in urban centres, where social unrest was much more likely. During the 1848 revolution Albert therefore reminded his brother Ernst to invite local policeman and talk to them about the eventuality that the "Citymob" (Stadtgesindel) could get out of control. In his opinion to be personally invited by the duke of Coburg would ensure the loyalty of every policeman in the region.

It would be cynical to see Albert's charity work solely as a PR stunt. He and Victoria were also driven by their religious convictions. Victoria was a patron of 150 charitable organisations and spent 15 percent of her income on charity. Though *Punch* claimed that Albert had only discovered his social conscience when his cousins lost their thrones in 1848, this was untrue. He had always supported many good causes, among them the international antislavery movement, housing and education projects for workers, and better hygiene schemes, like new sewage systems.[27]

Albert was also aware of the competition the monarchy faced. Charismatic politicians such as Palmerston and Gladstone styled themselves as national figureheads and were becoming more popular than the queen (one reason why Victoria despised them both). Therefore, the royal couple did their best to demonstrate great patriotic commitment. Royals had of course always been traditionally close to the church and the fighting services. But Queen Victoria went a step further: she saw herself as a female warrior, eagerly attending parades and inventing the Victoria Cross as the highest honor for all ranks of "her brave soldiers."[28] During the Crimean war she spent endless hours waving them off, knitting scarves, and handing out medals. To show their commitment to the navy, the Royal couple also developed the "Sailor Prince concept."[29] Their second son Alfred served from the bottom up in the navy, therefore displaying meritocratic and national commitments. How successful Albert's presentation strategy was is shown when one compares the press reports about royal receptions, royal trips, and charity events in the 1850s to critical reports of the royal family—the positive outnumber the negative by far.

While Albert was creatively turning his family into a success, the irony was that he himself did not profit much from the new image. Though he had become a British subject, his "Germaness" continued to be held against him. Of course "foreigner-bashing" and aggressive nationalism usually go hand in hand—every nation needs what Jean Bodin saw as the glue that seals the state. Yet Albert's critics even went so far as to see him as a security risk. His continental correspondence was viewed with great suspicion. Shortly before the outbreak of the Crimean War he was even accused of colluding with foreign powers and committing high treason. The accusations were without substance and hurt him deeply. He had always been well aware of the fact that his mail was not safe. To his brother he wrote in 1844: "I never write to Germany about English politics because everything is read."[30] Even 170 years before the invention of PRISM, international correspondence was already a risky business.

Though Albert avoided commenting on British politics, he had no qualms about giving advice on continental ones. Here his critics had a valid point—he did mingle. He also must have had some discrete couriers. One of his many interesting dynastic correspondences was with his relative and co-consort, Ferdinand of Portugal. It was Albert, the newcomer among the prince consorts, who approached Ferdinand and asked him whether they could start a "secret" political correspondence. Both were members of the House of Coburg and both shared the problem of being unpopular abroad. In the early years of his marriage Albert had envied Ferdinand who exerted a great influence over his wife, Queen Dona Maria II of Portugal. But once Albert had gained access to Victoria's red boxes, they were equals. As the queen's closest advisor, Albert now wanted to collect information that went beyond diplomatic dispatches. Ferdinand therefore had to inform him about Portugal's domestic affairs, social unrest, and constant ministerial crises. In return he was lectured by Albert in a rather direct way—the kind of directness you use only for relatives.[31] For Albert's detractors this correspondence might have been another incidence of secret networking, but a closer look shows that Albert did inform Prime Minister Lord Aberdeen about it. He wanted to achieve two things: to help his relative to stabilize the Portuguese throne and at the same time to help British interests in Portugal.

Albert felt convinced that foreign affairs were an important traditional field of monarchical influence. He remained adamant that his knowledge of continental politics and his closeness to European monarchs could be of great use. He would not live to read Bagehot and if he had, he would have certainly disagreed with him. According to David Craig, "it was a common view in the late nineteenth and early twentieth centuries that 'show' was the best way of transfixing the imaginations of the 'masses,' who were suffering a rationality deficit."[32] The monarchy certainly had to offer "theatrical show," yet despite all his artful presentation, Albert also defended the queen's prerogatives. He saw the monarchy's role as that of an arbiter, that is, above party politics. This was however a rather vague concept and it has often been turned against him. Even Disraeli—who became Victoria's favourite Prime Minster—once talked about Albert's idea of "absolute power." David Cannadine agrees. He claims that Albert "wanted to be a sovereign who governed as well as reigned."[33] If this had been Albert's intention, Palmerston certainly destroyed any such illusions. He clashed repeatedly with Albert over foreign affairs—a field in which Palmerston did not endure any competition by a young princeling.[34] Things came to a head when in 1848 Palmerston believed in supporting revolutionary movements *abroad* (not in Ireland of course!) while Albert feared for the survival of his correspondents, and a knock-on effect in Britain. While Palmerston supported Italian nationalism—Albert wanted the Habsburg Empire—despite criticising its faults—to stay intact. During the 1848 Schleswig-Holstein crisis, Albert backed the German nationalists who wanted to incorporate the duchies into a united Germany, while Palmerston instead favoured Denmark. Palmerston also did not share Albert's long-term plans for the German states. The prince worked for a united Germany under Prussia's leadership, not because he was a reactionary, but because he knew that only Prussia was strong enough to achieve such a goal. His long-term plan was an Anglo-German alliance which would have "westernised" Prussia—a plan that might have saved a lot of bloodshed.

Though he was often a lone fighter, in his 22-year struggle to establish a role as prince consort, Albert was not completely alone. He had several advisors: the Coburg network (his uncle Leopold, the king of the Belgians, and Stockmar), occasionally politicians such as Peel, and most importantly his wife who fought for his status. Victoria was outraged at every slight her husband endured, especially his lack of a proper title. To Palmerston she wrote: "it is a strange omission in our Constitution that while the wife of a King has the highest rank and dignity in the realm after her husband assigned to her by law, the husband of a queen regent is entirely ignored by law."[35] In the end it was Victoria who had to give Albert the title of prince consort by royal patent in 1857.

It was the Cambridge weather that killed Albert a few years later. As Chancellor of the University, he should have been used to it, but despite being highly enervated he travelled to Madingley Hall to sort out his son Bertie. The future Edward VII was supposed to study at Cambridge, but he had involved himself in other activities and was in danger of being blackmailed. On his return, Albert developed a fever. At first the queen did not understand the gravity of the situation and complained that men were such difficult patients. It was, however, typhoid fever and Albert was not fighting it. He was warning Victoria not to overdo the postmortem adulation—a wish she famously ignored. The warning was not false modesty on his part, but common sense. He knew all too well that the British public could not be manipulated into any kind of forced hero worship. After his death on December 14, 1861, the queen kept the illusion of Albert alive: by constantly talking and writing about him, by sleeping next to a cast of his hand, even having his clothes and shaving foam put out every day. In aristocratic circles such excessive grieving was highly unusual. *Not* to show emotions was seen as the highest form of self-control—one simply did not bother other people. Victoria had never been a good psychologist and her determination to "canonise" Albert did not go down well. But she was right in seeing him as an outstanding prince consort. Over the years Albert's role had varied between successes and failures. Yet despite all the drawbacks of his position, he kept finding backdoors to power that the royal family uses to this day.

For a man who officially had no power, he used it brilliantly.

Notes

1. Frank Lorenz Müller, *Our Fritz. Emperor Frederick III and the Political Culture of Imperial Germany* (Cambridge, Mass 2011). See also: Eva Giloi, *Monarchy, Myth, and Material Culture in Germany 1750–1950* (Cambridge 2011); Edward Berenson and Eva Giloi (eds.), *Constructing Charisma: Celebrity, Fame, and Power in Nineteenth Century Europe* (Oxford, 2013).
2. Karina Urbach, "Introduction," in Theodore Martin, *The Life of the Prince Consort: Prince Albert and His Times, Vol. 1* (London, 2012), viii.
3. See Charles Beem's chapter, "Why Prince George of Denmark Did Not Become a King of England."
4. Nancy Mitford, "Die Englische Aristokratie," *Der Monat: Internationale Zeitschrift*, vol. 9, no. 97 (1956), 40–9.
5. A biography of Prince Albert's mother has uncovered new details of this bizarre affair: Ulrike Grunewald, Luise von Sachsen-Coburg-Saalfeld (1800–1831): *Lebensräume einer unangepassten Herzogin* (Cologne, 2013).
6. Albert to his brother Ernst, LA A 6971: vol. III, 1841–43. State Archive Coburg.
7. Ibid. June 1843.
8. Princess Augusta Caroline, eldest daughter of the duke of Cambridge, married Frederick, hereditary grand duke of Mecklenburg Strelitz.
9. Prince Albert to his brother Ernst, July 30, 1843, LA A 6971: vol. III, 1841–43. State Archive Coburg.
10. See for this in more detail, Karina Urbach, *Queen Victoria* (Munich, 2011), 80ff.
11. John Davis, *The Great Exhibition* (London, 1999).
12. Quoted in: David Newsome, *The Victorian World Picture* (London 1997), 10.
13. Roy Strong interview in: Queen Victoria. A Royal Lovestory, BBC 1, March 14, 2010.
14. *Manja Wilkens*, Liebesgaben für den Prinzgemahl. Gemälde Franz Xaver Winterhalters als Geburtstags-, Hochzeitstags- und Weihnachtsgeschenke von Victoria an Albert und von Albert an Victoria, in Franz Bosbach, Frank Büttner (eds.,) *Künstlerische Beziehungen zwischen England und Deutschland in der viktorianischen Epoche* (Munich, 1998).
15. 838 V 16, RA VIC/Add A 6 nr 3, Royal Archives Windsor.
16. Count Bentinck to his daughter Mechthild, 27.4.1909. Papers of Mechthild Fürstin zu Castell-Rüdenhausen (born Countess Bentinck, 1877–1940). Fürstlich Castell'sches Archiv Castell (Franconia).
17. See Karina Urbach (ed.), *Royal Kinship: Anglo-German Family Networks 1815–1918* (Munich, 2008).
18. Roger Fulford (ed.), *Dearest Child: Private Correspondence of Queen Victoria and the Crown Princess of Prussia 1858–1861* (London, 1964); Ibid., *Dearest Mama: Private Correspondence of Queen Victoria and the Crown Princess of Prussia 1861–1864*, (London, 1968); Ibid., *Your Dear Letter, Private Correspondence*

of Queen Victoria and the Crown Princess of Prussia 1865–1871 (London, 1971); Ibid., *Darling Child: Private Correspondence of Queen Victoria and the Crown Princess of Prussia 1871–1878* (London 1976); Ibid., *Beloved Mama: Private Correspondence of Queen Victoria and the Crown Princess of Prussia 1878–1885* (London, 1981).

19. Philip Mansel, *Dressed to Rule: Royal and Court Costume from Louis XIV to Elizabeth II* (London, 2005).

20. April 13, 1848. Letter from Albert to Ernst, LA A 6974, vol. VI. 1848–49. no. 45. State Archive Coburg.

21. F. Airplay, *Prince Albert: Why is he so unpopular?* (London 1857), 8.

22. March 17, 1848, Albert to Ernst, LA A 6974, vol. VI, 1848–49. State Archive Coburg.

23. Albert to Ernst, LA A 6971: vol. IV, 1844. State Archive Coburg.

24. See Miles Taylor's forthcoming book, *Queen Victoria and India.*

25. See Gareth Stedman Jones, *Languages of Class, Studies in English Working Class History, 1832–1982* (Cambridge, 1983), 77.

26. Albert to Ernst, LA A 6971: vol. III, 1841–43. State Archive Coburg.

27. Stanley Weintraub, *Albert: Uncrowned King* (New York, 2001).

28. Walter Arnstein, "The Warrior Queen: Reflections on Victoria and Her World," *Albion* 30 (Spring, 1998) 1–28.

29. Miriam Schneider, *Royal Naval Education, Sailor Princes, and the Re-Invention of the Monarchy*, MPhil thesis, University of Cambridge 2011.

30. "Ich schreibe nie nach Deutschland über englische Politik, da alles gelesen wird." Albert to Ernst, LA A 6971: vol. III, 1841–43. State Archive Coburg.

31. For this correspondence, see Franz Bosbach, John Davis (eds.), *Common Heritage: Dokumente aus den Royal Archives Windsor und Staatsarchiv Coburg* (Munich, 2014).

32. David M. Craig goes on to show that this view is one-sided. Craig, "The Crowned Republic? Monarchy and Anti-Monarchy in Britain, 1760–1901," *The Historical Journal*, 46, 1 (2003), S. 167–85.

33. David Cannadine, The Last Hanoverian Sovereign? The Victorian Monarchy in Historical Perspective, 1688–1988, in A. L. Beier (ed.), *The First Modern Society: Essays in English History in Honour of Lawrence Stone* (Cambridge, 1989), 127ff.

34. See Karina Urbach, "Prince Albert and Lord Palmerston: Battle Royal," in David Brown and Miles Taylor (eds.), *Palmerston Studies, Vol. 1* (Southampton, 2007).

35. Quoted in Weintraub, *Albert*, 337.

CHAPTER 9

Commemorating the Consort in Colonial Bombay

Simin Patel

B y the time Australia received the news of the death of Prince Albert, the citizens of Bombay had already held a public meeting in the Town Hall to vote an address of condolence to Queen Victoria. The address, with well over 1000 signatures, was shipped to England. At the meeting it was agreed to include the prince's name along with Her Majesty's in the title of a proposed museum and set up a local fund in his memory.

Bombay's market economy responded equally briskly. Memorabilia commemorating the prince, lately shipped from England, filled city stores. At the top of Chesson and Woodhall's list of new books was the *Life of the Prince Consort* (1862), by Edward Walford, a former Balliol scholar. Largely a compilation of articles from the British press following the demise of the prince on December 14, 1861, the text offered Bombay readers the minutiae of a bereaved royal domestic: the family members at the prince's side during his last moments, Queen Victoria's afflicted state, the pattern of her sleep, names of the early visitors to Windsor Castle offering their condolences.[1] As Bombay audiences consumed these household happenings, two months after their actual occurrence, Australia was informed of the prince's passing.[2] By early March 1862, booksellers and agents, Thacker, Vining and Co. were advertising their stock of carte de viste of Prince Albert alongside the engraved portraits of Earl Canning.[3] Canning, governor general of India, was shortly due to retire to England, ample cause for the commemorative machinery to restart.

It is to this brisk culture of commemoration in Victorian Bombay that we turn in this chapter. Orchestrated by an influential and wealthy native citizenry, international, national, and local actors all fell within its ambit. Those honored were often British—royalty, statesmen, officials, and professionals at significant junctures of their lives or more commonly on their retirement, departure from Bombay, or death—allowing the state to comfortably and without controversy participate and legitimize the recognition. A governor would agree to preside over a memorial meeting; a statue of the protagonist, funded by subscription, could find pride of place in the

Town Hall. No doubt, in a few years, the governor, at the end of his tenure, would look forward to a bust of his own. A sense of reciprocity, of carrying forward a tradition as well as the actualities of a native elite keen to deploy their monetary resources and a transient Anglo-Indian population otherwise unlikely to leave material signs of their presence in the city, were some of the forces that shaped the logic of commemoration in Bombay.[4]

By focusing on the reception of the news of the death of Prince Albert, this chapter demonstrates how tributes to British royalty were both in and out of step with Bombay's wider culture of commemoration. The citizenry's sense of somehow belonging to and partaking of royal domesticity, despite the long distance, occasioned a host of emotive responses to major events in the reigning family. Marriages, births (Victoria and Albert had nine children), illnesses, and deaths were all cues for native subjects to voice their claims to and care for an imagined and encompassing Victorian royal domestic. Most striking were the prayer meetings held by the city's religious communities at their respective places of worship, at times of royal bereavement and distress—the sudden passing of Prince Albert at the age of 42, the near fatal bout of typhoid from which his son, the Prince of Wales, suffered in 1871. A prayer of thanks was held on the latter's recovery. These rituals of worship and mourning or celebration and joy offered avenues for leveled participation in the empire's private and innermost domain of the royal home. Prayer gatherings unlike subscription funds, made emotive demands from every attendee, a reminder that an urban citizenry otherwise operating within a modern discourse of commemoration could resort to traditional forms of community specific association. What do the needs of each community to supplement citywide royal commemoration with their own specific offerings of sympathy, joy, and loyalty, tell us of effectively affiliating with the imperial centre? And must we turn to the well-worn debate of the separation of private and public spheres to gauge whether offerings made to homes are best articulated from similar private realms of belonging?

II

At the meeting held at the Town Hall to console the untimely death of Prince Albert, possibly by typhoid fever, and to vote an address of condolence to Queen Victoria, the Governor of Bombay was unable to preside. Sir George Russell Clerk suffered from indisposition, another reminder of powerful deterrents of sickness, disease, and death that operated at the Victorian centre and periphery alike.[5] Speakers at the meeting commented on how some of the parallel congregations held in England were marked by subdued silences. Sir Jamsetjee Jejeebhoy (second Baronet), the leading *sethia* (merchant prince) of the Parsi community, noted that such restraint befitted a bereaved nation: "How appropriate, under the circumstances such a mode of proceeding! How much in harmony with the melancholy occasion! No words of fervid oratory were needed. No bursts of impassioned grief were heard in these assemblies."[6] The display of an orderly national public was testament to one of Prince Albert's forgotten legacies. At the two extraordinary public spectacles he orchestrated in London a decade earlier, The Great Exhibition (1851), an international festival showcasing the arts and sciences of various nations and the grand funeral of the Duke of Wellington (1852), the presence of mass audiences had been encouraged, tested, and approved.[7]

Iain Pears sees both events as involving "the mobilization of a mass audience serving as a demonstration of national solidarity and unity."[8] By the time of Prince Albert's funeral on December 23, 1861, England's masses had adequate practice in solemn and often silent national participation. While the funeral was kept private, processions and church services were organized in numerous towns and cities in England.

A subdued Bombay citizenry, distanced from the displays of mourning Prince Albert's death occasioned in England, would have gone unacknowledged. Jejeebhoy, among the few at the meeting at the Town Hall to have previously had an audience with the queen and her consort in London, proposed that "we as an influential community raise our voices in accents of mourning."[9] The need to be heard and an acknowledgement that the centre was in fact listening were the mainstays of the logic of royal commemoration in Bombay. This almost filial relationship and demand set the tributes to British monarchy apart from the wider practices of colonial commemoration prevalent in the city. Colonial commemoration was characterised by a proximity between the subject being commemorated and those commemorating him/her, professional goodwill and etiquette, public gestures, and sense of reciprocity (prominent citizens that participated could assume and expect that they would be conversely commemorated at some point in the lives or at the end of it). Royal commemoration, which included multiple prayer gatherings, fervent odes to England, and a focus on the Victorian domestic, was less modern in form. It was also largely reserved for the British monarchy. Major events in the lives of native princes and consorts, a good number of whom visited Bombay in the mid to late nineteenth century, and were well received by city's elite, did not occasion significant commemorative acts.

Both in England and Bombay, tributes to Albert portrayed him at the helm of the royal household—overseeing his children's education, imparting the lessons of sound governance to his sons, an arbitrator of taste, and a "loving, devoted, and considerate husband" to a monarch whose position demanded an emotional tepidness.[10] John Wolffe notes that Albert "presented the public with a perceived ideal of male conjugal and familial devotion."[11] At a soiree hosted by the Mazagon Library and Mutual Improvement Society in Bombay, member J. Hornsby drew on the prince's example in his speech on the topic of "home." *The Bombay Gazette* of February 12, 1862, summarized the speech: "As a type of home he could not do better than refer to the royal family—there we saw what home was in reality—there the late lamented Prince Consort did everything to make his home happy, in the education of his family and thus set a noble example to the world."[12] Portrayals of a domesticated Prince Albert were supplemented with examples of his public pursuit of the arts and industry. The Great Exhibition, a colossal display of largely manufactured goods from across the world, received special mention. Several though comparatively less sophisticated items from India had thronged the various exhibits at the Crystal Palace in London, the Koh-i-Noor diamond, fabulous in size though poorly cut, ceramics, simple agricultural machines, a howdah and a elephant cloth for which a stuffed elephant was eventually acquired.[13] The traffic of goods was two-way. British manufactures, designed to expedite modern domesticity that had beat in friendly competition their French, Swiss, and American counterparts, were imported into the Bombay market. Such was the success of the Great Exhibition that took its visitors around the world in half a day and on as little as a shilling, that another was held a decade later in 1862.[14] The Bombay press reported on the "melancholy interest" the Great Exhibition in 1862 had generated owing to the sudden demise of its author, Prince Albert, and the absence of the queen as inaugurator.[15] At least six members of the city's influential Parsi community attended the event.[16] Advertisements for Keating's Persian Insect Destroying Powder in the English language daily *The Bombay Gazette* boldly announced the prize medal the product had recently won at the Great Exhibition.[17]

A museum dedicated to the memory of Prince Albert was considered a fitting tribute by the coterie of native and European elite at the forefront of the commemorative machinery in Bombay. Since a project for establishing a museum and garden named after the queen was already in the works, it was thought appropriate to include the prince's name in the title of the existing institution (itself intended to commemorate the transfer of power from the East India Company to the Crown in 1858). When the Victoria Museum and Garden's Committee, on which the same set of Bombay's elite sat, sought the queen's approval on the titular extension, her secretarial office clarified: "it is Her Majesty's wish that the Horticultural Gardens should be considered under her peculiar and personal patronage and protection."[18] On the sprawling property that coopted smaller government run gardens and had a new fountain dedicated to the then governor Sir Henry Bartle Frere, only the museum bore the prince's name. Further the colonial Government washed its hands off executing the design of the museum, after its contribution of a lakh of rupees toward the cost of construction.[19] Ambitious plans for a structure in Gothic design were abandoned for an Italian Renaissance style; such flippancy in taste in complete disregard of the prince's legacy. Interestingly, the more elaborate porticoed structure that served as an entrance to the Gardens bore the image of both Victoria and Albert in the central relief.

When Bombay's officialdom petitioned the authorities in London for the inclusion of the image of Prince Albert in civic spaces, the latter's responses reaffirmed Queen Victoria's authority. In a letter dated November 12, 1862, officials at the Bombay Castle noted that the Government House at Parell as well as public buildings in the city would benefit from a worthy portrait of the queen. Further "it would be enhanced if it were accompanied by a portrait of his late Royal Highness the Prince Consort, whose name is held in honoured and grateful memory by the inhabitants of Bombay, and ever associated in their minds with that of Her Most Gracious Majesty."[20] The India Office confirmed that a portrait of the queen, executed by Sir George Hayter, had been long dispatched to several Presidency towns including Bombay. A fresh batch of portraits were dispatched from England as was a gilt pier table for the Government House on which the likeness of the queen would be eventually placed. The inclusion of a possible portrait of the prince does not appear to be pursued in subsequent official correspondence.

III

With the opening of the Victoria and Albert Museum in 1872, eleven years after Prince Albert's death, and ten after the inauguration of the adjacent Victoria Gardens, the prince was finally at the centre of his own exhibition. Amid the museum's curiosities was a towering marble statue of Prince Albert. Commissioned by David Sasoon, the city's foremost Jewish *sethia* (merchant prince), and sculpted by Matthew Noble in England under the queen's supervision, the statue offered Bombay's public the first dimensional view of the body of the prince, previously known through photographic likenesses.[21] In the confined and controlled space of the museum, the figure was safeguarded from the worshipping masses found at the statues of other British worthies in the city's open spaces.[22] In fact, the museum, a secular shrine to Prince Albert, offered Bombay's public a hybrid compromise of modern and older forms of commemorative practice. The main hall of the museum contained a double height atrium-like central space that enframed the eight-foot statue of the prince, placed on a pedestal. It appeared to glow with the reflected light. And the bust of Earl Canning that the Museum also housed, was nowhere near the haloed centerpiece.

Notes

1. Edward Walford, *Life of the Prince Consort* (London, 1862), 86–121.
2. John Wolffe, *Great Deaths: Grieving, Religion, and Nationhood in Victorian and Edwardian Britain* (Oxford, 2000), 197.
3. *The Bombay Gazette*, March 4, 1862, p. 213 (Maharashtra State Archives, {MSA}, January to July 1862 stack)

4. For an analysis of the fragility of Anglo-Indian lives in India and the fervent exchange of portable gifts as a means to combat that fragility, see Margot C. Finn's, "Colonial Gifts: Family Politics and the Exchange of Goods in British India, c. 1780–1820," in *Modern Asian Studies,* vol. 40, no. 1 (Feb., 2006), 203–31. Central to Finn's argument is the role of the public auction house, where the possessions of departing or deceased Anglo-Indians were sold to the highest bidder, stripping the goods from the emotional and historical ties that bound them with their previous owner.

5. *The Bombay Gazette*, January 28, 1862, p. 90 (MSA, January to July 1862 stack).

6. Ibid.

7. For a vivid account of the spectacle of the Duke's funeral, see Cornelia D. J. Pearsall, "Burying the Duke: Victorian Mourning and the Funeral of the Duke of Wellington," in *Victorian Literature and Culture*, vol. 27, no. 2 (1999), 365–93.

8. Ibid., 370.

9. *The Bombay Gazette*, January 28, 1862, p. 90 (MSA, January to July 1862 stack).

10. Ibid.

11. Wolffe, *Great Deaths*,198.

12. *The Bombay Gazette*, February 12, 1862, p. 147 (MSA, January to July 1862 stack).

13. Michael Leapman, *The World for a Shilling* (London, 2001).

14. Ibid.

15. *The Bombay Gazette*, June 4, 1862, p. 528 (MSA, January to July 1862 stack).

16. *The Times of India*, March 22, 1862, 3.

17. *The Bombay Gazette*, July 10, 1863, 1.

18. Ibid., February 1, 1862, p. 107 (MSA, January to July 1862 stack).

19. Ibid.

20. General Department, Portraits, no. 592 of 1862/63, MSA. For an account of the queen and the prince's relationship with India see Miles Taylor, "Queen Victoria and India, 1837–61," in *Victorian Studies*, vol. 46, no. 2, Papers from the Inaugural Conference of the North American Victorian Studies Association (Winter, 2004), 264–74.

21. Preeti Chopra, *A Joint Enterprise: Indian Elites and the Making of British Bombay* (Minneapolis: University of Minnesota Press, 2011), 223. For a detailed account of the various statues and shrines for Prince Albert across the empire see Elisabeth Darby and Nicola Smith, *The Cult of the Prince Consort* (New Haven, 1983).

22. For an account of how statues of colonial officials were turned into public shrines see chapter 6, "Of Gods and Mortal Heroes: Conundrums of the Secular Landscape of Colonial Bombay," of Chopra's *A Joint Enterprise*, 191–230.

CHAPTER 10

Ferdinand II of Portugal: A Conciliatory King in an Age of Turmoil

Daniel Alves

Introduction

A biographical sketch about King Ferdinand II of Portugal will have necessarily to go through the analysis of the image that his contemporaries had of him regarding his relationship with Portuguese military and political affairs. Such an image takes into account the reminiscences of his family and colleagues in Portugal as well as those of European statesmen and royalty. Obviously, such a study must take into account the personal, familiar, and political path of the monarch himself, as well as the ideas which he defended and left expressed in personal correspondence, both in Portugal and abroad. And it will also be necessary to contextualize this image and experiences within Portugal's political and social life, a country that welcomed him, in mid-1830s, and that became, in his own words, his new homeland.

The work that is being presented here gives a particular relevance, precisely, to this last point, considering that in line with the features of his own character, it was Portugal's peculiar political and military situation, in the first half of the nineteenth century, to determine the political role played by the king, the contemporary idea of his historical relevance, and the image of respectability and balance that, nonetheless, he ultimately earned in the second half of the century, until his death in 1885.

I start by describing the Portuguese political environment between 1820 and 1870, and then analyze the role played by Ferdinand II during this time, especially until 1853, concluding with a possible interpretation on how his conciliatory character has revealed important for the maintenance in power of Braganza's dynasty and for the process of transformation of Portuguese politics in mid-nineteenth century.

The Historiography on Ferdinand II

Interestingly, the life of Ferdinand II only recently attracted the interest of historians. Even so, those that wrote about him tended to highlight his private life and his role as a patron of the art rather than his political career. But this approach, although focused on very relevant aspects of the life and personality of the consort of Maria II, tends to abate or to give a lesser emphasis to his political role between 1836 and 1855, valuing, perhaps in excess, the last years of his life and the more media driven aspects of his relationship with his second wife.

The exception which, in part, came to change this picture is Ferdinand's recently published biography by Maria Antónia Lopes, although the author was primarily concerned with the "private life" of the king.[1] But prior to this, between 1878 and 1935, studies on Ferdinand were essentially laudatory of his royal character.[2] In 1952 Ernesto Soares published a biography focusing almost exclusively his role as artist and patron of the arts.[3] In 1986, upon the centenary of his death, there appeared a series of exhibitions, sources' publications, and a biography by José Teixeira.[4] However, once again, the main historical memory remained the king's connection to the national artistic medium, as well as his role in the construction of the National Park and Palace of Pena in Sintra.

From the 1980s onward, most of what was written about Ferdinand was through biographies of other individuals with whom he was related, such as his two wives, Queen Dona Maria II and the countess of Edla (Elisa Hensler), and his two eldest sons, the Kings D. Pedro V and D. Luís.[5] Lastly, in 2013 the Lopes biography was published, a solid historiographical work with a comprehensive picture of the king and the man, although focusing on family life, certainly, but with new data collected from sources never explored before.

A Kingdom in Turmoil: Portugal between Civil Wars, Coups and Revolutions

For the Portuguese, and also for a part of those who come into contact with the Portuguese people, be it for tourism, for business, or academic reasons, the idea of a country in constant turmoil, deeply divided, with a violent everyday life, is an idea altogether strange and not coincident with the alleged national "brandos costumes." This alleged "gentle way" picture was already defended by the end of the nineteenth century in some political circles, but was encouraged by Salazar's dictatorial regime, who ruled the country for much of the twentieth century.[6] However, about 150 years ago, that violent portrait was actually true, because between 1820 and 1851, Portugal has gone through no less than two revolutions, two civil wars, a dozen military coups and conspiracies, some popular uprisings, and a deep economic, social, and political restructuring process.

The end of the ancien regime and the transition to liberalism were anything but peaceful in Portugal, and between the Liberal Revolution of 1820 and the military coup of the "Regeneração" in 1851, the kingdom lived in almost permanent alarm. In those troubled decades, the decisive event was the civil war between liberals and absolutists in the beginning of the 1830s, and also the political dissensions between the liberals that lead to a new revolution in September 1836, and to a new civil war called the "Patuleia" Civil War in 1846–47. Throughout the whole situation, the role played by the military was central, but also were the political choices of the Queen D. Maria II from 1834.[7] It is in this troubled times that we need to integrate Prince Ferdinand's role, through his marriage with D. Maria II in 1836.

In the period from 1851 to 1870, although the Portuguese political environment entered a much more consensual period, problems still occurred such as riots due to the cost of living in the 1850s, uprisings against taxes in 1868 and a last military coup in 1870, in addition to several controversies about topics as diverse as reintroduction of female religious orders or the Iberian Union.[8] The power and influence of the monarch in this period tended to fade away due to the queen's death, which occurred in 1853, but in several occasions and for different reasons, Ferdinand did not fail to make its contribution to national and even international politics. After 1870 and until his death in 1885, the country experienced one of its most stable periods in economic, social, and political terms, and the monarch's private life, since his marriage with the opera singer Elisa Hensler in 1869 eventually eclipsed his earlier role as king consort.

Ferdinand and Portuguese Politics: The Breeding Process of a Conciliator King

Prince Ferdinand Augustus Francis Anthony of Saxe-Coburg-Gotha-Koháry was born in Coburg in 1816, son of Ferdinand George Augustus of Saxe-Coburg-Gotha and Mária Antónia Gabriella Kohary of Saxe-Coburgo-Gotha. "D. Fernando," as he was to be known by the Portuguese, died in Lisbon in 1885. Contemporaries considered Prince Ferdinand as the ideal choice for the second marriage of D. Maria II, because his family relations guaranteed from the start the maintaining of a moderate constitutionalism. Ferdinand was nephew of the Belgian monarch, Leopold I, and first cousin of Prince Albert, future husband of Queen Victoria of England, nephew of the reigning duke of Saxe-Coburg and of the duchess of Kent, sister of the Belgian king and mother of Queen Victoria.[9] His uncle Leopold played an important role in the negotiations that led to the proxy marriage of the young prince with the Portuguese queen, on January 1, 1836, followed by another ceremony on April 9, when Ferdinand arrived in Lisbon.[10] The marriage was a bolster to the position of the young queen, as well as a country that just ended a civil war. Additionally, the marriage provided a connection with the more liberal wing of nineteenth-century European royalty.

On September 16, 1837, the prince, who acquired the title of king after the birth of D. Pedro V, heir to the throne, had not been prepared for a political or military life, and that was a concern for the family, in particular for King Leopold. In a letter to Princess Victoria, of March 4, 1836, he confessed his need to have "written down for him everything which he ought to know about the organisation of a government in general," so he could "carry on successfully the Government in Portugal."[11] While his education had been devoted to the arts, Portugal still experienced instability resulting from the Civil War, and the marriage contract with D. Maria stated that Ferdinand would have to take over as commander in chief of the army.[12]

This last provision, which was not foreseen in the Portuguese Constitutional Charter, revealed the instability that still existed within the Portuguese military, which in part explains the troubled process of his appointment as commander.[13] By the decrees of January 29 and February 27, 1836 the Portuguese government made the appointment that was enshrined in the marriage contract, but it only became public on April 15, after the arrival of Ferdinand to the country. At that time, it was already another government in office, and his appointment to the post of commander in chief of the army would eventually be confirmed definitely only on the 30th of the same month.[14]

Shortly after his marriage to D. Maria II, the young and unskilled prince, still eager to distinguish himself, had the first contact with the political and military instability that Portugal was living. Already as holder of the office of commander in chief, he witnessed the so-called September Revolution in September 9, 1836. Feeling unable to change the course of events, he offered his resignation to the queen while strongly criticizing the revolutionary events. Under pressure from the *Septembrists*, D. Maria eventually convinced the Prince to give up on his intention to make public his resignation, but she could not prevent the young husband from supporting, more or less discreetly, the following countercoups, the Belenzada, in November, 1836, and the Marshalls's Revolt in July, 1837.[15] Informed by Van de Weyer, Belgium's Plenipotentiary Minister which had been in Portugal during the events of *Septembrism*, the Princess Victoria was under the impression that D. Maria was ill-advised in the Court and that Ferdinand had already a certain ascendancy over the queen who had for him enough respect and a "real obedience."[16]

The king opposed the reduction of royal prerogatives advocated by the *Septembrists* and would not have been very pleased with the fact that they extinguished the post of commander in chief of the Portuguese army. This edginess of the monarch would lead even to a "sour" exchange of words with Passos Manuel, the political chief of the *Septembrists*, during the negotiations to end the Belenzada coup attempt in November 3, 1837.[17]

But the rush of political and military events in the early years of his stay in Portugal, and probably the notion that he could do very little to intervene directly in them, forced the now King Ferdinand to fall back on a position of greater reticence regarding the kingdom's military and political matters. Contemporaries would later view this attitude as a mere facet of his character, in the sense that he was never comfortable with the military function that he was committed to under the marriage's contract.[18]

However, his position as the husband of the queen could not exempt him from responsibilities, and he was called to them by D. Maria II several times, the most relevant of them when she appointed Ferdinand again commander in chief of the army, in October 17, 1846, at the beginning of the movement that would lead to the Patuleia's Civil War (1846–47).[19] Apparently, during the crisis he always maintained a very active stance and uncompromising defence about the queen's interests, which was almost the same as those of the *Chartists*, the political party that opposed the *Septembrists* during the war events.[20]

But Ferdinand was above all a conciliator, convinced that this new crisis would only be resolved through negotiations. To some extent, the impetuous young prince (he was 19 when he arrived in Portugal), gradually gave way to a more thoughtful king that sought to put the Royal House above party factions. In this sense, he was the first to accept as reasonable the proposals of England from April 5, 1847, which led to the London Protocol signed on May 21. This protocol would become an essential document for the English intervention and the civil war resolution, which, among other measures, granted a general amnesty to all the players. And it was also he who managed to convince the queen to accept the English agreement and to dismiss the government so strongly opposed by the Patuleias.[21]

However, the idea that some of his contemporaries had of him, with regard to his military capabilities, was still very negative. One of the ministers, the Marquis of Fronteira, relates in his memoirs that the monarch, during the crisis of the Patuleia, preferred the "arias and duets," instead of "military parades" or revising of "daily orders."[22]

The same opinion would be recorded some years later, in April 1851, during the military coup of the "Regeneração" when, once again, the king has shown not to have been tailored to the military life and prefer the moderation and the dialogue instead of confrontation. In front of the troops that should fight Marshal Saldanha (the leader of the movement and a man with whom the king always had a certain complicity), Ferdinand left Lisbon but lingered in Santarém and then in Coimbra, giving Saldanha the opportunity to move north, to Oporto. The king was reluctant in the sense that he was not convinced, in his own words, about the "fairness and usefulness of his mission." That is, he could not find enough motivation to defend a minister, Costa Cabral, with whom he had not always agreed, and who attracted the country's largest political opposition, as had already happened in the crisis of 1846–1847.[23]

His stand, however, was complicated because by assuming the leadership of the armies that would confront Saldanha, he would eventually provide arguments to all who would confront the queen and see Costa Cabral removed from the government. Meanwhile, Oporto stood up in support of Saldanha and Ferdinand wrote to the minister Costa Cabral urging him to resign "immediately" and then to D. Maria insisting that the queen dismiss the disputed minister, which she eventually did on April 26.[24] Ferdinand's actions not only displayed his political foresight, as is a further evidence of his traditional aversion to political and military conflict, and his ascendancy over Queen D. Maria at this stage of the couple's life.

However, these events and the victory of the "Regeneração" movement meant an end to his military life, because in the wake of the military coup he requested the queen to dismiss him as commander in chief of the army, in a letter still written in the city of Coimbra on April 28.[25] The country had been through one more political and military crisis, the last of the reign of D. Maria II and Ferdinand II. The conciliatory spirit of the monarch and the great complicity built by the royal couple since the early days were finally paying back, helping them to preserve the dynasty and the country's constitutionalism. This was reinforced in subsequent years through a series of political reforms, and a period of economic and social development that Portugal underwent until the end of the 1880s, known generically as the Regeneration Era.[26]

The Death of the Queen and the Regencies of Ferdinand

Only two years after these events, and at a time when the country was still healing from the still gaping wounds of three decades of political and military upheaval, Ferdinand was compelled to assume new responsibilities. With the death of Queen D. Maria, after giving birth to her eleventh child, in November 15, 1853, Ferdinand assumed the regency during the minority of the future King D. Pedro V until September 1855, having taken the oath only four days after his wife's death.[27] Despite the resentment that he probably could feel about the events and protagonists of the past decades, some of them still active in Portuguese politics at the time, he did not break his neutrality and kept the government running, surpassing without any fright the two years of this first period of regency. In essence, Ferdinand understood "after years of surprises and inconveniences," that the monarchy could only survive if it were above the parties and above the political factions. He tried to inspire this perspective in his sons, D. Pedro and D. Luís, the two following Portuguese kings, which ultimately may have contributed to the strengthening of the political consensus and for the peaceful military and social times of the next decades.[28] By this time Ferdinand had evolved far beyond the teachings of uncle Leopold, and a rather harsh experience of nearly 20 years produced a definitive maturity which was decisive in conducting the political affairs of the kingdom.

Ferdinand exercised the regency again in short periods of absence abroad of King Luís, his second son, who became king after the unexpected death from typhoid fever of D. Pedro V on November 11, 1861. D. Luís was travelling in France and Ferdinand assumed the Regency until his return, when the new monarch was acclaimed on December 22.[29] He was still at the helm of the country, between October and December, 1865, when D. Luís and his Queen Maria Pia undertook a European tour, and again in July 1867 when the young monarchs went to Italy for the wedding of Maria Pia's brother.[30]

In addition to the regencies, he continued to wield influence over his sons concerning the governance of the kingdom as he did during the reign of his wife. The relationship with D. Pedro V, although sometimes difficult due to a difference in personalities, never took a break from the family's "harmony" that Ferdinand always sought to pursue.[31] Some of the existing letters demonstrate a close proximity between father and son, in particular with regard to the education of D. Luís, for instance.[32] In addition, D. Pedro recognized in the "system of tolerance that was characteristic of my father" a political advantage, assuming that it was Ferdinand's achievement "the foundation" of the system that guaranteed the proper "distance between the monarch and the parties."[33]

Ferdinand also subtly dispensed advice to his second son, D. Luís, following his ascension to the throne. An example of this happened before the last period of Regency in 1867, precisely. The monarchs' journey to Italy was considered an "affront" by the Portuguese political press, taking into account the financial difficulties of the State at the time. This led Ferdinand to draw the son's attention to the touchiness of the situation. While the king did not cancel his trip to his brother-in-law's wedding, he did not fail to take into account Ferdinand's advice and eventually ended up travelling later than was predicted, being less time away from the country.[34]

Whether on personal matters, on state affairs, or on domestic politics, the informed and experienced voice of Ferdinand and his conciliatory personality represented to a certain extent, an asset that transmitted the ideals of monarchical constitutionalism to Portuguese politics. These characteristics also explain the prestige of his figure in international terms, which led him to being invited or proposed to assume two foreign thrones throughout the 1860s.

Ferdinand II and the Succession to the Greek and Spanish Thrones

After a few years of struggle Greece saw its independence recognized by the Ottoman Empire in 1832. International pressure exerted by Britain, France, and Russia, led the new nation to adopt the monarchy as a political regime, having been chosen Otto of Wittelsbach, Prince of Bavaria, for first monarch in 1833. In 1862 a military rebellion ended his reign and negotiations immediately began to find a new monarch. After some proposals not approved internationally, the choice was a young Danish Prince who ruled with the title of George I.[35]

Ferdinand was one of the presumptive candidates to whom the Greek crown came to be offered. Apparently, the initiative came from England, being supported also by Belgium, which sought support from other great powers, such as France or Russia in December 1862.[36] The English press highlighted the political qualities of the Portuguese monarch, including his role in the Regency during the minority of King Pedro V, when the monarch demonstrated a "strong will, much judgment and great experience in dealing with the Southern population."[37] In essence, Ferdinand's experience with a kingdom in almost permanent political and military turmoil as Portugal had been in the first half of the nineteenth century, and the fact that the country was now facing peace and economic development, seemed to grant to the former king consort of D. Maria II sufficient political attributes to qualify him for a hotly contested throne. However, Ferdinand was not interested in the proposal, valuing precisely that quiet phase that the country's political life and his own personal life went through, and declined the proposal in mid-January 1863, justifying the refusal, apparently, "on account of his affection for his sons."[38] In a letter to his cousin the Duke Ernest II he wrote that "at no point has he had the idea" of accepting the Crown of Greece.[39]

The second invitation to occupy a foreign throne at the end of the 1860s was more meaningful and generated more controversy. Indeed, between 1868 and 1870, Ferdinand was one of the most serious candidates to the Spanish crown.[40] The idea of an Iberian Union that the candidacy of Ferdinand obviously placed on the agenda, was widely publicized by the press after the events of September 1868 in Spain that led to the deposition of Isabel II. The Spanish revolution transformed a theoretical issue, which sometimes was a mere academic discussion or argument of political combat, into a clear achievable feature in the near future. The Spanish constitution ratified after the revolution required the choice of a king. However, the rebels did not have a specific candidate and in this context emerged as a hypothesis of the application of Ferdinand II. The first news began to be delivered in the Portuguese press as early as October 1868. Apparently it was the French Emperor, Napoleon III, who initially backed Ferdinand's candidacy, and the Portuguese press widely publicized this: "Is it true, says the [French] government gazette that the Emperor Napoleon protects the candidacy of D. Fernando, father of the king of Portugal, to the throne of Spain."[41]

In January 1869, after an interview with an envoy of General Prim, leader of the Spanish revolt, Ferdinand politely refused the offer. Despite this, the Spanish "progressistas" did not give up their intent and in February and March were able to gather support in the government and parliament of Spain, so that in early April it was decided in the council of ministers to officially offer the crown to Ferdinand. The king and the Portuguese government, however, took the initiative to address a telegram to the minister of Portugal in Madrid on April 6, to inform the Spanish government about a new refusal to the offer.[42]

In this response, the major influences were the political issues, in particular, the risks that the acceptance of the Spanish throne placed to Portugal's sovereignty as an independent state. Not even the reaffirmation of Prim in the Spanish parliament that Spain had not, with that proposal, any intention that Portugal would be part of the Spanish nation, has modified King Ferdinand's determination, after all, closely connected to the full enjoyment of his magnificent palace in Sintra. Along with his patriotic concerns, Ferdinand was more interested in his private life and the role of patron of the arts than to any political ambition.

Nevertheless, the Spanish diplomacy continued to promote the candidacy of Ferdinand and in May 14, 1870 a new contact came through the Spanish ambassador Férnandez de los Ríos. After some negotiations and an exchange of letters, Ferdinand imposed a set of conditions that clearly were intended to make the Spanish government give up. He demanded a written guarantee about the independence of Portugal and the impossibility of any Iberian union. As he wrote later, Ferdinand did not want to be responsible for "the union of the two peoples of the peninsula,"[43] which had little support in Portuguese public opinion. In addition, he demanded that his hypothetical candidacy was approved by three-fourths of the members of the Spanish Constituent Assembly, and a "clear agreement" from France and England. The Spanish government was not in a position to guarantee these conditions and Ferdinand's position had not changed, thus putting an end to the issue.[44]

Conclusion: Royal Complicities

Ferdinand liked consistency in his life, and was most comfortable within his family life and his patronage of the arts. In June 1836, he was elected president of the Royal Academy of Sciences, a position he held until his death. In October of the same year, together with the queen he became protector of the Royal Academy of Fine Arts, which, through funds granted by the monarch, would eventually acquire a wide range of art works, many of them today exposed at the Museu Nacional de Arte Antiga (National Museum of Ancient Art). It was also partly as a result of his commitment that the recovery and preservation of monuments took place. For example, important monasteries of Batalha, Mafra, and Tomar, the monastery of Jerónimos or the Belém Tower, in Lisbon, in addition to the construction of the Pena Palace in Sintra. This Maecenas role was also recognized abroad and his connections to the European cultural and artistic milieu were undoubtedly significant, as it is possible to illustrate by the fact that Franz Liszt had dedicated one of his works, *Heroischer Marsch im ungararischen Styl*, of 1840, to the Portuguese monarch.[45]

The king's inaptitude for military life, and the difficulties he had in the political field, especially in early years in Portugal, when he did not possess the power to intervene in kingdom's internal affairs, did not prevent him from playing a significant role in Portugal's destiny. Often this influence was conducted informally, such as advising the queen. But sometimes he was called to greater responsibilities by the queen, either because she often resorted to his advice, or delegated to him the responsibility of managing the diplomatic channels to various European courts and even with some important actors of the domestic politics, while she preferred to occupy herself with more informal and family correspondence.[46] This would eventually be one of the most important roles of Ferdinand as king consort, because the correspondence maintained regularly with family members in other courts put him in a very well-informed position about national and international politics and diplomacy. For example, through "a lively correspondence with his cousin," Prince Albert, Ferdinand was always aware of the British diplomatic initiatives and the position of English politicians facing the Portuguese political situation, something that had been decisive in 1847, as was mentioned.[47]

This close working relationship between the queen and her consort resulted largely from an intimate relationship based on real affection that the couple expressed from the first moment until the queen's death, as attested by the private correspondence between the Portuguese queen and Queen Victoria, as well as other sources. In April 1836, the future queen of the English welcomed the fact that Ferdinand was "much pleased with the good Queen, and she is delighted with him." Years later it was the turn of D. Maria assert Victoria that if "Albert soit comme Ferdinand... vous serez parfaitement heureuse."[48] Ferdinand himself claimed in a small private diary written after the queen's death that "there has never been a wife like her."[49]

But the relationship between Albert and Victoria was never exactly the same as the one between Ferdinand and Queen D. Maria, at least in what concerned the participation in the political affairs. While the queen of England, apparently, did not allow her consort to "see the state papers which were sent to her by the various government departments," Ferdinand participated and influenced the political life of D. Maria. According to a statement from Prince Albert, "all her visitors before they were allowed to see her and then [allow them] to do little more than to kiss her hand."[50]

Beyond the personal and private relationships, this complicity and the attitude of the Portuguese king consort early secured to the queen a decisive political support to allow the royal family to overcome the difficulties encountered and the lack of good political advice that they sometimes felt. Over time, though not always in a linear way, of course, those features allowed also for the assertion of a certain independence from the political quarrels and the maintenance of a relative equidistance toward the various political parties and factions. In this respect, Ferdinand's role—that everyone recognized, had a more conciliatory personality than the queen—eventually made him gain the respect of the population and the political class, both national and internationally. If after the queen's death Ferdinand did not play a more active political role, it was simply because he chose to focus on other facets of his life that he had not had the opportunity to truly enjoy between 1836 and 1853, because if he had proved to be a politically ambitious man, he would certainly have had the opportunity to move to the front of the throne regarding the international invitations made to him in subsequent years.

Notes

1. Maria Antónia Lopes, *Portugal e o Piemonte: a Casa Real Portuguesa e os sabóias: nove séculos de relações dinásticas e destinos políticos (XII–XX)* (Coimbra: Universidade de Coimbra, 2012).
2. F. J. Pinto Coelho, *Contemporâneos Ilustres. D. Fernando II de Portugal* (Lisboa: Imprensa Nacional, 1878); Visconde de Benalcanfor, *Elogio histórico de Sua Magestade El-Rei o Senhor D. Fernando II, presidente da Academia Real das Sciencias de Lisboa: recitado na sessão pública de 19 de Dezembro de 1886* (Lisboa: Typ. da Academia Real das Sciencias, 1886); Marquês de Valada, *Elogio historico de Sua Magestade El-Rei o Senhor D. Fernando II proferido em sessão solemne na Real Associação dos Architectos Civis e Archeologos Portuguezes* (Lisboa: s.n., 1886); Azevedo Neves, *El-Rei D. Fernando II: discurso pronunciado no Parque da Pena de Sintra* (Lisboa: s.n., 1935).
3. Ernesto Soares, *El-Rei D. Fernando II, artista* (Lisboa: Fundação da Casa de Bragança, 1952).
4. Lígia Cruz, *Algumas cartas de D. Fernando para seu filho o Rei D. Luís* (Coimbra: Universidade de Coimbra, 1985); Marion Ehrhardt, *D. Fernando II – Um mecenas alemão regente de Portugal* (Porto: Paisagem Editora, 1985); Palácio Nacional da Pena, *D. Fernando II e a ópera no século XIX: exposição* (Sintra: Palácio Nacional da Pena, 1985); Palácio Nacional da Pena, *D. Fernando Saxe Coburgo-Gotha: comemoração de 1o Centenário da morte do rei-artista* (Mem-Martins: Europam, 1985); Francisco Alberto Fortunato Queirós, *Carta de D. Pedro II, Imperador do Brasil, ao Rei D. Fernando II* (Porto: s. n., 1985); "Passagem por Montemor-o-Novo da rainha D. Maria II e rei D. Fernando II em Outubro de 1843," *Almansor – Revista de Cultura* no. 3 (1985): 179–189; José Teixeira, *D. Fernando II: Rei-Artista, Artista-Rei* (Lisboa: Fundação da Casa de Bragança, 1986).
5. António Cordeiro Lopes, "D. Fernando II e a condessa de Edla, um germânico e uma suíça na corte dos Bragança: do escândalo privado à contestação da monarquia (1869–1889)," *Revista da Faculdade de Letras* 21/22 (1997): 103–18; Maria de Fátima Bonifácio, *D. Maria II* (Lisboa: Círculo de Leitores, 2005); Teresa Rebelo, *Condessa d'Edla: a cantora de ópera quasi Rainha de Portugal e de Espanha (1836–1929)* (Lisboa: Alêtheia, 2006); Maria Filomena Mónica, *D. Pedro V* (Lisboa: Círculo de Leitores, 2006); Luís Espinha da Silveira and Paulo Jorge Fernandes, *D. Luís* (Lisboa: Círculo de Leitores, 2006).
6. Oliveira Martins, *História de Portugal*, vol. 1, 3rd ed. (Lisboa: Livraria Bertrand, 1882), 5–6; Luís Reis Torgal and Amadeu de Carvalho Homem, "Ideologia salazarista e «cultura popular» – análise da biblioteca de uma casa do povo," *Análise Social* 18, no. 72/74 (1982): 1439; Filipe Ribeiro de Menezes, *Salazar: A Political Biography* (New York: Enigma Books, 2009), 83–6.
7. A. H. de Oliveira Marques, *History of Portugal* (New York: Columbia University Press, 1972); Vasco Pulido Valente, *Os militares e a política (1820–1856)* (Lisboa: Imprensa Nacional-Casa da Moeda, 1997); Bonifácio, *D. Maria II*.
8. José Miguel Sardica, *A Regeneração sob o signo do consenso: a política e os partidos entre 1851 e 1861* (Lisboa: Instituto de Ciências Sociais, 2001); Carlos Guimarães da Cunha, *A Janeirinha e o Partido Reformista: da Revolução de Janeiro de 1868 ao Pacto da Granja* (Lisboa: Edições Colibri, 2003); Luís

Doria, *Correntes do radicalismo oitocentista: o caso dos Penicheiros (1867–1872)* (Lisboa: Imprensa de Ciências Sociais, 2004).

9. Fortunato Almeida, *História de Portugal*, vol. 6 (Coimbra: Edição do Autor, 1929), 259–60; Bonifácio, *D. Maria II*, 55–6 and 67; E. J. Feuchtwanger, *Albert and Victoria: The Rise and Fall of the House of Saxe-Coburg-Gotha* (Continuum International Publishing Group, 2006), 56.

10. Arthur Christopher Benson, ed., *The Letters of Queen Victoria. Vol. I – 1837–1843* (London: John Murray, 1908), 45; Jacques Willequet, "Léopold I et le Portugal. Une mission de Van de Weyer en 1836," *Revue belge de philologie et d'histoire* 28, no. 1 (1950): 97 and 101; Brison D. Gooch, "Belgium and the Prospective Sale of Cuba in 1837," *The Hispanic American Historical Review* 39, no. 3 (August 1, 1959): 426.

11. Benson, *The Letters of Queen Victoria. Vol. I – 1837–1843*, 45.

12. Ehrhardt, *D. Fernando II*, 8–10; Bonifácio, *D. Maria II*, 69; Lopes, *D. Fernando II*, 78–9.

13. Valente, *Os militares e a política (1820–1856)*, 39; Bonifácio, *D. Maria II*, 70.

14. Almeida, *História de Portugal*, 6:260; Damião Peres, *História de Portugal*, vol. 7 (Barcelos: Portucalense Editora, 1935), 251.

15. Teixeira, *D. Fernando II*, 53–7; Almeida, *História de Portugal*, 6:271.

16. Benson, *The Letters of Queen Victoria. Vol. I – 1837–1843*, 58; Willequet, "Léopold I et le Portugal. Une mission de Van de Weyer en 1836."

17. Lopes, *D. Fernando II*, 87.

18. Teixeira, *D. Fernando II*, 57–8.

19. Ibid., 59.

20. Arthur Christopher Benson, ed., *The Letters of Queen Victoria. Vol. II – 1844–1853* (London: John Murray, 1908), 117 and 134–5; Lytton Strachey, *Queen Victoria* (New York: Harcourt, Brace and Co., 1921), 116–7; Bonifácio, *D. Maria II*, 213.

21. Benson, *The Letters of Queen Victoria. Vol. II – 1844–1853*, 117; Maria de Fátima Bonifácio, *História da Guerra Civil da Patuleia, 1846–1847* (Lisboa: Editorial Estampa, 1993), 88–9 and 93–4; Lopes, *D. Fernando II*, 121–6.

22. José Trazimundo Mascarenhas Barreto, *Memórias do Marquês de Fronteira e d'Alorna D. José Trazimundo Mascarenhas Barreto ditadas por ele próprio em 1861*, vol. VII–VIII (Coimbra: Imprensa da Universidade de Coimbra, 1931), 228.

23. Maria de Fátima Bonifácio, *A Segunda Ascensão e Queda de Costa Cabral, 1847–1851* (Lisboa: Imprensa de Ciências Sociais, 2002), 253–7.

24. Sardica, *A Regeneração sob o signo do consenso*, 122–4; Maria de Fátima Bonifácio, *Um Homem Singular – Biografia política de Rodrigo da Fonseca Magalhães* (Lisboa: Leya, 2013), 211.

25. Bonifácio, *A Segunda Ascensão e Queda de Costa Cabral, 1847–1851*, 257; Bonifácio, *Um Homem Singular – Biografia política de Rodrigo da Fonseca Magalhães*, 212.

26. Sardica, *A Regeneração sob o signo do consenso*; Mónica, *D. Pedro V*; Silveira and Fernandes, *D. Luís*.

27. Almeida, *História de Portugal*, 6:320.

28. Peres, *História de Portugal*, 7:334–5; Sardica, *A Regeneração sob o signo do consenso*, 180–1.

29. Almeida, *História de Portugal*, 6:380–4; Christopher Hibbert, *Queen Victoria: A Personal History* (Cambridge: Da Capo Press, 2001), 279.

30. Teixeira, *D. Fernando II*, 82–3.
31. Lopes, *D. Fernando II*, 253.
32. Ruben Andresen Leitão, ed., *Cartas de D. Pedro V aos seus contemporâneos* (Lisboa: Livraria Portugal, 1961), 182.
33. Mónica, *D. Pedro V*, 184–5.
34. Cruz, *Algumas cartas de D. Fernando para seu filho o Rei D. Luís*; Teixeira, *D. Fernando II*, 83.
35. Adolphus William Ward and George Peabody Gooch, eds., *The Cambridge History of British Foreign Policy*, vol. 1 (Cambridge: Cambridge University Press, 1922), 611.
36. The National Archives, Lord John Russell: Papers 30/22/100/16, n.d., f. 33–8; Lord John Russell: Papers 30/22/105/40, n.d., f. 146–8; Lord John Russell: Papers 30/22/114/41, n.d., f. 90–5; D. Dawson, "The Archduke Ferdinand Maximilian and the Crown of Greece, 1863," *The English Historical Review* 37, no. 145 (January 1, 1922): 107 and 110; Ward and Gooch, *The Cambridge History of British Foreign Policy*, 1:611.
37. *The Spectator*, n.d., no. 1798, December 13, 1862.
38. *Hansard's Parliamentary Debates*, vol. CLXIX (London: Hansard, 1863), col. 1485.
39. Marion Ehrhardt, "D. Fernando II visto através das suas cartas à família," in *Romantismo: figuras e factos da época de D. Fernando II* (Sintra: Instituto de Sintra, 1988), 12.
40. Já em 1855 o monarca tinha sido sondado para ocupar o trono espanhol, mas sem grandes consequências. Lopes, *D. Fernando II*, 304–307.
41. *Revolução de Setembro*, n.d., no. 7904, October 10, 1868; Marques, *History of Portugal*, 438–9.
42. António Rodrigues Sampaio, *A União Ibérica e a candidatura de El-Rei Dom Fernando* (Lisboa: Off. Typ. de J. A. de Mattos, 1877), 133–6; Marques, *History of Portugal*, 439.
43. Ehrhardt, *D. Fernando II*, 24.
44. Sampaio, *A União Ibérica e a candidatura de El-Rei Dom Fernando*, 139–75; Peres, *História de Portugal*, 7:395–6.
45. Keith T. Johns, *The Symphonic Poems of Franz Liszt* (Pendragon Press, 1997), 73–4.
46. Bonifácio, *D. Maria II*, 56.
47. Frank Eyck, *The Prince Consort: A Political Biography* (Houghton Mifflin, 1959), 48–51; Feuchtwanger, *Albert and Victoria*, 72.
48. Benson, *The Letters of Queen Victoria. Vol. I – 1837–1843*, 47 and 200.
49. Bonifácio, *D. Maria II*, 74.
50. Hibbert, *Queen Victoria*, 126. Impression surely transmitted to the English royal family by the Duke Ernest II after his visit to Portugal in 1840. *Memoirs of Ernest II, Duke of Saxe-Coburg-Gotha. Volumes I-II. Embracing Period 1815–1850*, vol. I (London: Remington and Co., 1888), 99.

CHAPTER 11

Gaston d'Orléans, Comte d'Eu: Prince Consort to Princess Isabel of Brazil

Roderick Barman

In May 1871, the Emperor Pedro II who had by then ruled Brazil for over 30 years was about to depart on a trip to his beloved Europe. During his absence, his daughter and heir, Princess Isabel, was to act as regent with full powers. A key passage in the instructions he gave her ran: "So that no ministry will have the least suspicion of my daughter's role in public affairs, it is indispensable that my son-in-law, otherwise the natural adviser to my daughter, behaves in a way that gives no hint that he influences even by his councils my daughter's opinions." He was sure, the emperor added, that his son-in-law, Gaston d'Orléans, comte d'Eu, "would follow the example of the spouse of Queen Victoria, Prince Albert."[1]

Pedro II's advice reveals the dilemma that husbands of female rulers have long faced. On the one hand, women, no matter how exalted their rank, were until recently generally deemed to be weak, emotional creatures, lacking the constancy of purpose, the capacity for rational thought and the physical resilience that characterized males. They required husbands who could control and guide them and no one more so than a female ruler. On the other hand, in monarchies the ruler, regardless of gender, has been regarded as the embodiment of legitimate authority, the font of honour and the ultimate decision maker. Anyone who preempts the sovereign's roles is a usurper who undermines the monarchy's viability. This contradiction has meant that prince consorts could not be seen to be running the show while, due to the very nature of women, they were expected to do just that.

Two further factors could make the prince consort's role even more demanding and complicated. He was typically a foreigner and, when the marriage occurred, his wife was no more than heiress to the throne. He was faced with an unfamiliar language and culture and with a ruling monarch, usually his father-in-law, who was in no way inclined to share his authority with a novice and outsider. His new wife would probably not be of great assistance in either task, having been raised in seclusion from the larger world and accustomed to being a dutiful and admiring daughter.

All of these challenges faced Louis Philippe Marie Ferdinand Gaston d'Orléans, comte d'Eu, when, on October 15, 1864, he married at Rio de Janeiro Princess Isabel, the elder daughter and heir of Pedro II, emperor of Brazil. This chapter discusses first how the comte d'Eu, termed here "the count," dealt with the three critical issues of gender, foreignness, and familial tensions. Second, it considers how the count's actions contributed to the overthrow of the Brazilian empire on November 15, 1889. Given that the Emperor Pedro II did not die until after his dethronement, the count was never formally prince consort but, since Princess Isabel acted as regent three times—1871–72, 1876–77, and 1887–88—during her father's absences abroad, the count did in practice so serve.

But, first, let me provide some necessary background as to who the count was and how he came to be the husband of the heir to the Brazilian throne. Born at the château of Neuilly in April 1842, he was the child of Louis, duc de Nemours, the second son of King Louis Philippe, and of Victoire de Saxe-Coburg-Gotha et Kohary, "die röschen"—"the little rose."[2] Through his mother he was first cousin once-removed of Queen Victoria and Prince Albert. For his first six years the count enjoyed the privileged life of a royal prince. The 1848 revolution drove the Orléans clan into exile in England where the Nemours family enjoyed close relations with the British royal family. As an adolescent, the count embarked on a military career in Spain, serving in the Spanish-Moroccan war of 1859–60.[3]

The count's link to Brazil came through his uncle, François, prince de Joinville, who had married Pedro II's sister, D. Francisca. In September 1863, the emperor wrote to Joinville: "I have to arrange the marriage of my daughters, and our long acquaintance makes me count on you in every way." Pedro II's two sons having died in infancy, his heirs were his two daughters, then in late adolescence. No male in Brazil possessed the rank and standing to be bridegroom. Joinville's task was to find two suitable spouses from the royal families of Europe.[4] He eventually recommended two of his nephews, August of Saxe-Coburg-Gotha, the son of his sister Clementine. The two young men arrived at Rio de Janeiro at the start of September 1864, "entirely free of commitment" on either side.[5] Although their families had designated August for Isabel and Gaston for Leopoldina, Pedro II chose the comte d'Eu, then aged 22, to be husband of his elder daughter and heir, aged eighteen. Gaston and Isabel married just six weeks after their first encounter. August and Leopoldina wed two months after that.

In respect to the count's character and capacities, Joinville recommended him thus: "As a match for one of your daughters, that would be perfection. He is tall, strong, handsome, good, kind, very friendly, well educated, loving study and, what is more, already possessed of a certain military renown. He's 21. He is a little hard of hearing, it's true, but not so much as to constitute an infirmity." [6] Much of what Joinville claimed was accurate. His nephew was tall and fit. He was also highly intelligent, well educated, and hard working. But despite Joinville's assertion that his nephew was "handsome" and Princess Isabel's characterization of him as "charming," the count's large Bourbon nose and his gawky features made it difficult to regard him as good looking. [7] Nevertheless, for Princess Isabel, it was every bit the love match as that enjoyed by her husband's cousins, Victoria and Albert. In the words of a French physician, "Jamais je n'ai vu ménage plus tendre et plus uni; ils s'aiment comme des bourgeois."—"I have never seen a more united or tender couple; they love each other as if they were middle class."[8] The count would be a devoted if somewhat severe father to their three sons. In sum the count's personal character and private conduct were both laudable and fulfilling.

The count also showed some capacity in state affairs. As his correspondence demonstrates, he possessed considerable powers of observation and analysis. His talents as a soldier were displayed in 1869 when he was called to assume command of the Brazilian forces which had, since 1864, been fighting a territorial war with Paraguay. The count reorganized the Brazilian troops and led them to complete victory in a well-planned campaign. During Princess Isabel's three regencies, the count managed in quiet fashion the business of government for her, which she acknowledged. "As to the affairs of government I was very afraid that they would torment me more than they have...But I would be in difficulties if I did not have beside me my good Gaston who helps me so much and gives me such good advice."[9]

When all is said and done, however, the comte d'Eu cannot be accounted a success as a prince consort. He became intensely unpopular in Brazil, an unpopularity which endures to this day. The influence he exerted on public affairs was nugatory. What may be termed his "public persona" contributed significantly to the regime's loss of legitimacy and to its overthrow. An analysis of the causes for his failure provides a case study of the qualities necessary in a successful prince consort.

Postulating a root psychological cause to explain the insufficiencies of a historical figure is always debatable, but in the count's case, the evidence supporting such an interpretation is very strong. In a letter sent in 1877 to his former tutor, the count remarked "in regard to these moments of discouragement, if your physical problems make them inevitable, my bizarre and little enviable character makes me, I believe, far more often subject to them." In the same letter the count mentioned his "taste for solitude, a taste that comes close to being misanthropy."[10] In 1869 Princess Isabel identified the cause of her husband's "moments of discouragement": "you know how agitated you become during these moments of altercation."[11] In other words, any form of tension induced stress attacks which the count could not handle. Moments of intense stress caused psychological depression and triggered psychosomatic illness, usually respiratory or digestive.

The most serious incidence occurred in Paraguay late in 1869. The campaign he led achieved two decisive victories but failed to capture the Paraguayan president. "The abominable task of chasing López God knows where," to use the count's own phrase, became more than he could handle and he suffered a psychological and physical collapse that largely incapacitated him.[12] In June 1870, back in Rio de Janeiro, he informed his father: "The Paraguayan war has provided me with some good memories; but it has wiped me out intellectually and has created an invincible repugnance for any prolonged business or work."[13] The inertia and constant illnesses persisted for over a decade. He did not regain psychological equilibrium and physical health until the early 1880s.

The inability to handle stress and some physical limitations explain the count's incapacity to manage social relationships. As he himself wrote to his father, "I know how awkward I am in converse with those I don't know."[14] It was not just that he could not exude warmth, show interest, and make polite conversation, all indispensable for securing popularity. In his public conduct he was frequently brusque, haughty, and peevish. Part of the trouble was physical. His growing deafness meant that he could not follow and so participate in group conversations. Deafness also meant that, even though his command of Portuguese became excellent, he never lost his French accent which so grated on Brazilian ears. No wonder he became known as "*o francês*"— the Frenchman. Further, he was not impressive physically—gangling in posture, gawky in movement, and unkempt in clothing.

Compounding these psychological and physical drawbacks were the count's cultural upbringing and outlook. It was not that he was a reactionary in a political sense, indeed, he identified with Liberalism and favoured reforms, but in outlook he never assimilated or accepted Brazilian cultural norms. In 1877 lamenting the death of a senior member of his household, the count remarked: "his education in Europe and his contacts with the diplomatic world made him familiar with more exalted horizons, the which his compatriots usually don't share."[15] The count was never less than an aristocratic European—which many Brazilians realized and resented.

This sense of superiority and entitlement was to involve the count in considerable if covert difficulties with his new father-in-law, a relationship that was central to the success of the role he was intended to play. The count arrived in Brazil clearly expecting that he would be given a large share in governing the country. Pedro II was not accustomed to sharing power with anyone, and certainly had no intention of so doing with a family member. The basic incompatibility between the two men became apparent when, early in the Paraguayan war, the two spent three months in each other's company. Following the two men's return to Rio, the issue that divided them was the count's desire to serve in the Brazilian forces fighting in Paraguay. The count presented his repeated demands in so ham-handed a fashion as to permit the emperor, skilled at deflecting all challenges to his authority, to block the requests without appearing to do so and also as to leave the leading politicians unimpressed by the count's political capacity and disenchanted with his personality.

Although the antagonism between the count and his father-in-law never became overt, the disagreement did take on a political dimension—with the radical wing of the Liberal Party supporting the count. There could have emerged, at that moment a "dynastic opposition," centring on the count and his wife, such as existed as in Georgian England when the heir to the throne attracted the disaffected and served as an alternative to the political status quo. Early in 1869 the sudden need to find a new commander of the Brazilian forces in Paraguay caused the emperor to change tack, virtually beseeching his son-in-law to accept the post. As already discussed, the count gained decisive success as commander before collapsing into despair and inertia. The count's conduct earned him the contempt of his officers who hunted down and killed López, much to the count's surprise, confirming his sense of inadequacy. He at once wrote to the emperor:

> At this moment of such great and so unexpected emotion I cannot fail to think of Y. M. and to kiss your hand, asking you to forgive me for my lapses in faith and other childish acts
>
> Your loving and submissive son
Gaston[16]

From this moment onward the count eschewed any attempt to create an independent political position or to participate in the governing of Brazil. Not until May 1889, almost 20 years later, did the count seek to offer the emperor advice on public affairs, noting "it is the first time that I have spoken to him about politics."[17]

The count's passivity and withdrawal had a considerable impact on the imperial regime and its prospects for survival after Pedro II's death, because Princess Isabel, by no means unintelligent, concurred in the gender assumptions of the day, viewing politics and public affairs as a male, specifically her father's preserve. When not being a dutiful daughter, she depended on her husband, using him as her interface with the ministers and taking his advice on the conduct of business. Ideally, the couple should have used Princess Isabel's regencies to prepare the way for their future reign by signalling through their handling of state affairs and their public behaviour that Pedro II's death would bring the significant changes desired by many in Brazil. Instead, especially during the first regency, the couple copied Pedro II's style of governing and conduct as monarch precisely, down to the phraseology used in his official speeches.

By the time of the second regency in 1876–77, the count and his wife had, for various reasons including the princess' reputation as a fervent Catholic, become highly unpopular. They were subjected to endless and ruthless denigration, the count being denounced, quite unjustly, as the owner of slum properties in Rio de Janeiro, as the ruthless exploiter of the poor.

The couple virtually buckled under the onslaught, making no attempt to respond and deliberately retiring into private life. "When the Princess is no longer seen every day in the streets of Rio, she is forgotten for a while and there is less temptation to denounce each of her acts and decisions to a discontented public."[18] In 1878 the couple withdrew from Brazil and spent almost four years in Europe.

Princess Isabel's third regency differed markedly from the first two. She took over from her father when he was forced to seek treatment in Europe for an illness so serious as to raise questions about his survival. Inspired by her religious beliefs, the regent played a decisive part in achieving the abolition of slavery on May 13, 1888. She thereafter enjoyed a considerable but transitory popularity, from which her husband did not benefit. In the middle of 1889, the count, being in his own words "sick and tired of the press making me a scapegoat and holding me responsible for everything without in reality having either input or influence," undertook a three month tour without his wife through the north of Brazil.[19]

To the disaffected, his travels simply confirmed that, once Pedro II died, it would be the count, not his wife, who would be the real ruler of Brazil. Further his journey made him appreciate how deeply the propertied classes were alienated from the empire. The ex-slaves and people of African descent gave him a rapturous welcome but, he commented, "no regime that depends solely on the proletariat can survive or, more importantly, achieve any good."[20]

The count's diagnosis was justified more swiftly than he anticipated. On November 15, 1889, just three months after his return from the North, a coup by the garrison forces of Rio de Janeiro replaced the empire with a republic. The imperial family was bundled off to Europe, bringing the count's life as prince consort to an end. Only in 1921 did he revisit Brazil, accompanying the coffins of the emperor and empress for reburial there. A year later, in August 1922 he sailed again for Brazil to participate in the centennial celebrations of the country's independence. Seated at dinner on board the steamer, he leaned against his daughter-in-law and gently passed out of this life. A silent death in the mid-Atlantic was a fitting end for a man who, despite his exalted birth, intelligence, high culture, and good intentions, either did not possess or could not develop the talents required in a prince consort.

Notes

1. Pedro II, *Conselhos à regente* (Rio de Janeiro, 1958), 60.
2. Information from the deceased Isabelle, comtesse de Paris, the comte d'Eu's granddaughter, interview at Paris, February 25, 2001.
3. The best biography of the count remains Alberto Rangel, *Gastão de Orléans (o ultimo conde d'Eu)* (São Paulo, 1935).
4. In his reply to Pedro II's letter, Joinville stressed the difficulties of his assigned task, observing: "As Queen Victoria remarked to me, not so long

ago, there is nothing so difficult as marrying off a princess"; see AGP XXIX François, prince de Joinville, to Pedro II, Claremont [Surrey], November 6, 1863.

5. AGP XXXVIII Pedro II to François, prince de Joinville, Rio, May 8, 1864, copy in the hand of the Empress Teresa Cristina.

6. AGP XXIX François, prince de Joinville, to Pedro II, Claremont [Surrey], February 7, 1864. Joinville added: "What I know for a fact is that nowhere you will find anyone better than he," an encomium which revealed more about the paucity in number and poverty in quality of available royal princes than about the count d'Eu's own merits.

7. AGP XLI-4 Princess Isabel to Louis, duc de Nemours, São Cristóvão, September 3, 1865.

8. "Le Docteur DePaul au Brésil," *Le Figaro* (Paris), December 1, 1875.

9. AGP XL-4 Princess Isabel to Louis, duke of Nemours, Laranjeiras, June 26, 1871, (quoted in L. L. Lacombe, *Isabel*, pp. 143–4).

10. AGP XI-30 Gaston, comte d'Eu, to Jules Gauthier, Rio de Janeiro, March 28, 1877.

11. AGP XL-1 Princess Isabel to the comte d'Eu, Petrópolis, February 21, 1869.

12. Rangel, *Gastão de Orléans*, p. 206.

13. AGP Comte d'Eu to Louis, duc de Nemours, n. 105, Laranjeiras [Rio], June 22, 1870.

14. Comte d'Eu to Louis, duc de Nemours, October 25, 1875, in Rangel, *Gastão de Orléans*, p. 420.

15. AGP XLI-5 Comte d'Eu to the Luísa Margarida de Barros Portugal, comtesse de Barral, Petrópolis, January 12, 1877. The sentence quoted continues "so that he could judge for himself certain doctrines which, accepted here as the law and the prophets, have so greatly contributed to undermining the spirit of order and morality."

16. AGP XLI-1[1] Comte d'Eu to Pedro II, March 4, 1870.

17. AGP XLI-5 Comte d'Eu to the comtesse de Barral, Petrópolis, May 28, 1889.

18. AGP XLI-5 Comte d'Eu to the comtesse de Barral, Petrópolis, January 17, 1877.

19. AGP XLI-5 Comte d'Eu to the comtesse de Barral, Petrópolis, May 14, 1889.

20. AGP XLI-5 Comte d'Eu to the comtesse de Barral, Maranhão, July 29, 1889.

CHAPTER 12

The Rise and Fall of Siddiq Hasan, Male Consort of Shah Jahan of Bhopal

Caroline Keen

To assume the position of nawab consort in Bhopal at the end of the nineteenth century in anything but a purely passive role was in many ways courting disaster. Sayyid Siddiq Hasan Khan al-Qannauji al-Bukhari (1832–90), married to Shah Jahan, the third ruling begam[1] of the central Indian state, was seen through the influence he exerted over his wife to be subverting the existing political order of Bhopal in which women literally reigned supreme under the benign umbrella of the British Raj. Siddiq Hasan's steady, calculated assumption of power appeared to challenge both parties to the harmonious relationship which had been built up over generations between a ruling dynasty and the imperial power. To the royal family of Bhopal he was an evil force causing a deep schism among its members concerning the birthright of the family of Dost Mohammed Khan, its founder, to rule the state. To the British he was a scheming, immoral adventurer who, having succeeded at total emotional domination of the begam, attempted to control all aspects of the government of Bhopal by forcing his wife to adopt *purdah* while using the state's finances and machinery to propagate his anti-British "Wahhabi" campaign. Condemned by both British officials and the local dynasty, the nawab consort was subjected to a relentless witch hunt until hounded out of the Bhopal court.

This chapter examines the contributing factors to the downfall of Siddiq Hasan: the intense family and court resentment at the excessive power wielded by an outsider; the personal vitriol of an eccentric, irrational British political officer; and imperial circumstances which engendered a fear of the Indian Muslim response to pan-Islamism. It attempts to establish whether his activities in governmental and religious spheres within and without India warranted his disgrace and eventual removal or whether, as many Muslim historians believe, Siddiq Hasan was a highly distinguished religious scholar who engineered his personal aggrandisement as consort as a necessary requirement to promote within the Muslim world his beliefs in a return to Islamic roots, and whose writings were neither extremist nor seditious.

From its establishment in 1709 by the Pathan, Dost Mohammed Khan, the central Indian state of Bhopal produced prominent female figures who were active in public and political life. Women's political influence in Bhopal was carried a stage further in 1819 when Nawab Nazar Mohammad Khan died suddenly, leaving his 18-year-old widow, Qudsia Begam, to be invested with the supreme authority of the state. Appointed regent by the British political agent, Major Henley, until her daughter, Sikander, came of age and married, Qudsia emerged from behind the veil, hired a tutor to instruct her daughter in the "arts of war," and proceeded to introduce wide-ranging reforms. Sikander Begam followed in this tradition, forcibly claiming the throne from her husband and proving to be a highly competent ruler. She distinguished herself in particular for her loyalty to the British during the 1857 Mutiny and for significant improvements in the administration of the state. As a result the British withdrew their proviso that the husband of the succeeding begam should become nawab, naming Sikander's only daughter, Shah Jahan, as sovereign in her own right upon the death of her mother.[2] On November 16, 1868, Shah Jahan was crowned Begam of Bhopal. She was in a different mold to her mother and grandmother, who had ruled in a sense as "unisex Pathan chiefs," wearing male dress and known for their talents in riding, shooting, and directing their own troops.[3] Shah Jahan was petite and feminine, if feisty, an aspiring poet and patron of the arts. When widowed at 29 after an unsatisfactory arranged marriage to Baqi Mohammad Khan, the son of the commander in chief of the Bhopal army twice her age and twice married with children, she was not averse to being feted by ambitious courtiers. It proved to be Siddiq Hasan Khan, acting as tutor to the young begam, who succeeded in overcoming all rivals.

Sayyid Siddiq Hasan was born in the city of Bareilly in northern India on October 14, 1832. He was from a distinguished family of theologians who, as Sayyids, traced their ancestry back to the Prophet. His Shiite ancestors first settled in Bokhara and then migrated to Multan, where they became guardians of mosques and holy places until moving to the centres of Shiite culture, Bareilly and Kannauj. Siddiq Hasan's grandfather was an acclaimed scholar who was employed in a high post in Hyderabad and owned land and property. The family was involved in the doctrinal debate between various Muslim schools of thought and Siddiq Hasan's father, Sayyid Awlad Hasan, who converted to Sunni Islam in the early 1800s, was a strong supporter of the Muslim reformers Sayyid Waliullah and Sayyid Ahmad Barelvi. From the legacy of these scholars the Ahl-i Hadith movement emerged, adhering to the original Islamic texts of the Quran and the *hadith* (traditions based on the deeds and sayings of Muhammad), the promotion of individual judgment regarding the scriptures, and the eradication of what was perceived to be the polytheistic sanctification of holy men and the Shi'a *imams*. The Ahl-i Hadith, many of whose adherents had come from once great Muslim families who had fallen on hard times, were also millenarian, believing in a transformation of the world with the turning of the thirteenth Islamic century, a perspective which added urgency to their teachings. In an attempt to stamp out the oppression of Muslims on the North-West Frontier, Sayyid Ahmad Barelvi had famously marched to the area in 1826 to fight the Sikhs and the English, and Siddiq Hasan's father had accompanied him.[4]

Siddiq Hasan was five when his father died, but with the aid of his late father's friends was able to study Arabic grammar, jurisprudence, logic, philosophy, and theology at Farukhbad, Kanpur, and Delhi, and to become proficient in Arabic, Persian, and Urdu. In order to help his mother financially he moved to Bhopal in 1854, initially selling perfume before becoming a schoolteacher and augmenting his small income by preaching at mosques where he opposed the commentarial tradition of the schools of jurisprudence and propagated the return to a literal interpretation of Islamic scriptures. However in 1857 Siddiq Hasan was banished from Bhopal to the state of Tonk. His supporters claimed that he incurred the wrath of a leading *maulvi* (expert in Islamic law) of the Hanafi school of law,[5] Abbas Chiryakoti, who opposed the tenets of the Ahl-i Hadith and forced him out of the state, although Siddiq's detractors maintained that his behaviour had already attracted the unfavourable attention of Sikander Begam.[6]

In the aftermath of the Mutiny, the prime minister of Bhopal, Sayyid Jamal-al Din Khan, persuaded Sikander Begam to allow Siddiq Hasan to return, when he took up a position as clerk in the minister's office and married his widowed eldest daughter. By the mid-1860s, apparently enthusiastically sponsored by his father-in-law, Siddiq Hasan began to climb the administrative ladder and assumed the responsibilities of tutor to Shah Jahan, then still heir apparent. When Shah Jahan was installed as begam in 1868 she promoted Siddiq Hasan to her chief secretary and, as private meetings between the couple proliferated, rumours were widely circulated that begam and secretary were emotionally involved. In the circumstances, marriage into the Bhopal royal family was an essential requirement to ensure the unhindered political progress of the relatively poor and unconnected Siddiq Hasan. To further such an alliance, word was allowed to reach Colonel Edward Thompson, the political agent in Bhopal, that Shah Jahan was pregnant with her lover's child and that honour could be saved only by an immediate wedding.[7] Such an alliance was by no means an unsatisfactory option for the government of India which, faced with the awkward dilemma of a ruling begam carrying an illegitimate child, made it clear that it would be helpful for Shah Jahan to have a nonexecutive consort by her side to assist her in the duties of head of state.

However to her family the marriage was far from ideal. Marriages were historically arranged by "family elders concerned with issues of property, power relationship and status" as had been the case with Shah Jahan's first wedding. Moreover Hindu and Muslim elites alike looked down upon widows' remarriage as vulgar, even impure. In marrying Siddiq Hasan, Shah Jahan Begam "broke both the taboo on widow remarriage and the abhorrence of marrying outsiders," a move that was seen as potentially undermining the material interests of family property, and in this case, royal succession.[8] Shah Jahan's marriage to Siddiq Hasan took place on May 8, 1871, and a public function was held at which the British formally gave their seal of approval, underlining the fact that Siddiq Hasan was to play a nonexecutive role as consort. After this event the agent to the governor-general in Central India, Colonel Richard Meade, took Siddiq Hasan to Qudsia Begam's palace, where the bridegroom received an icy reception from the 70-year-old dowager who openly resented the latest relationship and subsequent marriage of her granddaughter, Shah Jahan, offended by the fact that "the husband was a man of alien race, and qualified neither by rank, position, nor character to be the consort of the ruler of a State."[9] For Sultan Jahan, daughter of Shah Jahan and heir apparent, the wedding marked "the commencement of one of the unhappiest periods of my life. Intrigue became rife in the palace and every kind of attempt was made to undermine my Mother's affection for me."[10]

Siddiq Hassan began immediately to consolidate his position and succeeded in procuring British agreement to his assumption of the title of Nawab Wala-Jah, Amir-ul-Mulk and a 17-gun salute in Bhopal.[11] He further insisted that Islamic orthodoxy required Shah Jahan to adopt *purdah*. Shah Jahan dutifully obeyed, thereby reversing the practice of her mother and grandmother of interacting open-faced with the opposite sex. To add to the strains within the Bhopal royal family the nawab consort attempted unsuccessfully to marry his son, Nurul Hasan, to Shah Jahan's daughter, Sultan Jahan, who had effectively grown up with Ahmad Ali Khan, the consort selected for her by her grandmother. Assembled in 1874 to adjudicate on the matter, the family elders and nobles of the state declared unanimously that there should be no deviation from the original decision, demonstrating the extent of aristocratic opposition to Siddiq Hasan. As Shah Jahan heaped ceremonial honours on the nawab consort and gave him increasingly important appointments at court, Bhopal's *jagirdars* (grantees of hereditary states) and Barru-kat[12] elite strongly resented their loss of control. The fact that Siddiq Hasan was not a Pathan, and had arrived in Bhopal as a peddler made him "a target of condescension and jealousy" on the part of Bhopal's gentry.[13]

Nine months after the wedding of Sultan Jahan and Ahmad Ali Khan in 1875, a first child was born and three other children followed in rapid succession, while, despite the rumoured pregnancy behind her marriage to Siddiq Hasan, Shah Jahan proved unable to carry his child. Bhopal's society was divided into two camps with court intriguers fuelling enmity between mother and daughter. On the side of the begam and nawab consort were the establishment Muslim reformist sympathizers and *jag-irdars* who sought to benefit from those in immediate power. Coalescing around Sultan Jahan, and her husband, Ali Ahmad Khan, were the Baqi-khel (Baqi Mohammad Khan's powerful family from his first wives) and the Jalalabadi clan that had arrived in Bhopal with Ahmad Ali Khan. The strongest support for Sultan Jahan came from her great-grandmother, the highly respected Qudsia Begam, tilting the backing of the Bhopal public in favour of the heir apparent.[14]

During the following years, matters between the two parties of the royal family dramatically deteriorated. At a durbar in 1877 convened in the name of his wife, Siddiq Hasan launched into unbridled criticism of the reign of Sikander Begam, describing it as "a period of barbarism and oppression," followed by a violent attack on Ahmad Ali Khan and family members of Baqi Mohammad Khan, calling them conspirators and a danger to the state.[15] Mother and daughter were further estranged in 1881 when, at a viceregal audience in Calcutta, the heir apparent took precedence over Siddiq Hasan in the seating plan, enraging Shah Jahan at her husband's humiliation. During the following years, although living in a palace with a *jagir* (hereditary estate), servants, and the outer paraphernalia of royalty, Ahmad Ali Khan and Sultan Jahan were subject to continuous hostile pressure and privation at the hands of Shah Jahan and Siddiq Hasan. Moreover, in a measure "void of reason" the heir apparent and her husband were forbidden to visit Qudsia Begam with their children or to accept her grandmother's gift of a dowry, which eventually, with the rest of Qudsia Begam's property, fell into the hands of the nawab consort when she died in 1881.[16]

With the death of the prime minister, Sayyid Jamal-al Din Khan, in the same year, Siddiq Hasan accelerated his attempts to gain control over the state, placing his own appointees in key positions such as *Mir-Munshi* (Chief Clerk) and Chief of Police. Shah Jahan remained in *purdah*, rarely going out to meet her subjects, a task that she increasingly left to her consort. British officers were increasingly alarmed at the arrogation of power by the nawab, the dissipation of government funds, and the promotion of his family members in the state hierarchy. More alarmingly his articles, books, and pronouncements appeared to border on sedition. Giving a financial boost to his literary activity, Siddiq Hasan received a handsome *jagir* worth Rs. 75,000 a year as a result of his promotion to the post of *Mu'tamad al-Mahamm*, second only to that of the prime minister, and the support of an efficient team of *ulama* (Muslim legal scholars) of the royal court of Bhopal.[17] It was suspected by the government of India that state funds were being used to encourage the more politically active *ulama* into creating a groundswell of opposition against the British based on religious grounds. In addition it was reported that the nawab's emissaries had established contact with counterparts abroad, notably in the Sudan where the Mahdi was active against the British, and also in Arabia, Turkey, and Burma.[18]

Nevertheless the political agent in Bhopal, William Prideaux, was of the opinion that the nawab consort did not pose a serious threat, declaring that he was merely

> a bigoted Muhammedan and a man of great vanity. It would appear from his writings that he is desirous of enhancing his reputation for sanctity among his co-religionists, and at the same time posing before the eyes of foreigners as a great temporal prince... [with] a string of pompous titles which he gives himself in the books printed at Constantinople, ending with the usual designation of "Malik Mamalakah Bhopal," King of the Kingdom of Bhopal.

In the view of Prideaux, although Siddiq Hasan was prepared to distribute "Wahabi [sic] tracts" he was "confident that the Nawab would not risk a hair of his head to give them practical effect."[19] Sir Henry Daly, agent to the governor-general in Central India, was in agreement with the political agent that the government of India should not overreact to the nawab consort's activities, fearing that the result of degrading Siddiq Hasan in an attempt to "stamp out sedition" would be "the loss of Bhopal as a friend to the British government" and the creation of the idea worldwide that "dangers exist in India, which in fact have no existence."[20]

British sensitivity to the ramifications of the work of Siddiq Hasan has to be placed in the wider context of the rise in Indian Muslim dissatisfaction with British rule. During the eighteenth and early nineteenth centuries, East India Company servants, particularly Muslims, had become involved in preexisting pilgrimage networks of shipping, lodging, and financial transactions. With the growth of the steamship era *hajj* these routes increasingly provided outlets for Indian Muslim activists, merchants, and radicalized members of the *ulama*, many of whom had been displaced by the advance of European interests in India and after undertaking a pilgrimage to Mecca had settled in Aden, the Hijaz, Egypt, Syria, and Istanbul. Among these immigrants were growing numbers of Afghans who, with bitter experience forged by years of fighting with the British, provided a volatile anti-imperialist and anti-Christian element.[21]

The potential for the spread of anticolonial resentment was fuelled dramatically by events of the Indian Mutiny of 1857. British officials were quick to label the rebellion as an example of Muslim fanaticism and, despite the oversimplified assumptions behind such views, much of the symbolism of the Mutiny was undeniably Muslim; when they captured the Mughal capital of Delhi the mutineers fashioned the elderly Mughal emperor, Bahadur Shah, as the leader of the revolt, and uprisings followed in predominantly Muslim areas, such as the North-West Frontier and the recently annexed province of Awadh. In the wake of 1857, defeated and deprived of Mughal power and prestige, Indian Muslims turned increasingly toward the Ottoman Caliphate "in search for an alternative psychological and spiritual center."[22] Gradual political decline and loss of economic privileges, together with a creeping British disregard of the genuine differences of opinion that often accompanied *sharia* law (the religious law of Islam) in favour of a rigid colonial legal process, added to Muslim discontent over the following decades. At the same time the surge in growth of India's vernacular press, particularly in Urdu, provided Muslims with greater access to news from around the Islamic world, much of which was translated from Turkish and Arabic newspapers, and the government of India became increasingly sensitive to the trans-imperial networks being forged between Indian dissidents and the Porte.[23] However diffuse these links may have been during the 1850s and 1860s, by the accession of Sultan Abdul Hamid II in 1876 they had coalesced into a more substantial pan-Islamic movement and British officials in India began to express concern at the scale of the Indian Muslim diaspora in Mecca and the Red Sea region, and its potential as a conduit for far-reaching radicalism.

The instability of the region induced the Viceroy of India, Lord Lytton, to point out to Queen Victoria in 1876 that "If either by pressure of public opinion at home, or political difficulty abroad, Your Majesty's government should be forced into a policy of prominent aggression upon Turkey, I am inclined to think that a Mohammedan rising in India is among the contingencies we may have to face."[24] The Eastern Crisis of 1875–78 precipitated such a change in policy, when the British Liberal statesman William Gladstone spearheaded a public denunciation of the "Bulgarian horrors" perpetrated by the Ottomans against their non-Muslim subjects in the Balkans, sparking off an anti-Turkish crusade in the press which effectively ended Britain's pro-Ottoman policy. When Russia invaded Turkey in 1877, Britain failed to respond and was no longer able to tout itself to Indian Muslims as the Sultan's ally and protector, leaving many Indian Muslims further disillusioned with colonial policy.

With the Ottoman empire's significant loss of both territory and the majority of its non-Muslim population in the Balkans as a result of the Russo-Turkish War, Sultan Abdul Hamid placed more emphasis on the Islamic foundations of the Ottoman state, stressing his position as defender of the Holy Places, the *Haram al-Haramayn*, in Mecca and Medina.[25] Fuelled by the assumption of this role, the pan-Islamic response to imperialism started to grow into a conscious, focused activity as the Ottomans began aggressively to assert the Sultan's ecumenical claim of jurisdiction over Muslims living under the rule of non-Ottoman governments. The social and political fabric of the entire *dar al-Islam* (Islamic world) had come under increasing pressure from the imperial powers of Europe, especially Britain, France, the Netherlands, and Russia, and in response to these encroachments, disparate groups of Muslims from Central Asia to Indonesia rallied around the Ottoman Caliphate, giving impetus to the idea of a broad based movement to coalesce under the auspices of loyalty to Sultan Abdul Hamid.[26] To widen the appeal of such a movement, the concept was piloted of Islamic solidarity based not only on traditional religious and ethnic principles, but also on Tanzimat-inspired[27] notions of equity, justice, rule of law, and constitutional ideas of protecting minority rights. In his belief in the urgency of uniting Muslims by standardizing norms of deportment, discipline, and notions of morality around the template of the Quran and the *hadith*, Siddiq Hasan proved to be one of the prime movers in an intellectual current that connected modernist *ulama* and reformist bureaucrats of the Middle Eastern and North African provinces of the Ottoman empire to similarly oriented scholars in India.[28] It was the proliferation of "inflammatory" material circulating within this current which so alarmed the government of India.

The nawab's literary activity was powered by the introduction and expansion of printing technology in India and the private presses that became available to local elites, and he had his own printing presses in Bhopal, the most famous being the Shahjahani. Influenced by contacts he had established en route to performing the *hajj* in 1869, the nawab consort was ideologically linked to one of the most influential Islamic thinkers of the time, the great Yemeni scholar Muhammad ibn 'Ali ash-Shawkani (1759–1834). There were already Yemeni followers of Shawkani enjoying patronage at the Bhopal court when Siddiq Hasan arrived in the state and he became part of their circle, printing and disseminating his translations and editions of Shawkani, and other scholars outside India, within the Hejaz, Cairo, Istanbul, and other Ottoman cities.[29] While the nawab consort did not travel extensively himself, he was acutely conscious of his audience across the British and Ottoman worlds when he wrote some 80 books in Arabic, Persian, and Urdu. The emphasis in most of his work was on consultation, self-judgment (*ijtihad*), reason, and rationality. As a disciple of the Ahl-i Hadith he remained committed to the principle of purifying Muslim behaviour of all practices not in accordance with the *sharia* and argued[30] for the rejection of the decisions of the medieval law schools[30] and a return to jurisprudential techniques sanctioned by the textual sources of the Quran and the *hadith* (such as *qiyas*, or argument by analogy, and *ijma*, or the consensus of *ulama* on a point of law).[31] He had a well-financed and sophisticated network of traders, scholars, and activists to distribute his books, which were published from India, Mecca, Medina, Istanbul, and Cairo. At the same time his agents also sourced manuscripts in these areas and this material was published by the Shahjahani press.[32]

The stress upon independent thought expressed in Siddiq Hasan's writing and the impressively wide dissemination of his texts raised alarm in British circles where his literature was deemed "seditious," anti-British, and with the potential to raise pan-Islamic opinion against their rule.[33] As a result the nawab consort was labelled a Wahhabi, a term derogatorily employed by the British to describe men of religion whom the British suspected of being followers of the religious reformist Ibn Abd al-Wahhab (1703–1792) of Najd in the Arabian Peninsula, who had challenged both Ottoman and British control of Arab provinces. The Indian civil servant William Wilson Hunter, in his semi-official history *The Indian Musalmans* (1871) in tune with other contemporary British observers blamed Sayyid

Ahmad Barelvi's Wahhabi-inspired religio-political activism in North India as the inspiration behind the Indian Mutiny and other earlier frontier incidents in India, vividly describing Wahhabi influence as a "chronic conspiracy" and "a standing rebel camp" which threatened both India's frontiers and its internal security. Hunter's readers were left to assume that external influences, rather than heavy-handed British policies, were the primary source for Muslim radicalization in India.[34] The term Wahhabi conjured up fanaticism, although in its embrace of violence in alliance with political power the Arabian movement differed notably from Indian movements. However the label in India had first come into use for Islamic thinkers such as Sayyid Ahmad Barelvi whose works had remained influential for the Ahl-i Hadith, thereby apparently creating a lasting association between violent activism and Islamic movements such as the Ahl-i Hadith in British eyes.[35]

In his defense, Siddiq Hasan wrote the *Tarjuman-I Wahhabiyah*[36] (An Interpreter of Wahhabism) in 1884 against the charge of being called a Wahhabi. The nawab consort objected to the term being used, not only because of its anti-British connotations and its association with the use of violence, but also because the Najd Wahhabis had "stamped Islamic universalism with territorial localism" that went against the Islamic concept of *tawhid*, the idea of a universal God rather than a local, tribal, or parochial deity.[37] Siddiq Hasan maintained that he wished to widen his outreach by benefiting from the new imperial and maritime networks of the late nineteenth century to dispense literature to uphold the scripturally sanctioned idea of Muslim unity, unfettered by an adherence to a single leader such as Muhammad Ibn Abd al-Wahhab. Indeed passages from the *Tarjuman* suggest that Sadddiq Hasan was far from eager to destroy the British supremacy which provided him with communication channels through which he could forge reformist links.[38] Seema Alavi points out that it is interesting that Siddiq Hasan devotes an entire chapter of the *Tarjuman* to caution Indian princes and nawabs not to break their agreements and treaties with the British. He invokes the *hadith* to argue that God and the Prophet desired that, for the sake of universal peace, treaties and agreements should not be violated on superficial pretexts. Moreover he was prepared to intervene in the case of Muslim *jihadis* on the North-West Frontier to convey to the rebels that the taking of arms against the British was un-Islamic and was disappointed when the lieutenant governor of the Punjab did not agree to send his messages to Hazara.[39]

However British officers and in particular Sir Lepel Henry Griffin, agent to the governor-general in Central India, chose to ignore any apparent indications of loyalty on the part of Siddiq Hasan, and it was under Griffin that the Bhopal crisis escalated in the 1880s. Up to his arrival in central India, Griffin's career had been impressive despite the fact that he was a highly provocative character.[40] In 1878 his perceived brilliance had earned him the appointment of chief secretary to the Punjab and in 1880 the viceroy, Lord Lytton, entrusted him with the job of unravelling the disastrous aftermath of the second Afghan War. Fresh from success in Afghanistan and appointed a knight commander of the Star of India, Griffin was despatched by Lytton's successor, Lord Ripon, to the central Indian agency in 1881. Ripon was warned against making the appointment on the grounds that an agency of 148 states required "great tact and firmness" and it was argued that Griffin should be kept in the secretariat and not given serious responsibility in such a wide political sphere.[41] The Viceroy chose to ignore this advice, dramatically affecting the course of the reign of Shah Jahan Begam.

From the outset, Griffin displayed "a visceral dislike for the scholarly, cowardly, and arrogant outsider in Bhopal," Siddiq Hasan, whereas he took a great liking to Sultan Jahan and her husband who was an old-style Pathan.[42] Griffin also wished to see a begam of Bhopal ruling according to the traditional martial stance of her female forebears, regretting Shah Jahan's decline into the role of the "degraded" Oriental woman existing in submissive subordination to her husband.[43] He dismissed the ruler as "a weak misguided woman… [who] had permitted her State and her subjects to become the prey of an adventurer" and reported that since her second marriage the begam had become "a mere cypher in the hands of her husband."[44] Nothing short of banishing Siddiq Hasan from the state would provide an effective remedy for the existing maladministration of Bhopal; as long as her husband was allowed to remain in the state, the begam would be entirely unable to shake off his authority and govern on her own account through responsible ministers. In Griffin's view:

> It is impossible to exaggerate the ascendancy which he [Siddiq Hasan] has acquired over the Begam. All her attendants and relations attribute it to charms which he has given her, and which she wears in her hair and there is, indeed, something almost miraculous in her steadfast adherence to a man whose forgeries, perjuries and tyranny are thoroughly known to her. She cannot plead ignorance and she is as fertile as her husband in inventing lies to screen offences and crimes of his, which she is unable to deny.[45]

To British officers the inaccessibility of the Begam was much to be regretted since she had adopted *purdah*, moreover her female visitors had been discouraged from coming to the palace with the result that she was "virtually a prisoner." All information on state affairs "she has heard with the ears of the Nawab and seen with his eyes alone."[46]

Griffin's concern was not confined to the situation within palace walls. Under his eagle eye British intelligence outside India was alerted to every sign of intrigue on the part of Siddiq Hasan, convinced that in the books being taken out of India, "very startling disclosures of the Nawab's treachery, and his secret agencies will be made."[47] Egypt proved to be a fertile destination for reformist literature as Cairo connections with Indian Muslims were strengthened considerably after the British takeover of Egypt in 1882. The anti-British political feeling among ousted Ottoman officials in Egypt added to the popularity of authors such as the nawab consort, whose works setting out universal frames of belief, etiquette, and norms for the unity of the *ummah* (Islamic community) were printed on private and imperial printing presses in Cairo and Istanbul. Indian publications on these themes were welcome not only in Cairo but also in the larger Ottoman world that was "energised with similar ideas of Islamic solidarity based on Tanzimat inspired reformist modernism."[48] The fear of British surveillance made their distribution and return into India difficult, however via the Ottoman administration in the Hijaz small numbers were smuggled to Mecca where they were distributed to Indian and other *hajjis*.[49]

Anxious reports from Austen Henry Layard, the British ambassador at Constantinople, pointed to Mecca as the main point of contact for anti-British activities, warning that "ex-mutineer Indians at Mecca were in communication with the Porte and that through them the Ottomans could make an attempt to bring about a rising in India."[50] In 1885 Abdur Razzack, the British vice-consul at Jeddah, had four men arriving from Bombay followed and eventually arrested in Mecca. These men were ostensibly carrying the nawab's books and periodicals for distribution to Indian *hajjis*, and it was believed that the material they carried had already been circulated in the area before their arrival by "disaffected people from India, relics of 1857 and of the later wahabi [sic] movement."[51] Three other men from Bhopal had also set off for Mecca but apparently had changed route and opened communications with Osman Digha, the Mahdi of Sudan's son-in-law,[52] British fears that the Sudan was attractive both for forging anti-British political alliances and for dipping into the profits of the slave trade were increased by the arrest of two *maulvis* from Bengal and Meerut on suspicion of being involved in "treasonable" correspondence with the Mahdi party. These men had lived in Mecca for two years and had licences from the Ottoman administration to act as religious guides to Indian pilgrims. On their arrest they were found to be in possession of the Mahdi's proclamations and many works on reformist Islam written by Siddiq Hasan.[53]

Finally Griffin was supplied with more concrete grounds for action. In 1885 he reported that one of the nawab consort's emissaries, Din Muhammad, had been despatched to the Sudan to assess the potential of the North African network. Din Muhammad was a Hindu convert to Islam who had been employed as the favourite servant of Shah Jahan's grandmother, Qudsia Begam. He failed to deliver the required information and was dismissed by Siddiq Hasan. As a result he turned to Griffin, who predictably viewed the nawab consort's search for local knowledge as a political move to forge an anti-British alliance with the Mahdi.[54] Din Muhammad's deposition revealed the vast network of contacts which existed in the Ottoman world, stretching from the Hijaz to North Africa, and the fact that many personal agents of the nawab consort existed in the area. Alighting upon the potential sedition which these contacts were capable of fostering and citing widely circulated literature such as the *Hidayat ul Sail*[55] and a collection of *khutbas* (sermons), the *Diwan al-Khutub*,[56] as calls to *jihad*, Griffin bombarded Siddiq Hasan with demands for his material to be withdrawn and delivered a series of memoranda to members of the viceroy's council calling for the nawab consort's removal.

Siddiq Hasan defended himself against the accusation that he was involved in subversive activity in the Ottoman world and Afghanistan by declaring that he was "a scholar and could read Arabic" and that in itself should explain why he was part of the intellectual energy in the Ottoman lands and beyond.[57] He insisted that his writings stimulated religious debate rather than inciting violence, declaring that "The practice of refuting one another's religion is carried on among Muhammedans and Christian men of learning and religious books are compiled, and discussions on religious matters are made by others in other places in India; but no disturbance of the peace appears to have been created thereby."[58] The nawab consort argued that he was oblivious to the legal framing of British India as separate from the wider Islamic literary world, stating that most of the time since he arrived in Bhopal had been devoted to translating and compiling books which he would not have undertaken had he known that such works were prohibited by British law.[59] Moreover, as his supporters claimed, rather than expressing his own opinions his books were compendia of knowledge culled from other authors without reference to its correctness or otherwise. By combining the new facilities of print and faster communication with the older Muslim networks of traders, scholars, and activists he was simply facilitating the dissemination of scriptural commentary to a greater Muslim audience.[60]

However Siddiq Hasan's protestations and his agreement to the withdrawal of the most "offensive" works failed to diminish Griffin's determination to rid the state of "a traitor exciting his coreligionists to open opposition to the British Government."[61] To achieve such a goal some delicacy was required. Sir Henry Durand, foreign secretary to the government of India, advised Griffin that "more harm than good would be done by directing public attention in India to the matter, that the feeling in England was against punishing a man for his writings, [and] that the case might be misunderstood in Europe and magnified into a great Mahommedan conspiracy among the Native States." The unanimous opinion of the government of India was that if the nawab were to be removed, it must be done on the grounds of his "evil influence" in Bhopal rather than his seditious writing.[62]

There were undoubtedly grounds for Siddiq Hasan's dismissal as far as the maladministration of the state was concerned. Griffin had reported that the nawab's control, particularly in the criminal department, was "tyrannical, corrupt, and oppressive" with no "reasonable security for life and property" and there was ample corroborated evidence of torture and imprisonment without trial. In addition there had been dramatic increases in customs and transit duties, and a corrupt system of revenue collection had resulted in the emigration of over 7,000 cultivators.[63] Moreover, despite extolling the virtues of free speech, Siddiq Hasan was allegedly attempting to bribe *The Pioneer* newspaper in Allahabad and to shut down the local Bhopal press which criticised his rule.[64] In the view of the agent to the governor-general, "unless the Government were prepared to break the power of the nawab, a popular rising against him would probably take place in Bhopal."[65] However Sir Steuart Bayley, a member of the viceroy's council, mistrusted Griffin's judgment, suspecting that the agent had "exaggerated the amount of misgovernment" and "underestimated the effect which the deportation of the Nawab will produce on the Begam's mind and in other Native States."[66] Sir Henry Durand agreed, citing examples of gross misgovernment in other states, such as Indore and Kashmir, where there was no attempt to punish the ruler concerned. Nevertheless it was feared that the "disloyal and seditious" nawab consort, even if "hated" in Bhopal, would in all inevitability conspire in some form against the government of India and it would be advisable to prevent him from doing "further mischief" if the government had a sufficient case against him.[67]

Having received official sanction for limited disciplinary action against Siddiq Hasan, Griffin called a restricted meeting in Bhopal in August 1885 to which ministers and leading officials were summoned. He then catalogued the charges against the nawab consort while praising the begam for her administration and loyalty to the British Crown. The following day Griffin called a smaller gathering at which he insisted that the begam and her husband be present. At this meeting he read out passages from books which were considered seditious if not treasonable. He also produced evidence of misgovernance and corruption, accusing the nawab consort of taking decisions while Shah Jahan was denied access to information in *purdah*. After the agent departed, Shah Jahan issued a *yaddasht* (memorandum) in which she publicly proclaimed that Siddiq Hasan would not interfere further in state affairs.[68] However by October 1885 intelligence sources revealed that there was no decrease in either his control over his wife or the amount of Wahhabi material which continued to emerge, albeit by a more underground route. As a result at a durbar summoned by Griffin on October 27 with the approval of the viceroy, Lord Dufferin, the nawab consort was stripped of all his honours, including the 17-gun salute, the honorary gifts, and the title "nawab." He was also barred from any further role in governing the state. Griffin reported to Henry Durand that the begam, although shocked, took the decision silently and with dignity. Siddiq Hasan "maintained an impassive appearance and did not raise his eyes: his agitation being alone visible in his rapid breathing, which he could not control, especially at the mention of punishment" which, no doubt to his relief, did not include deportation.[69]

For the following five years Shah Jahan never ceased in her efforts to bring about the restitution of her husband's titles, writing to Lady Mayo, General Sir Henry Daly, and Lords Northbrook, Lytton, and Ripon regarding her "grievances" and visiting the viceroy, Lord Dufferin, in Calcutta in

March 1886 in an unsuccessful attempt to bring about a reinvestigation of the case.[70] Fuelling her campaign, in 1887 the Education Steam Press produced a 51-page long pamphlet in defence of Siddiq Hasan. This was an appeal from his supporters to Griffin and Dufferin, urging them to drop the charges of corruption, of exhortations to *jihad,* and of the publication of seditious literature, adding a plea for his writings to be understood in their proper context. The pamphlet underlined the consort's status as both a loyal subject and a man embedded in the literary culture of the Islamic world that extended beyond British India.[71] However it failed to convince the government of India that Siddiq Hasan had lost his appetite for power. It was suspected that soon after the durbar depriving him of governmental duties he attempted to gain control over the incoming British minister, Colonel Saurin Brooke, in an effort to have his case brought before Parliament. Moreover Griffin's successor, Francis Henvey, reported in August 1888 that, in spite of efforts to accommodate Siddiq Hasan in a different palace to his wife, for all intents and purposes the couple were "one and indivisible" and with his wife's collusion the consort was succeeding in collaring government officials each evening to overturn to his advantage decisions made during the day.[72]

At the same time the royal family rift deepened over the case of Bilqis Jahan, the eldest daughter of Sultan Jahan, who, in keeping with the tradition of most Muslim families in which the firstborn grandchild was brought up by the grandmother, had lived with Shah Jahan from the age of four. Animosity was caused by attempts on the part of Siddiq Hasan to groom his younger son, the 19-year-old Ali Hasan who was already married with children, to marry Bilqis, attempts which failed when the young princess died from typhoid after her removal from the begam's palace by Sultan Jahan. As tension between the ruler and the heir apparent had increased over the years, Bilqis had become the only link between her mother and grandmother, and her death irrevocably ended any possibility of reconciliation.[73]

By the end of the 1880s there were signs that the government of India was weakening over the restitution of the consort's honours. A note from the office of the viceroy, Lord Lansdowne, dated February 22, 1890, stated that the case of Siddiq Hasan had been discussed at length in council. The points considered in his favour were the "constant loyalty" of the begam, the condition of Siddiq Hasan's health, and the fact that he had suffered five years' degradation, and the accepted view that affairs in Bhopal were being administered in "a satisfactory manner." Given that sufficient punishment was seen to have been inflicted on the consort, it was now possible without loss of face on the part of the government of India to recommend to the secretary of state for India that Siddiq Hasan might be given back, not a right to "active interference" in the government of Bhopal, but the honours of which he was deprived in 1885.[74] However this final concession came too late. The note concluded with the news that a telegram had been received from central India announcing the death of the consort from hepatitis. Although death put an end to Shah Jahan's plans for reinstating her husband, she determined that, although the government of India had refused to honour him while living, in future correspondence Siddiq Hasan should be referred to as "the late Nawab and husband of the Ruler," a title which after some deliberation was granted by the viceroy, Lord Lansdowne.[75]

On February 28, Francis Henvey reported to the foreign secretary of the government of India, William Cuningham, that Siddiq Hasan's funeral had been "very largely attended, notwithstanding his alleged unpopularity." In Henvey's opinion the government of India had in Bhopal, as elsewhere, been seriously misled and that "Muhammedan sentiment is on the side of Siddiq Hasan to an extent we never dreamt of," tending to give him "the dignity of a Shahid or Martyr."[76] Henvey's analysis of the situation proved to be prescient and the persecution and humiliation that the consort was seen to have suffered at the hands of the British became increasingly viewed as a badge of honour by his followers.

Conclusion

As the most prominent and certainly most prolific spokesman of the Ahl-i Hadith, the depth and legacy of Siddiq Hasan's work bear witness to the fact that he was a religious scholar of considerable standing. Although modern Muslim historians regard him as one of the earliest anticolonial stalwarts in his support of Muslim nationalism there is no evidence that he personally wished to subvert British rule. His misfortune in attracting what appears to be disproportionate attention to his output was due largely to timing. Having academic feet in two empires in the latter part of the nineteenth century aroused the suspicion of British officials, who mistrusted Indian Muslim activists and were particularly wary of Muslim scholars who in their espousal of Islamic solidarity were courted by Ottoman Turkey. No doubt in the wrong hands some of Siddiq Hasan's publications could have been used in an inflammatory context, however it appears that his material was never adopted to incite violence. In the centres in and immediately adjacent to India where he concentrated his efforts, such as Benares, Dinapur, Patna, Rangoon, Dacca, and the North-West Frontier regions of Swat and Sittana there was no evidence of uprisings. Moreover it appears that, ironically, far from engendering violence as the British feared, pan-Islamism removed the necessity for extreme action by providing Indian Muslim activists with a good case against British condemnation. Given Queen Victoria's post-Mutiny guarantees of religious freedom,[77] such activists were able to argue that their organizational and financial efforts to support the Ottoman Sultan-Caliph and the protection of the Holy Places were wholly legitimate expressions of religion rather than seditious acts of *jihad* or nationalism.

However from the British standpoint there could be no room for complacency. Lepel Griffin was not alone in his reaction to the influence wielded by the nawab consort and the decision to depose him and to withdraw his titles was taken by consensus, not by one man. Griffin was undoubtedly abrasive and tactless in his vindictive personal pursuit of Siddiq Hasan, but his views were in line with the most senior officials in the government of India and the India Office in London who repeatedly stressed their concern at the possibility of an anticolonial Muslim response in India engendered by a lack of confidence in British policy and the Sultan-Caliph's increasing status in the eyes of non-Ottoman Muslims. The government of India was also particularly sensitive to the erratic policing of the Indian states with "leaking" borders easily accessed by undesirables with the potential to incite unrest, enabling material by potentially subversive authors such as Siddiq Hasan to be exported with relative ease. As Muslim states, not only Bhopal but also Hyderabad was watched intently during this period.

However it is quite possible that the British would have been forced to tolerate Siddiq Hasan's problematic literature albeit with limited dissemination had he performed more appropriately as nawab consort. The threat of the impact of pan-Islamism in India determined that his work would continue to arouse British disapprobation, but government of India officials failed to acquire sufficient evidence of sedition to formulate a watertight case against him. Even had such evidence existed they had grave concerns on one hand about using scholarly activity as a basis for disgrace and on the other about the ripple effect that disciplinary treatment could create, potentially unleashing instability and disorder in the state and neighbouring areas of princely and British India. Had Siddiq Hassan been content to remain tied to scholarly pursuits to the exclusion of political activity his legacy could have remained relatively unsullied. However his delusions of grandeur in the political arena nailed his downfall as far as the British were concerned, providing the government of India with grounds to remove him from power and thereby to suppress his flow of literature.

The grounds for Siddiq Hassan's removal were undoubtedly well-founded. There is little doubt that, having achieved a hypnotic hold over Shah Jahan, the nawab consort proceeded to use his advantage to gain financial and administrative control of the state. In pursuit of this goal he was unscrupulous, devious, and hugely ambitious, appointing his followers and members of his family who were mostly corrupt and inflicted severe hardship upon the subjects of Bhopal. It would appear that he perceived Sultan Jahan as the sole hurdle standing in the way of achieving his objective and was ruthless in attempting to undermine her position and that of her great-grandmother, Qudsia Begam. Despite the fact that Siddiq Hassan appears to have supported his wife in her most significant achievements, including major architectural projects and an impressive literary output, the status of the line of female rulers in Bhopal was greatly diminished by the loss of Shah Jahan's authority in affairs of state during her second marriage. This loss of authority placed a considerable burden on Sultan Jahan who upon her mother's death was forced to claw back control to deal with a state mired in corruption and crippled by debt as a result of the dissipation of state finances by Shah Jahan and the adherents of her husband. Siddiq Hassan's contribution to Islamic scholarship was without doubt formidable and, as his admirers would claim, he used the power of the pen rather than the use of violence in his support of the early stages of Islamic nationalism, but as consort his vanity and arrogance tarnished the Bhopal monarchy for a generation.

Notes

1. The title of the Muslim rulers of Bhopal was nawab, however female nawabs were also known as begams, their official title being Nawab Begam of Bhopal.
2. See Siobhan Lambert-Hurley, *Muslim Women, Reform and Princely Patronage: Nawab Sultan Jahan Begam of Bhopal* (New York, 2007).
3. Barbara D. Metcalf, "Islam and Power in Colonial India: The Making and Unmaking of a Muslim Princess," *American Historical Review*, 116 (1) (2011): 6.
4. Saeedullah, *The Life and Works of Muhammad Siddiq Hasan Khan, Nawab of Bhopal 1832–1890* (Lahore: Sh. Muhammad Ashraf, 1973), 13, 32. Sayyid Ahmad Barelvi was killed by the Sikh army in Balakot in 1831.
5. The largest and most prominent school of legal jurisprudence in South Asia.
6. Shaharyar M. Khan, *The Begums of Bhopal: A Dynasty of Women Rulers in Raj India* (London, 2000), 121–2.
7. Report by agent to the governor-general in Central India [hereafter AGG CI], Sir Lepel Griffin, to secretary to the government of India, foreign department [hereafter Sec. GoI FD], Sir Henry Durand, September 1885, British Library, Asian and African Studies, India Office Records [hereafter BL IOR], R/1/1/33.
8. Metcalf, "Islam and Power in Colonial India," 7.
9. Sultan Jahan Begam of Bhopal, *An Account of My Life* (London, 1912), 78.
10. Ibid.,31.
11. This salute was upgraded to 17 guns throughout India when Siddiq Hasan and Shah Jahan attended the Imperial Assembly in Delhi in 1877 to celebrate Queen Victoria's assumption of the title of Empress of India. Sultan Jahan reported that on this visit Siddiq Hasan made strenuous attempts to become regent of Bhopal with no success. Sultan Jahan, *An Account of My Life*, 75.
12. The Barrru-kat Pathans of Bhopal (literally the shrub-dwellers), who originally made their homes with thatched reeds, fought for and served Dost Mohammed Khan to become the original pioneering families of Bhopal. Khan, *The Begums of Bhopal*, 11.
13. Ibid., 127.
14. Ibid., 130.
15. Sultan Jahan, *An Account of my Life*, 93–4.
16. Ibid., 78–9.
17. Seema Alavi, "Siddiq Hasan Khan (1832–90) and the Creation of a Muslim Cosmopolitanism in the 19th century," *Journal of the Economic and Social History of the Orient*, 54 (2011): 6.

18. See telegrams and memoranda dated October to December 1885, BL IOR R/1/1/33, for the British assessment of Siddiq Hasan's activities during the first half of the 1880s.

19. Lt. Col. W. F. Prideaux, Political Agent Bhopal, to A. C. Lyall, Sec. GoI FD, 9 March 1881, BL IOR R/1/1/32.

20. Gen. Sir H. D. Daly, AGG CI, to Lyall, 20 January 1881, BL IOR R/1/1/32.

21. Michael Christopher Low, "Empire of the Hajj: Pilgrims, Plagues and Pan-Islam under British Surveillance, 1865–1926," (PhD diss., Georgia State University, 2007), 77.

22. M. Naeem Qureshi, *Pan-Islam in British Indian Politics: A Study of the Khilafat Movement, 1918–1924* (Leiden, 1999), 17, 176–7.

23. Particularly worrying for British authorities was the elite group of Indian exiles who took up residence in Istanbul alongside pan-Islamic activists, including Sayyid Jamal al-Din al-Afghani (1838/9–1897), who began to lobby for an Ottoman-supported *jihad* against European imperialism. Nikki R. Keddie, *Sayyid Jamal ad-Din "al-Afghani": A Political Biography* (Berkeley, 1972), 60; Azmi Ozcan, *Pan-Islamism: Indian Muslims, the Ottomans and Britain, 1877–1924* (Leiden, 1997), 90–4.

24. Lytton to Queen, October 4, 1876, Lytton Collection, BL MSS Eur 218, vol. 18.

25. See Ozcan, *Pan-Islamism*, 52–3, 74–5.

26. Low, "Empire of the Hajj," 88.

27. The Tanzimat reorganisation (1839 to 1876) consisted of a series of reforms undertaken in the Ottoman empire to modernize society along secular and bureaucratic lines in an effort to integrate non-Muslims and non-Turks more successfully into Ottoman society.

28. Alavi, "Siddiq Hasan Khan," 3, 6.

29. Metcalf, "Islam and Power," 12. For more information on the Yemeni connection see Claudia Preckel, "Wahhabi or National Hero? Siddiq Hasan Khan," *International Institute for the Study of Islam in the Modern World, Newsletter* 11 (2002): 31.

30. The followers of the Hanafi school were particularly vocal in accusing Siddiq Hasan of causing dissent within the community. However his book *al-Ikhtiwa ila mas'ala al-istiwa* written in 1869 argued that on some issues based on the *hadith* the four legal schools of Sunni thought could find consensual points of agreement between them. Alavi, "Siddiq Hasan Khan," 13.

31. Francis Robinson, "Varieties of South Asian Islam," Research Paper delivered at the University of Warwick, September 1988, 4–5.

32. Claudia Preckel, *Begums of Bhopal* (New Delhi, 2000), 129. For the impact of print upon the Muslim community in South Asia see Francis Robinson, *Islam and Muslim History in South Asia* (New Delhi: Oxford University Press, 2000), 66–104.

33. Saeedullah, *The Life and Works of Muhammad Siddiq Hasan Khan*, 195–8.

34. W. W. Hunter, *The Indian Musalmans* (London, 1871), 1, 11, 36; W. W. Hunter, *A Brief History of the Indian Peoples* (Oxford, 1893), 222–9.

35. Metcalf, "Islam and Power," 13. It was as part of this brief attempt at *jihad* that Siddiq Hasan's father had fought in the 1830s alongside Sayyid Ahmad Barelvi, although the British appear to have failed to make the connection when composing their case against Siddiq Hasan 50 years later. It is hard to

believe that Griffin would not have relished this piece of information had he found it. In his biography of the Sikh ruler Ranjit Singh the agent to the governor-general refers to the "Indian Wahabis [sic], who have at different times given much trouble to the Indian Government." Sir Henry Lepel Griffin, *Ranjit Singh* (Oxford: Clarendon Press, 1892), 210.

36. Siddiq Hasan Khan, *Tarjuman-I Wahhabiyah* (Bhopal, 1884).
37. Alavi, "Siddiq Hasan Khan," 9.
38. Alavi, "Siddiq Hasan Khan," 11.
39. Alavi, "Siddiq Hasan Khan," 12.
40. According to the *Dictionary of National Biography*, Griffin was "a dandyish, Byronic figure, articulate, argumentative and witty" with "an irreverent tongue" and an "overt disdain for modesty." C. W. Walton, "Sir Henry Lepel Griffin," in Sir Sidney Lee ed. *Dictionary of National Biography: Second Supplement* (New York, 1912).
41. David Gilmour, *The Ruling Caste: Imperial Lives in the Victorian Raj* (London, 2005), 202–3.
42. Metcalf, "Islam and Power," 23. Sir Henry Daly agreed that the nawab consort appeared somewhat spineless, labelling him "quiet in demeanour with little physical power or courage." Gen. Sir H. D. Daly, AGG CI, to A. C. Lyall, Sec. GoI FD, January 20, 1881, BL IOR R/1/1/32.
43. See Caroline Keen, *Princely India and the British: Political Development and the Operation of Empire* (London, 2012), 120–1.
44. Memorandum by FJH (Frederick James Halliday, first Lieutenant-Governor of Bengal 1854–1859 who served as a member of the Council of India 1868–1886), March 28, 1886, BL IOR R/1/1/33.
45. Griffin to Sir Henry Durand, Sec. GoI, FD, March 10, 1886, BL IOR R/1/1/33.
46. "History of Bhopal," Griffin to Durand, September 1885, BL IOR R/1/1/33. Sultan Jahan maintained that her mother knew little about her husband's activities and when Shah Jahan's opposition seriously alarmed Siddiq Hasan "he used the counter-threat of divorce, and against a Muhammedan lady of high rank he could wield no weapon more powerful." Sultan Jahan Begam, *An Account of My Life*, 201.
47. Griffin to Sec. GoI FD, August 14, 1885, BL IOR R/1/1/40.
48. Alavi, "Siddiq Hasan Khan," 20.
49. In 1888 Abdur Razzack, the British vice-consul at Jeddah, provided details of two of the nawab's books in circulation in the Hijaz. Abdur Razzack to Sec. GoI FD, July 17, 1888, BL IOR R/1/1/98.
50. Ozcan, *Pan-Islamism*, 90–3.
51. H. S. Ahmad Raja to Griffin undated, BL IOR R/1/1/39.
52. Ibid.
53. Alavi, "Siddiq Hasan Khan," 25.
54. "Note on Din Muhammad" attached to Griffin to Durand, June 22, 1886, BL IOR R/1/1/39.
55. As reported by Griffin, Siddiq Hasan stated in 1885 that only about 300 copies of the *Hidayat ul Sail*, a "particularly offensive and violent work," had been printed and not circulated outside Bhopal, but at the time 800 or 900 copies were discovered in Lahore. Memorandum by FJH, 28 March 1886, BL IOR R/1/1/33. See also Note by C. E. Pyster, January 21, 1890, BL IOR R/1/1/106.

56. As early as 1881 General Sir Henry Daly, AGG CI, had informed A. C Lyall, Sec. GoI FD, that the nawab consort's compilation of *khutbas* "breathes a spirit of direst fanaticism." Daly to Lyall, February 8, 1881, BL IOR R/1/1/32.

57. Daly to Lyall, January 20, 1881, BL IOR R/1/1/32.

58. Translation of the "Defence of Nawab Sadik Hasan against charges brought against him" attached to Griffin to Durand, September 10, 1885, BL IOR R/1/1/33.

59. Ibid.

60. *Affairs in Bhopal. A defence of the Nawab Consort* (Bombay, 1887), 12–13, BL IOR R/1/1/106. For example, Siddiq Hasan maintained that the *khutba* on *jihad* in the *Diwan al-Khutub* was not his view, but a citation from the *maulvi* Muhammad Ismail who had compiled most of the writings of the martyred Sayyid Ahmad Barelvi. Alavi, "Siddiq Hasan Khan," 30.

61. Griffin to Durand, September 25, 1885, BL IOR R/1/1/33. Griffin also demanded to know "whether English officers and gentlemen and the direct representative of His Excellency the Viceroy [should] be required to transact business with a man whom they know to be a traitor to Her Majesty the Queen-Empress." Ibid.

62. Durand to Griffin, September 25, 1885, BL IOR R/1/1/33.

63. Memorandum by FJH, March 28, 1886, BL IOR R/1/1/33.

64. See BL IOR R/1/1/42.

65. Memorandum by FJH, March 28, 1886, BL IOR R/1/1/33.

66. Memorandum by Sir Steuart Bayley, October 4, 1885, BL IOR R/1/1/33.

67. Durand to Viceroy, September 30, 1885, BL IOR R/1/1/33.

68. Khan, *The Begums of Bhopal*, 135

69. Griffin to Durand, October 29, 1885, BL IOR R/1/1/33.

70. Sultan Jahan Begam, *An Account of My Life*, 130. Undeterred, Griffin continued in his efforts to persecute Siddiq Hasan. A lengthy article in *The Times* of December 27, 1886, revealed sordid details regarding the begam's second marriage. The article declared that the begams, in the mold of female rulers such as the Czarina Catherine, had never been famous for their "domestic virtues" and Siddiq Hasan had been a "too successful lover." The article leaked confidential official exchanges, suggesting that Griffin himself was responsible. Keen, *Princely India and the British*, 120.

71. *Affairs in Bhopal: A defence of the Nawab-Consort* (Bombay 1887), R/1/1/106.

72. Note by C. E. Pyster, January 21, 1890, BL IOR R/1/1/106.

73. Khan, *The Begums of Bhopal*, 138–9.

74. Note from Viceroy's office, January 21, 1890, BL IOR R/1/1/106.

75. Saeedullah, *The Life and Works of Muhammad Siddiq Hasan Khan*, 79.

76. Francis Henvey, AGG CI, to William Cuningham, Sec. GoI FD, February 28, 1890, BL IOR R/1/1/106.

77. Queen Victoria's Proclamation, November 1, 1858, in C. H. Philips, H. L. Singh, and B. N. Pandey (eds.), *The Evolution of India and Pakistan, 1857–1947: Select Documents* (London, 1962), 10–11.

CHAPTER 13

Royalty, Rank, and Masculinity: Three Dutch Princes Consort in the Twentieth Century*

Maria Grever and Jeroen van Zanten

In her last speech as head of state on Dutch television, April 29, 2013, Queen Beatrix revealed that her choice to marry Claus von Amsberg was probably the best decision she had ever made.[1] It is unthinkable that Queen Juliana and Queen Wilhelmina would have made a similar statement about their spouses. But Beatrix lives in quite another time with other cultural values about kingship, rank, and gender relations. She could marry someone from a modest aristocratic background, which should have been impossible for her mother and grandmother. Nevertheless, in the mid 1960s her choice had been no less problematic: the fact that she wanted to marry a German caused quite a stir among the Dutch.

Up till now, in the Netherlands three female monarchs have been inaugurated as head of state: Queen Wilhelmina (1898), Queen Juliana (1948), and Queen Beatrix (1980). After their marriage their respective husbands received the status of prince consort (in Dutch: prins-gemaal): Hendrik, Duke of Mecklenburg-Schwerin in 1901, Prince Bernhard zur Lippe-Biesterfeld in 1937, and Claus von Amsberg in 1966. Queens and princes consort figured in a constitutional monarchy. In 1848 King William II had accepted a new constitution with the ministerial responsibility as one of its main principles: the ministers are responsible for acts of government and are accountable to parliament for government policy; the cabinet is politically responsible for what the monarch says and does.[2] In other words: "the King can do no wrong." Hence, David Cannadine argues, the constitutional monarchy is in fact an "emasculated monarchy, a feminised version of a male institute with an emphasis on family, domesticity, maternity, and glamour."[3] He suggests that female monarchs in modern society had smoothed the way to a constitutional monarchy because of their gender. The English Queen Victoria, for instance, functioned in the public domain as the nation's wife, and as the happily married wife of Prince Albert with nine children. In this way the British royal family incarnated the First Family of the nation. Photographic techniques offered the court new possibilities to distribute domestic images of the monarchy. The effect of this media strategy was, what Linda Colley has called, "the myth of royal ordinariness," generating an attractive combination of both distance and proximity.[4]

Yet ceremonies and royal rituals became highly important in inverse proportion to the decreased king's power. In the Netherlands, particularly the more conservative liberals increasingly valued the monarchy as an important symbolic institution to forge a national identity, and thus to prevent the series of uncontrollable revolutionary events which had afflicted France.[5] However, in contrast with other constitutional monarchies such as the United Kingdom or Denmark, since the 1880s the Dutch monarch played an important role in the formation of the cabinet.[6] As the electoral struggle between the many political parties in the Netherlands did not always result in a clear winner, often vulnerable and complex coalition governments had to be formed. The Dutch monarch appointed the premier-designate, after consulting the vice president of the council of state and the leaders of parliamentary parties. Therefore, despite parliamentary limitations, until 2012, the Dutch queen figured as intermediary in the formation of a government and during political crises.[7]

The issue now is what kind of meaningful tasks were possible for a prince consort in the context of the Dutch constitutional monarchy, which seems slightly less "emasculated" compared to the United Kingdom. To what extent did they support or undermine the performances of the queen and the execution of her traditional rights, as formulated by the English political scientist Walter Bagehot: the right to be consulted, to encourage, and to warn? What was the influence of their (perceived) gender, their rank, and family background? Although they shared the German nationality, the three princes consort differed significantly in social hierarchy, wealth, personality, political views, and the public's appreciation. Regarding the last aspect, several studies on female political leaders stress the problematic position of men in their entourage, such as male spouses, lovers, sons, and political advisors, who often show difficult behaviour ranging from greed, envy, competition, and gender insecurity. In the case of *dominant* or successful female leadership, husbands are often marginalized or domesticated, while struggling with their masculinity.[8]

At first sight the public images of the Dutch princes consort affirm this gender pattern. Prince Hendrik coincided with the stereotype of a marginalized insignificant figure in the shadow of a sturdy queen; from the very start Prince Bernhard represented the jovial modern sportsman, a fearless masculine adventurer, admired by a sweet Juliana; Prince Claus fulfilled the role of a supportive advisor of the perfect manager Beatrix, but he suffered from not being allowed to continue his work in the field of developing countries and was troubled by severe depressions. But it is also possible that the public roles of the princes consort have been canonized into frozen images. Let us not forget that particularly gender is a dynamic category that shapes people's imagination, political regulation, and cultural change in societies, such as a constitutional monarchy.[9] The challenge is to integrate gender in the analysis of changing social practices and power relations around men and women. An important changing practice with respect to monarchies in the nineteenth and twentieth century was the growing disparity between dynasty and state: the priority now lay with the nation.[10] Since the late nineteenth century the Dutch royal family became more and more identified with "The Netherlands." Hence, their duty was to be a visible and virtuous example to all Dutch. With the increasing influence of the media, this transformation put a lot of pressure on the individual members of the royal family.

This chapter analyses the position of the three Dutch princes consort while critically assessing the above outlined gender pattern. Apart from some primary sources we use secondary literature, such as the recently published biographical studies by Cees Fasseur and Annejet van der Zijl.[11] We compare how these male spouses performed their gender publicly, and—to some extent—in the royal family. In this way we hope to illuminate the dynamic interplay of changing views on rank, royalty, and changing concepts of masculinity in twentieth-century society.

In the Shadow of Queen Wilhelmina: The Escapism of Prince Hendrik

After the death of King William III in 1890, his ten-year-old daughter Wilhelmina officially became queen of the Netherlands. Her mother Emma took charge as the queen regent. Of the once large royal family, nothing was left but a young girl and her mother. The Dutch monarchy almost drifted into a monarchical crisis with "only these two vulnerable women at the helm of State."[12] Obviously, at the time the majority of the political and intellectual elite did not trust a female monarch. Despite the old concept of the King's Two Bodies, which justified a female reigning monarch,[13] in the nineteenth century, legal discourse categorized a "woman" as a child in need of tutelage, while female political leadership was considered an anomaly.[14]

This negative attitude toward Queen Wilhelmina completely changed in the following years. The determined Emma succeeded in preparing her daughter for her future tasks as a constitutional monarch, in creating a bond with the Dutch people, and in transforming the monarchy into a social and national kingship. This became particularly evident during Wilhelmina's inauguration, when she was staged as a young virgin queen. The initial distrust of politicians about a "vulnerable women's government" was transformed into enthusiasm and even euphoria. Eager to defend their queen, Dutch men appropriated her as an important emblem of their country. Wilhelmina had become a vessel for the national spirit and incarnated the "civilized nation." According to the Dutch historian

Henk te Velde this nationalism was shaped by men who projected their national dream upon a politically powerless woman.[15]

In 1900, Wilhelmina became engaged to Heinrich Wladimir Albrecht Ernst (Hendrik), the second son of the grand duke of Meckelenburg-Schwerin (1876–1934), an old and high ranked though not wealthy noble family in a rather conservative sovereign member state of the German empire. After consultations with several German princes, the engagement was arranged by Emma. Wilhelmina could hardly influence her mother's choice, whose main objective was to secure the dynasty with offspring. The demands set by the queen regent for her daughter's future husband were high. First, he had to be a protestant. Second, the House of Orange needed "fresh blood," so the prince had to be a distant, and not a close relative. The third prerequisite was of a more particular nature: the future husband of the young queen would have to have no political ambitions or interests whatsoever.

Hendrik fulfilled all these criteria. He was not a close relative; he and Wilhelmina were second cousins and shared great-grandparents, Tsar Paul I and his wife Maria Fjodorovna. Hendrik was also protestant and more important he showed no real interest in politics. After his gymnasium, Hendrik followed a military training and became lieutenant in the Königlich Preussische Garde-Jäger-Bataillon in Potsdam. Already after three years, in 1899, at his own request he was released from active duty. He preferred the quiet life of a country gentleman, spending much time in his great passion: hunting and fishing.[16]

But before the wedding could take place, some business matters had to be arranged. First, on request of the government, Hendrik had to renounce his German nationality in favor of his new Dutch nationality. Anticipating a royal offspring, the government also adapted some rules in the civil code with respect to a female spouse. Although a wife should obey her husband, Hendrik was not allowed to act accordingly. Next, with the permission of the grand duke of Luxemburg Adolf as head of the House Nassau-Weilburg, Queen Wilhelmina could transmit her family name Orange-Nassau to her children.[17] These measures not only hampered the traditional rights of a husband, but also in constitutional terms, Hendrik remained inferior to his wife as he became one of the subjects of the female monarchial head of state. Finally, it must have been humiliating for a son of a grand duke to depend on the annuity of hundred thousand guilders, provided by his wife Wilhelmina, as the government had refused this.[18] On the level of rank and gender, Hendrik was subordinated to his wife. This situation was mitigated to some extent, as Hendrik became a member of the Dutch council of state and received some high ranks both in the army and the marine.

At the occasion of their engagement when they visited The Hague, October 20, 1900, Hendrik himself guided the horses of their carriage with a proud Wilhelmina beside him on the box.[19] This kind of manly performances made the future consort very popular at the time. They married in The Hague, on February 7, 1901. A day before, he had received the title Prince of the Netherlands. After the civil wedding in palace Noordeinde, the happy couple was driven in the golden coach to the St. Jacobs Church where the religious ceremony was carried out.[20] The future of the young married couple looked rosy.

Although the marriage was arranged by her mother, initially Wilhelmina was very fond of Hendrik. "You can not even faintly imagine how frantically happy I am and how joy and sunshine has come upon my path," she wrote to her former English governess, Miss Elizabeth Saxton Winter (1857–1936). "It will always be my highest aim in life to try to be for him a wife worthy of him."[21] For Emma this compliantness of her daughter out of love and adoration for Hendrik was a problem. In a letter to Miss Winter she expressed her worries. As the head of state, the young queen stood above her husband, but emotionally she seemed to depend on him. The queen mother worried that her daughter was blinded by love. Wilhelmina's passion for Hendrik, Emma wrote, "did not allow her to reason in a wholesome manner." Her daughter was "overexcited" and lived in a "continual strain." "She licks the dust of his shoes… she is childish with him… treats him as if he were of a higher order than herself and [as if] she [is] not his equal but far beneath him."[22] To Emma's great relief Wilhelmina did not neglect her duties as a queen. "Only in the affairs of state, she is her usual self, the gifted, intellectual woman with very much tact."[23] But otherwise she behaved as a "stupid little goose without any own judgement." Emma wrote in her letter to Miss Winter that it hurt her "as a mother *and* a woman" to see that Wilhelmina gave up her female dignity toward her husband. A middle class, bourgeois, and conventional marriage, where the man was the master of his house, and the wife had to yield and care, was not suitable for a queen. "Will it ebb away gradually and settle down in wholesome love?" Emma asked. "Will it cease suddenly because she has been awakened to reality?"[24]

It did not take long, indeed, that reality started to sink in. After several miscarriages, the only child, Juliana, was born in 1909. Soon after, Wilhelmina and her husband began to drift apart which—to a great extent—resulted in a reversal of traditional gender behaviour. Perhaps Wilhelmina's isolation and loneliness, especially in her years as a young queen, stimulated an already present tendency to identify completely with the Dutch nation and her ancestors, the Prince-Stadholders and Kings of the House of Orange. Strongly convinced of being queen by the grace of God, she wanted to lead "the Dutch Fatherland." She also appreciated to be pictured as the soldier queen, inspecting her army, which she regularly did during the First World War.[25] In the meantime Prince Hendrik had several affairs with women, including prostitutes, and he had at least one illegitimate child. His escapades had to be covered up by the court's aides, while his wife had to pay his enormous financial debts due to blackmail and gifts to mistresses.[26] As a prince consort, he became chair of the Red Cross and honorary president of the Dutch Boy Scouts Association.[27] This was all Wilhelmina allowed him. Her frantic love during the first years was turned into a rational and somewhat detached attitude toward her husband.

In 1915 several American newspapers even wrote of divorce, but after a while this story proved to be based on rumours. After the birth of Juliana and despite continuous gossip about Hendrik's promiscuity, queen and prince consort found more or less a way to publicly preserve their marriage in dignity and duty. Emotionally and intellectually, however, they differed greatly. While Hendriks daily life was limited to the management of the court, hunting and light ceremony, such as inspecting troops and opening exhibitions, Wilhelmina devoted all her time to national and international politics.

In the summer of 1934 Hendrik died of a heart attack. "His heart gave up, just when I was talking to a nurse," Wilhelmina wrote years later in her autobiography. This was all she had to say about her husband in her memoirs. "I would have to go in great detail to explain what Hendrik meant to Juliana and me," she justified herself.[28] Hendrik would have known why. "I am only the luggage," he used to say when he was traveling with his wife.[29]

Queen Wilhemina deliberately had kept Hendrik in the background, emphasizing that he had to obey her which contrasted sharply with the marital power of the husband articulated in the legally institutionalized marriage relationship since the introduction of the Code Civil in the Netherlands in 1810.[30] It contrasted no less with the traditional and conventional gender relations, cultivated in the private and public sphere of bourgeois and aristocratic classes at the time: while masculinity corresponded with paternalism, maturity, strength, rationality, and courage, femininity was related to submission, vulnerability, emotion, and insecurity.

Hendrik had no clear rank or status and his position as prince consort more or less unmanned him. The German historian Heinz Dollinger explained this "inherent emasculation of being a prince consort" by focusing on the "embourgeoisement" of the monarchy.[31] Dollinger emphasized that with the so-called *Trennung von Amt und Person* in the second half of the nineteenth century, the private sphere of a king or a queen increasingly determined the public and political achievements of monarchs. Moreover, it also constituted the legitimacy of the monarchy and the appropriation by the middle classes of the royal family as the first family of the nation. This domestic ideology—which was prescribed by the bourgeois in almost all European countries—meant that the prince consort could only be "respectable" when he committed himself to the private sphere, as a loving, patient, and caring family man, and not as "a lad" for "the club or the pub."[32]

Zest for Adventure: The Ambitions of Prince Bernhard

After the death of Prince Hendrik in 1934, Queen Wilhelmina seemed to reproach herself—at least partly—for the failure of her marriage.[33]

She had excluded him from all the affairs of state she had to deal with. Constitutionally and financially he could do little. Perhaps as a response, the queen conceded that her son-in-law should have more freedom to perform meaningful tasks than her own husband had ever had. Hence, when Crown Princess Juliana married Prince Bernhard zur Lippe-Biesterfeld, she and her mother had insisted that Bernhard should have an independent income from the state and enough space to develop his talents. The government agreed. In 1936, after some revisions of the constitution, the future husband would receive an annuity of 200 thousand guilders.[34]

Apart from their different formal positions, the differences between the characters of the two princes consort were no less remarkable. While Hendrik was a rustic, passive, and simple "Landjunker," not up to his dominant wife,[35] the clever and active Bernhard played with visible pleasure a vital role in the public sphere.[36] To many Dutch the appearance of Juliana's young fiancée symbolized hope and energy in the context of the severe economic crisis, the threat of a war and the perceived fragile "women's monarchy." For seven years, the twenty-six-year-old Juliana and her widowed mother had been looking in vain for a spouse.[37] When she met Bernhard for the first time on February 11, 1936, the crown princess was delighted about his independent attitude, and his flexibility in dealing with the protocol of the court.[38] Within a year they married in The Hague; due to that occasion, similar to Prince Hendrik, Bernhard received the title Prince of the Netherlands.

Although some relatives warned of the superficial and frivolous behaviour of Prince Bernhard, and for his ambition to marry a wealthy woman,[39] according to the queen and the Dutch government, Bernhard had met all the requirements for a suitable husband for Crown Princess Juliana. His antecedents were examined. It was found that he held the title of Prince and belonged to the German aristocracy, he had studied law at the University of Lausanne and in Berlin, he was a hardworking young man with a promising job at the IG Farben in Paris, and he had not actively supported the Nazi-regime. Particularly this last element was important, as the queen and her cabinet were fierce opponents of Hitler.[40] Recent studies, however, have shown that this assumption was not correct.

Van der Zijl discovered that the princely suitor came from a rather modest aristocratic background. Born as count Bernhard von Biesterfeld, he only received the status of Prince, elevated with the predicate His Serene Highness, when he was five years old and only after interference of his uncle Prince Leopold IV von Lippe.[41] He was indeed a prince charming, but it turned out for more women than only his fiancé. When he took the initiative to arrange a first meeting with Juliana—after being stimulated by his mother Princess Armgard and the second wife of the German emperor in exile, Princess Hermine—he performed simple tasks as a trainee at the IG Farben (typing and correcting letters). Later, his biographers upgraded this "job" to mythical proportions: Bernhard would have held the position of executive secretary or even deputy director.[42] Regarding the Nazi regime, in October 1932, Bernhard was a candidate member first of the SA motor corps and, after the SA crisis in 1934, of the SS motor corps (a Nazi paramilitary automobile club); on May 1, 1933, when Hitler already had dictatorial powers, he reported himself a member of the NSDAP.[43] Three years later, when his contacts with Juliana became serious he quickly quit these memberships. During his life Bernhard concealed these facts in contradictory and tough stories. He became especially angry about later accusations that in April 24, 1942 he had sent a letter to Hitler or Himmler with the proposal to appoint him as governor (stadholder or Gauleiter) of the Dutch state as part of the German Reich. The existence of the much discussed stadholder's letter, however, has never been proved.[44]

When the war broke out, the royal family fled to England. Queen Wilhelmina appointed Bernhard head of the Royal Military Mission in London. After they were safely settled, his wife Juliana and the two children travelled to Canada; they returned to the Netherlands after the liberation. For Bernhard, the years in London were been the time of his life. He moved freely around and cultivated a loose lifestyle, set on luxurious comfort.[45] Moreover, he could celebrate his adventurous spirit in society life and as an active RAF wing commander. Several times he took risks in flying fighter and bomber planes into combat. In 1944 he became Commander of the Dutch (Interior) Armed Forces with the assignment to unite the various Dutch resistance groups. In May 1945, he was present at the negotiations on the surrender of the German army in Wageningen (the Netherlands). Although in retrospect Prince Bernhard sometimes had exaggerated his contributions to the war and the British government had suspicions because of his contacts with relatives and friends in Nazi-Germany, to the Dutch he had proven military bravery and loyalty to his new fatherland. After the war he was appointed inspector general of the royal army, a prestigious job especially created for him but that took little effort.[46] Queen Wilhelmina awarded him in 1946 with the high commander in the Military William Order and gave him the symbolic knightly blow on the shoulder.[47]

In 1948, Juliana was inaugurated queen. Bernhard, prince consort now, escorted her into the church. They had four daughters: Beatrix, Irene, Margriet, and Marijke (renamed later Christina). The popular and masculine Bernhard maintained close contacts with war veterans and appreciated military parades and uniforms. He participated in many supervising boards of great companies, corporations, institutions, and charity organizations. In the 1950s he coorganised the famous annual Bilderberg meetings with leading politicians, intellectuals, and CEOs to discuss economic, political, and other global issues. Among his friends were captains of industry in the United States and political leaders in South America, such as Argentina.[48]

In those years the royal marriage began to disintegrate. Already in London, Bernhard had had extramarital relationships. Perhaps more important, he and Juliana had opposite political interests which were highly gendered. The queen cherished democratic, pacifist, and progressive leftist ideals that built upon prewar views of femininity expressed by influential leaders of the Dutch women's movement.[49] The prince consort looked down on the democratic process; he loved adventurous military actions to prove his masculinity and enthusiastically supported NATO. After the birth of their youngest daughter Princess Christina in 1947, who had severe eye problems, the tensions in the marriage gradually culminated in a palace war. Bernhard had started a vendetta against a personal friend and advisor of Juliana, the faith healer and hand layer Greet Hofmans. It was Bernhard himself who originally had invited her to the court to treat the eye sickness of the youngest daughter. After a year or so, he considered Hofmans a Rasputin figure, as someone who had too much influence on his wife, encouraging her with pacifist and other "unrealistic" ideas. Particularly in the context of the Cold War the political views of the queen seemed a risk for the ministerial responsibility. In 1956, when newspapers published about the affair—after Bernhard himself had informed them—the crisis in the royal household became public. The tensions were so high that the desperate queen wrote to Bernhard that she wanted to live apart from him. The prince reacted cautiously, perhaps afraid of losing his privileges.[50] Despite these marital tensions, a divorce was absolutely impossible as it would cause a monarchical crisis.

It was rumoured that Queen Juliana was insane.[51] The prince would have wished to send his wife forcibly to the St. Ursula clinic in Wassenaar for mentally ill and depressed people.[52] Historian Cees Fasseur, who alone has had the privilege to research the royal archive on this issue, has debunked this rumour resolutely as a myth.[53] Fasseur, however, ignores the fact that in the 1950s in the Netherlands (potential) psychiatric patients had less legal rights than today.[54] Only a hint in that direction might be experienced as a threat. Another rumour, unmasked by Fasseur as well, was that Juliana feared a German "putsch," that Bernhard plotted a coup with his mother Princess Armgard in order to be in charge as regent on behalf of Crown Princess Beatrix.[55]

Despite all the unproved rumours, some documents in Fasseur's double portrait of Juliana and Bernhard disclose the cunning strategies of the prince consort and the nasty ways he sometimes treated his wife. For instance, in several letters during the war he had patronized and insulted her.[56] Much later, in November 1956, he wrote to the prime minister about another disagreement between him and Juliana regarding the organization of a secretariat for the youngest three princesses. If the situation would not improve, Bernhard argued, he would intend to deprive his wife from parental control.[57] This never happened. However, to avoid a constitutional crisis, a solution had to be found to minimize the tensions between the spouses. In consultation with the Social Democratic Prime Minister Willem Drees, a committee of three elder statesmen was set up. The aim was to provide the royal couple with advice. In July, 1956 they spoke to several involved persons, including the queen and her husband.

After a month, August 8, 1956, they offered their report to the queen and the prince consort. Its full text is published for the first time as an appendix in the work of Fasseur in 2008.[58] In their report the elder statesmen advised to banish Greet Hofmans from the court. Juliana had to break all relations with her, and various friends and supporters of the queen in the royal household had to give up their office. Bernhard was only reprimanded for informing the international press; he also had to promise to treat the queen more respectfully.[59] And so it happened. To the outside world they now lived in harmony.

However, 20 years later, in 1976, Prince Bernhard himself was the center of a big scandal: the so-called Lockheed Affair.[60] An American newspaper revealed that the prince had accepted a bribe of about 1.1 million US dollars from the US aircraft manufacturer Lockheed for influencing the Dutch government to buy a fighter aircraft. Again a prime minister of the Social Democratic Party, Joop den Uyl, was involved in a potential crisis of the Dutch constitutional monarchy. He ordered an inquiry and appointed a committee of three "wise men." A devastating report on Prince Bernhard's activities—presented to the prime minister on August 12, 1976—confirmed that the prince himself had demanded "commissions" to be paid to him for his lobby activities. Behind the screens Queen Juliana threatened to resign if the government would sue her husband. It seems that she wanted to protect Bernhard, but perhaps more likely is that she strove to pass the throne safely to her eldest daughter, Crown Princess Beatrix.[61] When it concerned the monarchy, Queen Juliana could be very determined. The cabinet refrained from prosecution. After a long impressive speech by the prime minister in the Dutch parliament, the majority agreed with this decision.[62] But Bernhard had to resign as inspector general of the Dutch army, he was not allowed to wear a military uniform in public anymore, and he had to turn down his positions in various institutions and organizations, such as the international World Wildlife Fund (WWF).

The reputation of the prince was damaged. In the meantime, the royal couple lived separately in Palace Soestdijk each in a wing of the palace until their deaths in 2004. Bernhard still played some role in society, for instance by being present during every Liberation Day on May 5 in Wageningen and by supporting cultural organizations such as the Prince Bernhard Culture Fund and the Foundation Premium Erasmanianum. When he died, he received a state funeral with military symbols. The coffin with his body—dressed in a military uniform as he had wished—was transported on the undercarriage of a cannon. The funeral procession was accompanied by military marches and guards of honour with veterans of Second World War; a spectacular tribute of three modern F-16 jet fires and a Second World War Spitfire performed during the funeral a missing man formation.

Shortly after his death, a newspaper published a report based on nine secretly held conversations with Prince Bernhard, very likely arranged without any knowledge of Queen Beatrix. The deceased prince admitted that he had accepted a large bribe from Lockheed, but that most of the money went to charities, such as the WWF.[63] He also confirmed having fathered two illegitimate daughters in 1952 and 1967.

Companion and Queen's Advisor: Prince Claus

While Prince Bernhard cultivated a hypermasculinity, the husband of Crown Princess Beatrix seemed to lack this kind of ambition at all. Although his image might seem a bit soft, Prince Claus behaved in an independent and quiet way with both dignity and dry humour. In the 1960s, due to the experiences with Nazi Germany, the Dutch did not like the idea of another future German prince consort. Hence the initial fierce resistance against Claus von Amsberg, illustrated by several protests and public slogans such as "Claus—raus" or "Clauschwitz."[64] On request of the Dutch government, historian Loe de Jong—a specialist in the history of the Netherlands during the Second World War—investigated the background of Claus with respect to the Nazi regime. As he did not find anything that would link Claus to Nazi preferences, the government gave permission to marry. In sharp contrast with the royal marriages of Queen Wilhelmina and Queen Juliana, this marriage in Amsterdam in 1966 was not exactly a rosy start: young protesters threw smoke bombs at the golden carriage extensively broadcast by television.

Claus was of modest background. His father was a member of the untitled German nobility and operated a large farm in Tanganyika from the late 1920s until the Second World War. During his youth, Claus lived with relatives in Bad Doberan, a town in Mecklenburg-Vorpommern. In 1936 his parents called him back to Tanganyika and sent him to boarding school (Deutsche Schule) in Lushoto, also known as Wilhelmstal, in the German part of Tanzania. During the war he was called up for military service, the German "Wehrmacht." After a training in the armored troops in Germany and Denmark, in March 1945 he was sent to the ninetieth armore division in Italy but he never was actually involved in military operations.[65] Two months later a military American unit made him a prisoner. After the war, Claus studied Law in Hamburg and pursued a short diplomatic career. In 1958 he joined the German diplomatic corps and was sent to the Dominican Republic. Two years later he was appointed second secretary to the German representative in Ivory Coast.[66]

When Claus became engaged to Princess Beatrix, he made good use of his diplomatic skills and talents. It is remarkable that within less then four years he became one of the most popular members of the royal family. In 1967, he joined the famous four days walking tour of the city of Nijmegen among thousands of walkers.[67] His increased popularity became obvious when he visited Nijmegen again two years later. He attended the celebration of the old restored Saint Steven's church which had been destroyed by a mistake bombardment of the allied forces in 1944.[68] The press reported in a positive and respectful way about this visit. The most likely reasons for the complete reversal of the public's appreciation of Prince Claus were his knowledge of the constitutional rights and duties of the monarch, and the distance he always kept toward military display. Unlike his father-in-law, Prince Claus never wore a military uniform. He was also actively involved in educating his children. In that way he symbolized a new type of husband: caring for his children and supporting his wife Beatrix. But what kind of professional tasks did he and could he perform as a prince consort?

After his marriage, the Dutch government had allowed Claus to become a member of the National Advisory Council for Development Cooperation, to chair the Foundation of Volunteers in Third World Countries, and to chair the National Committee for Development Strategy (1970–1980). Because this National Committee became involved with political controversial issues, such as the boycott of oranges from the apartheid regime of South Africa, he had to resign this post. Instead he became an advisor in the field of development strategies at the ministry of foreign affairs. When Queen Beatrix was inaugurated in 1980, he seriously fulfilled the task of a supportive advisor. As a prince consort, Claus played an important role in what is best described as the professionalization of the Dutch monarchy. Like Beatrix he was very aware that the head of state had little room for manoeuvre. He had—more or less with the burden of Bernhard's mistakes on his shoulders—to fulfill the task without giving rise to public insult or scandal. Claus presented himself as a charming and intelligent man of the world, committed to human rights and the development of Africa and other poor regions. In contrast to Queen Beatrix who had upgraded the Dutch royal rituals and traditions, such as the reintroduction of the Majesty's title and the use of carriages with horses for the ambassadors as an offer for their credentials to the crown, he downplayed the monarchy as an institution to some extent. He even considered the Dutch monarchy as a kind of crowned republic.

The royal couple successfully performed the image of a professional team. Yet, at the same time Prince Claus suffered from not being allowed to continue his work in the field of development cooperation in third world countries in the way he originally wanted to do. Probably as a result, he began to suffer from severe depressions. After the first period of mental depression, in the early 1980s, his public appearance changed. His behaviour became more and more restrained. Dutch newspapers speculated that this change in presence was not only due to Claus' depressions, and later, Parkinson's disease, but primarily caused by restrictions laid upon him as prince consort. What probably mostly frustrated Claus was not so much being in the shadow of his wife, Queen Beatrix, but the limits of his position as prince consort that was subordinate to the ministerial responsibility. Moreover, it is not unthinkable that he had underestimated not only the constitutional limitations of this position, but also the large amount of daily tasks his wife performed with great passion and ambition. He acknowledged and respected the democratic rules, but he wanted to do more in society. Claus' hatred of neckties– he more than once publicly ridiculed the male dress code, such as in 1998—was also seen in this light.[69] At the end of his life, however, his popularity increased even more because of his irony and openness about his disease. On one occasion, again in the presence of television cameras, he explained, without flinching, that the core business of the monarchy is the cutting of ribbons. That he expressed his feelings candidly was by the Dutch public not experienced as weak or unmanly, but as a strength.[70]

The marriage between Claus and Beatrix seemed to be a happy one. "I owe so much to my wife. And I am so happy you are here. And you cannot—ladies and gentlemen—imagine what I am feeling," he once said during an award ceremony.[71] On February 2, 2002, he attended the marriage of his son, Crown Prince Willem Alexander, visibly ill but happy. Eight months later, after new problems with his health, he died, leaving behind his wife and children in deep sorrow.

Concluding Remarks

Until the mid-nineteenth century, the premodern bond between dynasty and state had implied that a dynastic crisis in marriage, procreation, or succession was immediately transformed into a state crisis.[72] The growing disparity between dynasty and state in the nineteenth century did not make an end to this problem, as the loss of political significance of dynastic marriages was replaced by national moral relevance. The royal family became the first family of the nation and its members national symbols of virtue, health, prosperity, and conduct. The abdication in 1936 of King Edward VIII, for example, became a political crisis after doubts were ventilated about the morality and intentions of Wallis Simpson. Married twice, she had been intimate with other men and was therefore seen as immoral and not virtuous. Months before the political crisis became apparent, questions were raised about her influence on Edward and her own ambitions. How could she be a good mother to the future king? The abdication crisis of 1936 illustrates more than anything else that women who became formally associated with royals had to be of inpeccable behaviour and background, and more importantly: assumed to be fertile, virtuous, and self-sacrificing.

The national and moral significance of the royal family also meant that the prince consort had less and less room to manoeuvre in the course of the nineteenth and twentieth century. He was not only bound by political boundaries and rank—after all his wife, as head of state, stood above him—but he was also limited by the moral and national (self-)depiction of the monarchy. As a husband and father his conduct had to be exemplary. In this respect there is a significant gender difference between a male and female consort of a reigning monarch: the prerequisites set for the prince consort at the time conflicted with traditional gender conventions and the ascribed status of the male within society and family. In other words, being a prince consort did not only result in political emasculation but also in a strong degradation in male rank and social status.

In the Dutch case the male consort seemed only to be able to function when this public "demotion as a man" was compensated in private life. The way the three Dutch princes consort dealt with these limitations was determined both by the modern moral function of a royal family, including the role of the media, and by their personality to accept their position and to adjust to a hostile and changing political climate. Obviously all three men did not like a ceremonial life as a prince consort and somehow tried to compensate "the inherent emasculation of being a Prince Consort."

Prince Hendrik performed escapist behaviour in hunting and love affairs, entrusting Queen Wilhelmina with the task covering up all his sexual excesses and to solve the huge debts of her husband. Hardly any of this became publicly known; the court still could control the mass media. Prince Bernhard indulged in his role as military liberator of the German occupation during the Second World War; for the Dutch people he became a national symbol of resistance and the example of "true masculinity." Yet after the war he almost destroyed the Dutch monarchy with his illegal financial transactions, political assertiveness, and lavish lifestyle. In the 1950s Bernhard succesfully used his contacts with the newspapers to impose his will on Queen Juliana. However, with the Lockheed Affair in 1976, the same mass media revealed his illegal transactions. Eventually even the tough Bernhard was "emasculated" and had to live a life as a domesticated prince consort.

Prince Claus behaved quite differently. Before his marriage he had built a diplomatic career and he could use his working experiences to support his wife. His position as advisor to Queen Beatrix was however not only due to his personality and his diplomatic and intellectual skills. When he became a prince consort traditional gender relations had changed fundamentally. In the 1970s and 1980s it became much more accepted that a married woman had her own career. He and Beatrix presented themselves as a professional couple. Prince Claus more or less (re)invented himself as a modern family man who took care of the children, and played his part as advisor to his successful wife, the queen. But it still remains to be seen, if he and Queen Beatrix were really forerunners in women's emancipation, or creators of a useful public image fit to a modern royal family in the context of the Dutch nation. Yet, also Claus struggled with the constitutional limitations of his role as prince consort, which he probably had underestimated before his marriage. In that sense his ironic attitude seemed to articulate an emasculated masculinity as well.

Notes

* Parts of this article are based on Maria Grever, "Meer dan zichzelf: Politiek en sekse bij koningin Beatrix," in *De stijl van Beatrix. De vrouw en het ambt* ed., C. Tamse (Amsterdam: Balans, 2005) 73–96. We would like to thank Jeroen Koch, Coen Tamse and Froukje Stiekema for their valuable help and advice.

1. Speech Queen Beatrix, April 29, 20.30 hrs. Dutch quote about Prince Claus: "Wellicht zal de geschiedenis uitwijzen dat de keuze voor deze echtgenoot mijn beste beslissing is geweest." See http://nos.nl/koningshuis/artikel/501189-beatrix-plaatst-zich-in-traditie.html

2. Jeroen van Zanten, *Koning Willem II: Een biografie* (Amsterdam, 2013), 524–70.

3. David Cannadine, "From Biography to History: Writing the Modern British Monarchy," *Historical Research* 77 (2004) 197, 289–312, 300, 303.

4. Linda Colley, *Britons: Forging the Nation 1707–1837* (New Haven, 2005) 232–3, 235. See also John Plunkett, *Queen Victoria: First Media Monarch* (Oxford, 2003).

5. Siep Stuurman, *Wacht op onze daden: Het liberalisme en de vernieuwing van de Nederlandse staat.* (Amsterdam: Bert Bakker, 1992) 169; Henk te Velde, *Gemeenschapszin en plichtsbesef: Liberalisme en nationalisme in Nederland, 1870–1918* (Den Haag: SDU, 1992). See also Maria Grever, "Staging Modern Monarchs: Royalty at the World Exhibitions of 1851 and 1867," in *Mystifying the Monarch: Studies on Discourse, Power and History*, ed., Jeroen Deploige and Gita Deneckere (Amsterdam, 2006), 161–80.

6. G. Lammers, *De kroon- en de kabinetsformatie* (IJmuiden, 1952).

7. After the elections in 2012, for the first time since the late nineteenth century, the Dutch parliament itself appointed the premier-designate.

8. Anton Blok, "Weduwen, maagden en virago's: prominente politieke vrouwen en hegemonische masculiniteit," in *Wetenschap en partijdigheid: opstellen voor André J.F. Köbben*, ed. F. Bovenkerk et al. (Assen, 1990) 153–76; Maria Grever, "Koningin Wilhelmina en het feminisme of de ogenschijnlijke onverenigbaarheid van karakters," *Tijdschrift voor genderstudies* 2 (1999) 3, 4–19; Anneke Ribberink, "'I don't think of myself as the first woman Prime Minister': Gender, Identity and Image in Margaret Thatcher's Career," in *Making Reputations. Power, Persuasion and the Individual in Modern British Politics*, ed. R. Toye and J. Gottlieb (London, 2005), 166–79.

9. See particularly Joan Scott, "The Uses and Abuses of Gender," *Tijdschrift voor genderstudies* 16 (2013) nr. 1, 61–77, 74.

10. Heinz Duchhardt, "The Dynastic Marriage," in *European History Online (EGO)*, published by the Institute of European History (IEG), Mainz 2011-08-04. URL: http://www.ieg-ego.eu/duchhardth-2010-en URN: urn:nbn:de:0159-2011080407 [2014-01-27].

11. Cees Fasseur, *Wilhelmina: De jonge koningin* (Amsterdam, 1998) vol. I; Idem, *Wilhelmina: Krijgshaftig in een vormeloze jas* vol. II (Amsterdam, 2001); Idem, *Juliana en Bernhard. Het verhaal van een huwelijk. De jaren 1936–1956* (Amsterdam, 2008). Annejet van der Zijl, *Bernhard: Een verborgen geschiedenis* (Amsterdam/Antwerpen, 2010).

12. Henk te Velde, "Het 'roer van staat' in 'zwakke vrouwenhanden.' Emma en het imago van Oranje," in *Koningin Emma: Opstellen over haar regentschap en voogdij*, ed. Marcel Verburg (Baarn, 1990) 169–95; see also Te Velde, *Gemeenschapszin en plichtsbesef*, 134–7.

13. Ernst Kantorowitz, *The King's Two Bodies: A Study in Medieaeval Political Theology* (Princeton, 1957). See also Maria Grever, "Colonial Queens: Imperialism, Gender and the Body Politic during the Reign of Victoria and Wilhelmina," *Dutch Crossing. A Journal of Low Countries* 26 (2002) nr. 1, 99–114.

14. Marianne Braun, *De prijs van de liefde: De eerste feministische golf, het huwelijks-srecht en de vaderlandse geschiedenis* (Amsterdam, 1992) 161–80; Maria Grever and Berteke Waaldijk, *Transforming the Public Sphere: The Dutch National Exhibition of Women's Labor in 1898* (Durham NC, 2004) 128–34.

15. Te Velde, Gemeenschapszin en plichtsbesef, 151; see also J. P. de Valk, "Caught between Modernism, Pilarization, and Nationalism: Dutch Liberals and Religion in the Nineteenth Century," in *Varieties of Liberalism in Past and Present: Britain and the Netherlands XII*, ed. Simon Groenveld and Michael Wintle (Zutphen, 1997) 102–15, 106.

16. Fasseur, Wilhelmina, vol. I, 212–13.

17. M. G. Schenk and Magdalena van Herk, Juliana. *Vorstin naast de rode loper* (Amsterdam/Brussels, 1980) 33–34; Fasseur, *Wilhelmina*, vol. I, 241–3.

18. Fasseur, *Wilhelmina*, vol. I, 220.

19. Ibid., 231.

20. Ibid., 248.

21. E. van Heuven van Nes, *Dear Old Bones: Brieven van Koningin Wilhelmina aan haar Engelse gouvernante Miss Elizabeth Saxton Winter 1886–1935* (Bussum, 2012), 245–6; Fasseur, *Wilhelmina*, vol. I, 230.

22. Van Heuven van Nes, *Dear Old Bones*, 252–6.

23. Ibid., 252–6; Fasseur, *Wilhelmina*, vol. I, 270.

24. Van Heuven van Nes, *Dear Old Bones*, 252–256.

25. Mieke Aerts, "Om het lot van de krijgsman te delen: Koningin Wilhelmina en het martiale perspectief op burgerschap," in *Sekse en oorlog: Jaarboek voor vrouwengeschiedenis*, eds., Mineke Bosch et al. (Amsterdam, 1995).

26. Fasseur, Wilhelmina, vol. II, 94.

27. About Prince Hendrik, see also Grever, '"Meer dan zichzelf."

28. Wilhelmina, prinses der Nederlanden, *Eenzaam maar niet alleen* (Amsterdam, 1959), 251–2; J. A. de Jonge, *Hendrik, Prins der Nederlanden* (Amsterdam, 1988), 137.

29. De Jonge, Hendrik, 139–48.

30. Braun, *De prijs van de liefde*, 9–12.

31. Heinz Dollinger, "Das Leitbild des Bürgerkönigtums in der europäischen Monarchie des 19. Jahrhunderts," in *Hof, Kultur und Politik im 19. Jahrhundert. Akten des 18. Deutsch-französischen Historikerkolloquiums Darmstadt vom 27–30. September 1982*, ed., Klaus Ferdinand Werner (Bonn, 1985), 325–64; see also Clarissa Campbell Orr, "The Feminization of the Monarchy 1780–1910: Royal Masculinity and Female Empowerment," in *The Monarchy and the British Nation, 1780 to the Present*, ed., Andrzej Olechnowicz (Cambridge, 2007), 76–107.

32. Campbell Orr, "The Feminization of the Monarchy," 96.

33. Fasseur, *Wilhelmina*, vol. II, 103.

34. At the same time the government reduced Juliana's intended annuity of 400 thousand, with 200 thousand guilders. see Fasseur, *Wilhelmina*, vol. II, 113–4. Schenk and Van Herk, *Juliana*, 122, state that it was Juliana who wanted to avoid the mistakes her mother made with respect to her father.

35. Fasseur, *Juliana and Bernhard*, 19.

36. Maria Grever, "Schrijven in opdracht? Een koninklijk huwelijk op drift," *Tijdschrift voor geschiedenis* 122 (2009), 223–7; Maria Grever, "Prins Bernhard: biografie van een Personage," *Bijdragen en Mededelingen betreffende de*

Geschiedenis der Nederlanden / The Low Countries Historical Review, 126 (2011), nr. 2, 82–92.

37. Fasseur, *Juliana en Bernhard*, 24.
38. Schenk en Van Herk, *Juliana*, 98; Fasseur, *Juliana and Bernhard*, 17.
39. Fasseur, *Juliana and Bernhard*, 35–7.
40. Ibid., 22 and 38.
41. Van der Zijl, *Bernhard*, 87.
42. Ibid., 227–8, 237.
43. Fasseur, *Juliana and Bernhard*, 41–3. His membership number of the NSDAP was 2.583.009. See also Van der Zijl, *Bernhard*, 203–4. She reconstructed that Bernhard became a candidate member of the Motor SA in October 1932.
44. According to Schenk and Van Herk, *Juliana*, 223, Princess Armgard's friend Aleksei Pantchulidzev had proposed to the Germans to appoint Bernhard as a governor already before 1940. The publication about the stadholder letter by Wim Klinkenberg, *Prins Bernhard: Een politieke biografie 1911–1979* (Amsterdam, 1979) caused fierce debates; see also Gerard Aalders, *Leonie: Het intrigerende leven van een Nederlandse dubbelspionne* (Amsterdam, 2003) and Fasseur, *Juliana and Bernhard*, 77.
45. Fasseur, *Juliana and Bernhard*, 116–7.
46. Ibid., 122.
47. See original film of the ceremony in 1946: http://nos.nl/video/34386-prins-bernhard-krijgt-militaire-willemsorde-1946.html
48. For the adventures of Bernhard in Argentina in 1951, see Joseph A. Page, *Peron: A Biography* (New York, 1983) 250; and Grever, "Prins Bernhard," 90. Thanks to Ton Robben for this information.
49. Maria Grever, "Koningin Wilhelmina en het feminisme of de ogenschijnlijke onverenigbaarheid van karakters," *Tijdschrift voor genderstudies* 2 (1999) 5–29; Berteke Waaldijk, "Tussen moeder en dochter: Juliana en het koningschap als maatschappelijk werk," *Tijdschrift voor genderstudies* 2 (1999) 20–32.
50. Fasseur, *Juliana and Bernhard*, 280–1.
51. Schenk and Van Herk, *Juliana*, 215.
52. Klinkenberg, *Prins Bernhard*, 401. See also for the same rumour television documentary OVT on the Hofmans affaire, December 11, 2001.
53. Fasseur, *Juliana and Bernhard*, 343.
54. Henk Leenen en Sjef Gevers, *Handboek gezondheidsrecht: deel 1. Rechten van mensen in de gezondheidszorg* (Houten, 2007); and also Harry Oosterhuis en Marijke Gijswijt-Hofstra, *Verward van geest en ander ongerief: Psychiatrie en geestelijke gezondheidszorg in Nederland (1870–2005)* (Houten, 2008), m.n. 858.
55. Schenk and Van Herk, *Juliana*, 222–3; Fasseur, *Juliana and Bernhard*, 392–3.
56. For examples see Fasseur, *Juliana and Bernhard*, 101, 103, 114.
57. Ibid., 394.
58. See appendix 2 "Aanbiedingsbrief door de commissie-Beel van haar rapport aan koningin en prins, 8 augustus 1956" and appendix 3 "Tekst van het rapport van het driemanschap (de commissie-Beel)" in Fasseur, *Juliana and Bernhard*, resp. 431–2 and 433–49.

59. Fasseur, *Juliana and Bernhard*, appendix 3, 445.
60. See for the Lockheed Affair Annet Bleich, *Joop den Uyl 1929–1987. Dromer en doordouwer* (Amsterdam, 2008) 334–46.
61. Bleich, *Joop den Uyl*, 338; see also Grever, "Schrijven in opdracht?" 227.
62. Ilja van den Broek, *Heimwee naar de politiek. De herinnering aan het kabinet-Den Uyl* (Amsterdam, 2002) 81–2.
63. According to Bleich, *Joop den Uyl*, 335, the WWF never received any money.
64. Mariette van Staveren, "Moraliteit, sekse en de Natie: Een geschiedenis van het Monument op de Dam en de oorlogsherinnering 1945–1969," in Mineke Bosch et al. ed., *Sekse en oorlog: Jaarboek voor vrouwengeschiedenis* (Amsterdam, 1995) 94–116, 106. See also http://weblogs.vpro.nl/radioarchief/2007/07/04/rudi-dutschke-en-thabo-mbeki/
65. "Claus der Nederlanden," *Encyclopedie van het Koninklijk Huis: Winkler Prins*, ed. by F. J. J. Tebbe et al (Utrecht, 2005) 62–4.
66. Frans Bieckmann, *De wereld volgens prins Claus* (Amsterdam, 2004) 36, 60–5.
67. "Claus der Nederlanden," 63.
68. Picture of Prince Claus and his little son Willem-Alexander, *De Gelderlander*, September 13, 1969; article on the ceremony of the opening of the St. Stevens church with Prince Claus, "Stevenskerk, symbool van de ware vrijheid," *De Gelderlander*, September 20, 1969; picture of Prince Claus on the occasion of his birthday with subscription about his great popularity, *De Gelderlander*, September 4, 1970.
69. See http://nos.nl/koningshuis/video/261282-prins-claus-werpt-stropdas-af-1998.html
70. Jutta Chorus, *Beatrix. Dwars door alle weerstand heen* (Amsterdam, 2013) 209–21.
71. Chorus, *Beatrix*, 212.
72. Duchhardt, "The Dynastic Marriage."

CHAPTER 14

Prince Philip: Sportsman and Youth Leader

Ina Zweiniger-Bargielowska

Prince Philip, president of the National Playing Fields Association, led its silver jubilee appeal with the slogan, "The Battle for Recovery will be won on the Playing Fields of Britain." Linking the association's postwar relaunch with Britain's recovery, the prince referred to the well-known adage that the battle of Waterloo was won on the playing fields of Eton. In his first speech as president, Prince Philip maintained that playing fields could do a "great deal" to teach young people to become "well-balanced citizens" who were "mentally" and "physically" able "for the tasks they will be called upon to perform."[1]

In 1956 the prince initiated the Duke of Edinburgh's Award for young people to develop leisure pursuits, improve their physical fitness and become involved in service projects. Acknowledging the "many difficulties" faced by young people, Prince Philip hoped that the scheme would add "purpose and pleasure in their lives, and that sense of satisfaction which comes from successfully overcoming a challenge."[2] The scheme was intended to meet the "increasing need, under modern conditions, to provide incentives and opportunities for young people to achieve a balanced development of their character and physique, in preparation for citizenship."[3] By the mid-1960s the scheme, which had been launched in the face of considerable opposition and doubts about its viability, was clearly a success. The director Sir John Hunt, leader of the 1953 Everest Expedition, attributed this to its intrinsic appeal coupled with the "great inspirational effect on the young people of Prince Philip himself, with his personal example and known belief in the capabilities of youth."[4] In 2012–13 over 140 countries were operating the scheme and over eight million have participated since its inception. In the United Kingdom, about 300,000 young people and 48,900 adult volunteers or leaders were taking part and over 2.24 million awards have been gained since 1956.[5]

This chapter examines how Prince Philip defined his role as consort by establishing himself as a sportsman and youth leader following his marriage to Princess Elizabeth in 1947.[6] Drawing on dominant codes of masculinity, Prince Philip became an indefatigable activist in the sporting world, serving as president or patron of numerous organizations. The focus here is on the National Playing Fields Association (NPFA), which campaigned for more playing fields, the Duke of Edinburgh's Award (DofE) and related organizations. Prince Philip was clearly not just a figurehead. He galvanized adult volunteers, he inspired young people and his success as a fundraiser made a critical difference. These organizations provide case studies of the prince's ability to mobilize resources and his relationship with the government and voluntary youth organizations. Prince Philip's youth and sporting initiatives reached across the party political divide and he met and brought together people from a wide range of backgrounds.

Prince Philip revitalized the royal family's campaign for playing fields and outdoor recreation among youth, which had been led by George VI as duke of York in the 1920s and 1930s.[7] This endeavour formed part of the modernization of the monarchy in the wake of the collapse of the European monarchical system and the advent of mass democracy in Britain after the First World War. An examination of these initiatives extends Frank Prochaska's concept of the "welfare monarchy" from hospitals and social services to areas such as sport and youth organizations.[8] The underlying purpose of promoting sport and outdoor recreation was to encourage young people's physical, mental, and moral welfare and, thereby, foster good citizenship, loyalty, and social cohesion.

Prince Philip's activism needs to be located within the specific context of the early postwar period. The election of the Attlee government in 1945 and the creation of the welfare state marked a low point for the voluntary sector. Charities did not disappear but they were forced to redefine their role, which had implications for the monarchy's leadership in the sector.[9] With the election of a conservative government in 1951, there was a shift to the right in British politics. Following the accession of Queen Elizabeth II there was extensive talk of a "New Elizabethan" age. The young queen's dashing consort was portrayed as a modernizer who embraced the latest in science and technology. These were crucial to the success of the Everest expedition, of which Prince Philip was patron. The news, announced on coronation day June 2, 1953, transformed Edmund Hillary, Tenzing Norgay, and Hunt into national heroes.[10]

Prince Philip's role as consort to some extent parallels that of Prince Albert, who was also seen as a modernizer and promoter of science and technology. Nevertheless, there were major differences, most importantly due to the reduced political power of the monarchy. David Cannadine has portrayed the constitutional monarchy as "emasculated," describing George VI as the "ultimate castrated male."[11] Where does this approach leave a prince consort? Cannadine's argument depends on understanding masculinity in terms of unbridled domination, whereas a restrained masculinity among royal men was in tune with Sonya Rose's notion of a tempered masculinity at mid-century.[12] As historians of masculinity have demonstrated, masculinity is constructed not just in relation to women, but also in all-male settings. Sport functioned as a site of cross-class and cross-generational male bonding where masculinity is constructed and affirmed.[13]

Prince Philip's initiatives addressed long-standing anxieties about the socialization of youth and, particularly, their consumption patterns and leisure activities. These concerns were heightened by fears about increasing juvenile delinquency in the early postwar period and gang culture exemplified by the Teddy Boys.[14] The DofE aimed to reach the so-called unattached, adolescents who did not participate in any organized youth group or club and who were thought to suffer from lack of leadership, especially after leaving school at 15. Another concern was the "gap" until call-up for National Service at 18 and the potentially deleterious effects of its abolition in 1960. Of course sport and outdoor recreation were not a male preserve, but youth was frequently conflated with boys, who benefited disproportionately from the expansion of playing fields. The DofE was initially confined to boys, who accounted for the bulk of participants in the early years, but it was extended to girls after the pilot phase and has been updated and modernized on a regular basis. For over half a century Prince Philip has spearheaded this award, campaigned for playing fields and promoted active leisure pursuits among young people.

Prince Philip was an active sportsman who had excelled in games and athletics at Gordonstoun, his school, and whose sporting interests ranged from cricket and polo to sailing, hunting, carriage driving, and gliding. Helen Cathcart's *H. R. H Prince Philip Sportsman* details these and numerous other activities, noting that by the early 1960s Prince Philip was patron, president, member, or honorary member of 200 sporting organizations.[15] One biographer described him as a "sporting prince" whose popular image conveyed "unrelieved tough masculinity."[16] One of the prince's earliest patronages was the London Federation of Boys Club, from 1947, and he was an active president of the NPFA. However, his sport and youth leadership really took off following Queen Elizabeth II's accession, which effectively put an end to his naval career. These interests, along with the promotion of science, technology, and conservation, provided an outlet for the prince's abundant energy.

Prince Philip's efforts enhanced his popularity. According to Mass Observation in the early 1960s the prince was perceived as a "fine chap" who was "natural and easy and popular with all classes." He was "no stuffed shirt." He mixed with and talked to "ordinary people," but was also seen as "a bit nosey" and "too quick-tongued."[17] Richard Weight has described Prince Philip as a "role model for young Britons" who "repeatedly topped the popularity polls, beating pop stars and politicians alike." For example, the prince was "top of the royal pops" in a survey of young people's attitudes to the monarchy published in the *Daily Mirror* in 1962.[18] The prince's popularity is confirmed in another Mass Observation survey in which he was named "favourite royal person" by 31 percent, just ahead of the queen (28 percent), with other members of the royal family trailing far behind. Prince Philip topped the poll among men (50 percent), the 16–24 age-group (48 percent) and the lower middle- and skilled working class (33 percent and 35 percent respectively).[19] Comments replicated those of the earlier survey with respondents commending the prince for his "outstanding work for youth," which had "captured the imagination of the youth of this country" and given them "something to aim for."[20]

Prince Philip's "enthusiasm for the cause of youth [which] had already won the hearts of the people" was lauded by *Playing Fields*, the journal of the NPFA, which welcomed the association's new president as a "sportsman" and a "leader."[21] The silver jubilee appeal was supported by goodwill messages from Prime Minister Clement Attlee and George VI. Herbert Morrison, speaking on behalf of the government, paid a "tribute to the cooperation" between the NPFA and government departments. Morrison stressed the need for young people to "develop as reasoning responsible individuals" in work and play and, thereby, acquire a "sense of civic responsibility" which was necessary for the "safety of democracy." This required more playing fields, a task in which the NPFA was "taking a full and worthy share."[22]

According to Prince Philip's cousin, it was "Uncle Bertie," that is George VI, who "saw that presidency of this organization could help forge civic links for Philip throughout Britain's intricate national life."[23] The NPFA, which brought together representatives from sports governing bodies, youth, welfare, and public health organizations, worked closely with local authorities which generally owned and maintained the playing fields. It had long-established links with the royal family. George VI as duke of York had initiated the association and he served as its president from 1925 until his accession when he became patron. The queen took over patronage in 1952.[24] Prince Philip served as president of the association, renamed "Fields in Trust" in 2007, until 2013 when he was succeeded by the duke of Cambridge.[25]

Initially, Prince Philip became very actively involved, serving "in effect, as a whole-time 'Director General'" for six months during 1949.[26] The prince raised the association's public profile in the media and he initiated new approaches to fundraising and recognition of volunteers. He featured frequently on the front cover of *Playing Fields*, which reported on his attendance at countless charity sporting events, balls, gala performances, and other fundraisers. Prince Philip drew attention to the movement by opening numerous new playing fields, many of which were sponsored by the King George's Fields Foundation. For example he opened King George's Field Stepney, later renamed Mile End Park, in 1952.[27] This park, a site of 65 acres, was the most expensive project supported by the King George's Fields Foundation which decided in 1946 to expand East Enders' access to open space where "claims" for "more playing-fields were outstanding."[28] The foundation had been established in the wake of an appeal in memory of George V in 1936. Apart from funding a statue of the late king, most of the money raised was designated for "Playing Fields for the use and enjoyment of the people."[29] Clement Attlee chaired the foundation's administrative council until he became prime minister in 1945. The foundation, which had over £557,000 at its disposal, worked closely with the NPFA. Only a handful of fields had been completed by 1939 and work was suspended for the duration. The foundation sponsored a total of 471 schemes throughout the UK, which were mostly completed in the 1950s and 1960s. The foundation was wound up in 1965 and the NPFA took over its remaining functions, including overseeing the fields.[30]

By the late 1950s, the prince was inundated with requests to open playing fields. Most of these were rejected, but he maintained a tightly controlled schedule of visits throughout the country.[31] An innovative approach, first suggested in December 1958, was for the prince to open several playing fields simultaneously in a live television broadcast.[32] Prince Philip was actively involved in planning this programme which also included a different radio version.[33] Broadcast as part of "Grandstand" in May 1960, the prince's opening remarks drew attention to the work of the NPFA in providing greater opportunities for "healthy outdoor exercise" which was essential in fostering "physical fitness and the right moral outlook." This was followed by footage showcasing a variety of schemes supported by the association, including an athletics arena, a large King George's field, a cricket ground, and children's playgrounds in different parts of England, Scotland, and Wales.[34]

In 1962 Prince Philip introduced a "President's Certificate" which recognized local organizers, many of whom had served the association voluntarily for decades.[35] This certificate, presented annually by the prince to around ten activists, paid tribute to their "special contribution" to the NPFA. Signed by Prince Philip, the text acknowledged that there was "no adequate reward for many years' devoted service... Thousands of people throughout Great Britain have cause to be thankful to the Association, and therefore to you, for help and guidance freely given. This is a token of their gratitude." This event provided an attractive photo opportunity for *Playing Fields*, which regularly featured the recipients proudly holding their certificates in the company of the prince.[36]

Above all, Prince Philip led the NPFA's fundraising campaign. The silver jubilee appeal was supported by the archbishop of Canterbury, who preached at a special service held in the presence of the prince, Princess Elizabeth and other members of the royal family. The archbishop of York also appealed to the public on behalf of the appeal.[37] Regardless, only just over £33,500 had been raised by the end of 1949, but when the appeal closed in 1951 this figure stood at £228,000.[38] This achievement was the result of new approaches to fundraising initiated by the prince who forged links with iconic exemplars of popular culture—the cinema and holiday camps.

In September 1950, Prince Philip attended a dinner with leading cinema exhibitors, producers, and managers organized by the chairman of the NPFA. Earlier in the year, Carol Reed had agreed to produce an appeals film in collaboration with Alexander Korda's London Film Productions.[39] The five-minute film "Playing Fields" (1951), featured well-known actors Wilfred Pickles and Kathleen Harrison and included an appearance by Prince Philip. It follows a group of London boys who are chased out of a park by a policeman and end up playing football in the street because they have nowhere else to go. One of the boys breaks his leg in a car accident, which prompts the others to seek help from the NPFA and Prince Philip who explains the association's aims. The film concludes with an appeal for donations by Pickles.[40] The cinema collection was a tremendous success, accounting for over half of the money raised in the silver jubilee appeal (£115,000).[41]

At a luncheon celebrating the association's disbursement of £1m in 1955, Prince Philip called for raising another £1m.[42] A key fundraiser was a second cinema appeal, organized in collaboration with cinema exhibitors. The Prince participated in a new appeals film directed by Guy Hamilton which featured Bob Hope, Kenneth More, and Peggy Mount, released in 1956. *Playing Fields* applauded the cinema industry's "generous cooperation," noting the low production costs and the fact that 1,000 copies were made "without charge." The film yet again depicted children with nowhere safe to play, who made a personal appeal to Prince Philip.[43] This appeal raised £125,000. [44]

Prince Philip established a long-term relationship with Billy Butlin, a vice president of the NPFA from the 1960s, who received a knighthood in 1964. The early postwar years were the heyday of Butlin's camps, which provided an affordable all-inclusive holiday for lower middle- and working-class families from the late 1930s.[45] An annual scheme of donations, mostly collected by campers themselves and augmented by Butlin, started following Prince Philip's visit to Butlin's Skegness Holiday Camp in 1949.[46] A large cheque was presented during Butlin's annual reunion at the Royal Albert Hall. *Playing Fields* appreciated these collections, which by 1957 amounted to over £56,000, because they "produced much wanted cash" and because they brought the "aims and objects of the Association to the campers' 'notice.'"[47] In 1961 the prince attended the reunion to receive the cheque in person and two years later he accompanied the queen on a visit to Butlin's Pwllheli camp, where they also met young people training for their DofE gold award in Snowdonia.[48] By the end of the decade more than £153,000 had been donated by Butlin and his campers, amounting to one of the most important regular sources of income.[49]

Prince Philip's activities were of course not confined to the NPFA and in 1951 he became president of the Central Council of Physical Recreation (CCPR), a national umbrella body of sport and youth organizations which campaigned for more teachers and greater opportunities for sport and outdoor recreation. It worked closely with the NPFA and there was considerable overlap in membership. The council, founded in 1935, had strong royal connections, receiving the patronage of George V, Queen Mary, and George VI. Following her father's death, the queen became patron.[50] The

CCPR's work expanded considerably in the 1950s as a result of increased government funding and a £400,000 donation from the George VI Foundation, created in the wake of a memorial appeal following the death of George VI.[51] The money helped to finance several outdoor training and recreation centres, including Plas y Brenin, in Snowdonia, which opened in 1955 under Hunt's chairmanship. This centre organized the first training courses for leaders of the DofE expedition section in the late 1950s.[52]

To celebrate the council's twenty-first birthday in April 1956, Prince Philip spoke on television in front of an estimated audience of ten million about "active leisure." He had "no objection" to those who liked "doing nothing," but expressed concern that people "should not be forced to do nothing or take to criminal activities" because of lack of opportunity. The prince praised the council for introducing people to "all forms of physical recreation," based on the belief that exercise made people feel "better and happier." He also referred to the work of the NPFA and mentioned the DofE which was "still rather in the early stages." The prince hoped the scheme would "eventually" be available to all young people offering them the "satisfaction" of mastering a challenge and providing a service to others. This was particularly relevant to lads in "trouble with the POLICE," who could become "our best citizens" if they found an outlet of "something more useful than crime."[53]

The DofE, Prince Philip's most important initiative, was launched on an experimental basis with Hunt as director in February 1956.[54] Initially confined to boys, the scheme consisted of achievement tests in four areas, namely "Pursuits and Interests," "Physical Fitness," "Service" and an "Expedition." These were graduated to three standards of increasing difficulty: bronze, silver, and gold. To enter the scheme, a boy had to acquire a record book issued by the award office, where his progress was entered by an adult volunteer, who was part of an operating authority or organization taking part in the scheme. Participants had to demonstrate a sustained interest in a hobby, a period of service in a voluntary organization, pass fitness tests and successfully complete an unsupervised expedition in a small group. For gold, this involved a 50-mile trip, with three nights camping, in "wild country."[55] The bronze award was open to 14–17-year-olds and intended to reach those still at school. The gold award covered the 16–20 (later up to 24) age-group. Participants who reached the gold standard received a badge, a certificate and an invitation to a Buckingham Palace reception attended by Prince Philip. The scheme's underlying purpose was to relieve boredom by providing a challenge and sense of adventure. The different sections aimed to encourage balanced development, foster self-discipline, and counter irresponsible and anti-social behavior.[56] As the first issue of the DofE magazine *The Gauntlet* put it, "No Badge or Certificate has value of itself; the importance lies in the qualities called forth in the process of deserving it."[57]

The DofE built on the Moray Badge, devised by Kurt Hahn, Prince Philip's former headmaster at Gordonstoun in 1936. Hahn, an educationalist and headmaster of Salem School, was a German Jew who had been imprisoned by the Nazis in 1933. As a Rhodes scholar before the First World War, Hahn had close connections to the British establishment. Ramsay MacDonald helped to negotiate his release and he opened Gordonstoun in 1934. The Moray Badge, based on the German (pre-Nazi) sports badge and Hahn's ideas, was intended as a personal challenge for boys at the school and in the wider community. It consisted of a fitness test, a project or hobby, a service element and an expedition. The latter was inspired by Hahn's romanticism and spirit of adventure.[58] Indeed, Prince Philip was one of the first boys to win the badge.[59]

Hahn advocated an extension of his scheme in the late 1930s and he revived the introduction of a nationwide county badge during the war.[60] This suggestion was considered by the Board of Education but in the face of opposition from established youth organizations and doubts within the board, it was rejected as "not within the sphere of practical politics" in 1941.[61] By contrast, another of Hahn's ventures, Outward Bound, was rather more successful and the first school opened in Aberdovey in 1941. Outward Bound offered four-week courses of fitness training, seamanship, and mountain craft for boys and young men with the underlying purpose of character-training. The Outward Bound Trust was set up in 1946, several new schools opened in the 1950s and Prince Philip became patron in 1953.[62]

In 1954 Hahn assembled what later became known as the "Originating Committee" of the DofE which met for the first time with Prince Philip in the chair in October of that year.[63] Hunt, who had corresponded with Hahn about youth education during the war and given talks about the Everest expedition at Outward Bound schools, was a member.[64] Other members included Lieutenant General Sir Frederick Browning, Prince Philip's comptroller, the athlete Roger Bannister, Spencer Summers MP, chairman of the Outward Bound Trust and Major General T. N. F. Wilson, secretary of the King George's Jubilee Trust. The trust, established in the wake of George V's silver jubilee in 1935, awarded grants to youth organizations and sponsored research with the aim to promote young people's physical, moral, and mental development.[65] The committee agreed that the introduction of a "Royal Badge" consisting of four elements, namely athletics, expedition, project, and service was "desirable." Initially, the scheme was to be limited to boys, but girls were to be brought in later. No decision was reached on the age range and many questions were raised with regard to organization, administration, and finance. The scheme was expected to be "expensive to operate," raising "sufficient voluntary money" was "unlikely" and it "would be difficult to obtain public money," although a "strong case" could be made for a subsidy in the "form of direct grants." Several subcommittees were appointed to "draft more detailed proposals" which would be "coordinated" by the Jubilee Trust.[66] These were brought together in a document which estimated annual expenditure of £100,000.[67] At the next meeting Prince Philip insisted that the "cost must be kept to an absolute minimum" and he hoped that the scheme would operate "as far as possible on the basis of voluntary services."[68]

The scheme was subsequently scaled down and in early 1955 it was decided to launch a limited three-year pilot experiment at an estimated cost of £30,000 per year. It was hoped that funding could be obtained from "voluntary sources" with the money vested in the Jubilee Trust.[69] In the following weeks Wilson and Browning developed a procedure for consultation, which Prince Philip divided into three groups, namely "people without whose active cooperation the scheme would fail" including the Minister of Education, those "whose active disapproval" might "endanger" its success such as youth organizations and those whose "help and backing would be useful."[70] Wilson and Browning approached "Pop" (Sir Arthur) Dowler, secretary of the George VI Foundation, who "held out every hope" that funding would be made available from the foundation.[71]

Prince Philip's interest in youth was widely welcomed, but there was considerable opposition to and doubts about the scheme among established youth organizations and in the Ministry of Education.[72] The secretary of the Standing Conference of National Voluntary Youth Organizations was "very unhappy" not to have been consulted and feared that the scheme would divert resources from "useful activities" to "testing and examination." John Wolfenden warned that Prince Philip was "running a risk" of associating himself with a possible "failure," whereas success was "bound to be at the expense of similar work already being done."[73] The ministry's initial response focused on "serious objections" including the scheme's high cost and the danger of duplication and waste of effort. Civil servants had the "gravest doubts" about the scheme's "feasibility" and they questioned whether the "formation of a badge-wearing elite [was] socially desirable and according to English traditions."[74] Phyllis Coulson, secretary of the CCPR, was "extremely doubtful" about this revival of the county badge scheme. She disapproved of the attempt to introduce a single national fitness badge which was "unlikely" to "ever become an accepted factor among young Britishers" and which "would run counter to the accepted principles of youth work in this country."[75]

According to a memorandum of a meeting with Sir David Eccles, the minister of education, Prince Philip was "personally deeply convinced" that the award scheme "could be made a success" and that the "association of his name ... might be decisive." He maintained that the scheme was not "unsympathetic to the English tradition" of youth work, emphasized that "no boy would be compelled" and hoped that an "individual test" would provide a "way to break up street gangs and cliques."[76] In subsequent correspondence, Eccles noted that existing youth organizations were "either lukewarm or hostile" and he warned that the proposal appeared to "many people" to be "on the lines of the German youth schemes before the war." The scheme might "be a failure" and "attract adverse comment" to Prince Philip. Nevertheless, Eccles accepted that youth service work was in "poor shape" and he was "very keen" not to frustrate the prince's interest which should be steered into a more "acceptable and constructive proposal."[77] Wolfenden thought that Prince Philip "will want to make a splash" and he doubted that this would be successful.[78] Indeed, the prince was not diverted and he obtained at least tacit support from representatives of youth organizations who were "rather taken aback by the extremely modest way in which he put his proposals forward" at a meeting.[79] It was subsequently agreed that the scheme should go ahead as a pilot experiment, but there was no public funding.

The DofE could not have been launched without the support of the Jubilee Trust and the George VI Foundation which provided a grant of £50,000 for the pilot experiment.[80] The DofE initially operated from the offices of the Jubilee Trust, which administered the grant and also provided annual funding.[81] In 1955 the trust published *Citizens of To-Morrow*, a report on the influences and opportunities of young people, which criticized a lack of provision, particularly among those no longer at school against a background of rising rates of juvenile delinquency, widespread apathy, and lack of purpose among young.[82] The Originating Committee agreed on the link between this research, which provided a "diagnosis," and the award which was envisaged as a "remedy."[83] Indeed, the report was invoked in the official press release in February 1956, which announced the DofE as a new opportunity for "young people to develop their whole character."[84] Hunt maintained that the scheme was "particularly designed to attract the boy" who did not belong to an existing youth movement, and he stressed that participants did not have to join a movement which he considered an "encouragement for 'Teddy Boys' and other individualists." Hunt was "confident that as the scheme succeeded, fewer boys would want to put on 'Teddy Boy' suits, though he had great respect for the 'lone wolf' type of boy."[85]

The initial skepticism proved wrong and the DofE was a success as demonstrated by the rapid growth of new entrants in the first decade. By the mid-1960s the figure stabilized at about 60,000 annually and over 145,000 awards (12,400 gold) had been achieved.[86] A key factor accounting for this success was the decision to lower the starting age from the original 15 to 14, which made the scheme available for use in schools. By 1961 most Local Education Authorities operated the DofE and the scheme was also increasingly embraced by voluntary youth organizations.[87] There was a fairly good retention rate and about 30 percent of entrants continued after leaving school. The numbers of "unattached," who were considered most likely to be antisocial, was low. On a more positive note, over a third of gold award holders were "actively engaged in training younger boys," thereby providing the next generation of youth leaders.[88] The scheme's success further depended on large numbers of adult volunteers who taught participants, supervised their progress, and conducted tests. For Hunt the DofE was an "immense exercise in partnership among all" who were "concerned to help our youth to play their part in society."[89] Prince Philip was "delighted" by the "number of people who have come forward to help" by giving the "younger generation a lead along the road of life."[90] In the early twenty-first century, over 660 licensed organizations, supporting 10,636 local centres, run the scheme. The bulk of these are either voluntary and community organizations (4,883) or secondary schools (2,830) with most of the remainder accounted for by independent and special schools and youth clubs.[91]

After the pilot stage, the scheme's funding situation was precarious. From 1960 onward the Department of Education, initially rather reluctantly, provided grant aid of £13,500 per annum.[92] This grant and ongoing support from the King George's Jubilee Trust were not sufficient to keep the scheme afloat. The DofE depended on Prince Philip's fundraising in its early years when donations received as a result of his personal attendance at charity sporting occasions, gala performances, and other fundraisers accounted for nearly half of the income. For example, the prince raised just under £40,000 in 1965–66.[93] This unsustainable situation came to a head in summer 1965, when Prince Philip's private secretary became increasingly alarmed at the spiraling costs and shortfall of income which could not be resolved by "continually exhibit[ing] Prince Philip at so much a peep like the Fat Lady at the Fair!"[94] Subsequently, new funding sources were developed, including Local Education Authorities which contributed a levy based on participants in their area. Supplemented by increased support from business and wealthy individuals, the DofE's finances were gradually placed on a more secure footing.[95]

Building on the successful pilot, the DofE was made available to girls in a separate scheme in 1958. Initially, the numbers were low, but by the mid-1960s girls accounted for just under half of new entrants.[96] Perhaps not surprisingly, an award established for boys and largely run by former army officers, outdoor enthusiasts and mountaineers was adapted rather awkwardly to girls. The girls' scheme was conceived on the basis of traditional gender roles, exemplified by the fact that "Physical Fitness" was replaced by a section called "Design for Living." This consisted of activities such as "Grooming and poise," "Setting up your home," and "Running your house." The expedition section was scaled down and, indeed, could be substituted by "some special worthwhile" voluntary project for gold.[97] According to the 1961 annual report, the expedition was the DofE's "main appeal" for boys whereas girls were attracted by "design for living" which offered "opportunities for the girl to make the most of her feminine and home-making instincts."[98] However, these differences were reduced in 1969 when the DofE was relaunched as an award for young people. In 1980 gender differences were eliminated and all participants had to take some form of physical recreation. In subsequent decades the scheme has continued to adapt and modernize.[99] In the early twenty-first century, the scheme appealed almost equally to both sexes and, indeed, in some years girls outnumbered boys among new entrants.[100]

One of the DofE's aims was to counteract antisocial behavior and to contribute to the rehabilitation of young offenders. A handful of Home

Office Approved Schools participated in the pilot and the scheme was considered to be a "valuable incentive" and a "steadying influence" on the boys in the early 1960s. [101] Likewise, it was thought to be a "worthwhile aid" to their leisure time in girls' schools. For one girl participation was "rewarding" and she felt empowered by doing "that little bit extra."[102] A group of girls who met Prince Philip during a visit to Exeter described their experience as "thrilling" and a "never to be forgotten evening," hoping that there would be "many more" in connection with the award.[103] While the scheme did make a difference to a handful of young people, the number of participants remained relatively low with fewer than 500 in 54 Approved Schools and Borstals running the scheme in the late 1960s.[104] In 2011 the DofE operated 135 centers in Young Offender Institutions and prisons, where it provided a vehicle for achievement, resulting in positive changes in attitudes and hopes of better chances after release according to a recent study.[105] Positive outcomes were not confined to young offenders and a recent study of the scheme's impact noted that the overwhelming majority of participants reported increased motivation, greater independence, and self-esteem. The bulk of young people welcomed the opportunities to help others and over 80 percent felt their communication, leadership, and decision-making skills had improved.[106]

The DofE exemplifies the continued influence of interwar or even Victorian conceptions of character training among voluntary youth organizations in the UK. It was originally conceived as a challenge to help young men to cultivate a physically fit, tough masculinity, tempered by voluntary service and pursuit of a hobby, which functioned as a model of conduct for good citizenship. The female counterpart similarly drew on established notions of femininity, although this has changed since the 1980s. The DofE has periodically been modernized and updated, but its underlying purpose remains essentially unchanged. According to the 2011 annual review, the DofE's aim was to develop the "whole person – body, mind, and soul."[107] To quote from a recent report on the scheme's impact, the DofE was "created to give young people a framework for becoming active citizens" and "to recognize their achievement" by means of an honours system validated by the monarchy.[108] This remained unchanged for over half a century and in the 2010s Prince Philip still attended many fundraisers and Gold Award presentations.[109]

The DofE has provided a challenge for generations of young people. The original idea can be traced back to Kurt Hahn, but it is inconceivable that the scheme would have become a universally accepted and popular aspect of voluntary youth service without Prince Philip's leadership, status, and access to resources. The prince won approval for the scheme, he played a crucial role in fundraising and his ongoing interest during tours and at award ceremonies served as an inspiration for young people and adult volunteers. Similar factors operated with regard to the playing fields campaign and Prince Philip's wider engagement in the sporting world which brought him into contact with large numbers of people from a variety of backgrounds. Prince Philip does not come across as an emasculated figure. He refused to stay in the background and was not overshadowed by the queen in every aspect of public life. The prince used sport to shore up his masculinity and he forged a distinctive public role for himself in which sport and youth leadership figured prominently. These initiatives were intended to foster not only health and fitness, but also to promote social cohesion and good citizenship. Prince Philip's activism, which resulted in the provision of new facilities and opportunities working in collaboration with local authorities, schools, and voluntary organizations, played a key part in the modern "welfare monarchy."

Notes

1. *Playing Fields*, January 1949, 8–9; June 1949, 115. Prince Philip became president of the association in October 1948.
2. The National Archives, Kew, (hereafter TNA), ED 124/403/2, The Duke of Edinburgh's Award, Leaders' Handbook, n.d. [1956], Message from Prince Philip.
3. TNA, ED 124/403/2, The Duke of Edinburgh's Award, The Pilot Scheme, n.d. [1956], p. 1.
4. Modern Records Centre, University of Warwick, (hereafter MRC), Trades Union Congress Archive, MSS. 292/826.37/5, The Duke of Edinburgh's Award Scheme (DofE), Annual Report 1961, 5.
5. http://www.dofe.org/go/stats/ [accessed January 28, 2014]
6. On his marriage in November 1947, Prince Philip of Greece (Philip Mountbatten) [1921–] was made H. R. H The Duke of Edinburgh. In 1957, Queen Elizabeth II granted him the title, Prince of the United Kingdom. Henceforth, he was formally known as H. R. H. The Prince Philip, Duke of Edinburgh. I refer to him as Prince Philip throughout. For details on the Prince's background, life, interests, and activities, see http://www.royal.gov.uk/thecurrentroyalfamily/thedukeofedinburgh/thedukeofedinburgh.aspx [accessed January 28, 2014]
7. Ina Zweiniger-Bargielowska, "Keep Fit and Play the Game: George VI, Outdoor Recreation and Social Cohesion in Interwar Britain," *Social and Cultural History* 11:1 (2014), 111–29.
8. Frank Prochaska, *Royal Bounty: The Making of a Welfare Monarchy* (New Haven and London, 1995), xi–xii. For an overview of recent scholarship on the monarchy, see Andrzej Olechnowicz, "Historians and the Modern British Monarchy," in Andrzej Olechnowicz (ed.), *The Monarchy and the British Nation, 1870 to the Present* (Cambridge, 2007), 6–44.
9. See Melanie Oppenheimer and Nicholas Deakin (eds.), *Beveridge and Voluntary Action in Britain and the Wider British World* (Manchester, 2011).
10. John Hunt, *The Ascent of Everest* (London, 1953), vii, foreword by Prince Philip; James Morris, *Coronation Everest* (London, 1958).
11. David Cannadine, *History in Our Time* (New Haven and London, 1998), 65–6. For a more nuanced reading of the gendered meaning of constitutional monarchy, see Clarissa Campbell Orr, "The Feminization of the Monarchy 1780–1910: Royal Masculinity and Female Empowerment," in Olechnowicz, *Monarchy*, 76–107.

12. Sonya O. Rose, *Which People's War: National Identity and Citizenship in Wartime Britain 1939–1945* (Oxford, 2003), 196.

13. On masculinity see John Tosh, "What Should Historians do with Masculinity? Reflections on Nineteenth Century Britain," *History Workshop* 38 (Autumn 1994), 179–202; Martin Francis, "The Domestication of the Male? Recent Research on Nineteenth- and Twentieth-Century British Masculinity," *Historical Journal* 45:3 (2002), 637–52.

14. John Davis, *Youth and the Condition of Britain: Images of Adolescent Conflict* (London, 1990). For recent overviews, see Bill Osgerby, "Youth Culture," in Paul Addison and Harriet Jones (eds.), *A Companion to Contemporary Britain, 1939–2000* (Oxford, 2005), 127–44; Penny Tinkler, "Youth," in Francesca Carnevali and Julie-Marie Strange (eds.), *Twentieth-Century Britain: Economic, Cultural and Social Change* (Harlow, 2007), 214–30.

15. Helen Cathcart, *HRH Prince Philip Sportsman* (London, 1961), 22. See also Denis Judd, *Prince Philip: A Biography* (London, 1980).

16. Tim Heald, *The Duke: A Portrait of Prince Philip* (London, 1991), 205, 224, 226.

17. Tom Harrisson, *Britain Revisited* (London, 1961), 250.

18. Richard Weight, *Patriots: National Identity in Britain 1940–2000* (London, 2002), 320.

19. Leonard M. Harris, *Long to Reign Over Us? The Status of the Royal Family in the Sixties* (London, 1966), 96, 98–100.

20. Ibid., 110–11.

21. *Playing Fields*, January 1949, 5.

22. Ibid., 6.

23. Alexandra, Queen of Yugoslavia, *Prince Philip: A Family Portrait* (New York, 1960), 128.

24. Zweiniger-Bargielowska, "Keep Fit and Play the Game"; TNA, CB 4/1, National Playing Fields Association (hereafter NPFA), Report and Accounts, 1925/7, pp. 3–5; *Playing Fields*, April-June 1952, 15; October-December 1952, 14.

25. http://www.fieldsintrust.org/FAQ.aspx#royal [accessed January 29, 2014]

26. Private Papers H. R. H. The Duke of Edinburgh, Archive, Buckingham Palace, London (hereafter PPA), National Playing Fields Association, Box 12, Executive Committee, Minutes of Special Meeting, January 25, 1949. These private papers are cited with permission of H. R. H. The Duke of Edinburgh.

27. *Playing Fields*, January-March 1953, pp. 14–6.

28. Campbell Stuart, *Memorial to a King* (London, 1954), 64, 87.

29. London Metropolitan Archives, London (LMA), F/CST/II/1, King George's Fields Foundation Trust Deed, November 1936, 4.

30. George V National Memorial, King George's Fields Foundation, Final Report, London, 1965.

31. TNA, CB 3/ 215 provides extensive correspondence on this issue from 1957–62.

32. TNA, CB 3/216, correspondence, Luke to Norman, December 30, 1958; Norman to Luke, December 31, 1958; note, January 14, 1959; Craxton, BBC, to Norman, April 7, 1959.

33. TNA, CB 3/216, correspondence Orr to Hicks, November 5, 1959; Craxton to Hicks, November 9, 1959.

34. TNA, CB 3/217, circular Norman to county secretaries, March 7, 1960; Opening by His Royal Highness of Playing Fields, n.d.
35. *Playing Fields*, July 1962, 17.
36. Ibid., October-December 1964, pp. 46–7; see for example, January-March 1969, 21; January-March 1970, front cover.
37. Ibid., October 1949, p. 204; 4th Quarter 1950, 390.
38. Ibid., 3rd Quarter 1951, p. 16. For the 1948–49 figure, see PPA, National Playing Fields Association, Box 12, Annual General Meetings, NPFA Annual Report, 1949, p. 10.
39. *Playing Fields*, 2nd Quarter 1950, 326.
40. For a link to the film on Prince Philip's official website; see http://www.royal.gov.uk/ThecurrentRoyalFamily/TheDukeofEdinburgh/Publicwork.aspx [accessed January 29, 2014]
41. *Playing Fields*, 3rd Quarter 1950, 16.
42. Ibid., July-September 1955, 15.
43. Ibid., January-March 1956, p. 56; April-June 1956, 14–6.
44. Ibid., July-September 1957, 35–6.
45. For a recent account, see Sandra Trudgen Dawson, *Holiday Camps in Twentieth-Century Britain: Packaging Pleasure* (Manchester, 2011).
46. *Playing Fields*, January-March 1955, 19.
47. Ibid., July-September 1957, 40–1.
48. Ibid., April 1961, pp. 40–1; October-December 1963, 36.
49. Ibid., October-December 1969, p. 25.
50. The council was originally called "Central Council of Recreative Physical Training," see Ina Zweiniger-Bargielowska, *Managing the Body: Beauty, Health and Fitness in Britain, 1880–1939* (Oxford, 2010), 310, 314; H. Justin Evans, *Service to Sport: The Story of the CCPR, 1935–1972* (London, 1974), 25–34, 78–9.
51. LMA, COL/MH/AD/01/025, King George VI Foundation, Philanthropic Schemes (March 1954), pp. 5–6, 10, 23–4; Evans, *Service to Sport*, 76–8.
52. Evans, *Service to Sport*, 85–6, 108–14.
53. TNA, CB 3/ 216, Transcript of Broadcast Talk on "Active Leisure" by H. R H. The Duke of Edinburgh, April 30, 1956. [emphasis in original]
54. Hunt resigned from the army to take on this position, see John Hunt, *Life Is Meeting* (London, 1978), 131–2.
55. David Wainwright, *Youth in Action: The Duke of Edinburgh's Award Scheme, 1956–1966* (London, 1966), 19, see 13–23, 123–5 for an overview of the scheme in the mid-1960s.
56. See also TNA, ED 124/403/2, The Duke of Edinburgh's Award, The Pilot Scheme, n.d. [1956]. For the current scheme, see http://www.dofe.org/
57. MRC, MSS. 292/826/3, *The Gauntlet*, 1959, 5.
58. Cambridge University Library (CUL), S240.a.93.5, Kurt Hahn, *Education for Leisure* (Oxford: 1938); Hermann Röhrs and H. Tunstall-Behrens, *Kurt Hahn* (London, 1970), xix-xxi; Lynn Cook, "The 1944 Education Act and Outdoor Education: from Policy to Practice," *History of Education* 28:2 (1999), 159–60.
59. Cathcart, *HRH Prince Philip Sportsman*, 48–49.
60. Correspondence in *The Times*, April 5, 1938, p. 12; CUL, S240.a.93.5, Kurt Hahn, *The Badge*, From an Address at the Annual Conference of the National Association of Physical Education, London, September 1941;

James M. Hogan, "The Establishment of the First Outward Bound School at Aberdovey, Merionethshire," in Röhrs and Tunstall-Behrens, *Kurt Hahn*, 60–4.

61. TNA, ED 124/10, Memo on discussions for Parliamentary Secretary, September 8, 1941.
62. David James (ed.), *Outward Bound* (London, 1957); Mark Freeman, "From 'Character-training' to 'Personal Growth': The Early History of Outward Bound 1941–1965," *History of Education* 40:1 (2011), 21–43.
63. PPA, Duke of Edinburgh Awards Scheme, Box 1, Setting up of the Award Scheme 4 (hereafter Award Scheme Box 1:4), Award Office papers for 1954, Minutes of an Informal Meeting held at Buckingham Palace, October 15, 1954.
64. Hunt, *Life Is Meeting*, 128–9.
65. *The Times*, November 5, 1935, p. 17; March 6, 1936, 9.
66. PPA, Award Scheme Box 1:4, Minutes of an Informal Meeting held at Buckingham Palace, October 15, 1954.
67. PPA, Award Scheme Box 1:4, Coordinated Paper setting out the Proposal for the Badge in Greater Detail, Agenda, 2nd Meeting, November 16, 1954, Paper No. 2.
68. PPA, Award Scheme Box 1:4, Minutes of 2nd Meeting, November 16, 1954.
69. PPA, Duke of Edinburgh Awards Scheme, Box 1, Setting up of the Award Scheme 5, Award Office papers for 1955, Minutes of 4th Meeting, February 24, 1955, Paper No. 3, Financial Plan for the Badge Scheme, February 3, 1955.
70. PPA, Duke of Edinburgh Awards Scheme, Box 1, Setting up of the Award Scheme 1, October 1954-April 1955 (B.P. Office Files) (hereafter Award Scheme Box 1:1), Prince Philip, Memo to Browning, n.d.; correspondence Wilson to Browning, February 21, 1955, March 4, 1955, March 8, 1955; Browning to Wilson, March 7, 1955.
71. PPA, Award Scheme Box 1:1, Memo Browning to Prince Philip, March 14, 1955.
72. TNA, ED 124/403/1, Formal discussion of the award scheme in the ministry was initiated by Wilson, correspondence Wilson to Thompson, June 6, 1955, and enclosed Memo on the Award Scheme, May 1955.
73. TNA, ED 124/403/1, Minute on National Badge Scheme, June 8, 1955.
74. TNA, ED 124/403/1, Objections to the Proposed Scheme for the Duke of Edinburgh Award, n.d.; Minute, Duke of Edinburgh Badge Scheme, June 9, 1955.
75. TNA, ED 124/403/1, Letter Coulson to Kennedy, June 9, 1955, attached Notes on Fitness Badges, October 28, 1954.
76. TNA, ED 124/403/1, Interview Memorandum, June 10, 1955.
77. TNA, ED 124/403/1, Letter Eccles to Salisbury, June 10, 1955.
78. TNA, ED 124/403/1, Letter Wolfenden to Flemming, June 17, 1955.
79. TNA, ED 124/403/1, Minute to Eccles, October 14, 1955.
80. TNA, ED 124/403/2, The Duke of Edinburgh's Award Scheme (DofE), Report 1956–5, 3, 11;
81. MRC, MSS. 292/826.37/5, DofE, Report 1960, pp. 6–7; Wainwright, *Youth in Action*, 89–90, 95.
82. King George's Jubilee Trust, *Citizens of To-morrow: A Study of the Influences Affecting the Upbringing of Young People* (London, 1955).

83. PPA, Award Scheme Box 1:4, Minutes of 2nd Meeting, November 16, 1954.
84. TNA, ED 124/403/1, Press Announcement from Buckingham Palace, January 27, 1956.
85. *Times*, June 27, 1956, 6.
86. Wainwright, *Youth in Action*, p. 132; MRC, MSS. 292/826.74/2, DofE, Annual Report 1966, 11–2.
87. Wainwright, *Youth in Action*, p. 90; MRC, MSS. 292/826.37/5, DofE, Report 1961, pp. 5–7; 13, 28; MSS. 292/826.74/2, DofE, Annual Report 1966, 9–10.
88. MRC, MSS. 292/826.37/5, DofE, Report 1961, 14–15, 19.
89. Ibid., p. 1.
90. MRC, MSS. 292/826/3, *The Gauntlet*, 1959, 3.
91. DofE, Annual Review 2012, pp. 4–5, see http://www.dofe.org/en/content/cms/about-us/annual-review/ [accessed January 29, 2014]
92. TNA, ED 124/403/1, Correspondence, Martin to Gray, June 1, 1960, Gray to Martin, June 10, 1960.
93. MRC, MSS. 292/826.74/2, Memo on the Finances of the DofE, October 3, 1966; Budget Notes 1966/1967, n.d.
94. PPA, Duke of Edinburgh Award Scheme, Box 4, Finance General Correspondence 1955–66, Letter Christopher Bonham-Carter to Alexander Abel-Smith, August 18, 1965.
95. MRC, MSS. 292/826.74/2, DofE, Annual Report 1968, 14–6.
96. MRC, MSS. 292/826.37/5, DofE, Report 1961, p. 33; MSS. 292/826.74/2, DofE, Annual Report 1966, 10–11.
97. Wainwright, *Youth in Action*, 91, 124–5
98. MRC, MSS. 292/826.37/5, DofE, Report 1960, 17.
99. http://www.dofe.org/go/history/ [accessed January 29, 2014]
100. Information from Dame Anne Griffiths, archivist to H. R. H. The Prince Philip, email to author, December 10, 2013.
101. TNA, BN 29/2025, Memo, January 6, 1958; MRC, MSS. 292/826.37/5, DofE, Report 1960, pp. 9, 19; DofE, Report 1961, 17
102. MRC, MSS. 292/826.37/5, DofE, Report 1961, 22, 46.
103. TNA, BN 29/2025, Letter to Mr Jenkins, forwarded by headmistress, July 10, 1961.
104. MRC, MSS. 292/826.74/2, DofE, Annual Report 1968, 6.
105. DofE, Annual Review 2011, p. 4; DofE, Making a difference with young people in custody, Executive Summary (February 2009), see http://www.dofe.org/en/content/cms/about-us/our-impact/ [accessed January 30, 2014]
106. The study did not investigate those who dropped out, DofE, The Impact of the Duke of Edinburgh's Award on Young People, Executive Summary (January 2009), 6–10, see http://www.dofe.org/en/content/cms/about-us/our-impact/ [accessed January 30, 2014]
107. DofE, Annual Review 2011, 5.
108. DofE, Impact: Summary of Research Findings for Stakeholders (January 2010), 7, see http://www.dofe.org/en/content/cms/about-us/our-impact/ [accessed January 30, 2014]
109. http://www.dofe.org/en/content/cms/about-us/patron/; Prince Edward, a trustee, has become increasingly involved in the scheme in recent years.

CHAPTER 15

The Prince Who Would Be King: Henrik of Denmark's Struggle for Recognition

Trond Norén Isaksen

At a banquet celebrating the alleged 2500th anniversary of the Iranian monarchy in Persepolis in October 1971, the uneven number of male and female guests meant that Sovereign Prince Rainier III of Monaco found himself seated between Prince Bernhard of the Netherlands, the husband of Queen Juliana, and Prince Philip of Britain, the husband of Queen Elizabeth II. When Prince Bernhard wondered why there was a man rather than a lady between them, Prince Philip replied: "Because we are the only male queens."[1] Three months later the exclusive fraternity of male consorts got a third member.

Although the winds of both winter and radicalism swept over Denmark, Christiansborg Palace Square in Copenhagen was a sea of thousands of people as the clock struck 3 p.m. on Saturday, January 15, 1972. King Frederik IX had died the previous evening, and now, in a ritual dating back to at least 1699,[2] Prime Minister Jens Otto Krag stepped out on the palace balcony and, after a brief speech, shouted three times: "King Frederik IX has died. Long live Her Majesty Queen Margrethe II!"

For the 31-year-old woman standing next to the prime minister it was a moment of destiny. For Denmark it was history. It was the first time ever that a woman had inherited the crown of the nation which likes to think of itself as the world's oldest existing kingdom. Yet the new monarch had assumed the name Margrethe II. Strictly speaking, the first Margrethe was never queen regnant, but came to rule Denmark and Norway—and eventually to unite all the Nordic countries in the Kalmar Union of 1397—after the death of her son in 1387. She remained the actual ruler until her death in 1412, although she had her great-nephew, Erik of Pomerania, elected king in 1396.

That the new queen bore the name of her great predecessor was a coincidence, as she was named after her late maternal grandmother, Crown Princess Margareta of Sweden. Margrethe II was not born to be queen; indeed, at the time of her birth in 1940 women were entirely barred from inheriting the throne. Queen Ingrid bore King Frederik IX three daughters and suffered at least two miscarriages.[3] By the time of the accession in 1947 the queen had been advised that she might not survive further pregnancies.[4] The heir presumptive was therefore the king's brother, Prince Knud, who had two sons as well as a daughter.

The constitution of 1915 had become outdated and in 1939 a new constitution had been the subject of a referendum, but was defeated as participation was too low for it to receive the approval of the required 45 percent of the entire electorate. After the Second World War, the Liberal MP Poul Thisted Knudsen had the idea of linking the new constitution to a new Act of Succession whereby a princess would be allowed to inherit the throne if she had no brothers. This, it was believed, might interest people enough to make them go to the polls.[5] In a referendum in 1953 the new constitution and Act of Succession were passed, receiving the support of just above the required 45 percent of the electorate.[6]

When she heard that she was now heiress presumptive, the 13-year-old Princess Margrethe felt relieved that this meant that she could spend the rest of her life in Denmark, rather than moving to another country, as princesses normally did upon marrying foreign royals—and as her two sisters would do.[7] But eventually she also came to realise that her new status as future monarch might seem a hurdle to her prospective suitors.

An Heiress in Search of a Consort

If the woman standing next to the prime minister on the palace balcony that January day were a rare occurrence in Danish history, the man who soon joined them was something even rarer. As the first Margrethe had been a widow, Prince Henrik was the first male consort in the history of Denmark.

Margrethe II had by her own admission been afraid that she might ascend to the throne while still unmarried, "[s]o it was in many ways a miracle that we found each other at the right moment."[8] "I found it difficult to imagine a life without marrying, and yet I could not see how I would ever meet anyone in whose power I would dare place myself once I was Queen. Who on earth would take on the Queen? I wondered. This was my nightmare, because I knew it could make me very unhappy. I am only happy when I have someone to lean on."[9] She realised that anyone who made a commitment to her would have to be prepared "to give up his job, his country and in some ways even parts of his own identity."[10]

For, as the historian David Cannadine has written: "A king is by definition king regnant, and his consort is therefore queen; but the husband of a queen regnant is not therefore king. And so, with inexorable if superficially paradoxical logic, it is always better to be the woman playing the role of the man (with correspondingly increased scope as queen regnant) than to be the man playing the role of the woman (with much diminished opportunities as prince consort)...So being the husband of a regnant queen is even more of a non-job than being vice-president of the United States. To be so close to the presidency as to be only a heartbeat away from the White House is one thing; to be so near to the throne yet without prospect of ever occupying it is quite another."[11]

Thus it is perhaps understandable that Princess Margrethe "doubted if I would meet a man who would be able to say yes not only to me but to all that came with me."[12] She believes that her parents anticipated a Briton or a Swede, while a Frenchman was probably the last thing they expected.[13] They had made it clear that her husband need not necessarily be of royal blood, but that a Dane would not be acceptable.[14] And she was herself sure that if her parents disapproved of her prospective husband, she would have put up a fight, but that if their refusal was irrevocable, she would have put her duty to the nation above love.[15]

The man Princess Margrethe found who felt able to take on a future queen was Henri de Laborde de Monpezat, a French diplomat. In retrospect he has admitted that he did not know what he walked into. Henri-Marie-Jean-André de Laborde de Monpezat was born in Talence, a suburb of Bordeaux, on June 11, 1934, the second of nine children born to Renée Doursenot and André de Laborde de Monpezat, who later became her second husband. André and his children used the title of count, while his father and brother styled themselves marquis, but their noble status was disputable.[16] The family originated in Béarn, but in 1937 André de Monpezat bought an estate further north, Le Cayrou between Albas and Castelfranc in the Cahors area.[17]

By the time Henri de Monpezat came to Denmark he already had "both a Vietnamese and a French past."[18] His grandfather had significant business interests in French Indochina, which were inherited by his two sons in 1929. Renée de Monpezat had only returned to France to give birth and almost immediately brought her newborn son back to Indochina. Only in 1939, when the outbreak of the Second World War was imminent, did the family return to France. This felt as quite a cultural shock to the five-year-old Henri, whose Vietnamese was more fluent than his French.[19] It would not be the last time he had to adapt to a new country and a new culture.

Henri thus went to school in France, but in 1950 his father took him back to Indochina. Having graduated from the French upper secondary school in Hanoi in 1952, Henri returned to France to pursue his studies. He studied law at Sorbonne, but did not complete his degree. On the other hand he took a *licencié* degree in literature at Sorbonne and the same degree in Chinese and Vietnamese at l'École National des Langues Orientales. Having completed his studies he won a scholarship from Alliance Française (the Foreign Ministry's cultural department) and was for two years posted to the General Consulate in Hong Kong, where he continued his studies of Chinese at the university.

From 1959 to 1962 he did military service, working first in military intelligence in Paris and then seeing active service in the war in Algeria. Thereafter Henri de Monpezat joined the foreign ministry's Asia

Department. In 1963 he was posted to the embassy in London as third secretary. At the age of 32 he was, rather sensationally, offered the post of ambassador to Mongolia, but turned it down as he had then made up his mind to propose to the Danish heiress, whom he had first met at a dinner party in 1965.[20]

The couple became privately engaged on June 23, 1966 and on October 5, King Frederik IX and the Danish government gave their formal consent. The wedding took place in Holmen's Church in Copenhagen on June 10, 1967 and Henri de Laborde de Monpezat received a new identity as His Royal Highness Prince Henrik of Denmark. At that time, the Danish media was still full of praise for the country's new prince, but this would soon change.

Too French to Be a Dane

Princess Margrethe's choice of a Frenchman came as a surprise to her parents. There was a long history of cultural and diplomatic ties between Denmark and France,[21] but after the Second World War these historic links were eclipsed by an overwhelming Anglo-American cultural influence. By 1967 Denmark was, as noted by the prince consort's biographer Stéphanie Surrugue, herself the daughter of a Frenchman who settled in Denmark after marrying a Danish woman, a country where wine was something one drank at confirmation dinners and where only 29,000 out of 4.8 million inhabitants were immigrants—and only 621 of these were French.[22]

Asked in 1981 if he considered the Danes racists, Prince Henrik replied that he rather considered them xenophobes, explaining it with the country historically having been protected by its islands and its climate, causing a certain provincialism which clashed with the Latin way of life.[23] In his view most Danes expect immigrants to "become 100 % Danish. That is a law of life. One does not accept that people show off their roots, but almost upbraids foreigners— 'No-no, he has remained very German, she has remained very American, they will never become proper Danes.'" Command of the Danish language rather than citizenship or contribution to society is the key factor for being accepted, he believes.[24]

Before he met Princess Margrethe, Henri de Monpezat had only little knowledge of Danish history and culture. He knew that the country had been a great power centuries ago, he was familiar with the Vikings and had appreciated what he had read of Danish authors such as Hans Christian Andersen, Ludvig Holberg, and Søren Kierkegaard. But he immediately began to read French and English books on Danish history and culture, as well as on the royal family.[25]

"I came to Denmark wishing to integrate myself entirely into my new country," Prince Consort Henrik has said.[26] Yet, to many Danes he still appears more French than Danish and that is apparently something which rankles deeply with some of his countrymen. The prince consort himself realises this and acknowledges that language is his Achilles heel. He regrets his mistake in not learning Danish well and fast enough.[27] His failure to do so would cost him dearly, as his accented Danish remains a standing joke and appears to be one of the reasons why the Danes have never quite taken him to their hearts.

He was given a warm welcome back in 1966, but it did not last long. "A few months after my arrival everything I did was criticised," he writes in his memoirs. "My Danish was unsteady. I preferred wine to beer, silk socks to wool socks, Citroën to Volvo, tennis to football...I was different. It seemed I was happy to be so and not ashamed of it. Those were two errors!"[28] The "irrational and unfair" criticism annoyed his wife more than him, he has said.[29] And indeed Queen Margrethe has stressed in many interviews how important her husband is to her and how she relies on him. The prince consort himself thinks that the experiences of someone who did not sleep in a royal cradle as well as the perspectives of a foreigner are of great value to a royal family.[30]

The Role of the Consort

While the queen has naturally been the main person on the public stage, it seems the prince consort has been the dominant person in private. That a male consort to a female monarch takes the role of head of the family is not unusual; indeed the same seems to have been the case in Britain both in the current reign and in the reign of Queen Victoria. In neighbouring Sweden this was formalised in 1647 by a parliamentary committee which decided to distinguish between two roles if Queen Christina were to marry: while Christina as a monarch would be superior to her husband and retain her regal powers undivided, Christina as a woman would be subject to her husband's authority.[31]

Princes Frederik, born in May 1968, and Joachim, born in June 1969, were still very young when their mother inherited the crown in January 1972 and suddenly found herself with much less time for her children. "She was absolutely not the first person I thought of asking or searching [for support from]. That was the nanny or my maternal grandmother," crown prince Frederik has said.[32] "Our mother was not our true educator. That was our father."[33]

Prince Henrik's stated philosophy of how to bring up children— "Children ought to be raised somewhat like dogs. With firmness, consequence and love"[34]—caused a huge outcry in Denmark and has never been forgotten. That this had been not only theory was seemingly confirmed when the Crown Prince in his speech on his parents' silver wedding anniversary in 1992 addressed his father with the words "Papa, it is said that one punishes those one loves. We never doubted your love."[35] In an interview four years later, the crown prince stated his firm belief that his and Prince Joachim's upbringing would have been very different if their father had been Danish.[36] In recent years he has been more conciliatory, and

both he and Prince Joachim now play down the impression of rigid military discipline and stress "classic French upbringing," which they appear
to interpret as a certain distance and strictness coupled with unquestioned
parental authority.[37]

The prince consort has recalled that he found Princess Margrethe
insecure when they first met, but claims to have seen her potential.[38] The
queen apparently thinks he made her confident and contributed to releas-
ing some of her latent talents. For instance, speaking with admiration of
how her mother at the age of 26 decorated two palaces, she added: "She was
able to, but I could not have done that when I was 26! But I could when I
was 27, because then I had my husband by my side and he was as interested
in everything about colours and interior decoration as I am."[39] The newly-
weds were given the use of Christian IX's Mansion at Amalienborg, which
had been uninhabited since the death of the exiled Dowager Empress
Maria Fyodorovna of Russia in 1928 and had to go through a thorough
renovation. The Prince had been "forever marked by the reflection of the
refined and colourful Vietnamese culture"[40] and found the colours traditionally used in Denmark cold and boring. He managed to convince his
wife that their home should be decorated in strong colours, and she soon
came to share his view.[41]

Prince Consort Henrik has contributed strongly to the markedly cultural and artistic profile of the Danish monarchy in the current reign.
Like most European royals of today, the Danish royal couple do not have
the means necessary for being art collectors on a major scale, but the
prince consort collects African and Greenlandic art. To a certain extent
the queen and prince consort have upheld the tradition of commission-
ing works from contemporary artists, including their tomb intended for
Roskilde Cathedral, which will be in a modern, somewhat futuristic style
and is the work of Bjørn Nørgaard, a leading and often controversial artist
of their own generation.[42]

The prince consort has a great love for music and at one stage in his
early years considered a career as a pianist. He has written three books on
gastronomy, and in 1981 he and the queen translated Simone de Beauvoir's
Tous les hommes sont mortel into Danish under the pseudonym H. and M.
Vejerbjerg. In recent years he has published several volumes of poems
ranging from the melancholy to the erotic, making his debut with the
collection *Cantabile* in 2000.[43] The prince consort also expresses himself through sculpture. Starting in the late 1970s, he created many small
sculptures of mythical animals and abstract figures, some of which have in
later years been scaled up to large formats. In 2009 he made his exhibition
debut by taking part in the international open-air exhibition "Sculpture
by the Sea" in Aarhus.[44]

Bjørn Nørgaard observes that Prince Consort Henrik in his sculptural
work does not aim at creating "a specifically personal style, but to express
and to pass on his enthusiasm about encountering art including experience
from his own life. This is not eclecticism in the usual sense of the word, but

rather a *collectionneur* drawing inspiration and impressions from his own collection of African and Greenlandic art, his jade figures from China, and much else. We are dealing with a true amateur, a lover and admirer of art passing on his intense enjoyment. Attempts at describing the artistic activities of the prince consort would require the coining of a completely new ism, namely 'collectionneurism.'"[45] The results of his endeavours "represent an intelligent, perspective person's play with the elements of art."[46]

The queen and the prince consort share a deep commitment to the arts, but, as seems to be his destiny, the consort's artistic oeuvre has been overshadowed by his wife, who is ever present as a painter, scenographer, designer, and more. This has, however, been somewhat rectified in recent years, and his eightieth birthday in June 2014 will be the occasion for the publication of a book on his "artistic universe."[47] From October 2013 to February 2014 the art museum ARoS in Aarhus showed the exhibition "Pas de deux royal: An Artistic Meeting," in which the queen's and the prince consort's works were for the first time presented together. "We meet in almost all fields and have a deep common interest in literature, painting, sculpture, and decoration. It is a great fortune and it may also be therefore that the love is still so warm and alive," said the prince consort a few years ago.[48]

The two aesthetes preside over the most splendid court in Europe. Queen Margrethe's second job as a scenographer may have influenced this, but her husband has also put his mark on court life. He has for instance reintroduced the long-extinguished tradition of masked balls; he hosts concerts and presides over the royal hunts. In the current reign there is also a marked French flavour to the Danish court, not only in the literal sense through the prince consort's strong culinary interest and wine growing business in France. For instance, the lancier has been introduced at court, including at the artists' ball the royal couple host, and the royal website is available not only in Danish and English, but also in French, which is also one of the languages spoken by the royal family at home. The surprising choice of Hans Sølvhøj, general director of the public broadcaster DR and a former Social Democrat minister, as Lord Chamberlain in 1976 was Prince Henrik's idea. It turned out to be an inspired choice, and Sølvhøj has been credited with transforming the image of the queen and the monarchy into something more vital and accessible, including encouraging the monarch to go public with her artistic side.[49]

One of Prince Henrik's first public commitments was the time-consuming role as an advisor at the Danish Red Cross with responsibility for coordinating its work with that of the international Red Cross. Encouraged by his Dutch counterpart, Prince Bernhard, Prince Henrik in 1972 initiated the founding of the Danish branch of the World Wildlife Fund, whose President he remains. Another cause close to his heart is Europa Nostra, an NGO which aims at safeguarding Europe's architectural heritage and whose president he was from 1990 until handing over to Princess Pilar of Spain in 2007. At the time of writing (September 2013), the royal website lists the prince consort as president of two organisations, honorary president of a further five and vice-president of one, chairman of four, honorary chairman of three, member of the board of two, honorary member of 54, and patron of 70.

Yet, as former Lord Chamberlain Søren Haslund-Christensen has pointed out, "his most important role, which Denmark owes him much for, is that he has given the Queen the strength and security which has made it possible for her to do her work as well as she has done it."[50] Supporting the monarch is indeed the raison d'être of a consort, male or female. The prince consort himself sees it as being "a support, an adviser, an ally."[51] But except for supporting the queen, the role of a male consort had to be shaped from scratch by Prince Henrik himself. It is one of the trickiest roles there is, he insists: "to be prince consort one must be as sensitive as a seismograph under the skin of rhinoceros, that is, one must be thick-skinned, but still able to sense the slightest tremor."[52]

When Henri de Monpezat's father, who opposed his son's marriage to the Danish heiress, realised that he would not be able to change his son's mind, he firmly advised him to get his future role and duties clearly defined. "You must speak to the King about what position you will have," the father said. When Henri interjected that the King had said that he would receive the title of prince, his father shook his head and repeated his advice.[53] These days the prince consort admits that his father was right. "My wife also did not think of it then—we were just getting married and were so happy. But when one comes as a young diplomat from another country and sees the King sitting there on his throne, one does not say: 'So? What are you going to do for me?'"[54]

Looking back, the prince consort says he had thought that his role "was very important, and that it was up to me to define it," but that he soon realised that it was impossible to do so as "one had not made it clear what my function should be. I was a general without a general staff."[55] With no defined role, "the world sees a prince consort as his wife's shadow,"[56] "a shadow without substance."[57] "In the eyes of certain people I am like a child who must ask its mother's permission for everything."[58] Thus it has often happened that Prince Consort Henrik has felt ignored. Among the many examples he has mentioned over the years are the hostess of a dinner party to whom he had sent flowers in advance and who showed off to the guests "the flowers the Queen has sent me"; the ambassador who asked him if the queen had enjoyed her visit to his country, ignoring that Prince Henrik had also participated; how their children are habitually referred to as "the Queen's children"; and how even his dog and his estate in France and the wine it produces are referred to as the queen's.[59]

Something he found particularly galling was that he did not himself receive any money from the civil list, but only indirectly through his wife. "That is unnatural for a man. There is probably no one of the male sex who would be happy about such conditions," he said in 1981.[60] It was "an enormous relief" to him when the government three years later granted him a separate income from the civil list.[61] Speaking in 1996, Prince Henrik said that he could have been dissatisfied with his role, but that he was not, as he had willed himself not to be so.[62] Six years later, however, he had had enough.

A Consort's Crisis

In a tradition going back at least to the seventeenth century, the monarch starts the year by travelling in the gold coach to Christiansborg Palace, where diplomats and officials file past the senior members of the royal family to wish them a happy New Year. On January 3, 2002, Queen Margrethe had to pull out of the event after injuring her ribs when falling down the stairs during the Christmas holiday at Marselisborg Palace in Aarhus. The queen, who interpreted the New Year ceremony as one of her monarchical functions, deputised the crown prince to stand in for her, meaning that it was he who replied to the doyen of the diplomatic corps's speech and was greeted first by the well-wishers, his father taking second place. Prince Henrik, who saw it as a purely social event, thought he should have taken first place in his wife's absence.

"I and those people I confer with agree that what happened about the New Year court was correct," said the Lord Chamberlain, Søren Haslund-Christensen.[63] Later he would be more specific: "There is only one person who can make that decision. And that is Her Majesty. All these things are decided by the Queen."[64] The journalist and royal biographer Annelise Bistrup pointed out that there was a precedence from when King Frederik IX was ill in January 1972, and Princess Margrethe, not Queen Ingrid, deputised at the New Year celebrations.[65]

The news coverage of the event focused on the crown prince, who was described by one newspaper as "King for a day."[66] His pride injured, Prince Henrik virtually went on strike and retreated to his French estate, Château de Caïx. A month later, the prince gave an interview to Bodil Cath, a veteran royal correspondent of *B. T.*, generally considered the more respectable of the two national tabloids. The interview appeared in two parts on Sunday 3 and Monday 4 February, but it was the first instalment which was explosive. "I need time to think," the prince said. "For many years I have been number two in Denmark. That is a role I am satisfied with, but after so many years in Denmark I am not willing to be suddenly demoted to number three, as some sort of indifferent appendage." After 35 years in Denmark he still felt that he was disparaged and not accepted.

"Every society has a hierarchy," he went on. "That has been the case for tens of thousands of years. There is the government. There are the armed forces. And the monarchy also ought to have a hierarchy. One has a reigning couple, who are number one and two, and one has the Crown Prince... Now, after thirty [sic] years in Denmark, the impression is still given that I am number three... I do not want to be part of that game. I am number two. I shall be number two. In such a hierarchy one cannot simply change the order because someone thinks it is clever or sells more newspapers."

"Number three is there to fill number one's place in certain constitutional circumstances, because he is crown prince. But only in those cases which concern the executive power. He cannot take number two's place at social events. To say that number three should be number two when number one for some reason cannot be present is to humiliate any husband and any wife. I would never interfere when my son should take care of state affairs or assist his mother. But no one can expect me to agree automatically to being replaced by number three."

"Any father of a family wants to be the host in his own house. But also our people and the press have tried to say that it is the Crown Prince who is host. The Crown Prince was for instance at the New Year courts not the host, but his father's guest. If the Danes want to change the rules they may do so. But I do not want to play along on such wrong notes."

The whole affair of the New Year courts had made it necessary for him to take his life and role under consideration, he said. "I have come to doubt my place in the Danish society so much that I prefer to take a long, long break. It is not I who is fantasising. I have really started to wonder if one wants to change the rules without me. But as I am married to the monarch I expect that I am given the place next to her. There are still a lot of people who believe that I am not on the same level as for instance Queen Ingrid was. There shall be no doubt. We are a regnant couple." Declaring himself hurt and disappointed, the prince insisted that what had happened was not the crown prince's fault, before lashing out at attempts "to destroy my self-respect," which he now needed time to rebuild.[67]

The prince's personal crisis soon became the monarchy's existential crisis as his hurt feelings were splashed all over the media in Denmark and abroad and the possible repercussions were debated. Jørgen Langballe, Member of Parliament for the far right, anti-immigration Danish People's Party, blamed the prince's foreign birth: "Prince Henrik is and remains a Frenchman, and his whole way of thinking is French. And it is no unconditional benefit that he has marked the Danish royal house with the French attitude."[68] The historian Claus Bjørn would rule out neither abdication nor divorce, but interpreted the interview primarily as "a cry for help."[69] The constitutional expert Jens Peter Christensen found it all a non-issue: "But, Prince Henrik *has* no number at all...He is non-existing. At least in the constitutional sense. He is his wife's husband, quite simply."[70]

The queen and the Lord Chamberlain had both read the interview ahead of publication and strongly advised the prince to withdraw it. When he refused, the queen concluded that she would have to show her support.[71] On the very day that the first instalment of the interview appeared, Queen Margrethe, Crown Prince Frederik, and Prince Joachim all flew out to join Prince Henrik at Caïx. The next day the media were invited to an impromptu photo session in the sun-drenched garden, where the royals made some remarks about the weather and being together, the prince joking that one of the ceramic cats adorning the stairs was named for Bodil Cath. Little more was said, but the public were provided with images which suggested a united royal family at peace with each other. The following week Prince Henrik carried out his first public engagement since the New Year court, when he and the queen attended the reopening of La Maison du Danemark at Champs-Élysées in Paris before returning to Denmark some days later. Meanwhile the media had gotten other and happier news to write about when the court announced on February 9 that Princess Alexandra was expecting another child. Thanks to efficient crisis management things were swiftly brought under control.

In a book-length interview three years later, Queen Margrethe blamed herself for her husband's personal crisis, saying that things had "periodically been harder for my husband than I was aware of. And I have not helped him enough. I have not been aware of how I could help in the right way." Although he had also been master of the house in her eyes, she acknowledged that she had on too many occasions made decisions without consulting him, leaving him to be informed by others about what the queen had decided.[72]

At least for outward appearances, the prince's personal crisis changed little. When the 2002 edition of the Royal Danish Court and State Almanac was published it repeated that the prince was second in order of precedence, but a clarification had now been added: "However, when the Crown Prince carries out the functions of the head of state in the Queen's absence, the Crown Prince takes the Queen's place."[73]

In retrospect Prince Joachim thinks that it was quite simply necessary for his father to blow the lid on that occasion.[74] In an interview with the British newspaper *Sunday Telegraph* a year later, Queen Margrethe played down her husband's crisis: "He's got over all that. It's the sort of thing that happens to you occasionally when you really don't feel happy. He went through a very difficult period, but he's very well again now."[75] But although the storm had died down the prince's discontent kept simmering.

Prince, Prince Consort, or King Consort?

In his sensational 2002 interview, Prince Henrik played down the importance of his title in relation to his rank. "Can you imagine that one in the sixties would have said 'the King and Princess Ingrid?' But Ingrid became queen. Today one still says the queen and Prince Henrik, but Prince Henrik is still Prince Henrik—and now apparently number three. I do not care if my title is the prince, if one says 'the Queen and the crocodile' or 'the Queen and Ba-u-bab,' but Ba-u-bab should be number two."[76]

But it is his belief that his role not being understood is to a great extent due to his lack of a distinctive title. Upon marrying Princess Margrethe in 1967, he received the title His Royal Highness Prince Henrik of Denmark, a decision he says was made by his wife's mother. "My mother-in-law, Queen Ingrid, thought that one should follow the English and Dutch examples, which were the only current ones. One did not consider looking further to the south, [toward] Navarre, Naples, Portugal, Spain, all these kingdoms where there had been equality between the sexes."[77] Ingrid had herself received the title crown princess when marrying the then heir in 1935 and became queen upon her husband's accession in 1947. If Frederik IX had told his wife that her title should be "Princess Ingrid," she would have "slammed the door and gone back to Sweden," joked her son-in-law.[78]

The diaries of the then Prime Minister, Jens Otto Krag, reveal that a dukedom was considered during the final days of Frederik IX's life. The title one had in mind was duke of Fredensborg, after the palace north of Copenhagen which serves at the monarch's principal summer residence. However, Krag found the idea curious. "It would not be popular. On the contrary [it would be] artificial," he noted on January 3, 1972.[79] Without a dukedom, the new monarch's husband was officially referred to as "His Royal Highness the Prince"—a curious solution given that there were at the time six Danish princes in addition to the crown prince.[80] This was a title the prince himself disliked. "For what is a prince? Is it little Prince Felix [the second son of his youngest son]? Or is it the Queen's husband?"[81]

He eventually came to realise that the title of prince was insufficient. "I have wished to be utilised by the Danish society. But one has never discussed my title. And that has meant that people have not accorded me a well-defined position in the Danish society, if I may say so. One does not know what a prince does. Maybe he does nothing, as he has no official functions? We know what functions a crown prince, a hereditary prince, a prime minister, a national ombudsman or a national archivist has. But what is a prince? That question is to me an important psychological factor."[82]

"I am convinced that a married couple ought to be equals, no matter what role in society the couple might fill. Denmark could have made me state prince, prince of the realm, king consort, what do I know. It is an omission, maybe unwillingness. But it is not the title that is crucial, but the awareness that I have a role, a function."[83] He did concede that his work would have been the same with another title, but that he would have been seen in another way. "People would not say: 'He does nothing, he has no function in the royal house or in society.' Of course no one asks what my son, the Crown Prince, does. He is of course Crown Prince, and thereby classified in society."[84]

He told his biographer that he could not see what would have prevented his wife from declaring him King Consort and Majesty, but added that he did not blame her, but "that one neglected it back then, 30–40 years ago."[85] He resented being seen as "his wife's concern. I am my wife's concern. And one expects that I ask my wife for permission for everything… Roughly, it is as if I am not worthy of being at my wife's side."[86]

They did not discuss his title much after her accession, said Queen Margrethe in her book-length interview in 2005, also taking the opportunity to announce a new title for her husband. "We reached the conclusion that Prince Henrik was 'the Prince.' But later we have talked it over again, and during the past few years we have concluded that it would be quite natural to use the title 'Prince Consort.' It is a title which can only be used by the Queen's husband, and which he must not share with others. It is truly his, and it goes well along with those expressions one uses in foreign languages: 'Prince Consort' in French and in English and 'Prinzgemal' in German, and which we also use consistently in foreign relations. It is a title which we will quietly use more and more also in Danish, and which I find natural."[87]

In the prince consort's version, the decision was his and his alone: "It was *my* decision to take that title. Why? Because I was tired of being called 'the Prince.'" But he added that there were many who refused to use his new title. "They believe that Prince Henrik is Prince Henrik. In that case I would prefer that they call me *Monsieur Henrik*."[88] Indeed, the change from "the Prince" to "the Prince Consort" did not happen in such a quiet, gradual manner as the queen suggested. Rather, the court came to use "the Prince Consort" without exceptions from then on, while his group of male friends introduced a fine of 50 DKK for any one of them who lapsed into calling him just "Prince."[89]

Yet, nine years earlier, Prince Henrik had described the title of prince consort as "an abnormity which means that one compares a royal marriage with a morganatic relationship."[90] The prince consort has on a number of occasions made his own situation an issue of gender equality and considers equality between the monarch and her spouse important for Denmark's image. When the Act of Succession was made gender-neutral through a referendum on June 7, 2009, a journalist asked the prince consort what he thought about sexual equality. "I hope that men one day will be as equal as girls," he replied. "And then I would like to turn it around and ask the people: What do you think about equality?"[91]

His remarks sparked a new debate on his own role and title, and when the prince consort celebrated his seventy-fifth birthday a few days later the newspaper *Berlingske Tidende* reported a parliamentary majority in favour of granting him the title of king. The Conservative Party, the junior partner in the governing coalition, was joined by the centre-ground Danish Social Liberal Party and the Social Democrats and, with some reservations, the far right Danish People's Party in being open for complying with such a wish if it were put forward by the royal house. However, the Liberal Party, the prime minister's party, was firmly against the idea.[92] The far left Unity Party stated that as far as they were concerned the prince consort could call himself whatever he liked, including emperor, while a spokesperson for the Liberal Alliance preferred to let the issue rest in order not to lay the royal family open to ridicule.[93] However, the next morning the Danish People's Party changed their mind, now believing that such an idea would only undermine the monarchy and gain the republican cause. Søren Espersen, MP and one of the party's ideologues, encouraged the prince consort never to bring it up again.[94]

In Stéphanie Surrugue's authorised biography, which was published in September 2010, Prince Consort Henrik again spoke at length about his own position and his perception that his role was not being understood. Yet the prince consort insisted that his supposed wish to be king was a media invention. "I do not want to be king. One may call me Baobab, I do not care. I have only asked for a title with a function which gives me an identity in the Danish society. And I cannot help thinking of the future princesses who may one day reign in Europe—what about their spouses?"[95] But would he accept if he were to be offered the title of majesty and king consort, Surrugue asked. "Yes. Naturally. But I now think it is too late."[96]

Two and a half years later, the prince consort again raised the issue in a joint interview he and Prince Joachim's second wife, the French-born Princess Marie, gave to the French magazine *Point de Vue*. "You, my dear daughter-in-law, contracted a normal marriage, in which you are equal to your spouse. He is a prince, and you a princess. This was not the case with me. There is no reason why I should not be on an equal footing with my wife. I have the impression, and this impression will remain with me until the day I am laid to rest, that I am second choice. Nor am I alone in thinking so; Prince Philip shares my point of view. Such an inequality never existed before the twentieth century, even less in the twenty-first. It is some sort of reversed discrimination, modern-type. 5,000 years ago queens always made their husbands kings. The exception is simply an English fad, which was followed by Denmark and Holland. Please find out why! Even in Egypt and again in Byzantium empresses inherited the throne and made their husbands emperors. This injustice is quite hard to bear."[97] This time the prince consort's statement caused less of a stir than in 2009 and the Danish press quickly moved on.

Henri from Navarre

The prince consort reads a lot of history and is said to be something of an authority on the history of male consorts.[98] The concept of prince consort is a nineteenth-century invention, starting with his wife's great-great-grandparents, Queen Victoria and Prince Albert of Britain, he insists. Until then, "queens made their husbands kings consort and they governed the country together."[99] As this book shows, such was not always the case.

Among the exceptions are: the husband of Queen Mary I of England, the second and third husbands of Mary, Queen of Scots, and the consort of Queen Anne of Britain, two of whom became kings without independent authority[100] and two of whom received only dukedoms,[101] and the four husbands of Queen Giovanna I of Naples. Of the latter, two were created kings, while the third was a king in his own right, and the fourth of too low a rank to be deemed worthy of a kingly title. However, all four of them were denied royal authority, which was at least part of the reason for the power struggles and turmoil of Giovanna's reign.[102] But it was indeed usual in medieval Europe that a reigning queen's husband took part in the governance of her realm.[103]

Despite these exceptions, 1840 may indeed be considered a watershed. In 1830 the *Gazette de France* reported that Prince Leopold of Saxe-Coburg and Gotha had turned down the offer of the Greek crown as he planned to marry his niece, Princess Victoria of Britain, "and thereby become King of England."[104] The rumour was obviously unfounded, but it is interesting to note that it was still taken for granted in 1830 that a man would become king by marrying a future queen regnant. Leopold's nephew, Prince Ferdinand of Saxe-Coburg and Gotha, who married Queen Maria II of Portugal in 1836, did indeed become king consort when the Queen gave birth to an heir the following year.[105] After Maria's death in 1853, Ferdinand served as regent, but gave up the reins of government when his son, Pedro V, reached his majority in 1855.[106] In contrast, Ferdinand's first cousin, Prince Albert of Saxe-Coburg and Gotha, received no title when he married Queen Victoria of Britain in 1840, as the politicians would not allow her to create him king consort, and was only created prince consort after 17 years of marriage.[107] After Ferdinand of Portugal only one European male consort has received the title of king, namely Prince Francisco of Spain, Duke of Cadiz, who married his first cousin, Queen Isabel II of Spain, in 1846. In his case the title was purely honorary and he was denied any powers.[108]

One historical example of male consorts is perhaps particularly close to the heart of the prince consort of Denmark: that of Navarre. For although Prince Consort Henrik is widely regarded as French, his forebears were subjects of the monarchs of Navarre, the kingdom where queens regnant first ceased being an anomaly and where their husbands were kings. The Monpezat family hails from Béarn, an ancient viscounty in the south of France. Between 1134 and 1555 the viscounty passed six times through inheritance to women, who invariably shared power with their husbands (or sons). Through marriage Béarn eventually merged with Navarre, which saw six queens regnant between 1274 and 1572. Elena Woodacre tells the story of five of these queens and their consorts in a recent book as well as in an earlier chapter in this volume, demonstrating that they operated with three different modes of power sharing, but that the kings *jure uxoris* always took part in the governance of Navarre.[109]

With his Navarrese background in mind it is easier to understand how natural the concept of king consort is in the eyes of Prince Consort Henrik. He has on a number of occasions referred to his Navarrese heritage, for instance in explaining the ease with which he changed religion when marrying Princess Margrethe.[110] He has also introduced into the Danish royal house the tradition of rubbing the lips of newborn boys with wine and garlic, a custom the Monpezats have taken over from the Navarrese kings.[111] According to his authorised biographer, the Navarrese examples of kings consort have been known to Prince Consort Henrik ever since he was in school.[112] But a closer study might have told him that, as Elena Woodacre has found, the Navarrese kings consort who succeeded the best in their roles were those whose role was clearly defined. As a young man, Henri de Monpezat often rebelled against his heavy-handed, choleric father, but in his old age the prince consort has realised that his father was right when he insisted that he should have his position clearly defined before marrying the heiress to the Danish throne. It was a failure which has caused him much frustration through more than 40 years.

Notes

1. Empress Farah of Iran, *My Thousand and One Days: An Autobiography*, translated from the French by Felice Harcourt (London, 1978), 94.
2. Thomas Lyngby, Søren Mentz, and Sebastian Olden-Jørgensen: *Magt og pragt: Enevælde 1660–1848* (Copenhagen, Gad, 2010), p. 117. The ritual is first known to have taken place on August 25, 1699, when Christian V died and was succeeded by his son, Frederik IV. However, as Denmark had become an elective monarchy in 1660, it is possible that it might also have taken place on the death of Frederik III in 1670.
3. Jon Bloch Skipper, *Tre søstre: Samtaler mellem dronning Margrethe, prinsesse Benedikte og dronning Anne-Marie* (Copenhagen, 2008), 22; Annelise Bistrup, *Margrethe* (Copenhagen, 2005), 17.
4. Skipper, 27.
5. For the process leading to the new Constitution of 1953, see Søren Eigaard, *Idealer og politik: Historien om Grundloven af 1953* (Odense, 1993), where chapter 9 deals specifically with the succession issue.
6. In 2009 another referendum approved changes to the Act of Succession which made succession to the Danish throne gender-neutral.
7. Bistrup, 45–6. Princess Anne-Marie married King Konstantinos II of the Hellenes in 1964; Princess Benedikte married Prince Richard of Sayn-Wittgenstein-Berleburg in 1968.
8. Bistrup, 58.
9. Anne Wolden-Ræthinge, *Queen in Denmark: Margrethe II Talks about Her Life*, translated from the Danish by Liv Bentsen (Copenhagen, 1989), 58.
10. Bistrup, 82.
11. David Cannadine, *The Pleasures of the Past* (London, 1997), 12.
12. Stéphanie Surrugue, *Enegænger: Portræt af en prins* (Copenhagen, 2010), 105.
13. Surrugue, 96.
14. Wolden-Ræthinge, 55; Bistrup, 81–2.
15. Wolden-Ræthinge, 57–8; Anne Wolden-Ræthinge, *En familie og dens Dronning* (Copenhagen, 1996), 196–7; Bistrup, 86.
16. Prince Henrik with Philippe Viguié Desplaces, *Skæbne forpligter*, translated from the French by Else Henneberg Pedersen (Copenhagen, 1996), 34. See also Joseph Valynseele, *Les Laborde de Monpezat et leur alliances* (Paris, 1975), ch. 9.
17. Henrik, 34, 36, 64–5.
18. Lise Lander, *Prins Henrik: Samtaler med Lise Lander* (Copenhagen, 1981), p. 33.
19. Henrik, 113.
20. Surrugue, 94–5.

21. See Erling Bjøl, *Den franske forbindelse: Fra Holger Danske til Sarkozy* (Copenhagen, 2009).

22. Surrugue, 126.

23. Lander, 37.

24. Surrugue, 133.

25. Larsen, Larsen, and Ørsted, 123–4.

26. Surrugue, 2010, 14.

27. Henrik, 167 ; Surrugue, 14.

28. Henrik, 167.

29. Ibid., 169.

30. Ibid., 166–7.

31. Karin Tegenborg Falkdalen, *Kungen är en kvinna: Retorik och praktikk kring kvinnliga monarker under tidigmodern tid* (Umeå, 2003), 156. See also Erik Petersson, *Maktspelerskan: Drottning Kristinas revolt* (Stockholm, 2011), 149.

32. Gitte Redder and Karin Palshøj, *Frederik: Kronprins af Danmark* (Copenhagen, 2008), 55.

33. Jens Andersen, *M: 40 år på tronen* (Copenhagen, 2011), 371.

34. Quoted in Larsen, Larsen, and Ørsted, 129.

35. Quoted in Redder and Palshøj, 58.

36. Wolden-Ræthinge, 70.

37. Redder and Palshøj, 58–9. See also Andersen, 371–2.

38. Henrik, 190–5.

39. Henrik Lyding, *Dronningens teater* (Copenhagen, 2009), 21.

40. Henrik, 131.

41. Larsen, Larsen, and Ørsted, 69, 132–133.

42. Ulla Kjær, *Roskilde Domkirke: Kunst og historie* (Copenhagen, 2013), 344–7; Bjørn Nørgaard, "'Collectioneurisme?': Om H. K. H. Prinsgemal Henriks skulpturelle arbejde/ 'Collectionneurism?': About the Sculptural Work of H. R. H. Prince Consort Henrik," in Pernille Taagaard Dinesen, Jens Erik Sørensen, and Victoria Marie Christiansen (eds.), *Pas de deux royal: Et kunstnerisk møde/Pas de deux royal: An Artistic Meeting* (Aarhus, 2013), 51–71.

43. Stéphanie Surrugue: "Anarkistromantikeren/The Anarchist Romantic," in Dinesen et al., 103–16.

44. Jens Erik Sørensen, "Pas de deux royal: Prolog/Pas de deux royal: Prologue, » in Dinesen et al., 9–16.

45. Nørgaard, 54.

46. Ibid., 71.

47. Thyge Christian Fønss, *Åbent hjerte: Prins Henriks kunstneriske univers* (Copenhagen, 2014).

48. Larsen, Larsen, and Ørsted, 135.

49. Andersen, 137–40.

50. Surrugue, 142, 316.

51. Henrik, 204.

52. Ibid.

53. Surrugue, 98–9.

54. Ibid., 302.

55. Ibid., 131–2.

56. Bodil Cath, Henning Dehn-Nielsen, and Georg Vejen (eds.), *Samtale med Regentparret* (Copenhagen, 1992), 14.

57. Henrik, 204.

58. Lander, 39.

59. Henrik, 205; Cath, Dehn-Nielsen, and Vejen, 14–5.

60. Lander, 41–2.

61. Henrik, 206.

62. Wolden-Ræthinge, 62.

63. *Politiken*, February 5, 2002, quoted in Andersen, 378.

64. Quoted in Jørgen Eskild Høigaard, *Krisen i kongehuset* (Højbjerg, 2002), 90.

65. Claus Stolbjerg Hansen and Dorte Kofoed, "Det her er alvorligt for monarkiet" (*B. T.*, February 4, 2002).

66. Quoted in Surrugue, 306.

67. Bodil Cath, "Jeg føler mig kasseret" (*B. T.*, February 3, 2002).

68. Quoted in Andersen, 384.

69. Claus Stolbjerg Hansen and Dorte Kofoed, "Det her er alvorligt for monarkiet" (*B. T.*, February 4, 2002).

70. *Berlingske Tidende*, February 5, 2002, quoted in Andersen, 382.

71. Surrugue, 306–7.

72. Bistrup, 91–2.

73. *Kongelig Dansk Hof- og Statskalender 2002*, 137, quoted in Andersen, 389.

74. Surrugue, 312.

75. Gyles Brandreth, "Being Queen Is Just What I Do' (*Sunday Telegraph*, January 5, 2003).

76. Bodil Cath, "Jeg føler mig kasseret" (*B. T.*, February 3, 2002).

77. Surrugue, 300–1.

78. Ibid., 321.

79. Jens Otto Krag, *Dagbog 1971–1972* (Copenhagen, 1973), 114.

80. Prince Henrik himself, his youngest son Prince Joachim, the Queen's uncle, Hereditary Prince Knud, and the Princes Gorm and Georg of junior lines.

81. Surrugue, 320.

82. Ibid., 301.

83. Ibid., 302.

84. Ibid.

85. Ibid., 302–3.

86. Ibid.

87. Bistrup, 91.

88. Surrugue, 320.

89. Ibid., 296.

90. Henrik, 203.

91. Quoted in Amalie Kestler, "Prins Henrik vil have ligestilling for mænd" (*Berlingske Tidende*'s online edition, June 8, 2009, http://www.b.dk/danmark/prins-henrik-vil-have-ligestilling-maend).

92. Chris Kjær Jessen and Uffe Tang, "Politikere: Prins Henrik kan blive konge" (*Berlingske Tidende*'s online edition, June 11, 2009, http://www.b.dk/danmark/politikere-prins-henrik-kan-blive-konge).

93. Chris Jessen and Uffe Tang, "Kong Henrik kan skabe kaos" (*Berlingske Tidende*'s online edition, June 11, 2009, http://www.b.dk/danmark/kong-henrik-kan-skabe-kaos).

94. Uffe Tang, "DF trækker støtten til kong Henrik" (*Berlingske Tidende*'s online edition, June 12, 2009, http://www.b.dk/danmark/df-traekker-stoetten-til-kong-henrik).

95. Surrugue, 320.

96. Ibid., 322.

97. Adélaide de Clermont-Tonnerre, "Complicité au palais d'Amalienborg" (*Point de Vue*, no. 3367, January 30 - February 5, 2013).

98. Surrugue, 300.

99. Lander, 38.

100. Caroline Bingham, *Darnley: A Life of Henry Stuart, Lord Darnley, Consort of Mary Queen of Scots* (London, 1997), 99, 104–5, 108–11, 116–7, 120–1; Harry Kelsey, *Philip of Spain, King of England: The Forgotten Sovereign* (London and New York, I. B. Tauris, 2011), 69–70, 73, 82, 93, 97, 99–101.

101. Charles Beem, *The Lioness Roared: The Problems of Female Rule in English History* (New York and Basingstoke, 2006), 101–39; Mogens Højland, *Jarlen af Bothwell: Danmarks berømteste fange* (Copenhagen, 2007), 171, Bingham, 189.

102. Nancy Goldstone, *Joanna: The Notorious Queen of Naples, Jerusalem and Sicily* (London, 2010), 48, 77, 82, 93–5, 107–8, 110–1, 120, 125–8, 132–4, 207, 210, 216, 218, 226, 273–4, 328.

103. William Monter, *The Rise of Female Kings in Europe, 1300–1800* (New Haven and London, 2012) argues (p. 60) that what he calls "the Navarrese solution," that is the concept whereby a queen regnant and her husband "were jointly invested with sovereign powers" and the king consort "took primary responsibility for governing his wife's kingdom," was the norm in the fourteenth and fifteenth centuries. This is, however, an oversimplification, as for instance Elena Woodacre has shown in her studies of the Navarrese queens and their husbands [see n. 109 below], yet it was the norm that husbands of queens regnant were allowed at least a share in the rule of their wives' realms.

104. Cited in *Stockholms Posten*, May 25, 1830.

105. Edmund B. d'Auvergne, *The Coburgs: The Story of the Rise of a Great Royal House* (London, 1911), 139. Queen Maria's first husband, Duke Auguste of Leuchtenberg, had only been prince consort as he died within four months of the wedding and thus did not sire an heir.

106. Francis Gribble, *The Royal House of Portugal* (Port Washington and London, 1970), 229; d'Auvergne, 265.

107. Daphne Bennett, *King Without a Crown: Albert, Prince Consort of England, 1819–1861* (London, 1977), 127; Monica Charlot, *Victoria: The Young Queen* (Oxford, 1989), 178–80, 381–2; Stanley Weintraub, *Albert: Uncrowned King* (London, 1997), 87–8, 337–9.

108. John D. Bergamini, *The Spanish Bourbons: The History of a Tenacious Dynasty* (New York, 1974), 231.

109. Elena Woodacre, *The Queens Regnant of Navarre: Succession, Politics, and Partnership, 1274–1512* (New York, 2013. For the sixth and final queen regnant and king consort of Navarre, see Nancy Lyman Roelker, *Queen of Navarre: Jeanne d'Albret, 1528–1572* (Cambridge, 1968), chapters II-VII; Vincent J. Pitts, *Henri IV of France: His Reign and Age* (Baltimore, 2009), 2–26, Monter, 131–3.

110. Henrik, 201.
111. Roelker, 99; Henrik, 33; Prince Henrik and Philippe Viguié Desplaces, *Fotos fra prins Henriks private album*, translated from the French by Patricia Jouglas (Copenhagen, 2004), 63; Pitts, 7.
112. Surrugue, 300.

INDEX

Printed in the United States of America